The Purposes of Paradise

The Purposes of Paradise

U.S. Tourism and Empire
in Cuba and Hawai'i

Christine Skwiot

PENN

UNIVERSITY OF PENNSYLVANIA PRESS

PHILADELPHIA · OXFORD

Published by
University of Pennsylvania Press
Philadelphia, Pennsylvania 19104–4112

Printed in the United States of America on acid-free paper
10 9 8 7 6 5 4 3 2 1

Library of Congress Cataloging-in-Publication Data

Skwiot, Christine.
The purposes of paradise : U.S. tourism and empire in Cuba
and Hawai'i / Christine Skwiot.
p. cm.
Includes bibliographical references and index.
ISBN 978-0-8122-4244-7 (hardcover : alk. paper)
1. Tourism—Political aspects—Cuba—History—19th
century. 2. Tourism—Political
aspects—Cuba—History—20th century.
3. Tourism—Political aspects—Hawaii—History—19th
century. 4. Tourism—Political
aspects—Hawaii—History—20th century.
5. Cuba—Colonization. 6. Hawaii—Colonization.
7. United States—Territorial expansion. 8. United
States—Foreign relations—19th century. 9. United
States—Foreign relations—20th century.
10. Imperialism—History. I. Title.
G155.C9S56 2010
306.20973—dc22
2010004927

For Larry

CONTENTS

INTRODUCTION

Nowadays, Cuba and Hawaiʻi seem worlds apart. Beginning with Dwight D. Eisenhower, eight successive presidential administrations regarded Fidel Castro and the Cuba he heads as the archenemy of the United States and antithesis of all things for which the nation stands. In stark contrast, these same administrations and most mainland citizens have viewed Hawaiʻi as their "Aloha State" of love and affection and their nation's own South Seas paradise. The present circumstances of Cuba and Hawaiʻi and the ways U.S. citizens think about them render them so dissimilar as to seem incomparable. But for more than a century before the Cuban revolution and Hawaiian statehood of 1959, these islands figured as twin objects of U.S. desire, as possessions whose tropical island locales might support all manner of utopias, as necessary additions to the imperial republic, and as keys to the global projection of its power.[1] Cuba and Hawaiʻi occupied the same position or analogous places in the Atlantic and Pacific oceans and the mental and material geography of a U.S. empire in which they were contemporaries and neighbors between 1898 and 1959.[2] Only after 1959 did the connected histories and what many saw as the shared destinies of Cuba and Hawaiʻi come to seem so impossibly different.

This exploration of the ways travel and tourism reciprocally shaped U.S. imperialism in Cuba and Hawaiʻi sheds new light on the forces responsible for this divergence and for divergence as well as persistence in U.S. imperial thought and practice. Travel writers and tourism promoters from all three places collaborated with a wide variety of imperial and anti-imperial agents to imagine and debate, perform and transform, contest and protest the place of Cuba and Hawaiʻi in the U.S. imperium. Although especially focused on the period between 1898, when the United States took control of them, and 1959, when they respectively achieved revolution and secured statehood, this story begins in the early nineteenth century in order to trace the ways that century's dreams and policies shaped twentieth-century memories and practices.[3] As we untangle the histories of Cuba and Hawai'i as integral parts of the Union, as occupied territories that have known forcible interventions and violent memories, and as fantasy islands ripe with seduction and reward, travel and tourism emerge as sites where "the pleasures of imperialism" met the politics of empire.[4] That said, the book is less concerned with plumbing the mind of the traveler or explaining the culture of a privileged class of globe-trotters than it is with exploring the roles that travel narratives, rituals, and institutions played in making and remaking U.S. imperialism. There is plenty of sun, sea, and sex in *The Purposes of Paradise*, but it is not about tourism, leisure, or consumerism as such. It is an exploration of the mutually sustaining relationships between imperial fantasies and political practices in U.S. citizens' favorite tropical islands.[5] In a quest to understand the particular, and especially the political, purposes to which imperial and anti-imperial agents put travel and tourism in usually restless, always elusive quests to find, create, or regain some sort of paradise, this book follows historian Robert Campbell's lead in taking "seriously the reality of what was imagined."[6]

Desire, Duty, and Destiny

Nineteenth-century imperial desires and duties were bound up with one another and with the belief that destiny decreed that Cuba and Hawai'i would belong to the Union of States. In 1896, newspaper editor and politician Whitelaw Reid suggested how deeply these island societies haunted the imperial imagination. Asserting that possessing them was as important to national progress as the Louisiana Purchase, Reid told president-elect William McKinley, "To get both, in your administration, would place it besides Jefferson's in the popular mind, and ahead in History." Reid urged his managing editor at the *New York Tribune* to take advantage of an "admirable opportunity" afforded by some "recent Cuban excitement" in its creoles' latest war for independence. He advised, "One or two excellent articles might be made on Cuba as a winter resort for Americans, its advantages and drawbacks." After showing how Spanish misrule prevented Cuba from achieving its promise as a resort, "then some idea might be given of what the island . . . might become with an energetic population under good government."[7]

Whether promoting the annexation of Cuba or Hawai'i, Indiana or Montana, California or Canada, myriad expansionist travel narratives followed this formula: discuss the status of a desired land as a resort; then, imagine the realization of its potential as such once under the good government and in the hands of the energetic population of U.S. citizens and their allies. The conjoined terms seasonal resort, energetic population, and good government suggest something of the entanglements among travel, tourism, and empire. Presenting the delightful climate, natural beauty, and abundant resources of a desired land as ripe for exploitation, such travel narratives presented bad hotels, inadequate infrastructure, and poor public health as proof that the government in power was incapable of moral or material progress. U.S. citizens and the free whites of a desired land who sought belonging in the Union would cooperate to annex it, regenerate it, and transform it into a resort. The resort would reward those responsible for the regeneration and those who traveled there to witness their work and enjoy newfound opportunities and delights. As a project by and for agents of U.S. empire from many lands, the resort would stand in testimony to the consensual nature of U.S. imperialism, to annexation honorably achieved, and to the happy convergence of politics and pleasure.[8]

In such narratives, the unrealized potential of the resort sanctioned conquest in the name of honorable intentions and foretold a happy end to the morality-cum-fairy tale. While the resort represented the pleasures that were the reward of proper action, the acquisition of new territory with the consent of colonized and colonizer would confirm that destiny was the reward of duty. As President McKinley proclaimed in 1898, "Duty determines destiny. Destiny . . . results from duty performed." As the result and reward of the proper performance of duty, Hawai'i and the United States fulfilled their destiny by entering a consensual union. Cuba would soon do the same. In his 1898 and 1899 State of the Union addresses, McKinley averred that Hawai'i "has cast its lot with us and elected to share our political heritage" and declared that a "Cuba yet to arise from the ashes of the past" would choose to be bound to the United States "by the most singular ties of intimacy." He presented the recent annexation of Hawai'i and the anticipated addition of Cuba as "a natural and inevitable consummation."[9] McKinley and Reid needed all the help they could get in presenting the annexation of Cuba and Hawai'i as consensual. Most Cubans and Hawaiians opposed annexation.[10] They struggled against imperialism and for sovereign and independent nationhood. That so many U.S. citizens believed and continue to believe otherwise is a testament to the power of imperial histories indebted to travelogues in shaping enduring memories and amnesias.

The Politics of Empire

Over the nineteenth century, expansionist travel writers and tourism promoters in the United States, Cuba, and Hawai'i imagined these island states as part of the United States and tried to replicate the success of tourism-settlement schemes used in the U.S. West to recruit whites to them. They offered up the vision that as a result of these islands' progress under American civilization and white republicanism, U.S. statehood would be the eventual outcome in both places. By World War I, elites of all three places abandoned efforts to use tourism to attract permanent white settlers to Cuba and Hawai'i. They instead built tourist trades by and for privileged whites who were proud republicans but had long fantasized about living like aristocrats. The exclusive residential-resort communities they built in the outskirts of Havana and Honolulu became conjoined sites of tourism and governance. White elites who ensconced themselves in them reenvisioned the extension of republican principles and practices to Cuba and Hawai'i not as a matter of pressing urgency but as one of some hazy future. Travel and tourism helped legitimate a variety of different political, racial, and social regimes in Hawai'i and Cuba and stabilize relations between capital and labor. However, when tourism and politics became too corrupt, too repressive, or both, travel and tourism regimes provided a foil for anti-imperial nationalisms and social movements that ranged from reformist to revolutionary.

The dramatic divergence in the mid-twentieth century of two societies widely regarded as imperial twins in the second half of the nineteenth century is a story replete with ironies. The first made its appearance at the beginning of this story when expansionists deemed Cuba and Hawai'i the "apple" and the "pear," the first two fruits of and overseas twins in a tropical island "empire of liberty" by and for free whites.[11] To many contemporaries, it seemed as obvious that most people of Cuba and Hawai'i were not white as it did that their differences exceeded their similarities. The former was a colony of the Spanish Crown; the latter was a constitutional monarchy based on Polynesian and European forms and customs. In Cuba, mostly African slaves worked a large, lucrative sugar industry; in Hawai'i, free Hawaiians and Chinese and indentured Chinese worked a nascent sugar industry still struggling to survive. The former was officially Catholic; the latter was officially Protestant. The former lay but ninety miles off the coast of Florida; the latter was over twenty-five hundred miles from California.

Neither vast distances nor stark differences dampened the capacious comparative imaginations of imperialist whites in Cuba, Hawai'i, and the United States. Many claimed that the United States had a right to possess Cuba and Hawai'i by virtue of their being located closer to the United States than to any other nation. Invocations of physical propinquity merged with visions of global destiny. Possessing the "key to the New World" and the "crossroads of the Pacific" would enable the United States to become a commercial and military power rivaling the most powerful European nations and empires.[12] While Cuba and Hawai'i might join the Union respectively as slave and free territories (or states), both had the potential to become integral parts of a Union widely regarded as an expansive white republic in the making. After all, none of the North American colonies and few U.S. territories were all that Anglo-Saxon at their inception. Rather, whites emptied them of Natives, as they hoped to empty the nation of people of African ancestry, when or if slavery ended, and of Mexicans and Chinese and other racial "undesirables," when their labor was no longer needed.[13] Agents of U.S. empire believed that U.S. citizens and their allies too would one day empty Cuba and Hawai'i of people of color and transform them into white republics.[14] Yet most hoped that sufficient nonwhite people and barbarous ways would remain to give the "Pearl of the Antilles" and the "Paradise of the Pacific" the erotic and exotic ambiences and experiences white travelers associated with the tropics. This mad array of wildly contradictory goals and fantasies fueled deadly serious practices and beliefs.

After more than half a century of dutiful performances and carefully staged interventions, the shared destinies of Cuba and Hawai'i produced the annexation of only the latter, no doubt shocking the expansionists who had long deemed the former far more worthy of formal inclusion in the Union. They were incorporated into the U.S. empire in different ways, Hawai'i as a territory, and Cuba as a protectorate, statuses that half a century later structured their radically different forms of official decolonization, statehood and revolution. Even as the islands' different forms of imperial governance shaped their processes of divergence, many U.S. expansionists continued to believe that the future of Cuba and Hawai'i could be found in idealized visions of the United States' past, and they labored, or so they imagined, to make it so.

The logics and legacies of white republicanism and settler colonialism remained influential long after the United States *generally* came to prefer informal, commercial imperialism, or what scholars have called the "new" imperialism, over formal, territorial colonialism.[15] Just as the new imperialism often associated with offshore islands and linked to 1898 has important roots and precedents in the nineteenth century and on the North American continent, the ideologies and logics of the old white republican settler colonialism continued to shape U.S. imperialism deep into the twentieth century and hence long after its practice was formally abandoned.[16] Consider this study's endpoints. In the mid-nineteenth century, expansionist travel writers wrote the futures of Cuba and Hawai'i into romanticized versions of the United States' Pilgrim and Puritan pasts to demonstrate these islands' worthiness to become part of the virtuous republic and empire for liberty.[17] In the mid-twentieth century, self-identified anti-imperial travel writers and tourism promoters presented the Cuban revolution and Hawaiian statehood as national family romances rooted in the sort of moderate, orderly revolution that produced the U.S. nation and as noble causes U.S. citizens should support. In both instances and at numerous points in between, they averred that Cuba and Hawai'i were American enough, civilized enough, republican enough, and white enough to warrant the support of a U.S. nation and citizenry intimately bound to them by ties of affection and kinship, destiny and duty.[18]

The Pleasures of Imperialism

All this talk of white republican virtue, whether in 1898, 1959, or any other time, may seem to bear little relation to prevailing historical images of Hawai'i as a land of carefree "hula girls" and "beach boys" and Cuba as a "whorehouse with a view of the sea." Was it not visions of sensuous Polynesian women clad in grass skirts and *mulatas* clad in tight ones—not fraternal orders of white men—that made Hawai'i and Cuba U.S. tourists' two most popular tropical destinations overseas? Was it not desire for the erotic and exotic that drew U.S. citizens to Havana and Honolulu, rather than the opportunity to stand on one's republican or any other kind of virtue? The processes by which the answers to these questions both changed and endured in altered form are as complicated as they are contradictory.

Imperial fantasies and projects to transform Cuba and Hawai'i into white republics animated efforts to ban all manner of "vice," foremost among them hula in Hawai'i and gambling in Cuba, as barbaric relics of dying pasts and racially inferior peoples, despite the fact that they were wildly popular with tourists. Yet even some of the most determined crusaders against these and other "iniquities" came to argue that upstanding U.S. citizens could occasionally indulge in the vices of backward people as a way to maintain the "barbarian virtues" needed to prevent the overcivilization of modern people.[19] In other words, while remaking "them" into modern and civilized republicans capable of self-government, "we" might enjoy debauched delights in moderation.[20]

In the interwar era, travel writers and tourism promoters made excess the watchword and abandoned the golden rule of all things in moderation; they instead sought to bring to the forefront of U.S. empire the sorts of pleasures they associated with Spanish aristocrats in Cuba and Native monarchs in Hawai'i. In key ways, the exclusive enclaves that privileged whites built on the outskirts of Havana and Honolulu resembled hill stations, most famously those of British India which were, Dane Kennedy argues, at once "sites of refuge and sites of surveillance," places where wealthy whites withdrew from the societies they ruled and places from which they ruled them.[21] The exclusive, cosmopolitan communities of Cuba and Hawai'i similarly were sites where imperial politics and pleasures converged. Yet even as privileged whites modeled their modern and enlightened aristocratic societies in the "American" tropics on European lines, they insisted that unlike those corrupt, oppressive monarchical empires and imperialists, agents of the U.S. empire remained committed to the extension of universal rights and liberties and eventual self-government to all in Cuba, Hawai'i, and the world. The notion that imperial agents could act like decadent aristocrats without endangering the U.S. republic and its citizenry rested on a confidence in the incorruptibility of their collective and individual republican virtue (such confidence could and did coexist with doubts and fears), an example of the hubris and willful ignorance that is an especial privilege of powerful nations and peoples.[22]

The interwar-era strategy of practicing repression while preaching republicanism prefigured the Cold War practice of supporting right-wing dictatorships while overthrowing left-leaning regimes in the transformation of backward agricultural societies into modern liberal capitalist democracies.[23] In Hawai'i and Cuba of the 1930s and the 1950s, these practices

generated backlashes that took the form of interracial and cross-class movements against white power and privilege and for equality and justice and
representative self-government. While the resort served as a central site for
the sociability and reproduction of cosmopolitan white elites and those
accorded honorary whiteness, it became a leading symbol used by movements against racism and imperialism and for democracy across lines of
class and color.[24] During the interwar period in Cuba, tourism was of central importance to an authoritarian-developmental political regime that
depended on securing massive loans from the United States (which happened in different form in the 1950s). At the same time in Hawai'i, tourism
served a repressive oligarchy determined to govern without interference
from Washington and to keep U.S. capital out of Hawai'i in order to maintain its monopoly of the political economy (a hold that was effectively ruptured during and after World War II). Dispensing with moderation in
practicing repression or indulging in delights imperiled political and pleasurable imperial regimes and led to revolts against them. They inspired
postwar travel writers and tourism promoters to reembrace commitments
to virtue and duty and seek to instill them in the business and recreational
travelers they charged with enacting the American Century and winning
the global Cold War.

Over the course of the nineteenth century and for much of the twentieth, religious and republican principles informed fears that unfettered leisure threatened the well-being of the U.S. nation, its citizens, and their
special destiny. Efforts to resolve the dilemma of enjoying actual or armchair travel without endangering moral and material progress generally
hinged on harnessing the pursuit of pleasure to the performance of duty. If
travel represented a way for white elites to improve their minds and bodies
while enhancing their power and prestige, promoters reasoned, why could
not these same people work to advance their nation's interests and enhance
its power and prestige in the process? Boosters labored mightily to render
travel and tourism "a kind of virtuous consumption," as Marguerite Shaffer
aptly phrases it.[25]

Travel writers and tourism promoters exploited U.S. citizens' ambivalent views of leisure, notions rooted in values bequeathed by the Puritan
colonials and republican nationals who saw the demands of destiny and
duty as inextricably linked. This ambivalence helped make the travel
account the most popular literary genre in the thirteen colonies and the
new United States. Educational and uplifting, travel writing peddled

"truth," unlike novels and other kinds of fiction, which were widely viewed as morally corrupting, if not outright sinful. Even as proscriptions against fiction disappeared, the travel narrative retained both its popularity and its purposefulness. The privileged, white nineteenth-century U.S. citizens who came to regard vacations as social and cultural entitlements and mental and physical health requirements continued to view leisure and idleness as "sources of moral, spiritual, financial, and political danger," Cindy Aron shows. Whereas the puritanical distrust of leisure had roots in the religious belief that hard work glorified God, the republican one had roots in the political belief that the nation's future depended upon the self-sacrifice and steadfast labor of its free white people.[26]

Here was another juncture at which the political imperatives of empire dovetailed with pursuits of imperial pleasure. At their core, travel writing and tourism promotion involve producing a place, its people, and their history and culture in order to profit from their consumption by readers and visitors from away and also by those who invested in travel and tourism to chase their own dreams of pleasure and power. Travel writers and tourism professionals took great pains to make mental and material trips to Cuba or Hawai'i irresistible to U.S. citizens. At the same time, they labored to transform actual and armchair travelers into agents of "manifest destiny" during the continental land rush and "diplomats without portfolio" during the Cold War.[27] Their goals eluded them perhaps as often as not. This should not be surprising. As Melani McAlister argues, "the end product of a successful discourse" results from neither a "conspiracy, nor a functional-ist set of representations in the service of power, but a process of conver-gence, in which historical events, overlapping representations, and diverse vested interests come together in a powerful and productive, if historically contingent accord."[28] Efforts to harness travel and tourism to imperial poli-tics did and did not produce the intended results. They became more prone to backfire or fail outright when anti-imperial agents appropriated, recast, and redeployed dominant travel and tourism discourses to advance their own goals. Neither the wealth nor the power of hosts and guests could change this equation.

Contrary to received wisdom, overseas travel remained an elite preroga-tive until after the mid-twentieth century. A recent generation of scholars has challenged the view held by an earlier generation who charged the mass, crass hordes of overseas tourists with debasing highbrow overseas travel in the late nineteenth century.[29] Overseas travel certainly became more accessible to the middle class over time, but as late as the 1950s, working and retired corporate executives and high-level managers, their wives, and their children dominated the U.S. overseas travel market.[30] Together they represented the past, present, and future of the nation's managerial elite. Instead of becoming a populist practice, overseas travel remained more a patrician privilege until the takeoff of the jet age in the 1960s. At the time of revolution and statehood, overseas tourists were more similar than not to a pair of Boston Brahmin peers of John Quincy Adams who visited and wrote travelogues on Cuba and Hawai'i. Their works confirmed Adams's view that the United States would possess both of them in due time. Once formed, "the habits of empire" endured all manner of change in remarkable ways.[31] This is a story of how the United States and many of its citizens came to regard these acquired habits less as privileges than as rights. It is also a story about the citizens and subjects who struggled for freedoms denied them by an imperial republic that proclaimed liberty the essence and purpose of its mission and destiny.

The first chapter explores how Cuba and Hawai'i became twinned in the U.S. imperial imagination as the apple and the pear, the "First Fruits of a Tropical Eden" empire overseas. Unable to establish that Cuba and Hawai'i were quantitatively white enough to warrant incorporation into the U.S. republic as territories or states, travel writers wrote them into New England's Pilgrim and Puritan pasts to whiten them qualitatively. Travel writers and tourism promoters argued that the white creoles of Cuba and Hawai'i were laying foundations that would hasten their transformation into republican settler societies emptied of indigenous and immigrant people of color, who would somehow die out or leave after annexation. Accepting travel writers' and tourism promoters' constructions of Hawai'i as American enough, civilized enough, republican enough, and white enough to warrant the privilege of eventual statehood, the United States made it a territory in 1900. After the United States failed to secure Cuban annexation after intervening in Cubans' war for independence in 1898, Cuban and U.S. annexationists adapted promotional schemes developed by *haole* (originally stranger, by the mid-nineteenth century applied particularly to Anglo-Saxon settlers)[32] in Hawai'i to pursue this time-honored goal in Cuba during the U.S. military occupation and early years of the Cuban republic. The boosters of both sought to attract tourists in the hopes that a visit would convince some of them to settle or invest in the United States' newest frontiers.

The U.S. abandonment of white settler colonialism in Cuba and Hawai'i and reconstitution of a U.S. overseas empire that came to prefer informal colonial control is the subject of Chapter 2, "Garden Republics or Plantation Regimes?" Elite whites failed to transform Cuba and Hawai'i into settler republics, and they failed to annex Cuba. But they succeeded in adapting narratives produced in pursuit of these aborted dreams to the construction of new political and pleasure regimes. On the eve of World War I, white elites from all three places embarked on what might be called social imperialism for themselves and their privileged peers. They built elite white enclaves in Havana's suburb of Marianao and Honolulu's Waikīkī. They designed them to keep social and racial inferiors at bay and conduct the important business of reproducing the dominant classes of Cuba and Hawai'i. Waikīkī Beach and the Havana Country Club emerged as models of the sites that came to serve as nerve centers of U.S. overseas relations around the globe, ones inhabited by white and whitened English-speaking elites presumably bound by common interests. No longer ideologically obligated to promote republican virtue and censure barbaric vice, white elites embraced for themselves and tourists a host of formerly forbidden pleasures. Foremost among them were the hula and surfing, and the gambling and prostitution, for which Hawai'i and Cuba remained famed even as imperialists condemned them as incompatible with American civilization and white republicanism.

The transformation of Waikīkī and Marianao into enclaves of white power, privilege, and pleasure coincided in 1920 with a strike by Japanese and Filipino workers and claims by Hawaiians to their native lands and a fraudulent and violent Cuban presidential election. These events potentially imperiled white rule. The United States intervened in Cuba and threatened intervention in Hawai'i. Chapter 3, "Royal Resorts for Tropical Tramps," compares the ways promoters of Cuba and Hawai'i transformed discourses of tourism to reconstitute white governance and convince the United States of their ability to maintain order without direct supervision or rule. They worked to convince U.S. tourists to invest culturally and politically, and in Cuba also financially, in tourist and political regimes imagined as modern aristocracies devoted, on the one hand, to the preparation of the masses for self-government, and, on the other hand, to the production of a host of decadent pleasures for their "betters." Promoters deployed narratives of the freedoms enjoyed by tourists to present authoritarian regimes as enlightened polities devoted to liberty and progress and dedicated to the extension of eventual republican self-government from above.

The fourth chapter, "Revolutions, Reformations, Restorations," traces the beginning of the demise of the "traditional" political classes that took form in turn-of-the-twentieth-century Cuba and Hawai'i. Cubans across class and color lines overthrew the Machado dictatorship in 1933 and worked to make Cuba a sovereign and inclusive democratic nation. After two trials resulting from a cross-racial rape accusation in 1931 blatantly exposed the dual structure of rights for haole and people of color in Hawai'i, its indigenous and its immigrant U.S. citizens and settlers moved to end haole hegemony and forge interracial democracy. In both places, emergent social and political movements targeted the tourism industry as a symbol and source of racism and imperialism. After World War II, Fulgencio Batista and haole Republicans sought to contain demands for equality and democracy. They promoted tourism as the safest and surest path toward economic and political development. Both promised prosperity and consumerism as a compensation for the lack of, or slow progress toward, democracy. To their dismay, most of the people of Hawai'i and Cuba rejected the rewards of consumer citizenship as a substitute for the civic and civil rights of political citizenship.

The final chapter, "Travels to Revolution and Statehood," explores the roles travel and tourism played in the Cuban revolution and Hawaiian statehood. Supporters of revolution and statehood made these movements appeal to U.S. audiences by interpreting them through historically informed travel narratives. Supporters cast the Cuban revolution in two ways. On the one hand, they presented it as a quest to rescue a nation and people prostituted by a dictator who had gambled their resources and again rebuilt the tourism industry on commercial vice. On the other hand, they described it as a struggle waged by rebels who modeled themselves on the U.S. founding fathers, with their virile republican manhood and virtuous republic. Tourism and statehood promoters in Hawai'i adopted a two-pronged strategy as well. They presented the beauty of its mixed-race people, particularly the women and children, as a leading reason for U.S. tourists to visit and, once there, see how the Asian-descended majority had become so thoroughly Americanized as to warrant the full rights of citizenship and national belonging that the mainland had not long ago extended to recently whitened European ethnics. Tourism promoters wrote Hawai'i into postwar narratives of normative whiteness with roots not in an old

"Plymouth Rock whiteness" but in a new "Ellis Island whiteness" that celebrated the United States as "a nation of immigrants," in the words of Matthew Frye Jacobson.[33]

Although by no means predetermined, the story in many ways came
full circle. Advocates of revolution and statehood updated old narratives to
cast the rebels of Cuba and the multiracial people of Hawai'i as American
enough, civilized enough, republican enough, and white enough to warrant
the support of these movements by a U.S. nation and people bound to
them by ties of affection and kinship, history and genealogy. Revolution
and statehood could hardly have represented more divergent courses of
decolonization (which Hawaiians did not experience as such). Yet both
resulted in the incorporation of hundreds of thousands of people from
Cuba and Hawai'i into the Union as full-fledged U.S. citizens, albeit in far
different ways than nineteenth-century imperial actors would or could have
imagined.

CHAPTER ONE

First Fruits of a Tropical Eden

There are laws of political as well as physical gravitation; and if an apple severed by the tempest from its native tree cannot choose but to fall to the ground, Cuba, forcibly disjoined from its own unnatural connection with Spain, and incapable of self-support, can gravitate only to the North American Union, which by the same law of nature, cannot cast her off from its bosom.

John Quincy Adams, 1823

The native population [of Hawai'i] are fast fading away, the foreign fast increasing. The inevitable destiny of the islands is to pass into the possession of another power. That power is just as inevitably our own. ... The pear is nearly ripe; we scarcely have to shake the tree in order to bring the luscious fruit readily into our lap.

Alta California, 1851

For the statesmen who imagined Cuba and Hawai'i as the first fruits of a tropical-island empire, providential and natural law foretold of their belonging to the United States. Writing in 1823, John Quincy Adams averred that biblical injunction and national honor prohibited the United States from plucking the forbidden fruit of Cuba from Spain. But when the inevitable storm caused the apple to fall, the law of gravity dictated that it would land on U.S. soil. Four years earlier, a group of Congregationalist missionaries, some of them direct descendants of John Winthrop, sailed from Boston to Hawai'i to build a "city on a hill" in the Pacific. Much as Winthrop had read the death of Native Americans from imported diseases as a sign that "the Lord hath cleared our title to what we possess," the San

Francisco newspaper *Alta California* interpreted the mass death of Native Hawaiians as a sign that the United States was fated to possess the imperial pear. In 1853 Cuba and Hawai'i became twinned objects of desire when guests at a party celebrating the election of Franklin Pierce as president raised their glasses to toast "Cuba and Hawai'i—May they soon be added to the Galaxy of States."[1]

The stars did not align, nor the fruits ripen, so as to bring Cuba into the U.S. empire before Hawai'i. In January 1893 a group of missionaries' descendants, backed by U.S. officials and troops, threw honor to the wind and overthrew the sovereign queen and independent Kingdom of Hawai'i. U.S. Minister John Stevens raised the Stars and Stripes over Honolulu and wrote Washington: "The Hawaiian pear is fully ripe, and this is the golden hour to pluck it."[2] Before his message even reached the capital, newspapers across the nation reencoded Hawai'i as the first fruit of overseas empire. The *New York Independent* asserted, "The ripe apple falls into our hands, and we should be very foolish if we should throw it away. . . . The soil is fertile, the climate wonderfully equable and salubrious; it has excellent harbors, and the most wonderful volcano in existence."[3] It did not take the likes of John W. Foster, secretary of state at the time of the coup, to know that Kilauea was the volcano in question and to list it among the reasons the United States must possess Hawai'i.[4] Well-read U.S. citizens knew, and expansionists among them believed, the same. Many with the means anticipated seeing a cyclorama of Kilauea at the World's Columbian Exposition in Chicago later that year. The best-informed readers would have recognized the annexationist Lorrin A. Thurston as a founder of the firms that operated the hotel at the volcano and would exhibit it in Chicago. After Thurston's annexationist-tourist promotional efforts helped produce the annexation of the Paradise of the Pacific in 1898, advocates of Cuban annexation adapted the promotional strategies of Hawai'i to pursue this goal for the Pearl of the Antilles.

Travel writers and tourism promoters helped spread and sustain desire for Cuba and Hawai'i when the United States was too weak and too divided to wrest them from Spanish and Hawaiian control. Scholars have explored how representations of Cuba and Hawai'i as barbaric, racially inferior, and childlike established their unfitness for self-government and need for imperial tutelage. But this is only part of the story. Travel writers and tourism promoters wrote Cuba and Hawai'i into narratives of American civilization to establish their worthiness to join an imperial republic governed by and

for free whites. They rendered their possession essential to the "continu-
ance and integrity" of the Union, as Adams said of Cuba.[5]

All empires enact and legitimize colonial conquest through ritual and
performance as well as violence and decree. Agents of U.S. empire sought
to create the appearances, if not necessarily the conditions, that enabled the
naturalization of forcible conquests as consensual acts. They staged elaborate performances and conducted time-honored "ceremonies of possession" designed to incorporate into the empire for liberty colonies that only
the founding generation called by that name.[6] Becoming a U.S. *territory*
required demonstrating that a desired possession and its people were or
were capable of becoming American enough, civilized enough, republican
enough, and white enough to warrant the privilege of joining the body
politic. Only by fulfilling or demonstrating the potential to fulfill these conditions could a land and its people show they had forged the "bonds of
affection and love" with the U.S. nation and citizenry needed to enter into
a consensual union with them.[7] Annexationists scripted travelogues and
designed tourism programs used to stage performances aimed at convincing U.S. citizens that Cuba and Hawai'i were capable of becoming integral
parts of the imaginary white republic.

Atlantic and Pacific Visions, Cuban and Hawaiian Dreams

In the antebellum era, visions of a United States that extended beyond the
continent into the "mighty Pacific" and "turbulent Atlantic" were more
widely shared than is typically thought. Thomas Jefferson for one drew
upon them to imagine peopling "all America, North and South" from the
"nest" of "our confederacy," linking the Atlantic and Pacific by land and
sea, and challenging rival powers for dominion over them. His conversa-
tions with Alexander von Humboldt, work with John Ledyard, and his and
his fellow citizens' voracious reading of the works of famous explorers and
investigative travelers shaped and sustained dreams of empire.[8]

U.S. citizens debated whether the nation should become a commercial
and naval power rivaling Britain, France, and Spain or a host of white
settler societies confederated into a "Union of many republics, comprising
hundreds of happy millions," as the coiner of the phrase manifest destiny,
John O'Sullivan, proclaimed in 1839. U.S. nationals disagreed over which
of these two forms U.S. imperialism should take, even as they, like European nations, practiced both. But most concurred that the U.S. empire for

liberty did not and would not resemble the oppressive colonialism practiced by European nations. They "conquer only to enslave," O'Sullivan's *Democratic Review* thundered in 1848. By contrast, the United States "conquers only to bestow freedom," an idea that policymakers embedded in the nation's legal frameworks for expansion.[9]

The founding generation established the methods by which to expand the nation's territory and make citizens of the "right" immigrants needed to settle it. The Northwest Ordinance of 1787 established the frameworks that the United States used to acquire new territories by consensual legal means that could and frequently did elide violent conquest. Territories would become eligible for statehood once they possessed a sizeable population of U.S. citizens and white settlers, demonstrated their capacity for republican self-government, and stated their desire to enter the Union. Aware from recent experience that colonies might become objects of desire by rival powers or seek their independence, the founders took care to design "the right kind of colonialism," one that "could lead to happy decolonization at some future, undetermined time," as Walter LaFeber observes. In 1790, Congress limited eligibility for naturalization to "free white persons." The twinned frameworks for enlarging the nation and restricting its citizenry enabled imperial architects to proclaim an empire for liberty by and for free whites while pursuing dominion over foreign lands and nonwhite peoples. Federal officials thereby institutionalized a racialized system of territorial and demographic expansion, one rhetorically devoid of vanquished colonies and subject peoples. In the process, they made empire and liberty as mutually sustaining as slavery and freedom.[10]

While public officials led the way in designing the empire, private citizens often moved ahead of the government in expanding the nation. The ideological, as well as practical, importance of pioneering whites to U.S. expansionism became regarded as a matter of fact. Writing in 1873, at the height of Cuba's Ten Years' War (1868–1878) against Spanish colonialism and slavery, the Italian travel writer and journalist Antonio Gallenga mocked U.S. ambitions in Cuba and ridiculed the U.S. travelers who constantly told him that the "'American annexation of Cuba was an event as desirable as it was inevitable.'" He found such views as astonishing as they were specious. For one, "the Creoles want 'Cuba for the Cubans.'" For another, he found no evidence of the "usual system of U.S. annexation," which required that a territory "be Americanized before it can become American." In Texas and California, Gallenga asserted, "swarms of adventurers, pioneers, squatters paved the way" for their annexation. But in Cuba, "no progress in the way of Yankee colonization is as yet perceptible, and none is practicable." U.S. settlement of a territory was a prerequisite of annexation. So was proof that the white creoles of a potential possession shared with U.S. citizens a desire for annexation and devotion to republicanism. When the United States extended policies to Cuba and Hawai'i designed to acquire them, it committed to incorporating them into its institutional frameworks of citizenship and colonialism and ideological frameworks of white republicanism.[11]

In 1823, Secretary of State John Quincy Adams established the Monroe Doctrine and no-transfer as official U.S. policies toward Cuba. The first forbade interference in its affairs by other foreign powers. The second proclaimed the right of the United States to annex Cuba if it ceased to be a Spanish colony, rendering Cuban independence compatible with, perhaps even a prerequisite of, U.S. annexation. Although Adams thought that the magnitude of Cuba's black population and the weakness of the U.S. military made annexation impossible at the time, he claimed that the United States had an unparalleled interest in a Cuba that could not and would not want to be independent. Its white *criollos* shared with their U.S. counterparts a hatred of monarchy and a devotion to "the republican spirit of freedom." This mutual devotion would propel the white creoles of a Cuba freed from Spain to choose union with the United States over what Adams believed its only alternative, incorporation into the monarchical empire of Britain. Adams asserted that what was needed to achieve annexation was time: time for the United States to become stronger, time for Spain to become weaker, time for Cuba's white population to increase, and time for its black population to decrease. Acknowledging the prudence of Adam's "patient-waiting" strategy, every subsequent nineteenth-century president reaffirmed the Monroe Doctrine and no-transfer as official policy toward Cuba.[12]

President John Tyler extended the Monroe Doctrine to Hawai'i in 1842. The then-congressman Adams wrote the report designed to establish U.S. relations with and recognize the Kingdom of Hawai'i as an independent nation. A decade later, the United States extended the no-transfer policy to Hawai'i, asserting that the United States would annex the kingdom if it somehow lost its sovereignty. As he had for Cuba, Adams proclaimed that the United States had an unparalleled interest in Hawai'i, in its case as a result of the labors of New England missionaries. They had brought to Hawai'i the Christianity, civilization, and constitutional government that entitled it to join the world family of nations and "be acknowledged by their brethren of the human race as a separate and independent community." Adams again contrasted the tyrannical British Empire, which recently had seized Hawai'i for a brief time, to an honorable U.S. empire. "The people of the North American Union [have a] virtual right of conquest" over Hawai'i, based not on "the brutal arm of physical power, but over the mind and heart by the celestial panoply of the gospel of peace and love." As in Cuba, bonds of affection between the people of the United States and Hawai'i would lead to a mutual desire to make it part of the Union. As in Cuba, all later nineteenth-century presidents affirmed the Monroe Doctrine and no transfer as policy toward Hawai'i.[13]

As policymakers settled in to wait, expansionist travel writers worked to stimulate desires for possessing Cuba and Hawai'i and making them part of the Union. The notion that these islands had ties to the nation's mythic Pilgrim and Puritan pasts crystallized in the imperial imagination over the nineteenth century. Abiel Abbot and James Jackson Jarves, two prominent Bostonians who traveled in the same circle as the Adams family, helped make these visions foundational with their respective travelogues on Cuba (1828) and Hawai'i (1843). Statesmen, journalists, travel writers, and other expansionists who worked to make Cuba and Hawai'i part of the Union drew inspiration and arguments from their travel narratives for the rest of the century.

In 1828, Abbot, a prominent minister and classmate of Adams at Harvard, published a collection of letters written during a four-month trip to Cuba, which apparently caused his death on his return voyage (he spent so many grueling hours in the saddle that his already poor health worsened). The travelogue demonstrated the prudence of his peer's patient-waiting strategy. Abbot accomplished this goal by locating Cuba's future in New England's Pilgrim past. He spoke with an authority rooted in his impeccable republican credentials: "His parents belonged to that truly respectable class, the yeomanry of New England" and instilled in him the "habits of simplicity, diligence, and religious propriety of conduct, which the descendants of the Puritans have maintained from the first settlement of the country."[14]

In comparison to "other slave-holding islands," Abbot found Cuba "strong in its *free* population," with a "numerous *yeomanry,* armed and mounted." Both foretold of high destinies. Although then "unprepared" to challenge Spanish rule, Cubans in time would "become more homogenous and patriotic." Abbot proclaimed the *monteros*, whom he asserted "chiefly cultivated" tobacco, the bedrock of a budding white republican yeomanry. Spaniards and Cubans would have corrected Abbot. Cuba's tobacco farmers were *vegueros* and easily distinguished from the often impoverished, renter class of *monteros* that elite Spanish *peninsulares* and Cuban *criollos* alike regarded as inferiors. Tellingly, Abbott's incorrect usage persisted in the United States throughout the century. It held profound significance to U.S. citizens, who associated fierce independence and armed and mounted free white men with republicanism.[15]

Abbot popularized the belief that the monteros represented Cuba's hope for the growth of the united and homogeneous patriots of a future republic. They were numerous and "increasing faster than any other species." By contrast, even maintaining the slave population required constant imports. Abbot decried the monteros' penchant for gambling and thought they could be "better disposed to labor." But he admired their physical and moral fiber: "A hardier, healthier, more muscular race of men cannot be found in the mountains of New Hampshire or Vermont." Indeed, he deemed the monteros more worthy than "many of the yeomanry of New England" of the appellation "virtuous progeny of the virtuous pilgrims."[16]

New Englanders like Abbot admired Jeffersonian republicanism. But they tended to regard Massachusetts as the true birthplace and home of the virtuous freeholding yeomanry and U.S. republic—not Virginia, where African slave labor fueled the growth of a tobacco-plantation society and a white landed elite that often looked and acted more like aristocrats than republicans. By contrast, Abbot's free, white, tobacco-growing monteros were fast propelling Cuba along a path that would soon raise it to the same plane as Massachusetts's more rustic neighboring states. In the mountains of both, the yeomanry devoted themselves to cultivating their own land and raising their own children as the producer-citizens of a white republic. Fellow citizens embraced Abbot's finding as one of great import: Cuba's yeomanry traced its cultural and political genealogy to mythic forebears of the United States.

Abbot wrote as white republicanism was beginning to unite some elite whites of Cuba and the United States around the idea of annexation. After rich criollos called for increasing white migration to reverse the island's "Africanization," Spain countered with repression and a "policy of importing blacks to scare whites into political acquiescence." This move drove many white Cubans into opposition to the peninsulares. They began to articulate a Cuban identity grounded in whiteness; some equated Cuban independence with U.S. annexation. Such disciples of white republicanism began to bond around the idea that annexation would hasten the end of slavery and attract the free whites who would empty a United States including Cuba of their blacks.[17]

Two decades after Abbot tied Cuba to a U.S. history that began at Plymouth Rock, the New England missionaries sent to Hawai'i by the American Board of Commissioners for Foreign Missions (ABCFM) inspired James Jackson Jarves's account of this second "city on a hill." He published *History of the Hawaiian Islands* and *Scenes and Scenery in the Sandwich Islands* in 1843. Like Abbot, he did not take a stand on annexation, but others later used both men's travelogues to promote this goal. Like Abbot, Jarves was from an old New England family that traveled in an elite Brahmin circle of merchants, ministers, and statesmen, which included John Quincy Adams. Like Abbot, Jarves traveled "in search of health and recreation." Unlike Abbot, Jarves was not a minister and admitted a predisposition to hostility toward the missionaries. However, he became so enraptured with "the wondrous changes which a christian benevolence has wrought" on Hawaiians and Hawai'i that he became an outspoken champion. He promoted U.S. interests in and representations of Hawai'i as an outpost of Anglo-Saxon civilization in his capacity as a travel writer and editor of a local newspaper, *The Polynesian*.[18]

Much of the credibility of Jarves's travelogues derived from the fact that they were not missionary accounts that glorified the mission and sought support for it. But like them, *Scenes and Scenery in the Sandwich Islands* presented the United States as a Protestant nation ordained to transplant its city on a hill overseas. Providence had situated the Kilauea volcano to serve as a beacon guiding ships to the safety of the "great ocean hotel." The flames of a "lighthouse tended by God's own hand" illuminated the missionaries' success at making Hawai'i "the central point of christianity and civilization in this portion of the globe." Jarves felt that Hawai'i owed its nationhood and Hawaiians their sovereignty to ABCFM agents: "The Anglo-Saxons are capable of teaching; the Malay of being taught; the one by its own native energies can conquer and rule the world; the very existence and advancement of the latter is dependent upon the forbearance and benevolence of the former." He ignored the fact that Hawaiians embraced

Christianity and civilization in no small part in response to the devastations
resulting from mass death by imported diseases and because of their determination to become and remain an independent nation and people recognized as such by the world family of nations.[19]

In helping constitute the kingdom as a modern nation-state, the missionaries situated Hawai'i in narratives of history and modernity equated
not abstractly with the West but concretely with the United States. Jarves
insisted that the continued existence of the Kingdom of Hawai'i required
the continued "aid of foreigners," specifically retired missionaries to serve
its government: "for its real interests no better class can be found, than
those who have been so instrumental in nurturing and sustaining them in
their progress towards civilization. . . . In pursuing this policy, they and
their children will become identified with the nation." In elaborating the
"debt of gratitude" that Hawai'i owed the missionaries for its nationhood,
Jarves ignored the fact that Hawaiians had enlisted the aid of foreigners to
preempt colonization.[20]

Jarves's and Abbot's works became foundational texts of subsequent
nineteenth-century travelogues and annexationist debates on Cuba and
Hawai'i. But linking Cuba to New England proved a tougher sell than linking New England and Hawai'i, which rejected slavery and became a land of
many Protestants and few Catholics. Many New Englanders visited and
settled in Cuba, but they obviously did not achieve positions of authority
in Spain's colonial bureaucracy. By contrast, a host of New England missionaries, merchants, and professionals settled in Hawai'i and became
important government officials. They built courts, churches, and schools
and introduced legal codes, religious communities, and educational systems
modeled on those of New England. Even as California supplanted Massachusetts as the leading trade partner of Hawai'i, haole ties to New England
endured. New Englanders predominated among annexationists in Hawai'i
and on the mainland, best symbolized by a key trio of men from Maine:
James G. Blaine, Sanford Dole, and John L. Stevens. Cuba boasted substantial and persistent New England connections, but they were not as broad
or deep as those in Hawai'i. Nonetheless, Abbot's construction of Cuba as
a nascent white republic whose virtuous yeomanry traced its cultural and
political genealogies to the Pilgrims acquired new importance in the mid-
nineteenth century. Then, as divisions over slavery began to tear the United
States apart, an alliance committed to Cuban annexation continued to hold
due to the willingness of many of its members to compromise on slavery.

A Piece of Plymouth Rock in the Tropics

By 1854, the annexationist Cuban travelogue was so common that the Harvard Divinity School graduate William Henry Hurlbert could summarize its main arguments in two sentences: "Spain is tyrannical, Cuba is rich, America is ravenously republican. From these propositions it has been deduced that Cuba must soon become a member of our great and glorious confederacy." His *anti*-annexationist travelogue appeared amid heated debates on the Kansas-Nebraska Act. By then, sectionalism had permeated every arena of public discourse, including empire, as Robert E. May's phrase the "sectionalization of manifest destiny" indicates.[21] Many scholars accept the idea that the "Cuban question" had become but part of the "southern question."

But the Cuban question never became just a southern question. Richard Henry Dana's famous declaration, "You cannot reason from Massachusetts to Cuba," appeared in his canonical anti-annexationist Cuban travelogue of 1859. Few scholars have entertained the notion that the line was anything but obvious. Fewer still have imagined that it might have expressed exasperation about how deeply associated Cuba and New England had become. After all, New England and abolitionism seemed synonymous, and a number of New England's most prominent abolitionists opposed the annexation of Cuba. They exploited the affinities the tropical, slaveholding colony shared with the South to distance Cuba from the North. Dana and Hurlbert located Cuba in the South to show that it had no place in a future republic that they believed must and would be modeled on the North.[22]

In doing so, they joined a literary war against editors and journalists, planters and politicians, and travelers from Cuba and the U.S. North, South, and West who found Cuba so desirable as to warrant compromise on the future of slavery.[23] Even as slavery was tearing the United States apart, many insisted that devotion to the white republicanism that underlay the empire for liberty was capable of reconciling the nation on the Cuban question. These annexationists did reason from Massachusetts to Cuba. Of course efforts to annex Cuba in the 1850s failed, and they did not prevent the U.S. Civil War. But cross-sectional discourses on annexation were not simply a cover that hid the real goal of annexing Cuba as a slave territory or state. Recognizing that emancipation was a global process and that perpetuating slavery forever was unlikely led many to embrace an alternative white supremacist tropical-island fantasy of Cuba as part of a free and united U.S. republic in an unknown future.

Abbot wrote Cuba into New England during a period of informal agitation for annexation there and in the United States, which blossomed into an organized bilingual, cross-sectional, transnational annexation movement at midcentury. In response to an aborted slave rebellion of 1844, the Spanish government instituted La Escalera, a brutal reign of death, torture, and imprisonment that drove into U.S. exile the white Cuban creoles who helped transform binational annexationist sentiments into transnational annexationist organizations headquartered in New Orleans and New York. Many believed that a leading British abolitionist and former British consul in Havana had plotted to foment a black revolution in Cuba to check U.S. expansion in the hemisphere. As a result, La Escalera renewed interest in the annexation of Cuba and Texas. It influenced the filibustering expeditions of Narciso López. It led to the founding of *La Verdad*, the longest-lived and most influential nineteenth-century Cuban newspaper in the United States. The paper brought together U.S. proponents of manifest destiny (including John O'Sullivan), English-speaking creole planters who commanded some influence in Washington (most notably, Gaspar Bentancourt Cisneros), and a variety of "patriotic" annexationist writers. Basil Rauch regards the paper as "by much the most effective to date of any propaganda vehicle of a foreign group" in the United States and gives it some credit for "the importance which the desire for Cuba began to assume in American politics after the Mexican War." Travel writers contributed to and drew so much information and inspiration from *La Verdad*, especially its pamphlet *A Series of Articles on the Cuban Question* (1849), that it deserves recognition as a leading archive on the subject.[24]

With diverse contributors divided over slavery and addressing multiple audiences, *La Verdad* was a multi-vocal production. It maintained two constant themes, which an early supporter, long-term Havana resident, and uncompromising advocate of slavery, John S. Thrasher, later called "national gain," the notion that trade with Cuba would enrich all sections of the United States, and "national power," the idea that Cuba was a key to U.S. preponderance in the Atlantic and Pacific. But these were not the issues that most divided proponents and opponents of annexation. Few disputed the riches the nation would reap from an annexed Cuba. Few doubted its acquisition would allow the United States to project its power across two oceans. Matters of wealth and power did not divide nearly so much as matters of race and republicanism did.[25]

La Verdad's editors and contributors presented annexation as a project that criss-crossed the levels of section, nation, and Atlantic world. Writing under the banner "A Journal Supported by the Patriots of Cuba, for the Dissemination of Republican Principles and Intelligence," contributors to the Cuban question pamphlet articulated a specific role for each section of the United States to play in resolving the slavery question, saving the union, and preserving republicanism in the New World. They held up New England, the first region in the United States to abolish slavery, as the model of gradual emancipation. A North and South united on annexation would use the New England model of emancipation to put a slow, orderly, and peaceable end to slavery once Cuba was made part of the Union. Contributors also viewed emancipation as an Atlantic-wide struggle between New and Old World political models. Accordingly, they insisted that only the triumph of American republicanism over European monarchism could preserve the nations and civilization of the New World from the corrosive forces of the Old World.[26]

The English-language section of La Verdad's first issue contrasted the "truth" of the Americas with the corruption of Europe, the former representing liberty and republicanism and the latter, despotism and monarchy. The journal presented Cubans and U.S. citizens as brothers-in-arms in a transatlantic clash of civilizations: "the interests of the monarquies [sic] of Europe and the interests of free America are opposed to each other." Old World "hostilities against America" would not cease until Europe was "driven from the last stronghold, the last refuge that remains to her in the New World." The "decisive event" in this clash was the contest over Cuba. Only U.S. triumph would remove all manner of European threats and "obstacles to American civilization" and ensure the "progress of liberty and humanity" throughout the hemisphere.[27]

Many annexationists asserted that the fate of republicanism in the Americas depended on the survival of the United States, which in turn hinged on the acquisition of Cuba. As La Verdad put it, "the cause of Cuban Emancipation is the only means of conciliating the opposite interests of the North and the South." But slavery threatened an alliance that sought to transcend sectional divisions. Fears of an impending clash of civilizations united many northerners and southerners in the desire to "emancipate" Cuba from Spain, but creating a cross-sectional alliance required really equating this emancipation with actually ending slavery.[28] Annexing Cuba would end the slave trade, causing its black population to enter into decline;

then, New England would provide the precedent and guiding light for emancipating slaves in a United States that included Cuba.[29]

To this end, *La Verdad* reminded its readers that all the "parent band of thirteen" colonies were "slave-holding when they joined hands at the altar of independence." New England began a process of gradual emancipation that all the original states in the North had emulated and some in the South were preparing to follow: "Seven of them are now free soil, and two more, Delaware and Maryland, within a step of it." Only gradual emancipation would allow Cuba and the United States to avoid the prospect of another Haiti, where "negroes have unlimited power," or Jamaica, where they have "unlimited equality." Both demonstrated the "evils [of] hasty emancipation." Thus, "for the individual States, for the Nation, and for the ultimate good of the races," it is "wisest and kindest to invite Cuba into the Compact of Union, and subject the crude and undeveloped negro family to the crucible of gradual emancipation."[30]

La Verdad popularized the notion of a triple emancipation: of Cuba from Spain, of the slaves in Cuba and the United States, and of both from blacks. After annexation the United States could, first, abolish the slave trade in Cuba, second, implement the New England emancipation model in a United States that included Cuba, and third, transform the expanded nation into a white republic. If abolition would cause Cuba's black population to decline, annexation would cause its white population to rise: "the superabundance of population which exhausted Europe pours daily into the New World will find a new, rich, and vast field which . . . has been closed to foreign emigration . . . by the oppressive and egotistical government of Spain." Betancourt Cisneros concurred, "Europe scatters its industrious and active population throughout all America, and even to the savage shores of Africa and Oceana [*sic*]; Cuba, the admired and coveted of all nations is not permitted to welcome a single colonist, nor to see one of the sprouts of the beautiful Caucasian tree take root in her soil." With contributors estimating the increase of white settlers from between one to one and a half million in ten years, readers could calculate that whites in Cuba should rise from about half to between three-quarters and four-fifths of its population, without even accounting for the anticipated decline of blacks.[31]

Meanwhile, two-way travel between Cuba and the United States would continue to affect a one-way transfer of republican ideas from the North to Cuba. Over the nineteenth century, the number of U.S. citizens visiting Cuba and of Cubans visiting the United States steadily rose. Although

Cubans were as likely to travel to the South as they were the North, many annexationists located Cubans, and Cuba, squarely in the North. According to "mistress of manifest destiny" Cora Montgomery, annexation would amplify the volume of this two-way travel: "Launched into free traffic with the Northern States, her children would send their children here by hundreds, for education, and come themselves by thousands, to enjoy the bracing air of a higher latitude, while in return thousands from the North would hasten there in winter, to enjoy her perpetual spring and ceaseless round of fruits and flowers, which are fairest and brightest in Cuba when our fields are buried under chilling robes of frost and snow." Annexation would accelerate the transformation of white Cubans of means into English-speaking republicans and naturalized U.S. citizens and speed Cuba's incorporation into the imperial republic.[32]

The proposition that two-way travel and a three-part emancipation would reconcile national divisions and strengthen New World republicanism spurred efforts to write Cuba into New England. Doing so offered a way to refute anti-annexationist arguments of homegrown New Englanders like Dana, or adopted ones like the Charleston-born Hurlbert. In 1854, Maturin M. Ballou, a son of the famous minister Hosea Ballou, a founder and later the editor-in-chief of the *Boston Daily Globe*, and the "father of the dime novel," published an important annexationist travel narrative that quickly ran through at least six printings.[33] It proclaimed that "the time has come when the progress of civilization demands" that Cuba "pass into the hands of some power possessed of the ability and the will to crush out" the slave trade. Ballou declared that the United States was the power "designated" by "Providence" to do so. Once a part of "this great national confederacy," Cuba "would immediately catch the national spirit and genius of our institutions, and the old Castilian state of dormancy would give way to Yankee enterprise, her length and breadth would be made to smile like a New England landscape." A "tide of emigration from the States will pour into the island," the "wastelands will be reclaimed" and a "new system of agricultural economy" would be built by a Cuban and U.S. yeomanry.[34]

Whereas Ballou saw a dynamic and progressive future for a Cuba incorporated into the United States, Hurlbert saw a forever torpid Cuba unworthy of admission into the Union, part of both a slaveholding regional South and a sultry global East that also included India, Italy, and Persia. Hurlbert declared "life in this tropic 'Castle of Indolence' more dreamy than the dream of Naples," a land "where thoughts vanish like vapors" and "the mind is as cloudless as the skies." For Hurlbert, Cuba would remain a "garden of dreams." For Ballou, it was a latent "garden of the world" that would "blossom like a rose" once under the influence of "liberal institutions." For Ballou, the monteros were fast fulfilling a destiny envisioned by Abbot, becoming "like the American farmer, the bone and sinew of the land" and preparing to assume their role as "the real masters of the country." For Hurlbert, "indolent beyond conception" and "lordly in their laziness," the monteros were "incapable of maintaining a free and orderly polity." These backward provincials "lounge[d] away" their mornings drinking, smoking, gambling, and gossiping. Such sights filled him with the "painful idea" that a member of "these barefooted, barefaced, disreputable assemblies . . . might perhaps, at no distant day, be inflicted upon our own unfortunate Congress, as a representative from the sovereign state of Cuba." For Ballou, the monteros, the criollos "educated at our colleges and schools," and U.S. tourists, merchants, and mechanics were "all . . . apostles of republicanism." They had aroused such a deep desire for annexation that "we can no longer wonder at the spread of the conviction that Cuba should belong to this country" as "soon as it can be honorably brought about."[35]

At the core of Ballou's and Hurlbert's opposing white supremacist analyses was the potential of Cuban and Cubans to become American enough, civilized enough, republican enough, and white enough to join the Union. While most travelogues regarded Cuba as a garden of sorts, Ballou and other members of the transnational, cross-sectional annexationist movement routinely employed phrases like Yankee enterprise, New England landscape, and reclaimed wastelands to invoke for it a white republican U.S. future rooted in Pilgrim and Puritan pasts.[36]

Travel accounts of the 1850s built on the pathbreaking work of Abbot and *La Verdad* and engaged Ballou and Hulbert in advocating or opposing annexation. For Richard B. Kimball, Cuba offered "every emigrant fond of labor, a vast field to exert his efforts in, and the prospects of a very brilliant reward." John S. C. Abbott found this idea preposterous: "None would go to Cuba but determined slaveholders." Dana similarly rejected a free-labor solution: "blacks must do the hard work or it will not be done." To the contrary, insisted Thrasher, on small farms and in the urban trades, "the manner of labor, tools, and style of work in Cuba, resembles ours" and has "given to her civilization a resemblance to that of the Anglo-American, not found elsewhere outside the United States."[37]

Point-for-point, blow-for-blow, mid-nineteenth-century travel writers argued the established issues. All commented on two-way travel between Cuba and the United States and pondered whether white creoles' U.S. travels and educations had prepared them for republican government. One test of this proposition was white Cubans' perceived ability and willingness to fight for independence, as their counterparts in the thirteen colonies had. Abiel Abbot began this debate with his assertion that delay would prepare the fiercely independent, armed, and mounted monteros with the will and the means to achieve their independence. Thirty years later, Hurlbert was certain that time had done no such thing: "They hate the Spanish government but dread the chances of an insurrection"; even if they so dared, the monteros would make a "despicable militia." Ballou noted that Spain kept one soldier in Cuba for every four white adults. Asking whether the North American colonists could have beaten Britain at these odds, he declared it "insulting and idle" to claim that white Cubans could have already achieved independence "if they had earnestly desired and made the effort for freedom." They "await only the means and the opportunity to rise in rebellion against Spain," for the "spirit is among her people." Kimball agreed: "Cuba has the power, as well as the will and wisdom, to be free." John Abbott and Dana heartily disagreed. John Abbott asserted that seizure or purchase offered "the only conceivable" means of annexation; he thought either unlikely. Dana expounded in a maritime metaphor: "When Massachusetts entered into the Revolution, she had one hundred and fifty years of experience in popular self-government. . . . The thirteen colonies were ships fully armed and equipped, officered and manned, with long sea experience, sailing as a wing of a great fleet, under the Admiral's fleet signals. They only had to pass secret signals, fall out of line, haul their wind, and sail off as a squadron by themselves. . . . But Cuba has neither officers trained to the quarterdeck, nor sailors trained to the helm, the yard or the gun. Nay, the ship is not built, nor the keel laid, nor is the timber grown, from which the keel is to be cut."[38] This passage provided the rationale for Dana's claim about the impossibility of reasoning from Massachusetts to Cuba, one grounded in the fallacious projection of stark divisions between an ostensibly free white North and slaveholding South at the time of the Revolutionary War.[39]

The U.S. Civil War dashed all hopes that a slaveholding Cuba could enter the Union. Not until nearly a decade after Cubans waged its Ten Years' War against Spain could the United States and Cubans again seriously contemplate annexation. In that war, Cubans failed to achieve the goal of independence from Spain but began the process of slave emancipation, which was completed in 1886. The war left the Cuban economy in ruins, the sugar industry destroyed. U.S. capitalists moved in and compelled many planters to exchange their property for shares of stock or managerial positions in U.S. firms. The end of slavery and increased U.S. investment renewed interest in annexation. By then Cuban and U.S. annexationists had to contend with a powerful separatist movement determined to achieve Cuba's independence from Spain, prevent its acquisition by the United States, and build a nation founded on racial equality. Because white republicanism remained central to annexationist projects, in the 1880s and 1890s, travel writers visited or revisited Cuba to update old narratives for use in new annexation movements.[40]

For different reasons, the Civil War proved as important for Hawai'i as it did for Cuba. It ended hopes of annexing Cuba but renewed them for Hawai'i, where slavery had never existed and which, like Cuba, was the object of several annexation schemes in the 1850s. During the war, Cuba's export of sugar to the United States fell as dramatically as that of Hawai'i rose, putting this industry on a secure basis for the first time in its brief history. The expansion of sugar pulled Hawai'i deeper into the economic orbit of the United States. The victory of the industrializing, urbanizing North resurrected dreams of U.S. commercial and military supremacy in Asia. Visions of how the fabled China trade would propel the United States to greatness inspired Secretary of State William Seward: "The nation that draws the most from the earth and fabricates most, and sells most to foreign nations must be and will be the greatest power on earth." Fulfilling this dream required a coaling and naval base in the Pacific. To this end, Seward wrote the U.S. Minister of Hawai'i: "a lawful and peaceful annexation of the Sandwich Islands is deemed desirable."[41]

In 1866, the *Sacramento Union* sent the then-little-known Mark Twain to Hawai'i to investigate how the nation could capitalize on Seward's dream of annexing Hawai'i and propelling the United States to global power. Twain's accounts of Hawai'i propelled him to transatlantic fame. His vision of it as a plantation regime worked by Chinese contract labor soon achieved canonical status in the United States, much to the alarm of the emergent annexationist leadership. Its members wanted to transform Hawai'i into a white republic and knew that making progress toward this goal was crucial to their cause. As with Cuba, debates on the annexation of Hawai'i turned more on issues of race and republicanism than on issues of wealth and power.

A Volcanic City on a Hill

Contrary to a belief popularized by Twain and other contemporaries, and later perpetuated by a host of popular and professional historians, most sugar planters opposed annexation until after the overthrow of Queen Lili'-uokalani in 1893, some as late as 1898. Although leading planters and leading annexationists were both descendants of New England missionaries, the "mission boys" did not then constitute the unified bloc that so many later observers presumed they always were. In fact, annexationists envisioned a future political economy inimical to planter interests. Planters believed that the profitability of sugar depended on Asian contract labor, which the kingdom guaranteed but which was illegal in the United States. By contrast, nonplanter haole imagined Hawai'i as a white republic governed by and for Anglo-Saxons engaged in diversified agriculture, tourism, and trade. Drawing support from small businessmen, professionals, mechanics, and farmers, they comprised but 2 to 5 percent of the population. Most Hawaiians opposed annexation. No one consulted the Chinese and Japanese.[42]

The businessmen, editors, lawyers, ministers, and publishers who led the annexationist movement in Hawai'i articulated their vision of the future in the twin contexts of the ascendancy of Twain's works on the "Sandwich Islands," the wholesale expansion of the sugar industry, and the devastating decline of Natives during the reign of King David Kalākaua. Between 1874 and 1891, sugar production expanded tenfold, while Hawaiians fell from 90 to 45 percent of the population. To Kalākaua fell the unenviable and ultimately irreconcilable tasks of promoting the planters' interests while reinvigorating the Hawaiian people and nation. His efforts to advance the contradictory agendas of planters and Hawaiians drove nonplanter haole into opposition to sugar planters and Native nationalists.[43]

On his 1866 visit, Twain asserted that lack of regular steamship service had left the United States "out in the cold" in the colonial competition for Hawai'i, playing "third fiddle" to Britain and France.[44] Such a service would help the United States "populate these islands with Americans [and] loosen that French and English grip." By filling "these islands with Americans," the United States would "regain her lost foothold." Marveling at the prosperity of the plantations and the investment opportunities they represented,

Twain reiterated the primary lament of industry leaders, the "loss" of a native work force: "day by day the Kanaka race is passing away." Twain revealed capital's solution to the presumably inevitable death of Hawaiians: "Chinese labor," the "cheapest, the best, and most quiet, peaceable and faithful labor" in the world. Chinese labor would enable California's investors to grow rich on Hawaiian sugar and the nation's capitalists to realize Seward's dream of the United States producing and selling its way to power while relieving white men from the "drudgery" of degrading manual labor: "You will not always go on paying $80 and $100 a month for labor which you can hire for $5." For Twain, the route from California to Hawai'i to Asia constituted the "true Northwest Passage" that would propel the rise of the United States to "almost the exclusive trade of 450,000,000 people—the almost exclusive trade of the most opulent land on earth." The United States needed Hawai'i to project its power in Asia.[45]

By the time Twain left Hawai'i, his letters to the *Sacramento Union* had begun appearing in Honolulu and its newspapers. The editor of the *Pacific Commercial Advertiser* and future annexationist leader, Henry Whitney, expressed shock at Twain's praise of Chinese contract labor and the many "lies" he told about Hawai'i. Unhappy that Twain stole a copy of one of Jarves's books, Whitney was aghast that Twain "pirated" Jarves's text. His angst likely had deeper roots. Twain had appropriated a commodity more valuable than a book: the power to represent Hawai'i. Whitney and his peers organized to counter Twain after Kalākaua came to the throne, via an election Hawaiians contested and planters supported, the latter after he pledged to negotiate the duty-free entry of sugar into the United States. Once he did, nonplanter haole moved to prevent Hawai'i from becoming any more demographically multiracial and agriculturally monocultural.[46]

The implementation of the Reciprocity Treaty of 1875 seemed to make many of Twain's predictions come true. It spurred the expansion of the sugar industry and the quest for a cheap, captive workforce of contract laborers, initially from China and later Japan. In four years, sugar production doubled, and the number of Chinese quadrupled. Reciprocity also brought the California-based sugar refiner Claus Spreckels to Hawai'i. He built the most technologically advanced and extensively irrigated plantations and achieved a monopoly on sugar marketing, transporting, and refining. Spreckels and an ally of his, Walter Murray Gibson, a self-proclaimed champion of Native rights, came to exercise power over the king. This perturbed Hawaiian-born haole, who considered foreign influence in government their own birthright.[47]

Hawaiians and haole both believed that the cultural and demographic decline of Hawaiians threatened the survival of the kingdom—with a key difference. Historian Jonathan Kay Kamakawiwo'ole Osorio shows that the former regarded the Hawaiian nation as real; the latter did not. As the *Pacific Commercial Advertiser* contemptuously remarked, "should your people continue to decline . . . the present *courtesy* of foreign recognition will be withdrawn." Seeking to reverse the demographic and cultural destruction wrought by half a century of Western colonial incursions, Kalākaua fostered Native nationalism and cultural revitalization under the banners "Hawai'i for the Hawaiians" and "Ho'oulu Lāhui" (Increase the Nation and Its People).[48]

The missionaries and their descendants had toiled for half a century to eradicate most things Native. Kalākaua revitalized Hawaiian culture, genealogy, history, society, politics, and religion. Seeking to stem the demographic decline of Hawaiians, he revived indigenous healing practices and launched a search for a "cognate people." He thereby sought to legitimize his rule and govern Hawaiians in resistance to Euro-American colonialism. But his need for the support of the haole community compelled him to validate his kingship through Western traditions as well. Like previous monarchs, Kalākaua sought, in Sally Engle Merry's wonderful formulation, "to purchase independence with the coin of civilization."[49]

On the first round-the-world tour made by any reigning monarch, Kalākaua secured recognition of the independence of the kingdom from the leaders of the world's most powerful nations. Making careful study of European monarchies and trappings of monarchical power, he and his advisors incorporated their findings in the construction of 'Iolani Palace, a coronation upon its completion in 1883, and a fiftieth-birthday jubilee in 1886. Intended to inspire nationalist pride among Hawaiians and demonstrate the civilized standing of a court modeled on Europe's best, both coronation and jubilee were hybrid affairs. At the coronation, the king was invested with a feather cloak worn by Kamehameha I and a jeweled gold crown. The state's German-inspired Royal Hawaiian Band played, and the king's retinue of hula dancers performed. For the occasion of the first performance of hula, banned by missionaries, at a high state affair in over half a century, court musicians and choreographers produced a new genre: *hula ku'i*. It combined elements of Hawaiian and Western music and dance.[50]

Nonplanter whites viewed the changes wrought by reciprocity, Native nationalism, and cultural renaissance as threats to Anglo-Saxon American civilization in Hawai'i. They did not oppose sugar production per se. They protested the conversion of Hawai'i into a typical plantation society composed of a white landed minority and a nonwhite working majority. Monocrop export agriculture threatened their dream of settling in Hawai'i an independent yeomanry whose members would support the establishment of a smallholder-republic.[51] Nonplanter haole cast the future as a choice between "flourishing farms" or "bloated monopolies," "homesteads" or "field gangs," and the commitment to "social" or "industrial" interests.[52]

Missionary descendant and lawyer William R. Castle summarized their vision of the ideal moral and political economy for Hawai'i: "that of a multitude of small farmers, each of whom will . . . possess sufficient property to make him a conservative supporter of stable government." Were action not taken, "our population will consist of a small landed aristocracy and a restless, discontented population of ignorant and idle laborers. Towards the latter we are tended today. . . . It would be a national blessing if the great plantations could be divided . . . and allotted to intelligent and sturdy farmers." Nonplanter haole agitated to restrict Chinese migration, recruit Portuguese families to work the cane (they viewed the Portuguese as white but not haole), sell or lease Crown lands to white small farmers, and attract Anglo-Saxons to the islands to visit, settle, and invest. These became the core of the annexationist platform. If nonplanter haole viewed the consolidation of plantation society as a threat to their interests, they concurred with the planters who came to regard Native nationalism as a menace to the interests of all Anglo-Saxons in Hawai'i.[53]

Haole did not object to Kalākaua's massive government expenditures for projects that served their interests, but they labeled his coronation and jubilee extravagant wastes of state funds. They denounced these affairs and the performance of hula at them as proof of a resurgence of barbarism that called into question Hawaiians' capacity for self-government and independent nationhood. The publisher and tourism promoter Thomas Thrum denounced the coronation as "silly, wasteful and provoking tomfoolery." Castle brought obscenity charges against the publishers who produced a program listing the 263 *mele* (chant) and *hula* performed. Among them was a *hula ma'i*. A song honoring the genitals of a chief, its reenactment of the genealogy of the king was crucial for establishing his legitimacy in the eyes of Hawaiians. Haole thought it "smut." After the jubilee, the *Honolulu*

Daily Bulletin said, "Let the Hawaiian be once fully saturated with American ideas of liberty and personal independence. . . . While the Hawaiian is wedded by ignorance to superstitious ideas and practices, he can never stand side by side, on the same plane with Bulgarian or American, as a free citizen of a free country." Haole regarded the civilizing process as a one-way street on which hybridity was tolerated only insofar as Western political and cultural forms encroached upon and replaced Hawaiian ones. They made it clear that the revitalization of Hawaiian culture and politics threatened Hawaiians' citizenship and independent nationhood. Some haole even began to claim that they were the true "Hawaiians" capable of promoting and defending the interests of Hawai'i.[54]

Several months after the jubilee, Castle and Thrum figured prominently among the planter and nonplanter whites who organized to fight the political influence wielded by "foreigners" like Spreckels and Gibson and what they viewed as the extravagance and corruption of the king. They joined Lorrin A. Thurston's Hawaiian League, a secret haole organization. The league's stated objective was "constitutional, representative government in fact as well as in form." Members interpreted this goal in two conflicting ways. The faction led by planters favored making the king a figurehead and transferring power to an elected cabinet. The faction spearheaded by Thurston favored abolishing the monarchy and establishing a republic that many anticipated would pave the way for U.S. annexation. Planter royalists prevailed.[55]

The league and its military arm, the Honolulu Rifles, then forced Kalākaua to sign the "Bayonet Constitution." It stripped him of his power to rule, transferred it to an elected cabinet, and reconstituted citizenship and suffrage along racial lines for the first time in Hawaiian history. The constitution disenfranchised many Hawaiians and rescinded the Hawaiian citizenship of Chinese and Japanese. It vastly enlarged the electorate of whites, even for those who were not citizens. The cabinet closed the king's genealogy, history, and health boards. In return for the renewal of reciprocity, it ceded Pearl Harbor to the United States. King and kingdom remained sovereign in name, but Hawaiian-born haole had taken control.[56]

Haole who had hoped to overthrow the monarchy and establish a republic began to coalesce around calls to pursue these goals by promoting diversified agriculture and the "tourist crop." Against the king's wishes, Thurston became the first minister of the interior under the Bayonet Constitution. He began construction of roads to leading attractions, most notably one from Hilo to Kilauea Volcano on the Big Island. He awarded Benjamin F. Dillingham the permissions needed to build a residential resort at the mouth of Pearl River and establish a sugar plantation nearby. Upon returning to the private sector in 1890, Thurston worked to make Dillingham's Oahu Railway and Land Company (OR&L) and the Kilauea Volcano House Company he and Castle founded in 1891 the centerpieces of a tourism industry devoted to increasing the population of taxpaying, property-holding, and ballot-wielding Anglo-Saxons.[57]

Dillingham's OR&L sought to demonstrate that profitable sugar production did not require Asian contract labor. Free whites could raise cane on a cooperative basis. Dillingham hoped to subdivide part of Ewa Plantation into plots for small farmers and develop Pearl City into a fashionable residential resort. Through this two-pronged strategy, the OR&L endeavored to affect a "Great Land Colonization" by prosperous whites. The Kilauea Volcano House Company adopted a similar strategy. It sought to lure tourists to a volcano that made "the wonders of Yellow Stone, Vesuvius and Popocatepetl rolled into one" seem "but a sideshow." The road they traveled to the volcano also showcased lands being opened for homesteading.[58]

Thurston argued that visiting would convince many tourists that Hawai'i was the rare tropical clime where white men and their families could survive, thrive, and enjoy unparalleled delights. A sizable number would buy land and build vacation homes, farms, and businesses. Those who settled would become voters, citizens, or both. Thurston worked to attract mainland tourists *and* sell nonplanter haole on his plan. He and Whitney proposed targeting a "blue list" of U.S. citizens who traveled abroad annually to convince some to join a haole society described as "cosmopolitan, educated, and refined, alike devoted to good works and having a good time." Nonplanter haole hoped that these efforts would enable them to acquire the clout needed to challenge Native and planter royalists and transform Hawai'i into a white republic. The treasonous word "annexation" was not spoken aloud at the time.[59]

Three events returned annexation to the realm of public discussion in 1891: the death of King Kalākaua, the ascension of Queen Lili'uokalani to the throne, and the revocation of reciprocity by the United States The queen vowed to reassert the power of the monarchy by promulgating a new constitution to supersede the Bayonet Constitution, which haole had not properly ratified under kingdom law.[60] The McKinley tariff ended preferential U.S. treatment of Hawaiian sugar, which brought immediate depression to the islands. Estimated losses reached $5 million for 1891 alone. Facing the twin specters of the restoration of monarchical power and the dependence of sugar's profitability on the United States, nonplanter haole rallied behind Thurston. They urged him to accept an invitation to exhibit Hawai'i at the World's Columbian Exposition in Chicago. A cyclorama of Kilauea Volcano would lure visitors to an exhibit that would also illustrate "the character, condition and prospects of the country."[61]

Royalists grew suspicious about the exhibit's intent when the *Pacific Commercial Advertiser* asserted that the "severe shock" to the sugar industry had "rudely awakened" the country "from its soft dreams of a fancied prosperity" and editorialized: "Our safety depends on our relations with the United States. . . . The bonds that unites [*sic*] us must be drawn more closely. . . . The tourist travel to these islands is capable of almost indefinite expansion. . . . If it comes, the country will be opened up by a network of roads which will give to thousands of acres of arable land a ready access to market. With the realization of these conditions the prosperity of the country will be assured and we can laugh at sugar tariffs. The World's Fair at Chicago is our great opportunity." A royalist from Canada demanded that the editor explain what closer U.S. relations meant, "annexation or free trade." He responded, "we believe a political connection" to the United States "would be a boon to the country." It would bring "American capital" and "American immigrants" to Hawai'i, "kill the contract labor system," and make "free labor a fact" and "healthful and general progress a certainty." But "we are still not prepared to commit ourselves publicly to a policy of annexation." In less than a year, the *Advertiser* publicly committed. Meanwhile, haole who had wanted to overthrow Kalākaua, proclaim a republic, and seek U.S. annexation regrouped in a clandestine Annexation Club. Its members turned to travel and tourism to raise support and funds. Led by Thurston, they made three key moves.[62]

The first commenced in 1892 when the Hawaiian government underwrote a visit to the United States by several commissioners of the World's Fair exhibit. It did not know that the Annexation Club also financed the trip. While in Washington to arrange the exhibit, Thurston met with Secretary of State James G. Blaine. President Benjamin Harrison had authorized Blaine to inform Thurston that "an exceedingly sympathetic audience" awaited an annexation proposal. This was crucial. To render annexation consensual, the invitation had to come from Hawai'i. Blaine urged Thur-

ston to take the necessary steps. Thurston later wrote him the annexationists would, once they achieved the means to do so, peacefully if possible but
forcibly if necessary.[63]

Upon his return from Washington, Thurston made his second move.
He organized the Hawaii Bureau of Information (HBI). Its stated purpose
was to advance the interests of the business community, support the
exhibit, and "encourage and induce tourist travel, the immigration of desirable population, the settlement of the country, the establishment of hotels,
sanitariums, and other resorts." Although the HBI claimed to represent "all
interests," all those appointed to organize it were annexationists. The secret
Annexation Club and the public HBI became twinned branches of their
movement: the former charged with plotting against queen and kingdom,
and the latter with making Hawai'i more like a white republic and a part
of the United States. The annexationists worked with U.S. Minister to
Hawai'i John L. Stevens, a protégé and former business partner of Blaine,
who had just stepped down as secretary of state.[64]

In the third move, Stevens employed annexationist travel and tourism
plans to prepare Blaine's successor, John W. Foster, for the arrival of a
treaty. Warning that Hawai'i had "reached the parting of the ways" and
"must now take the road" to "Asia or America," Stevens insisted that
ensuring the latter outcome required taking possession of Hawai'i and
implementing the annexationists' program to Americanize it: "assume control of the 'crown lands,' dispose of them in small lots for actual settlers and
freeholders." The result "soon will be to give permanent preponderance to
a population and a civilization which will make the islands like southern
California, and . . . convert them into gardens and sanitariums, . . . thus
bringing everything here into harmony with American life and prosperity."
Conjuring a "yellow peril" served as a call to action. Invoking white republicanism demonstrated the worthiness of Hawai'i to join the Union.[65]

The annexationists found their justification for a coup on January 14,
1893, when Queen Lili'uokalani unsuccessfully sought to promulgate a new
constitution designed to restore power to the monarchy. The Annexation
Club (renamed the Committee of Safety) and Stevens convinced Captain
Gilbert Wiltse of the U.S. Navy to land troops and artillery, even though
they lacked authorization from Washington. Two days later, they overthrew
queen and kingdom and established a provisional government. Stevens recognized it on the grounds that its members controlled the archives, the
executive building, and the treasury. The control of the archives was of

especial importance to the annexationists, for it held official state documents that would undermine their representations of the Hawaiian government as barbaric, corrupt, and inept. The Provisional Government sent a commission to Washington to negotiate an annexation treaty. This was not a fait accompli, given widespread Hawaiian and U.S. opposition.

Resistance emerged at sites official and cultural, political and performative. The queen led the way. Refusing to surrender to the Provisional Government, she yielded her authority under protest to the U.S. government, believing that it would "reinstate me in the authority which I claim as the constitutional sovereign of the Hawaiian Islands." Leading ali'i,[66] or chiefs and chiefesses, organized the opposition into hui, or societies, to demand restoration of queen and kingdom and prevent annexation. The Royal Hawaiian Band, scheduled to appear at the World's Fair, followed suit. The Provisional Government demanded that the band's members sign an oath of loyalty to the new government or face dismissal. Faithful to queen and kingdom, the musicians refused. Reorganizing as the Hawaiian National Band, they traveled to the mainland on their own to perform and protest. In their honor, Ellen Keko'aohiwaikalani Wright Prendergast composed a mele mocking the government official who told the fired band members that they would have to eat rocks to live: "No one will fix a signature / To the paper of the enemy / With its sin of annexation / And sale of native civil rights. / We do not value the government's sums of money / We are satisfied with the stones, / Astonishing food of the land." It became a rallying cry for the tens of thousands of Hawaiians who organized to restore queen and kingdom.[67]

In Washington, Secretary of State Foster and an annexation commission led by Thurston and Castle drafted a treaty. It did not come up for a vote before Congress's session ended and President Harrison left office. Days after President Grover Cleveland's inauguration, he withdrew the annexation treaty and appointed James H. Blount to investigate the U.S. role in the coup and the extent of support for annexation in Hawai'i. Cleveland ordered Blount to lower the U.S. flag and withdraw U.S. troops upon arrival. He presumed he had tabled the Hawaiian question. Instead, when Cleveland opened the World's Fair, his carriage passed the Kilauea Volcano Building, which flew five U.S. flags. On April 1, Blount lowered the Stars and Stripes from the government building in Honolulu to proclaim that Hawai'i was not a U.S. possession. On May 1, Thurston raised them above the Hawaiian Building in Chicago to show that Hawai'i was, in many ways, already part of the Union.[68]

The exhibit paid tribute to the work of the New England missionaries. Because the Royal Hawaiian Band refused to appear, Thurston had to content himself with exhibiting a quartet of Hawaiian singers. They sang patriotic U.S. tunes, intended to demonstrate the success of the conversion of heathens to Christianity and civilization and paper over the fact that virtually all Native Hawaiians opposed annexation. The hula that Kalākaua made a symbol of Hawaiian nationalism and anticolonial resistance was not performed at the Volcano Building. (It could be seen at the nearby South Sea Islanders' Village.) Beneath the cyclorama of an erupting Kilauea, Thurston distributed annexation tracts and tourism and settlement guides. He invited U.S. Anglo-Saxons to visit Hawai'i. He urged them to ask their editors and congressmen to support annexation.[69]

The Volcano Building appeared a microcosm of the struggle for civilization being waged by white Americans in Hawai'i. The Columbian Exposition was divided into two complementary sections: the Midway, which presented an evolutionary hierarchy of race and progress from savagery to the approach of civilization, and White City, which celebrated the millennial advance of white civilization and industrialization. Thurston may not have relished assignment to the Midway, but ironically the location dovetailed with the annexationists' representation of their cause. On the Midway, as in Hawai'i, the forces of barbarism pressed threateningly close from all sides. The cyclorama of Kilauea helped make this point. For civilized U.S. citizens, the volcano offered a science lesson on "the forces which have fashioned the crust of this earth." The statue of Pele, the goddess of Kilauea, at the building's entrance served both to entice visitors and to warn them of the dangers of a "heathen" revival that the annexationists argued King Kalākaua had begun and Queen Lili'uokalani continued. The imperialist press never tired of telling U.S. citizens that the queen routinely made offerings to Pele. The U.S. press interpreted said offerings as proof that she and her subjects were incapable of self-government. Denying the queen her devout Christianity and adherence to the rule of law complemented the annexationists' efforts to discredit Hawaiians' pursuit of restoration through legal means. It further enabled haole to ignore their illegal act of war against the queen.[70]

The closing of the world's fair coincided with the debates in the U.S. Congress on Blount's report. Asserting that the coup could not have succeeded without Stevens's and navy captain Wiltse's illegal assistance, it concluded that "the people" are "for the Queen, against the Provisional Government, and against annexation." Cleveland and most Democrats recommended restoring queen and kingdom. But in an inquiry and report led by Senator John T. Morgan, Republicans argued that Hawaiʻi seeks "what every American state has achieved," since the nation's founding: "release of her people from the odious antirepublican regime . . . [that] subordinates them to the supposed divine right of a monarch, whose title . . . originated in the most slavish conditions of pagan barbarity." Congress voted neither to restore the queen nor to annex Hawaiʻi.[71]

Forced to wait for a different administration, the annexationists returned to Hawaiʻi to proclaim a new government and redouble promotional efforts. On July 4, 1894, they transformed the Provisional Government into the Republic of Hawaii. It pursued annexation through expanded propaganda efforts and policies that sought, with not much success, to reduce Asian migration, increase Anglo-Saxon settlement and Portuguese migration, and open Crown lands to white farmers. It promulgated a constitution based on Mississippi's restrictive franchise laws that limited citizenship and suffrage to the white minority. It outlawed the Hawaiian language as a medium of instruction. The nationalist leader Joseph Nāwahī condemned the government at a mass meeting: "We have been ousted by trespassers who entered out house and who are telling us to go a live in a lei stand that they think to build and force us all into." His "lei stand" reference may have mocked efforts to promote annexation through travel and tourism. His protest did coincide with the publication of a key annexationist travel narrative.[72]

Picturesque Hawaii dramatically synthesized the narratives the annexationists had assembled over two decades. It cast the future as a drama in a millennial struggle: "The principles that underlie Christian civilization . . . are now battling against a drift back to barbarism." Its authors, former diplomatic minister Stevens and religious minister and educator William Oleson, embodied two mutually sustaining ideas of U.S. manifest destiny in Hawaiʻi. Oleson stood for the missionaries sent to build a Pacific city on a hill. Stevens represented the statesmen who claimed the right to annex Hawaiʻi if it "lost" its sovereignty. Pairing them underscored the mutual benefits of annexation. The United States would support white republican government in Hawaiʻi. Hawaiʻi would regenerate a United States corrupted by urbanization and inferior white immigrants by relocating the fount of republican virtue to a pastoral island eden cultivated by blood descendants of Winthrop and intellectual heirs of Adams and Jefferson.[73]

The travelogue proclaimed Christianity the spiritual and material foundation of American civilization in Hawai'i. The missionaries arrived at a "critical period," after the "breaking down" of the tabu system and "abandonment [of] idols [had left] the people without any religion." Having "come under the condemnation of the nation," the ancestral religion was "cast aside [as] worse than useless." The missionaries rescued bodies and souls: "Christianity saved the Hawaiian race from complete collapse and disappearance from the earth." The land discovered by the missionaries was as "worthless" as the moral state of Hawaiians. Stevens and Oleson encoded it as "arid" and "forbidding" and Hawaiian agriculture as "unproductive," a strategy for dispossessing the natives and institutionalizing land ownership. Christianity and capitalist property relations laid the foundation of the sugar plantations. Stevens and Oleson celebrated the irrigation works, modern machinery, and scientific agriculture as a continuation of the original mission: "The industrial development of Hawaii under American leadership marks an epoch hardly less phenomenal than the great religious awakening under the devoted labors of American missionaries." They held civilization to the highest standard by which westerners measured progress: technological achievement. Yet in the next breath, they warned that industrial monopoly and Asian migrants were about to derail the train of Anglo-Saxon civilization and white republicanism.[74]

Stevens and Oleson reiterated annexationists' critique of plantation society. Acknowledging the sugar industry's dependence on heavy capital investment and labor inputs, they rejected oligarchic organization and Asian contract labor. Whereas the "resurgence" of barbarism among Hawaiians and royalist haole threatened to set back the civilizing project, the "submergence" of American civilization would result from continued Asian immigration. Ewa Plantation was the institution poised to supersede the plantation system. Having completed capital improvements, Dillingham divided it into leaseholds, "attaching to the soil a permanent class of farmers." The authors argued that "adapted to all plantations it would obviate the necessity of importing laborers from abroad" and "conserve the interests of Anglo-Saxon civilization." Ewa Plantation, which bore the namesake of a mission Jarves described as a moral and physical oasis in the desert, was part of a providential plan revealed at Kilauea.[75]

This plan seemed to interrupt the civilizing narrative, but it advanced the plot by comparison. At the crater's edge, Stevens and Oleson witnessed divine creation: "At the brink of Kilauea . . . , we behold the mighty forces that have been building our world since the dawn of time. . . . We seem to come into touch with the hoary ages when God said, Let the dry land appear. We get glimpses into the past of this planet of ours, more luminous than the most graphic portrayals of the beginnings of creation. . . . Here is the water all about and here is the land emerging from the deep. Here are the mighty constructive forces at work building the basis for vegetation and the habitation of man." Moving from plantation to volcano, the narrators transported their readers back in time, not to the volcano's habitation by Pele but to the biblical origins of the world. The reenactment of the story of Genesis in the bowels of Kilauea paralleled and validated the history of the missionaries and their descendants. The Christian God and his Anglo-Saxon flock had labored to make Hawai'i an earthly Garden. The discussion of clearing and irrigating cane fields took up where the "constructive forces" of the volcano, building the "basis for vegetation and the habitation of man," left off, with missionary descendants transforming "forbidding" lands into thriving fields. The divine creation of the volcanic islands recalled the human engineering of the sugar plantations. Just as God made the islands fit for habitation by his Christian servants, so did planters build an industry that white farmers would work in the future. Yet neither the work of God or civilization was "completed." Only annexation would hasten to the grave the "dying forces" of monopoly and barbarism: "To spurn and reject this important and thoroughly American colony . . . would be cowardice and inhumanity, which no self-respecting Christian nation would be guilty of, least of all the great American nation." Annexation would result in the transformation of Hawai'i into a republic by and for resident whites and 400,000 to 500,000 new white immigrants.[76]

Picturesque Hawaii provided mainland annexationists with a valuable bank of images from which they drew to keep discourses of white civilization and republicanism central to pursuit of annexation. It offered a powerful counterargument to anti-annexationists like Carl Schurz, who wrote: "No candid American would ever think of making a State of this Union out of such a group of islands with such a population as it has and is likely to have." Its arguments were used to counter Hawaiian resistance, foremost among them the 1897 anti-annexationist petitions Natives sent to Washington. They bore more than 38,000 adult signatures at a time when there were 40,000 Hawaiians in Hawai'i. Finally, *Picturesque Hawaii* insisted that the United States remain true to its principles, by which it meant supporting the transformation of Hawai'i into a white republic.[77]

Senators Henry Cabot Lodge, John T. Morgan, and John R. Proctor utilized *Picturesque Hawaii* to advocate the annexation of Hawai'i as the first step in a mission to extend Anglo-Saxon American civilization and white republicanism overseas into the New Worlds of the Atlantic and Pacific. Travel writers figuratively and literally retraced Stevens's and Oleson's journey to take their story to new audiences. But the cultural production of Hawai'i as part of the United States was no substitute for annexation. And that power was a monopoly of the U.S. state.[78]

Only after April 1898, when the United States voted to intervene in Cuba's war for independence from Spain, and secured its first victory in Philippines, were annexationists in Congress able to secure the votes for a joint resolution (requiring only a simple majority) for Hawaiian annexation. Statesmen led by President McKinley, Alfred Thayer Mahan, Theodore Roosevelt, and Senators Lodge and Morgan argued that victory in the war required permanent control of Hawai'i for a naval base and coaling station. Their arguments won some converts, but race and republicanism remained more contentious issues than power and wealth. In a statement comparable to Hurlbert's commentary about the monteros, the Missouri congressman Champ Clark thundered: "How can we endure our shame when a Chinese Senator from Hawaii, with his pigtail hanging down his back, with his pagan joss in hand, shall rise from his curule chair and in pigeon [*sic*] English proceed to chop logic with George Frisbie Hoar or Henry Cabot Lodge?" The Senate Foreign Relations Committee insisted that white settlers would displace Asians and Hawaiians, invoking the "effort of the Republic to fill up the public domain with white people" as a first step in this direction. Once the House voted for annexation, the Senate followed.[79]

The U.S. entry into Cuba's war against Spain served as a catalyst for its conquest of the Philippines, Guam, Hawai'i, and Puerto Rico. But Hawai'i served as the benchmark for determining their forms of government. The architects of U.S. colonial governance celebrated the achievements of Anglo-Saxon U.S. civilization in Hawai'i in debates over whether to extend citizenship and the constitution to the nation's new colonies. Harvard professor of government A. Lawrence Lowell praised U.S. statesmen for recognizing that only Hawai'i warranted "territorial government," because "the element of Anglo-Saxon origin" is "to-day and is apparently destined to remain, the ruling class." Lowell plotted a course between those who claimed that citizenship followed the flag and those who held that the Constitution applied only to states. Taking the latter course would rescind citizenship and constitutional rights in U.S. territories then on the path to statehood. He created a legal fiction to distinguish "incorporated" from "unincorporated" territories and extend U.S. citizenship and constitutional rights only to the former. On the grounds that "centuries of discipline," had prepared "only the Anglo-Saxon race" for self-government, the United States made Hawai'i its only incorporated territory. Of all its new possessions, U.S. imperial architects deemed Hawai'i alone American enough, Anglo-Saxon enough, civilized enough, republican enough, and white enough to warrant self-government for whites and the promise of eventual statehood.[80]

But Hawai'i was neither very American nor very Anglo-Saxon nor very white at the time. In 1900, as in previous censuses, haole, mostly Anglo-Saxon, remained about 5 percent of the population, with those of U.S. origin or ancestry perhaps half of that. The Portuguese grew from four hundred people in 1872 to eighteen thousand in 1900, but this raised the total Caucasian population only to 17 percent.[81] Yet because a rising Anglo-Saxon ruling class from New England had steadily planted American civilization in Hawai'i over three-quarters of a century, it seemed to have the potential to become white, especially if Hawaiians continued to die and Asians, to leave. Hawai'i stood in contrast to islands that had not been written and performed this way. The United States made Puerto Rico an unincorporated territory and the Philippines a colony.

Cuba's status offered further complications. Since 1823 U.S. policy had held that if Cuba ceased to be a Spanish colony, the United States would annex it. But in 1898 the Senate enacted a joint resolution, the fourth article of which, the Teller Amendment, renounced "any disposition or intention to exercise sovereignty, jurisdiction, or control over said island, except for pacification thereof." U.S. annexationists including Whitelaw Reid and Senators Albert J. Beveridge and Orville Platt attacked the resolution as violating the no-transfer policy. Former Secretary of State Richard Olney demanded that Congress make "Cuba in point of law what she already is in point of fact, namely, United States territory." Annexationists believed historical productions of Cuba as American, civilized, republican, and white enough to deserve a place in the Union had laid the foundation for achieving their goal in the near future. Advocates took from the example of Hawaiʻi hope and lessons for making Cuba a U.S. territory.[82]

A travel narrative of two former U.S. consuls in Cuba, Pulaski F. Hyatt and John T. Hyatt, invoked Hawaiʻi to strategize the annexation of Cuba despite the Teller Amendment: "It is the desire of the Cubans to have as many Americans settle in Cuba as possible. Cuba Libre only asks to be given a chance to govern the island for five years, when it will be ready to apply for annexation to the United States. As in the Hawaiian Islands, the more Americans there are on the island, the easier it will be to bring about this annexation." The consuls lied blatantly about the goal of Cuba Libre, whose proponents had struggled for decades for a Cuban nation independent from Spain *and* the United States. But annexationists seized upon promoting tourism as a way to increase white settlement and the notion that five years of independence, the same period between the overthrow and annexation of Hawaiʻi, would be sufficient to Americanize and whiten Cuba and secure support for annexation. "It will not be long," Senator Joseph Benson Foraker predicted, "until Cuba will appeal for annexation just as Hawaii has done." Senator Chauncey Depew agreed: "Within five years from now there will be from two to three million Americans in that island. . . . Cuba, resembling the United States in its constitution, laws, and liberties, and in all which makes a country desirable to live in for people brought up and educated as are Americans, will have from five to six million people . . . worthy of all the rights of American citizenship. Then, with the initiative from Cuba, we can welcome another star to our flag."[83]

Explicit and implicit comparisons of Cuba and Hawaiʻi and the resurrection of the arguments made by travel writers in the 1850s bolstered beliefs that the United States would soon annex Cuba. If Hawaiʻi had managed to secure territorial status despite the fact that 80 percent of its people were not white, could not a Cuba, whose people of color constituted 30 percent of the population, do so more easily? If Native Hawaiians would soon die out, would this not also be the case with Cuban blacks? Travel writers drew upon earlier Cuban travelogues to reinvigorate the belief that maintenance of the black population required, in the words of Robert Hill, "constant renewal by immigration." With a chilling disregard for human life, he noted that 500,000 Cubans of color had perished during the war, significantly whitening the population in the process. Annexationists drew from the past to argue that two-way travel between Cuba and the United

States had produced a Cuban elite that would be an asset to the Union and would help white settlers remake Cuba and Cubans on U.S. lines.[84]

After 1898, Cuban and U.S. annexationists followed a path in many ways similar to the one taken in Hawai'i. They promoted U.S. tourism, investment, and settlement in a quest to make Cuba part of the United States—with a key difference. In contrast to Hawai'i, the United States and Cuban managers and shareholders of the increasingly U.S.-dominated sugar industry supported annexation and hence backed white tourism, immigration, and settlement schemes. Agents of the U.S. military occupation sought in three years to introduce to Cuba the same kinds of educational, government, and legal systems that had taken over three-quarters of a century to institutionalize in Hawai'i. There, planter and nonplanter haole struggled to reconcile their competing interests and consolidate rule by the Anglo-Saxon minority, for they agreed on the need to prevent any form of direct rule, like the military governance the United States imposed on Cuba between 1899 and 1902. In both places, travel writing and tourism promotion aimed to increase white tourism and settlement and build republican government. Committed to fostering virtue and eradicating vice, imperial agents worked to stamp out pastimes such as the hula and gambling that had long lured travelers to Hawai'i and Cuba. They were associated with the Old World aristocratic decadence and corrupt monarchies believed to be the antithesis of the virtuous republicanism and empire of liberty the U.S. founders forged in the New World.

The tension between republican and monarchical modes of imperial governance that animated so many nineteenth-century debates on empire and beliefs in the exceptional nature of U.S. empire persisted into the twentieth century. Such tensions escalated at the turn of the twentieth century and led the United States to experiment with different ways to exert imperial powers and pleasures without formal territorial control and extensive white settlement. As U.S. Anglo Saxons came to feel under assault at home and abroad by those they deemed class and racial inferiors, an always fragmented "white egalitarianism" developed fresh cracks. Privileged Anglo-Saxons looked at newly conquered islands, wondering if they might be able to make such bounded spaces utopian outposts by and for privileged whites. Tensions between mass and class, plebian and patrician visions of empire surfaced on the river leading to the heart of New York City after the United States waged war against Spain and Cubans for the control of Cuba.[85]

On August 20, 1898, New Yorkers lined the banks of the Hudson to welcome the U.S. Navy home from Cuba and celebrate the nation's victory over Spain. Unlike other recent naval exhibitions, the *New York Times* reported, those aboard the "floating palaces of the rich were few in number" compared to the throngs of ordinary people who packed every pier, excursion boat, and tenement rooftop. The masses gathered to cheer not the officers but the common sailors who helped "make history [and] brought respect from the nations of the Old World to the flag of Freedom and Liberty." This was "peculiarly a day for the common people." It was "not a New York Yacht Club affair." "So," the *Times* concluded, "they believed it was of the people and for the people. . . . And no one who saw the demonstration will dispute their right to the belief."[86]

So, even as it celebrated an empire by and for the people, the *Times* lent credence to the view it protested. In key ways, the naval parade and overseas empire *were* New York Yacht Club affairs. Numerous naval officers who belonged to the club fought in the wars of 1898. The club supplied its stations, communications networks, and twenty-one member yachts to serve, chiefly as gunboats, in the U.S. naval war in Cuba. Its roster boasted some of the best-known proponents of Cuban and Hawaiian annexation, including William Randolph Hearst, Alfred Thayer Mahan, and Theodore Roosevelt, as well as a number of travel writers whose "winter cruises" provided them opportunities to chart the course of U.S. overseas empire. In 1902, for example, former Vice-Commodore Anson Phelps Stokes published a travelogue in which he proposed to fellow members that winter Caribbean cruises offered the "best means" for them to enjoy a salubrious climate and beautiful scenery, provide the "Americans who are now called upon to consider colonial problems" with an opportunity to study them, expand U.S. investment and trade in the Caribbean to promote its "permanent prosperity," and train young yachtsmen for future service as U.S. naval officers. His was scarcely a vision of either egalitarian whiteness or republican empire, but of one by and for privileged whites. The form the U.S. empire should take in its new possessions was subject to a debate that focused on the question of which white U.S. citizens were the nation's ideal agents of overseas empire.[87]

CHAPTER TWO

Garden Republics or Plantation Regimes?

Mrs. Emma Metcalf Nakuina springs from bloodlines which touch
Plymouth Rock, as well as midseas islands. High priests, statesmen, and
warriors join hands in their descendants with pilgrims, lawmakers, and
jurists.

> Hawaiian Promotion Committee, *Hawaii,*
> *Its People and Their Legends,* 1904

Cuba's higher classes, as in New England, Pennsylvania, Minnesota, and
Louisiana, are gentlemen of education and refinement.

> Robert T. Hill, *Cuba and Porto Rico,* 1909

Once the United States made Hawai'i a territory in 1900, a number of
former annexation leaders helped organize the Hawaii Promotion Committee (HPC) to attract Anglo-Saxon tourists, settlers, and investors. Still they
insisted that the HPC was "not a tourist bureau" but an agency devoted
to advancing "the best interests of Hawaii." To promote their paramount
interests of the time, the legitimation of metropolitan rule and local white
governance, the HPC seized upon the genealogy of Emma Kaili Metcalf
Beckley Nakuina, daughter of a high-ranking ali'i and haole sugar planter.
In the preface to her *Hawaii, Its People and Their Legends,* the HPC asserted
that marriages between elite haole men and ali'i women had anchored
Anglo-Americans in Hawai'i and Hawaiians in the United States. It presented such marriages as proof that annexation came at "Hawaii's own
request," the consensual outcome of a long history of cross-cultural marriage and governance. The HPC rewrote recent history, negating the fact
that most Hawaiians opposed U.S. annexation and that ali'i women mar-

ried to haole men were prominent leaders of the movement that organized Hawaiians to protest it in Hawai'i and across the United States. Nakuina rejected haole interpretations of genealogy and history in a booklet of Hawaiian legends she retold and the HPC published, to its later regret. In it, she denounced haole efforts to present colonial rule as a project mutually desired and freely entered into by Anglo-Saxon Americans and Native Hawaiians.[1]

In Cuba, travel writers and tourism promoters invoked not ties of marriage but bonds of brotherhood to present annexation as a consensual project. Travel writers associated with the U.S. military government (1899–1902) and early Cuban Republic (1902–1909) helped reconstitute a fraternity of privileged white men dedicated to making Cuba part of the Union, a project challenged by separatists for three decades. They saw bonds of imperial brotherhood as the foundation of a pan-American unity between Latin Americans and Anglo-Americans.[2] In the quest for annexation, their shared devotion to expanding white republicanism in the Americas could level a hierarchy of whiteness ascribing superiority to Anglos.[3] Travel writer Robert Hill deemed the "higher classes" of U.S.-educated, English-speaking Cubans more worthy of U.S. citizenship than millions of immigrants: "Numerically inferior to the annual migration of Poles, Jews, and Italians into the eastern United States, Cubans are far too superior to these people to justify the fears of those who have been prejudiced by the thought that they might . . . be absorbed into our future population." Few *independentistas* had a chance like Nakuina's to withdraw the "cordial welcome" that mayor of Havana Perfecto Lacosta and his peers extended to the U.S. tourists they invited to settle and invest in agriculture and annexation. Cuban separatists resisted annexation on the streets, at the polls, and in print media other than travel writing.[4]

In second decade of the twentieth century, historic dreams of transforming Cuba and Hawai'i into white republics and of annexing Cuba foundered and died. As a result, the United States abandoned further attempts to establish white settler colonies overseas and came to prefer alternatives to territorial annexation and direct rule (but did not forsake them). As efforts to make Cuba and Hawai'i into white settler colonies met with frustration, then failure, interest in enjoying the sort of decadent pleasures associated with European colonizers and building exclusive enclaves of privilege and power like their hill stations soared. Privileged whites built exclusive residential-vacation resorts designed to keep social and racial inferiors at bay, enable U.S. citizens living in or visiting them to enjoy all manner of diversions, and reward hosts and guests for their service to the U.S. imperial state. Promoters lifted prohibitions against hula in Hawai'i and gambling in Cuba and made decadent pleasure rather than republican virtue central to tourism strategies. Even as U.S. imperialism changed, patterns of representation and interaction, ideologies and logics of governance, and memories and amnesias forged in the nineteenth century, particularly in Cuba and Hawai'i, endured and influenced U.S. imperialism around the world.[5] Indeed, at the same time that U.S. citizens embraced the kinds of imperial politics and pleasures that they denounced as corrupt, decadent, and oppressive in European colonial contexts, they insisted that the U.S. empire remained exceptional in its dedication to the extension of liberty and republican virtue.

Old Narratives for New Frontiers

Reimagining Hawai'i and Cuba as future white republics proved a daunting task in the United States at the end of 1898. By then countless cartoons, pamphlets, speeches, novels, and travelogues had purported that its "new possessions" were despotic feudal polities peopled by dark childlike savages incapable of self-government. Travel writers and tourism promoters joined other imperial agents in drawing on nineteenth-century narratives to reinstate positive images of Cuba and Hawai'i, particularly their elites, and stress their potential to become self-governing citizens of the imperial republic. Recasting violent conquest as consensual projects for belonging in the Union proved central to maintaining the fiction that the empire of liberty was extending universal freedoms to all. Unconvinced, most Cubans and Hawaiians continued to demand independence and oppose U.S. imperialism.[6]

When Spain surrendered Cuba to the United States in 1898, the demands by most Cubans for independence and the prohibitions on U.S. annexation laid out in the Teller Amendment collided with the no-transfer policy in force since 1823. Neither the wishes of the Cuban majority nor the amendment's restriction of U.S. "sovereignty, jurisdiction, or control" to "pacification thereof" seemed insurmountable. For one, U.S. occupiers and their allies held the power to define pacification. For another, the Teller Amendment forbade annexation during the pacification process but, one could plausibly argue, not necessarily at a later time, especially if Cubans were to invite it. U.S. officials, investors, settlers, and travel writers worked with conservative white Spaniards and Cubans to build a Cuban nation that would ask to become part of the Union. However, efforts to present Cuban freedom as a prelude to U.S. annexation had come to require the negation of three decades of Cuban struggles for everlasting independence.[7]

Naming proved essential, but insufficient, to efforts to transform Cubans' thirty-year struggle for independent nationhood into a two-month U.S. war against Spain. The most common U.S. names for its intervention, "America's War Against Spain" and the "Spanish-American War," ignored the fact that the Cuban Liberation Army had nearly defeated Spain in 1898, and that the United States had then joined the war to prevent Spain from surrendering Cuba to the Cubans. Cuba Libre's vision of a nation independent from Spain *and* the United States and dedicated to racial equality flew in the face of historic dreams of whitening and annexing Cuba. Cubans' struggles to transcend racial divisions and overturn racial hierarchies proved especially disturbing in the late nineteenth century, when the United States was preoccupied with enshrining segregation as the law of the land. It led North and South to renew old commitments to the annexation of Cuba in a common international cause not long after "separate but equal" Supreme Court decisions that united them in common national cause. Half a century before, the annexationist cause had not prevented the U.S. Civil War, but after war and Radical Reconstruction ended, the renewal of this quest helped northern and southern whites achieve reconciliation.[8]

Fears of racial equality had long existed in Cuba, not only against but within Cuba Libre. Beginning with the Ten Years' War, Cubans' struggles for emancipation and independence, historian Ada Ferrer argues, institutionalized enduring frictions between the forces of antiracism and revolution, on the one hand, and racism and reaction, on the other hand. The U.S. intervention in Cuba's war for independence convinced Cubans to restructure the leadership of the Liberation Army. Promotions brought to prominence officers of "refinement, education, comportment, civilization," qualities identified with republican manhood and white men. Demotions removed officers of color from positions of power and authority. Such personnel transfers constituted one scene in a multiact performance that Cuban separatists staged to convince the United States that Cubans were capable of independence and self-government, and that resembled Hawaiian efforts to "purchase independence with the coin of civilization." These moves compelled annexationists to rewrite the past to lend historic weight to their movement against the permanent Cuban independence demanded by most Cubans.[9]

Removing Cubans from accounts of their recent war and peace involved revising old historical narratives to suit changed circumstances and conditions. The United States excluded the entire Cuban Liberation Army, officers and men regardless of color, from participating in a surrender, victory, and peace in which Spain relinquished Cuba to the United States. These maneuvers enabled the United States to assume credit for "liberating" Cuba from Spain. Moreover, they helped annexationists cast members of the Cuban Liberation Army as black savages *and* white barbarians unfit for self-government. Travel writer Trumbull White offered a typical assessment: "If the Cuban soldier had been the equal of the American mentally and physically, he would not have needed our aid. It was because he was distinctly an inferior that we gave our assistance." White asserted that "the backbone of the revolution" was not the Cuban Liberation Army at all but "the professional class of Havana, and the other cities." Although its members "sympathized with the insurgent cause," he argued that few of them served, much less fought. But in stark contrast to the "illiterate four-fifths" who had, these elite white civilians understood the meaning and practice of "personal liberties" and "wise liberal government."[10]

White's assertion offered a stark contrast to the mid-nineteenth-century narratives that predicted Cuba's white yeomanry would demonstrate its republican manhood on the battlefield and secure Cuban independence before requesting U.S. annexation. The emergence of a powerful Cuban separatist movement that waged the Ten Years' War led annexationists to question Cubans' ability to win their independence. In 1885, Maturin M. Ballou recanted his previous view that Cubans had the will, the means, and the martial manhood needed to win their freedom. He faulted their lack of "self-reliance and true manhood" and expressed incredulity that such an "intelligent people . . . constantly visited by the citizens of a free republic and, having the example of successful revolt set by the men of the same race [had] never aimed an effectual blow at their oppressors. It would seem that the softness of the unrivaled climate of the skies, beneath which it is a luxury only to exist, has unnerved this people."[11] Ballou could have more nearly plucked these words from the anti-annexationist 1854 travelogue of William Henry Hurlbert than from his annexationist travel narrative of that same year. In 1898 U.S. annexationists concurred that the alleged failure of Cubans to win their war for independence demonstrated their lack of republican manhood and incapacity for self-government. White merely took this argument to its extreme in arguing that the Cubans who did in fact possess these qualities were the Cubans who had never fought.

Many of the privileged civilians of whom White spoke did view Liberation Army officers as their main political rivals and its men as threats to building a white republic. U.S. occupiers enlisted these men as allies committed to an independent Cuba that would seek U.S. annexation. The "pure white" members of the "higher" or "better class" of men "opposed above all an out and out Cuban government," the *New York Times* and travel writers insisted. The higher class men who had not demonstrated their manhood on the battle field embodied the restrained manhood that befitted their civilized status and qualified them to work with U.S. elites in rebuilding Cuba. As in the nineteenth century, at the turn of the twentieth, the so-called better classes were a crucial component of a multinational annexationist alliance. Having erased from the field the white republican monteros celebrated by earlier traveler writers, their turn-of-the-century counterparts insisted it was U.S. settlers who would form the backbone of the future republic. U.S. and Cuban annexationists even welcomed their longtime enemy into a reconstituted imperial brotherhood.[12]

Defining the war as a Spanish-American conflict served the project of transforming bitter enemies into affective allies committed to a Spanish-American peace. The travel narrative of Robert Porter, President William McKinley's agent in Cuba, was one of many to stress that the "rebuilding of Cuba" required the participation of Spaniards, who dominated the property-holding and merchant ranks and generally supported annexation. Those who transferred their loyalty from Spain to the United States aroused neither contempt nor suspicion. Instead, U.S. officials, travel writers, and others gladly incorporated these agents of conservatism and capital into the fraternal annexationist fold. The U.S. Army guaranteed their property and personal rights. Travel writer Franklin Matthews asserted that he journeyed to Cuba to find evidence to justify its "prompt relinquishment" but came to support the "merchants [and] every member of the pro-Spanish class" who wanted the United States "to retain control of the island." He argued that "only the members of the Cuban army," those of the Cuban Assembly, and "their immediate sympathizers [wanted] complete independence." Matthews deemed the Liberation Army barbaric and its desire for independence irrelevant and insisted that the civilian assembly members only wanted independence "for a year, or a year and a half." Travel writers joined official occupiers in making common cause between Spanish property owners and Cuban professionals, respectively symbols of capital and stable government. According to White, not even internecine war had ruptured affective bonds of brotherhood among them: "the many congenial associations, among Spanish officers, Cuban plotters, and Americans alike" continued to thrive during it. Spaniards and Cubans represented the Spanish side of a Spanish-American nation-building project that would lead to annexation.[13]

By virtue not of their New World birthplace but of their U.S. citizenships and educations, thousands of Cubans also belonged to the American side of the Spanish-American peace. Their upbringings made distinguishing Cuban-born and mainland-born U.S. citizens difficult, if not downright impossible. As Edward Atkins, a longtime resident planter from Boston, told the U.S. Congress in 1902: "There are so many naturalized Cubans, American citizens on the island that you can not tell, even by talking with them, whether they are Americans or Cubans." U.S. observers who denied most Cubans a place on the battlefield celebrated the military service of elite men who possessed U.S. citizenship and educations. Robert Porter asserted that their heroism was "not a surprise" given that the "most enlightened Cubans" and "active participants in the war for Cuban freedom carried individually, alike into battle and into conference, the grandest badge of freedom so far vouchsafed to mankind—United States citizenship." Such narratives echoed nineteenth-century travelogues in asserting that the two-way travel between Cuba and the United States resulted in the one-way transfer of U.S. republican ideas, identities, and citizenship to white Cubans. These Cuban-born U.S. citizens had joined U.S.-born U.S. citizens and Spaniards to extend this badge of freedom to all worthy of its rights and responsibilities.[14]

Members of this imperial brotherhood would Americanize and whiten the Cuban nation and citizenry so as to give rise to "annexation by acclamation." As Hawai'i had confirmed, and overriding the Teller Amendment seemed to require, honorable annexation would result from Cuba issuing an invitation that the United States could then accept. Like President McKinley, who rejected "forcible annexation" as an act of "criminal aggression" that would violate "our own code of morality," Porter asserted, "there can be no forcible annexation to the nation representing the absolute liberties of the people." Cuba would become part of the United States because Cubans "shall so decree." José Olivares similarly avowed, "When Cuba is ready to come to us, she may depend upon receiving a cordial welcome." Robert Hill called "absorption into the Union [a] fate . . . desired and prayed for by the people of the Island for over half a century." If an invitation from Cuba would produce honorable annexation, a period of independence would enable Cubans to restore an honor sullied by U.S. detractors, who cast them as criminals during the war. As the U.S. congressman Henry Cooper told the *New York Times*, many Cubans "said to me, 'We want to show the world that we are not thieves, bandits, and cutthroats.'"[15]

Along with Cuba's better classes, U.S. settlers would serve as "so many apostles of republicanism" dedicated to annexation, without the aid of Cuba's white yeomanry, as Ballou and other nineteenth-century observers had once maintained. Upon establishment of a "proper government," a U.S. official in Cuba declared, U.S. settlers would provide Cubans with "numerous teachers and exponents of republics and republicanism." To advance this goal, former president of the Canadian Pacific Railroad William van Horne founded the Cuba Company. He dreamed of making Cuba, along the lines of the western United States and Canada, into a land of "small farmers, owning their own land." Van Horne further claimed, "In countries where the percentage of individuals holding real estate is greatest, conservatism prevails and insurrections are unknown." A white yeomanry from North America would form the bedrock of a stable republic and help prepare Cuba and Cubans to join the Union.[16]

As predicted, U.S. settlers and investors flooded the island after 1898. But rather than advancing the cause of annexation, they seemed to undermine efforts to create a Cuban desire for it. Days after the signing of the peace, Matthews recounted, U.S. citizens descended on Havana. While many were respectable, the "motley" among them "seemed to outnumber the real American army of the occupation" much to the consternation of Cubans, "who wished that they had not come." Travel writers voiced alarm that Cuba was becoming "over-run" with U.S. citizens "of all conditions of life, of all professions, and of no professions" and of "swindlers, loafers, and topers." For White, the U.S. West offered an aptly disgraceful comparison: "Adventurers found their paradise and all sorts of frauds were attempted in competition with legitimate business enterprises." They "reminded one . . . of our own west in the bonanza days. Hotels were crowded and at every corner there were men with options worth fortunes, which they were willing to sell dirt cheap." Causing "endless trouble to American officials" and creating "a bad impression" among Cubans, these men fueled demands for independence. As the wrong U.S. citizens threatened the annexationist project, the better classes failed to secure the support of the Cuban electorate or write a constitution that satisfied the United States.[17]

The U.S. military gave government positions to both annexationists and moderate separatist Cubans it hoped to co-opt. Before the first municipal elections, held in 1900, the U.S. government enfranchised Cuban-born U.S. citizens, a group more annexationist than most Cubans. Using military-service, literacy, and property requirements, it disfranchised two-thirds of adult men, disproportionately Afro-Cubans, sparking mass protests across the island. Despite the diminution of the voting ranks, candidates representing the separatist Nationalist Party won far more seats than U.S.-backed candidates. The majority of even a restricted electorate declined to elect officials not dedicated to complete independence, universal suffrage, and at least the principle of racial equality. The better classes fared even worse in the elections for delegates to the constitutional convention. The convention's adoption of universal adult male suffrage then raised yet another obstacle to annexation. But its proponents did not waver from the goals of restricting the power of the *clases populares* and expanding that of the better classes.[18]

The next year, the United States declared independence contingent upon Cuba's acceptance of the Platt Amendment as an appendix to its constitution. The Platt Amendment gave the United States the power to intervene in Cuba "for the protection of life, property, and individual liberty," establish naval bases, and circumscribe Cuba's ability to negotiate treaties, incur debt, and nullify acts and "lawful rights" enacted during the occupation. Cubans protested the Platt Amendment across Cuba and the United States. Faced with the choice, as a constitution framer put it, of limited independence or no independence, the assembly accepted the Platt Amendment—by just one vote. The Republic of Cuba achieved its nominal national independence in May 1902. Its first president was a naturalized U.S. citizen who had lived in the States for three decades. With the help of the military government, Tomás Estrada Palma ran unopposed from his home in New York, from which he told the *New York Times* that the "natural destiny" of Cuba was to "be part of the United States." The U.S. occupation and the Platt Amendment had succeeded in creating two national constituencies of the Cuban state, one led by U.S. government and business interests centered in Washington and New York and the other, a Cuban electorate of adult men.[19]

After 1898, narratives of a Spanish-American war and a Spanish-American peace established myriad "debts of gratitude" that Cubans ostensibly owed the United States for its liberation of them from Spanish colonialism and the formation of the Cuban nation.[20] By contrast, by the time the United States annexed Hawai'i, over fifty years had passed since U.S. travel writers and policymakers popularized the notion that Hawaiians owed a debt of gratitude for their nationhood to the New England missionaries. Haole drew on these memories to portray annexation as a consensual decision, rather than an illegal act of war, as they worked to legitimize the new colonial state and stake claims to belonging to and rights of governance in Hawai'i. While most Cubans struggled to achieve sovereign nationhood, most Hawaiians dreamed of restoring it. The resistance of the majority in Cuba and Hawai'i to the extension and legitimation of U.S. imperial governance in these island states and societies frustrated already difficult projects to transform them into white republics. So too did the work of the very imperial agents charged with transplanting settler colonialism to the tropics, a goal about which they became increasingly ambivalent over time.

In 1900, a U.S. government official declared that "Hawaii would be governed by a 'ruling class' of 4,000 Americans and other Anglo-Saxons who were to have dominion over the remaining 145,000 residents of the Islands."[21] The metropole certainly gave haole the means and latitude to do so. Although the United States had the power to fill important offices in the territorial government, in practice this power largely remained in the hands of haole. As became custom, rather than appointing the territorial governor, the U.S. president generally allowed haole to select for themselves a governor with more power than that of any other U.S. territory or state. Still, proclaiming white dominion proved easier than legitimizing haole governance.

From the founding of the U.S. territory, Asian immigrants and settlers (many once citizens of the kingdom) and Native Hawaiians contested haole efforts to consolidate their power and authority. U.S. law took effect in Hawai'i in 1900, denying U.S. citizenship and the right of naturalization to Asian immigrants (their children who were born on U.S. soil were U.S. citizens) and rendering contract labor illegal. The Asian majority took advantage of a newfound freedom of action and movement as workers. The Japanese staged over twenty strikes that year, filling haole "with much solicitude and watchfulness . . . from the uncertainty of labor" and "the protection of established interests against ignorance of law and justice." Laborers voted with their feet in other ways. In droves they abandoned the plantations and plantation work, migrated to the United States, sought employment in the urban trades, or established small shops and farms.[22]

Despite efforts by whites in Hawai'i and the United States to deny citizenship and suffrage to Hawaiians on racial grounds, recognition of them as the indigenous people and citizens of a once sovereign nation recognized by the world family of nations in this instance overrode the legal equation of naturalization and whiteness. The extension of U.S. citizenship to whites and Hawaiians and the vote to white and Hawaiian adult men made the latter the electoral majority of registered voters. (It was a small electorate, comprising only 7 percent of the population, or 12,550.)[23] U.S. citizenship and suffrage rights represented part of the process of "forced inclusion" into the United States and "worked against collective assertions of political self-determination." But as far as possible, Hawaiians used these imposed rights to their advantage.[24]

Hawaiians could not prevent the consolidation of haole governance, but they did protest, delay, and set some limits on it. Nationalist societies urged Native Hawaiians to boycott the ceremony transferring sovereignty to the United States in 1898. Virtually all did. Even ardently expansionist travel writers conceded that "more tears than cheers" marked the event and that it "was more like a funeral than a *fête*."[25] In the first territorial elections of 1900, the Home Rule Party swept elections. Three years later, haole backed Prince Jonah Kūhiō Kalaniana'ole as the territory's nonvoting delegate to the U.S. Congress. As haole hoped, he split the Hawaiian vote, enabling a haole-led Republican Party to take control of the territorial legislature. His triumph was not just a victory for haole. The election of an ali'i, imprisoned for participating in the 1895 revolt against the republic and venerated for his role in defeating an 1897 annexation treaty, inscribed Native resistance and persistence into the colonial state. His victory compelled haole to govern more according to the wishes of Hawaiians than they would have otherwise. It also led haole to seek to legitimate their governance by staking genealogical claims to Hawai'i.[26]

On the eve of annexation, Queen Lili'uokalani rejected the claim made by annexationist haole that they were Hawaiians. She asserted the primacy of Hawaiian genealogical traditions in determining ancestry: Hawaiians are "the children of the soil—the native inhabitants of the Hawaiian Islands and their descendents."[27] In response to the queen's authoritative pronouncement, haole abandoned efforts to stake claims to Hawai'i and Hawaiianness by virtue of birthplace. They appropriated and wrote themselves into Hawaiian genealogies. Ideas of Thomas Jefferson provided them with ways to do this, while writing Hawai'i and Hawaiians into U.S. history and American civilization. Jefferson proposed that marriages between white colonials and Native Americans would legitimate the whites' ties to the land and forge bonds of affection that would render conquest consensual. For Natives devastated by disease and dispossession, such marriages would effect "their restoration" and "rebirth as Americans."[28]

As haole claimed rights of belonging to Hawai'i, they simultaneously worked to transform Hawaiians into assimilated, whitened U.S. citizens. They postulated that marriages between haole and Hawaiians resulted in the "dilution" of the Hawaiianness of their children and their distillation into an assimilated American body politic rooted in whiteness.[29] The author of the one-page preface to Emma Metcalf Nakuina's *Hawaii, Its Peoples, Their Legends*, likely a haole man connected to the HPC, asserted that her "bloodlines" linked "Plymouth Rock [to] midseas islands." He invoked bonds of blood to connect white U.S. citizen-settlers and the United States genealogically and geographically to Hawaiians and Hawai'i. Operating on the then-popular belief that Polynesians were Aryans, the author of the preface contended that her ancestors of Hawaiian "high priests, statesmen, and warriors" and Anglo-Saxon "pilgrims, lawmakers, and jurists" each had ties to an imaginary England, specifically late nineteenth-century discourses of a monarchical government over which king, church, and a martial aristocracy presided in both feudal and modern times.[30]

The Pilgrims fled this imaginary England in 1620 to escape post–Norman Conquest corruptions of true Anglo-Saxon culture, faith, and governance. They alighted in Massachusetts on or near Plymouth Rock. On the bicentennial of their landing in 1820, Daniel Webster consecrated this broken boulder as the birthplace of a free and prosperous Anglo-American people destined to spread their uncorrupted liberties to others. By coincidence, that same year New England missionaries landed in a Hawai'i the HPC proclaimed was "not more than four hundred years behind . . . England when the islands were discovered." Variously dating this moment with the arrival of Captain James Cook in the eighteenth century or the

arrival of Spaniards in the sixteenth century, haole argued that on the broad
eve of Western contact, Hawaiʻi resembled the imaginary England that their
Pilgrim ancestors had fled. Time and space collapsed, and destiny and history converged when the rulers of a newly centralized Hawaiʻi welcomed a
procession of New Englanders. Some married Hawaiians. Most labored to
Christianize, civilize, domesticate, and otherwise remake Hawaiʻi and
Hawaiians on Anglo-American lines.[31]

Nakuina's biographer used the same sort of elision of time and space.
He presented her as a domesticated, disenfranchised U.S. citizen who had
renounced her Hawaiian identity and the historic prerogative of female aliʻi
to govern. He did not name her aliʻi ancestors. He named only her haole
ones and attributed her upbringing, character, and loyalties to them.
"Broadly and liberally educated under the immediate care of her father,"
Theophilus Metcalf, "a Harvard man [and] nephew of the late Chief Justice
Metcalf of Massachusetts," Nakuina appeared principally as the domesticated descendant of a minor forefather of the United States. This upbringing prepared her to draw upon her chiefly heritage and made her as "fitted
to present" the legends of "her people," the "Hawaiian Race," to white
tourists and settlers as she was content to leave affairs of state to haole
men.[32]

This preface served as a bridge between haole HPC accounts of the U.S.
civilizing mission in Hawaiʻi and Nakuina's "legends," the lone Hawaiian-
authored HPC publication. Haole-authored HPC booklets of the time
argued that Hawaiians were "well fitted to appreciate civilization when it
came." After Cook's fatal visit, "the influence of white races rapidly altered
native customs." Kamehameha led the unification of the archipelago:
"counseled by white men and with the aid of gunpowder," Kamehameha
"united the islands into one kingdom." After subduing Maui, Molokai, and
Oʻahu, "the latter rebelled." Kamehameha returned "with a few white men
incorporated into his army" and triumphed in the Battle of Nuʻuanu. Unification marked the beginning of progress "from this time forward." King
Kamehameha and Queen Kaʻahumanu "built up the empire along modern
lines, [and] in rapid succession, political rights were granted, the lands . . .
were subdivided, the constitution was framed."[33]

Although haole narratives credited Kamehameha and Kaʻahumanu with
"administrative genius" for promulgating these measures, they simultaneously asserted that these same features of "permanent civilization" had
"followed the arrival of the American missionaries." Led by Kaʻahumanu,

Hawaiians "embrace[d]" Christianity. Haole deemed New England missionaries, lawyers, and teachers as the personages most "fitted to undertake
the rehabilitation of the aboriginal kingdom." Some of these haole married
aliʻi; some of these same and other men worked in government for aliʻi to
make Hawaiʻi into a modern constitutional monarchy and as teachers to
make Hawaiians into literate, law-abiding, Christians: "And so as the missionaries had laid the foundations for character, the lawyers and instructors
builded up good government and intelligent citizenship." Telescoping to
the future, the HPC presented annexation "at Hawaii's own request" as
the outcome of a process of collaborative governance and cross-cultural
marriage. It further asserted that Hawaiians had willingly relinquished the
rights and power of governance to haole men. Hawaiian women who wed
haole men and embraced Anglo-Saxon civilization voluntarily removed
themselves from the public sphere, even before annexation. Haole offered
as an example Princess Bernice Pauahi Bishop, "a daughter of the Kameha-
mehas who preferred domesticity to the throne." The same held true for
the "almost separate race" of part-Hawaiians, which "brings to American
citizenship [a] grasp of public affairs, much capacity for development, and
charming graces of hospitality." Their feminization and domestication into
educated, yet immature, citizens *and* genial hosts and hostesses content
with life in the private sphere affirmed that governance resided with Anglo-
American men.[34]

As best symbolized by Queen Liliʻuokalani, domesticity and marriage to
haole need not translate into Hawaiian women's withdrawal from the political sphere, acquiescence to colonial rule, or abandonment of Hawaiian
identities and loyalties. Nakuina and her peers challenged, in the words of
Ann Laura Stoler, the notion that "a demonstrated disaffection for one's
native culture and mother" was a condition upon which a woman's place
of privilege in the colonial community rested.[35] In *Hawaii, Its People, and
Their Legends*, Nakuina offered lessons of Hawaiian resistance and persistence in the face of mass death and devastation from imported diseases,
alienation from the land, and civilizing projects aimed at cultural annihila-
tion. She did not just write about "her people." She wrote to and for them.
She preserved select *moʻolelo* (histories, stories) by translating them into
English after haole banned Hawaiian as a language of instruction and public
discourse. Far from static legends, her moʻolelo offered "lessons from the
past intended to guide" behavior in the present, as Jonathan Kay Kamakawiwoʻole Osorio argues. Nakuina created useable pasts for Hawaiians in pres-

1. Princess Kaiulani, a niece of Queen Liliʻuokalani, represented the haole ideal of Victorian Hawaiian womanhood: assimilated and whitened, civilized and domesticated, titled and entitled. Reprinted from John L. Stevens and W. B. Oleson, *Picturesque Hawaii* (Philadelphia: Hubbard, 1894).

2. Hula dancers, Honolulu, c. 1900. To most haole at the time, the
Hawaiian hula girl represented Princess Kaiulani's polar opposite: barbaric
not civilized, debased not refined, racially inferior not racially elevated.
Author's collection.

ents rerouted but not erased by death and dispossession, colonialism and
conversion.[36]

Reflecting on whether Hawaiians "had descended from the great Aryan
race [or] the lost tribes of Israel," Nakuina pronounced Hawaiians more
like "the Israelites" who clung "to their beliefs in the face of persecutions."
Like them, Hawaiians became the "objects of envy" by those who sought
"either to expel them or attempt their destruction." Rejecting haole claims
that marriages between Hawaiians and haole placed the Kingdom on a path
toward annexation, Nakuina argued that such marriages resulted from
Hawaiians' loyalty to the ali'i who allowed some "unusually beautiful
Sarahs or Rebekas [to be] taken [by] the powerful and rich among whom
they sojourned." These marriages formalized ties between sovereign
peoples. She substituted for haole civilizing narratives histories of survival
and adaptation to a host of conquering strangers, from whom, like the
Israelites, Hawaiians were promised deliverance.[37]

Haole narratives of the progressive advance of civilization met their match in Nakuina's account of the destructive forces unleashed in its wake. She critiqued the haole belief in the progressive influence of Western law. Hawaiians had maintained "stringent laws and regulations of the taking of fish, looking toward their preservation." But then "the white man, with his alleged superior knowledge, prevailed on chief and commoners to throw down their wholesome restrictions." The application of a liberal faith in the inexhaustible supply of natural resources undermined old environmental laws, with "the result that fishes are very scarce in Hawaiian waters and getting more and more so every year." Nakuina spoke with authority. Educated in aquaculture and natural resource management, she served the kingdom as commissioner of water rights and ways for eighteen years, earning the reputation as "judge of the water court." The decimation of the environment and the people went hand-in-hand in the Hawaiian cultural imagination. Nakuina challenged haole appropriation of her genealogy to legitimate the rule of the few without accepting obligations to all, obligations conferred by Hawaiian ancestry.[38]

Nakuina reclaimed her Hawaiian ancestors to reinterpret postcontact history. Her history of Kamehameha's conquest of Oʻahu and founding of the nation featured no white men, unlike haole narratives that exaggerated their importance and ignored their acculturation into Hawaiian society.[39] She mobilized Hawaiian genealogy to highlight the persistence and adaptation of natives to usurping strangers: "A young chiefess, the daughter of the high priest Kanaloauoo, whose residence was on Punchbowl crater, and who was connected with the Hawaii chiefs by the father's side, but whose mother was one of the tabu princesses of Kukaniloko, the famous cradle of Oahuan royalty," Nakuina recounted, "was compelled to be married" to the general Kamehameha appointed to govern the conquered island. While the chiefess accepted this marriage "with unquestioning obedience, [she] displayed her fidelity to her slaughtered kindred and people by calling her first born Kaheananui," that is, "the great heap of the slain" in honor of those who perished in the Battle of Nuʻuanu. Kamehameha could have put her to death for this. Instead, "hearing of this covert act of feminine defiance, [he] only smiled indulgently and approved of her fidelity to the memories of the dead." Nakuina expressed special thanks for this dispensation. The chiefess, Kalanikupaulakea, was her great-grandmother. War by usurping strangers was a customary path to power in Hawaiʻi, but victory conferred obligations upon the conqueror to the conquered.[40]

Like her ancestors, Nakuina embodied "the sanctity of home, obedience to superiors and full justice" but not in the manner presumed by her unnamed biographer. She pledged allegiance not to the patriarchal authority of haole men but to the Hawaiian ancestors who empowered women like her great- and great-great-grandmother to govern. Nakuina's great-grandmother had not entered into an affective or consensual union with Kamehemeha's general. Rather, she acknowledged military defeat and accepted a marriage that enabled her to continue to protect and serve her people. Her defiant act of naming testified to Hawaiian endurance amid the ruptures of colonialism. Rejecting haole views of Hawaiian legends as static tales of a dying people, Nakuina plumbed a dynamic past to present contemporary lessons that permitted, historian Julia Clancy-Smith argues in a parallel context, "the survival of her cultural patrimony in a society literally and figuratively under siege."[41]

Nakuina illustrated that Hawaiian survival depended on a mixture of conformity and resistance. On the one hand, she accepted haole as the latest in a series of usurping strangers who had brought "four changes of government, or rather the personnel of the governing people" as she defiantly put it. On the other hand, Nakuina asserted that the failure of the most recent conquerors to accept obligations and loyalties conferred by Hawaiian genealogies undermined their authority. She lamented that "most of the stone" of Kamehameha's residence "had been carted away, evidently for the making of . . . the wharf that extends from . . . what was the entrance and altar to the temple."[42] Through the desecration of the seat of the nation and temple upon which it sat, haole demonstrated that they revered their ancestors who were pilgrims, lawmakers, and jurists but not those who were high priests, statesmen, and warriors. Their loyalties lay solely with their New England ancestors and their version of Pilgrims' progress. Nakuina contrasted the proper legitimating of power through genealogy and marriage by Kamehameha at the turn of the nineteenth century with the failure of haole to do so at the turn of the twentieth. Likely acknowledging the threat Nakuina's performative resistance posed to haole governance, the HPC and its two successors did not again publish a Hawaiian-authored narrative.

Narratives on the annexation of Hawai'i as the consensual outcome of collaborative governance and cross-cultural marriage, and those on the U.S. liberation of Cuba without the participation of Cubans, became entrenched in U.S. memory as Cuban and Hawaiian resistance to imperial state-building projects imposed limits on the projection and consolidation of U.S.

power in both places. Imperial authorities hoped that the predicted influx of U.S. settlers would extend the reach of their power and authority and help them transform Cuba and Hawai'i into integral parts of the white republic. For a variety of reasons, attracting white settlers proved difficult, a matter complicated by debates over just who was the "right kind" of white settler. These debates gave voice to imperial anxieties and shape to shifting imperial desires and designs in Cuba, Hawai'i, and the tropics more broadly. The wrong sort of white settler came to symbolize not just an obstacle to dreams of making them into white republics but an impediment to the growing desire of U.S. imperial agents and their allies to lead the sorts of lives of privilege and decadence that European colonizers across the torrid zones seemed to lead.

The "Right Kind of Island" Is White

Travel writers and tourism promoters invoked the closing of the frontier in the continental West to lure U.S. citizens to its newly opened frontiers overseas. Haole tourism promoters sought to replicate the success of the U.S. West's tourism, immigration, and settlement bureaus by attracting "her share of the tourist travel of the well-to-do class for the enjoyment of her climate and scenery and the investor for the development of her tropical resources." The *Havana Post* similarly invoked the West. It called for advertising in the United States "during the fall and winter, when the tourist travel is the largest" in order to "bring Cuba to the front as one of the most desirable countries in the world for the investment of capital and the coming of immigration." The HPC declared that "settlers are as desirable as tourists and we may as well consider both classes as one," but in the next breath, it cautioned that Hawai'i was not for the ordinary pioneer: "It is not a Klondike where gold can be picked up nor an Oklahoma where land can be had for the asking." Arable land was a scarce commodity in Hawai'i. But in seemingly land-rich Cuba, as well, travel writers, tourism promoters, and others divided over whether they wanted all manner of white pioneers or just privileged Anglo-Saxons.[43]

Whereas the promotion of U.S. investment would complete the integration of Cuba and Hawai'i into the U.S. economy, U.S. settlers would whiten their populations and integrate them into the Union of states. For the whites who long hoped to displace blacks from Cuba and Asians from Hawai'i, recruitment of an immigrant working class willing to work the cane and white enough to become U.S. citizens was a key counterpart to middle- and upper-class settlement. But first, promoters had to dispel the widespread belief that whites could not survive, much less thrive, in the tropics.[44]

Diseases, especially those of uncertain or unknown cause, offer potent metaphors for perceived social or moral ills.[45] For U.S. occupation officials, making Cuba physically, morally, and politically safe for U.S. investment and settlement required eradicating many "diseases" of Spanish colonialism: yellow fever, poor sanitation, feudal tyranny, and immorality of all kinds. Virtually all U.S. observers concurred that the occupation's greatest material challenges were eliminating yellow fever and building streets and sewers. More than matters of public health, they represented a moral and political struggle against Spanish feudal despotism and for U.S. capitalist republicanism. As Olivares put it, "Wherever Spain's yellow flag has rested . . . it has been accompanied by pestilence and death and decay. And on the contrary, it may be said with equal truth that health, happiness, and prosperity are the inseparable companions of the starry flag of the free." Porter agreed: "Spain in herself was a tyrant contagion and everything she touched became diseased and rotten to its vitals. And this terrible condition was not only physical, but moral, for moral uncleanliness is sure always to follow physical uncleanliness."[46] Eliminating yellow fever came to signify the power of the United States to rescue Cuba and Cubans from centuries of backwardness and place them on mental and material roads to civilization and modernity. These narratives did not go uncontested. The debate over whether the Cuban citizen Carlos Finlay or U.S. citizen Walter Reed identified the disease's cause escalated into a "struggle for power" in which U.S. actors strove "to establish the supremacy of 'triumphant' American medicine over that of a dominated nation" and Cubans, "to demonstrate their resistance to American ascendancy over Cuba."[47]

The eradication of yellow fever and the construction of roads would also open Cuba to U.S. investment and the U.S. settlement needed to pave the way for annexation. U.S. assertions that "four-fifths of the land" was "unoccupied," mostly in Oriente province in the east, dovetailed with the occupying forces' utter disregard for farmers and planters devastated by decades of war. The United States refused Cuban requests for recovery aid and instead spent over $15 million of Cuban revenues to make the tropics safe for white U.S. citizens and open lands for them to buy. U.S. military decrees worked to dispossess great proprietors and even more small farmers. In 1901, the U.S. military government revoked a moratorium on mortgage collection. Without access to capital or credit, with land prices and production at a historic low, farmers abruptly confronted with paying off years of debt were forced to sell their land at fire-sale prices. In 1902, a decree designed for "cleaning up the mess of titles that has entangled the properties" held in common or by custom destroyed Oriente's small farming class. Because most Cubans, disproportionately Afro-Cubans, could not afford surveys and deeds, U.S. occupiers in effect alienated them from their land and thereby opened it to U.S. firms and individuals.[48]

The work of the U.S. occupation forces laid the ground for real-estate agents, travel writers, and tourism promoters: the first produced saleable land with clear title, the last sold it to, and at times developed it for, U.S. settlers and investors. Even before war ended in 1898, a New Yorker traveled to Havana to invest in a hotel "in the hope that Cuba would eventually become an American possession" and center for "a profitable throng of wealthy guests," seeking pleasure and investment opportunities. During the first two months of 1899, the *Havana Post* reported, hotel registers listed "the names of men whose wealth mounts up into the hundreds of millions who came on no idle tour of inspection but who meant business." In the first days of 1900, the "vanguard of the first American colony" arrived to build the agricultural colony of La Gloria, lured by the Cuban Land and Steamship Company's promise of "a short road to competency and a life amid tropical delights."[49]

Ever fearful that the wrong sort of investors and settlers would derail the annexation project, travel writers and tourism promoters made special efforts to attract white men in good moral and monetary standing. Responding to the *Havana Post's* call to "advertise Cuba" through a tourism and immigration bureau staffed by the "right kind of men," James Dorman urged them to solicit the right kind of settlers: "This island is not a place for wild-cat schemes, dreamy speculations or chimerical projects, but a country where the energetic, industrious and vigilant can realize and earn the most on the least labor and output." Travel writers warned prospective settlers that despite the eradication of dread disease, the tropics remained enervating to whites. Hill advised that those "who seek investment have the means to return frequently to the native country." Whitening Cuba depended upon men in possession of character *and* capital, widely believed to be mutually reinforcing measures of manhood and future success.[50]

Although handpicking settlers and investors was impossible, tourism promotion presented an avenue for attracting well-heeled citizens. New York business groups, most prominently the New York Merchants' Association and the New York Produce Exchange, which handled three-quarters of U.S. commerce with Cuba, organized to promote investment and settlement and agitate for annexation. Backed by the *Havana Post* and Publicity League of Cuba, leading residents advertised "commercial and agricultural opportunities" to prosperous New Yorkers and midwesterners. Promoters recommended visiting Cuba as a tourist prior to investing and settling there, following the example of compatriots: "Mr. A. W. Scoville, architect and builder of Hartford, Conn., and his 8-year-old son Raymond embark for the States today, after an extensive visit to Cuba. He is very enthusiastic over the island and expressed his admiration of its people and their hospitality in no measured terms. He will return promptly to buy an estate and start orange culture on a large scale." Acting on the advice of Florida real-estate and development magnate Henry Flagler, William van Horne established luxury hotels at his railroad's terminal cities of Camaguey, Santa Clara, and Santiago de Cuba. Catering to "the many visitors who are seeking homes and investments," the hotels' rates and discriminatory policies limited guests to whites of means. Developers and travel writers cooperated to sell "winter homes" to "well-to-do Americans" in hopes such sales would generate "a great interest in industries with consequent additional investment in capital." Their work stood in contrast to the U.S. West, where promoters customarily welcomed all deemed white in order to displace Native and non-Native people of color and establish U.S. authority in disputed territory.[51]

As in Cuba, the promotion of investment, settlement, and tourism in Hawai'i became bound up with struggles to eradicate a disease identified with racial and social sickness and to open land to white settlement. Unlike Cuba, widely regarded as a death trap for whites before the elimination of yellow fever, Hawai'i held a reputation of being a temperate tropics free of dread disease, a land where whites would grow healthier and stronger. In a travelogue dedicated to Lorrin Thurston, Sanford Dole, and B. F. Dillingham, Caspar Whitney offered a typical view: "It would be difficult to improve on the physique of the boys and young men born of white parents in Hawaii," as attested by the athletic achievements of "members of the Hawaiian Club at Yale or Harvard." But in 1899 bubonic plague struck.

Although it did so across "race, class, and property lines," haole papers, led by former annexation leader Thurston and his *Pacific Commercial Advertiser*, insisted that Honolulu's Chinatown was the sole source of the plague. The chair of the Citizens' Sanitary Committee, Thurston editorialized that it was the "white man's burden" to disinfect Chinatown. The Board of Health decided to do so by burning its infected areas. Tragically, wind swept the fire out of control, razing thirty-eight acres and leaving four thousand people homeless. As the ashes smoldered, Thurston suggested appropriating Chinese-owned land for the expansion of the white business district. He preferred that "Asiatics" be "pressed back rather than the owner's of Honolulu's most beautiful and stately homes." No buildings outside Chinatown were burned. The Chinese protested the violation of their property and personal rights. Those who sued received only limited compensation, and Chinatown got only a new water and sewer system. Thurston's proposal died. But the white business community secured revenues from a "plague-born public health tax" on ships to use to attract Anglo-Saxon tourists, investors, and settlers to Hawai'i.[52]

To aid their promotional efforts, nonplanter whites counted on the U.S. federal government to help make land available to settlers and investors. After overthrowing queen and kingdom, the Provisional Government, and later the republic, took control of the Crown lands. Despite Hawaiian opposition, the U.S. state took title to them upon annexation. But the territorial government maintained control of their management. U.S. officials supported local efforts to promote white homesteading and diversified agriculture. They pressured the sugar industry to do the same. But good land was scarce, and planters wanted the best Crown lands for expanded sugar production. Noting the "excessive preeminence" of sugar, the United States established the Hawaii Agricultural Experiment Station in 1901 to diversify agriculture and attract "American citizens, white voters, freemen." For their part, sugar planters viewed mainland investors and settlers as unwanted competitors who might upset their pursuit of a monopoly of power and wealth in Hawai'i.[53]

So when tourism promoters from the Honolulu Chamber of Commerce and Merchants Association sought support from the sugar interests and the territorial government to "secure a trade that is admittedly large and profitable" and bring "us an increased and permanent population of the most desirable character," they argued that the sugar industry stood to benefit from an increase of tourists: "there would be sufficient of the

wealthier classes among them who would become interested in our securities . . . to obviate a necessity . . . of our capitalists visiting the United States
for the purpose of raising funds necessary to carry on the plantations."
They asked the Hawaiian Sugar Planters' Association (HSPA) for financial
support. After it declined, the Chamber and Merchants Association recommended the formation of a tourist committee financed by a voluntary
freight charge and the territorial legislature. Governor Sanford Dole argued
that a "recent depression" had shown the "vital importance" of developing
"productive enterprises along other lines" and that planters had an obligation to remedy a situation that the concentration of cane produced: "a
powerfully repressive influence upon all other productive enterprises."
Dole further insisted that planters had a racial obligation to help less fortunate haole secure and maintain a place of privilege and power in the colonial hierarchy. Eventually, the legislature appropriated fifteen thousand
dollars, a sum matched by business, to fund the HPC.[54] It worked to attract
tourists with the hopes some would become the "small and general farmers
upon whom rest the hope of the Territory." It focused on attracting prosperous men able to carry themselves and their families for the two and five
years, respectively, that pineapple and coffee took to reach maturity.[55]

In addition to recruiting wealthy white settlers, nonplanter haole
worked to increase the white laboring class. Whitney argued that "now"
was the time "to supplant Asiatic with white labor" on the grounds that
Asians could outcompete and undereat whites. Until this goal was achieved,
"Hawaii will remain undeveloped . . . for no competition is possible
between Eastern and Western men in the same field and operating on the
same basis. There must be the substitution of one by the other." In 1905,
the U.S. labor commissioner reported, "It is not easy to give an adequate
idea of the resentment and the bitterness felt by the white mechanic and
the white merchant who see themselves being steadily forced to the wall,
and even driven out of the Territory by Asiatic competition." Nonplanter
haole demanded help at home and from abroad.[56]

The U.S. government assisted nonplanter haole efforts to increase the
population of white laborers eligible for naturalization as U.S. citizens. Sub-
scribing to the belief that allowing Japanese immigrants to compete with
white U.S. citizens was tantamount to "race suicide," President Theodore
Roosevelt pledged to help Hawai'i "secure a white population of actual
landtillers who are small landowners." Beginning in 1905, the Hawaiian
Board of Immigration endeavored "to bring into Hawaii such persons as

would be capable of becoming American citizens," especially the Portuguese. Roosevelt celebrated the board's achievement of bringing thirteen hundred Portuguese to Hawaiʻi the next year: "That shipment" shows that "we shall succeed in turning Hawaiʻi into the right kind of island." For Roosevelt and nonplanter haole, both the right kind of island and the Portuguese were white. Roosevelt and haole agreed that the Portuguese were inferior whites. They were Caucasian but not haole, a distinction institutionalized in the territory's census categories of Caucasians (Spanish and Portuguese) and Other Caucasians (mostly Anglo-Saxon). The Hawaii Immigration Board and the HPC worked in tandem: the former to attract white worker-citizens who might eventually become small farmers; the latter to attract middle- and upper-class Anglo-Saxon gentlemen farmers.[57]

If planter and nonplanter haole disagreed over the need to increase the white middle- and working-class populations, their counterparts in Cuba agreed on the need but disagreed on the reasons. U.S. and Cuban annexationists worked to increase the white population to achieve the incorporation of Cuba into the United States, while Cuban separatists did so to resist it. The U.S. military governor of Cuba, General Leonard Wood, asserted that "the solution of both the *social* and *economic* problems in the Island of Cuba depends principally on endowing it with a population of 8 or 10 millions of white inhabitants." He and other annexationists envisioned recruiting a hierarchy of whites. Attracting white U.S. residents and settlers constituted a strategy for creating the independent producers who would demonstrate Cuba's capacity for republican government and make annexation possible. Recruiting Spanish immigrant workers represented a strategy for whitening Cuba yet satisfying capital's insatiable demand for labor. But U.S. planters protested bans on the importation of black West Indian workers. Perfecto Lacosta, a naturalized U.S. citizen and wealthy planter who was once the mayor of Havana, brokered a compromise to preserve the annexationist alliance. In violation of U.S. laws then in force, it allowed a return to contract labor, but with Spaniards rather than West Indians, keeping the workforce relatively cheap while making it whiter.[58]

In the early twentieth century, as in the mid-nineteenth, Cubans sympathetic to annexation supported recruiting whites from the United States and Spain. Lacosta proclaimed, "The policy of the new government is to strongly encourage the influx of American capital and brains, and the visitor from the north, be he capitalist or laborer, professional man or sightseer is assured of a cordial welcome." Cuba's "success" depended on "the colonization of lands by the sturdy, energetic farmers of the United States." White separatist Cubans regarded the promotion of U.S. settlement with alarm. In 1903 and 1909, their congressmen introduced legislation to prevent foreigners from buying land or establishing towns or agricultural colonies. Both failed. Reasserting a Latin whiteness against Afro-Cubans and Anglo-Saxons, Cuban separatists strengthened prohibitions on the immigration of "races of color." They especially encouraged the immigration of Spanish families to lower the proportion of blacks and erect a bulwark against Anglo-Saxon settlers and annexationist designs. Separatist congressman Rafael M. Portuondo declared, "Absolutely all Cubans agree on the need to approve of Spanish immigration as a means of saving our race and of saving our existence in America."[59]

By 1903, a year after the U.S. military occupation ended, U.S. businessmen, winter visitors, and vacation-home owners had helped transform the western Havana suburb of Vedado into a center of high society for the better class of U.S., Cuban, and Spanish whites. U.S. settlers had established no fewer than thirty-seven agricultural colonies across the island; their numbers doubled by 1912. Over two thousand foreigners held title to land on the Isle of Pines, an island promoted as U.S. territory, although whether it belonged to Cuba or the United States then remained a thorny diplomatic question. By 1905, U.S. citizens held title to agricultural, commercial, residential, and resort properties worth an estimated $50 million. The growth of U.S. settlement inspired a cartoon in the *Havana Telegraph*, reprinted in U.S. newspapers and travelogues. Depicting a U.S. citizen at work in his citrus grove, the caption read, "Hoeing an orange tree? Yes—and shaping up a new state for the Yankee Union, that's what he's doing."[60]

Such proclamations overstated the degree of Americanization of Cuba and the importance of U.S. settlers there. Promised quick returns, many cultivated citrus, only to learn that the trees took years to reach maturity and hence required more capital and income than most possessed. Thirteen thousand U.S. citizens held title to land in Cuba in 1905, but only six thousand resided there in 1907. Ironically, programs to make tourists into settlers often produced the opposite effect. Many U.S. citizens bought shares in the colonies, not to live in them, but have an excuse to visit Cuba, like others of the twenty to thirty thousand tourists who visited Cuba annually.[61]

But then armed rebellion led by Cubans horrified by the rigged reelection of Estrada Palma led to a second U.S. military occupation of Cuba from 1906 to 1909. Like the first occupation, the second produced a new wave of U.S. settlement. Commentators pointed to the maturation of agricultural colonies and the influx of a new wave of settlers as proof of successful Americanization. Wrote travel writer and journalist Irene Wright, "American residents have made the Isle of Pines an American community in everything but political status." U.S. citizens constituted the "majority of the population," U.S. dollars were the "currency of trade," U.S. ministers preached, U.S. architecture prevailed, and U.S. railroad cars transported produce grown by U.S. citizens to U.S. ships for export to U.S. consumers. Pictures and descriptions disseminated in the United States showed the sober settlers and tidy towns of Omaja and La Gloria as typical of the U.S. Midwest. They boasted of their Protestant churches, clapboard houses, picket fences, social clubs, and town meetings. Travel writers presented U.S. colonists as "stout, whole-souled hospitable Americans" or "the hardy pioneer type that made the winning of our West a triumph of civilization." Cuba offered a lifestyle much like that of the Midwest but with cheaper land, a superior climate, and an easier road to a competence.[62]

As some exaggerated the importance of U.S. settlers, others disavowed that annexation need follow from Cuban desire. Travel writer Charles Forbes Lindsay thought it "highly probable that Cuba will eventually come into the Union by a process similar to that which brought Hawaii under the flag. . . . It is not difficult to imagine a *coup d'etat*, resulting in a government in the hands of Americans."[63] Lindsay invoked Hawai'i to express frustration over the failure of Cubans to issue an invitation for annexation in short-order fashion, as predicted. Although the second occupation generated another wave of U.S. settlement, it also convinced the most powerful proponents of annexation, the U.S. government and capital and Cuba's better classes, that they did not need it. The political class and semisovereign state the United States helped create after 1898 had proved capable of advancing their interests without colonial control.

If limited U.S. white settlement in Cuba failed to generate support for annexation, in Hawai'i, annexation failed to produce an influx of white settlers. In its first decade, tourism increased faster than settlement. In the 1890s, an annual average of twenty-seven hundred tourists visited; the next decade, their numbers doubled to an annual average of five to six thousand. While nearly forty-three hundred people from the United States migrated to Hawai'i in the first decade of the twentieth century, the number that became or remained farmers was tiny. By 1909, half of all privately owned land belonged to haole corporations and one-sixth to haole individuals. A territorial government representing planter interests made "it very difficult for persons without influence" to obtain land, while planters' growing control of transportation and markets made it difficult to make a profit. The owners and lessees of many, perhaps most, "homestead lands" did not work them but leased them to planters. Few survived the expansion of cane. One rare success story was James D. Dole, a second cousin of Sanford Dole. He moved to Hawai'i in 1899, bought sixty acres, and planted them in pineapple. Dole and a few others expanded the area cultivated in pineapple from eighty acres to four thousand in the next decade and became wealthy members of a secondary planter class.[64]

There seemed cause for optimism in 1906 and 1907 when the emigration of eighteen thousand Japanese from Hawai'i to the United States produced a labor shortage. The next year, the United States negotiated the Gentlemen's Agreement, whereby the Japanese government agreed not to issue passports to workers for travel to the United States and its possessions. For nonplanter haole, the combination of rising Japanese emigration and the ending of Japanese immigration inspired hope. They limited the ability of sugar planters to expand cane production, opening opportunities for small farmers. The HPC stepped up efforts to lure white settlers, and the Immigration Board, white workers. But the hope that Japanese migration restrictions would pave the way for increasing white settlement proved as unfounded as the hope that the second U.S. occupation and wave of U.S. settlers would lead to the annexation of Cuba.[65]

Both wittingly and unwittingly, advocates of whitening came to focus on settling Cuba and Hawai'i with privileged whites who could farm or otherwise labor *with* money rather than *for* money. Not only was this at odds with the logic of settler colonialism that made western expansion a success for the United States and so many of its citizens, but it raised even higher all manner of barriers to white settlement in the tropics. The failure to attract enough of the "right kind" of whites to Cuba and Hawai'i gave elites a rationale for aborting efforts to install a white yeomanry in the tropics and an incentive for building white-only enclaves of power and pleasure and pursuing the kinds of decadent and aristocratic delights they associated with European colonizers and colonies. As they succumbed to these desires, privileged U.S. whites resurrected a variation of a moribund republican dream held by some of the nation's founders. They asserted that "leisured gentlemen" freed from the need of earning a living should assume responsibility for governance and political oversight, in this instance, of the U.S. overseas empire.[66] Without admitting as much, multinational agents of U.S. empire adopted the predominant Western belief that the tropics were places where whites ruled and recreated, not where they toiled and procreated.

Plantation and Pleasure Regimes

Efforts to extend U.S. republican-settler colonialism overseas came to an end in the second decade of the twentieth century. After the second military occupation of Cuba, the United States and its Cuban allies abandoned the promotion of white U.S. settlement and annexation, and Cuban government officials assumed greater responsibility for protecting and advancing U.S. interests. In 1909 in Hawai'i, the formal consolidation of the largest sugar agencies into the Big Five occurred when its members acquired the lone outside sugar and shipping interest. This purchase coincided with the great strike of Japanese workers. These events ushered in a new era of planter paternalism and haole solidarity. New tourism regimes began to take shape as the Big Five firm of Castle & Cooke invested in ships and hotels, and wealthy U.S. residents took the lead in founding the Havana Country Club. These actors placed private pleasure, not public virtue, at the center of new and exclusive tourism industries catering to the rich and powerful.

With the restoration of the Cuban Republic, the U.S. state and capital withdrew their support for annexation and embraced dollar diplomacy as official policy in the Caribbean and Latin America. In reinterpreting the Platt Amendment through the lens of dollar diplomacy, the United States came to favor political intervention and supervision over military intervention and occupation, in Cuba if not the Dominican Republic, Haiti, and elsewhere. The United States made economic dislocation a justification for intervention, and the ability of Cubans to advance U.S. capital interests a measure of their success and the nation's stability. With U.S. capital having achieved primacy in the Cuban economy, the Cuban state became Cubans' primary vehicle for accumulating wealth and capital and producing and reproducing the better classes. Bribery, graft, and the like became an institutional fixture of Cuban government. Paradoxically, at the same time, the new Plattist regime gave the better classes, who failed to win Cubans over to annexation, opportunities to restore a masculine honor compromised in the process. They redeemed their manhood through demonstrations of the managerial competence and financial expertise that dollar diplomats demanded.[67]

The new Plattist regime promised to offer the stability, protection, and commitment of Cubans to U.S. interests without the need or expense of annexation, a promise on which the Cuban government delivered in defeating a political challenge to the status quo. In 1912 it repressed and massacred participants in a revolt led by the recently outlawed Partido Independiente de Color (PIC). The government's brutal repression of the PIC demonstrated the ability of Cuban officials to guarantee political stability and racial order while protecting U.S. investments. Indeed after repressing the revolt, the government acquiesced to the demands of capital in ending its ban on black immigrant labor from the Caribbean.[68] Journalists, travel writers, and tourism promoters followed suit in abandoning the annexationist cause. But not until 1917, when crop disease, a hurricane, an armed revolt, and a draft instituted to raise the troops needed to fight the world war took place, did the mass exodus of U.S. settlers from Cuba occur.

By the time the Cuban government outlawed the PIC in 1910, many elected officials and media had reversed their opposition to the introduction of U.S.-style segregation in hotels, restaurants, and bars on the grounds that Afro-Cubans' "intrusions" into such spaces fomented "the animosity of Americans" and threatened tourist revenues. The year of the massacre, *The Cuba Magazine* also identified ordinary white U.S. citizens as impediments to dreams of making Havana a grand resort and praised the state's response to them. Not long ago, it argued, "The 'Pan-Handler' type of tramp used to wend his way" to Cuba. But with such people recently "ousted by a vigilant police force[,] now the well-to-do seeker of health and pleasure has taken possession of Havana." Promoters embraced the opportunity to focus on building luxury resorts for privileged visitors, residents, and citizens that catered to U.S. desires for more Jim Crow in Cuba. Well-to-do pleasure seekers soon had an exclusive enclave in a western suburb of Havana.[69]

The Havana Country Club (HCC) and adjacent Country Club Park transformed Marianao into the center of a new high society for wealthy businessmen, diplomats, politicians, and tourists. These institutions came to serve as a pivot upon which the new Plattist regime revolved. In 1911 the American Club had financed a search for property suitable for a golf course and country club. Its agents purchased a former tobacco estate in Marianao near the ocean and Camp Columbia, former headquarters of the U.S. military government. In 1912, the HCC opened its $150,000 club house and golf course and invited members of exclusive U.S. clubs to be their guests. Wealthy tourists flocked to the HCC, which earned glowing reviews in U.S. golfing magazines. The country club initially attracted few Cubans, who were unfamiliar with the game of golf. Two years after its founding, the HCC invited select Cubans to buy shares in the Country Club Park Investment Company to build a residential park for elite white Cubans, Spaniards, and Anglo-Saxons from America, Britain, and Canada (the ABC community).[70]

With the HCC, foreigners brought a favorite diversion and visiting friends and financiers to Cuba. Their vision of Country Club Park represented a far more ambitious plan. Its directors worked not only to build a profitable and exclusive suburban enclave but to create a "new society" and forge a "new kind of relationship" among wealthy and powerful Anglo-Saxons, Cubans, and Spaniards. The list of the firm's directors and shareholders read like the roster of the transnational power elite it was: the president of the Spanish Havana Yacht Club, the most politically connected Cuban lawyers and property owners, and the ABC and Cuban officers and managers of foreign-owned banks, railroads, sugar *centrales*, and engineering and contracting firms. Between 1914 and 1916, the Country Club Park Investment Company approved the sale of eighty lots to the "most prominent Americans and Cubans." Among them were members of the Liberal Party, which came to power in 1909. The U.S. ambassador acquired a residence in the park. Soon the HCC had a long waiting list. It and Country Club Park made Marianao a center of business, cultural, political, and social life for rich Cubans, Spaniards, and the ABC community. As they married, worked, and played together, the multinational members of this colony came to regard Cuba as "our country," as the HCC's second president later put it.[71]

Members of the ABC colony took the lead to secure the support of the Cuban state and U.S. and Cuban capital for expanding tourism and making country clubs, casinos, and a horse-racing track conduits through which U.S. visitors and capital would flow into Cuba. HCC members and Country Club Park residents proved pivotal in struggles to legalize gambling against the continued opposition of a bloc of U.S. occupiers and diplomats and

3. The Havana Country Club. This photograph was probably taken not long after the club opened in 1912, an event that marked the triumph of an empire and its pleasures for privileged whites. The American Photo Co., Havana. Courtesy of the Manuel R. Bustamante Photograph Collection, Cuban Heritage Collection, University of Miami Libraries, Coral Gables, Florida.

La Gloria, Cuba, 1914.

4. Central Avenue in the American colony of La Gloria in Camagüey, Cuba. Taken in 1914, this photographic postcard depicted a homesteading community on the tropical frontier only a few years before the demise of such communities. Courtesy of the Augustus Mayhew Photograph Collection, University of Miami Libraries, Coral Gables, Florida.

Cuban politicians who had prohibited games of chance on the grounds that gambling promoted decadence and vice and were incompatible with republican government. In 1904 Estrada Palma had vetoed a lottery bill, citing "the dictates of reason, the precepts of morality," and "the Revolutionary Program of the fathers of the present country, and of all who raised the flag of independence, as the only means of securing that political, social, and moral regeneration so much desired in the Cuban people." Backers of gambling legislation achieved their first victory on betting on horse races, paving the way for the opening of Oriental Park in Marianao in 1915.[72]

Similarly in Hawai'i, as efforts to transform it into a white republic finally collapsed with the consolidation of the Big Five and the strike by Japanese workers, haole united to build a residential resort enclave for white residents and tourists, as well as select Hawaiians, at Waikīkī. The sugar agencies collectively known as the Big Five officially earned this name in 1909 when C. W. Brewer took over the lone sugar and shipping outsider. By then, the Big Five had consolidated control over most of the sugar industry through an ever-tightening network of interlocking directorates, cooperative corporate governance, stock control, and intermarriage. The Big Five and the HSPA produced virtually all of the sugar in Hawai'i, financed its plantations, and refined planters' cane, handled their accounting, insured them, recruited their workers, sponsored research and development, and lobbied on their behalf in Washington. In 1907, Castle & Cooke became the agent for and major shareholder in Matson Navigation Lines, giving it monopoly control of U.S.-Hawai'i shipping. Generating more capital than sugar could absorb, the Big Five diversified. Castle & Cooke, the only Big Five firm on the HPC's original board, invested in tourism. By the time World War I began, it had financed and built four passenger-freighters.[73]

    With a newfound commitment to keeping ship cabins full, tourism promoters began to look anew at a hula that tourists knew through vaudeville, Tin Pan Alley, and Hollywood films and always demanded to see in Hawai'i.[74] Like the annexationist tourism promoters before it, the HPC prohibited the hula as barbaric, lewd, and a threat to white republicanism and Anglo-American civilization. Before the 1904 St. Louis World's Fair, for example, the HPC reassured the haole community that its "creditable exhibit" would not include the hula: "It is one of the chief desires of this community that the so-called hula-hula . . . shall not disgrace these Islands" and "discredit" the Hawaiian exhibit. Eight years later the *Paradise of the*

Pacific insisted that "the hula must go, and the sooner it goes the better," despite a great demand for it: "The reputation of Hawaii and Hawaiians has suffered a good deal from the hula. It has caused the islands to be pictured the world over as a land of women wearing waistbands of straw and men wearing less and far worse, it constantly brings tourists here." The HPC offered some financial support to what became a hit Broadway musical, *The Bird of Paradise*. It showcased Hawaiian-themed music and a hundred Caucasian actresses sporting grass skirts and dancing a New York choreographer's interpretation of hula. *The Bird* opened to rave reviews and traveled throughout the United States and Europe. The next year, lei-bedecked and grass-skirted women serving pineapple proved a hit among visitors at the Pan-Pacific Exposition in San Francisco, cementing the territory's capitalists' commitments to the hula girl and to hula.[75]

The same year that the Big Five officially acquired its name, Japanese workers staged what became known as the great strike. The Gentlemen's Agreement ended the flow of Japanese laborers but permitted travel by former residents, relatives, wives, and picture brides. Their migration reduced historic gender imbalances and fostered the Japanese's identification of themselves as settlers and Americans, not immigrants and foreigners. With the support of the urban Japanese professionals who organized the Higher Wages Association, seven thousand Japanese workers on Oʻahu struck in 1909 for higher wages, the elimination of racialized wage scales, and the overturn of the "present undemocratic, un-American condition of Hawaii." Strikers averred, "We have decided to permanently settle here, to incorporate ourselves with the body politique [*sic*] of Hawaii." They demanded the rights and wages needed to become "a thriving and contented middle class—the realization of the high ideal of Americanism." Planters evicted striking workers, hired scabs and spies, made arrests, banned mass meetings, and finally waited the strikers out. The four-month strike ended without negotiations, much less concessions. But it transformed social relations. The solidarity across class lines exhibited by the Japanese majority inspired the same in the haole minority. Haole unity suddenly seemed crucial to minority white rule. Haole could call upon the United States to defend them from internal threats, but to do so risked the sort of unwanted military occupations the United States had imposed in Cuba and other states in the Caribbean and Central America.[76]

For labor historians, the great strike marks the beginning of planter paternalism. After it ended, the HSPA raised wages, claimed to eliminate ethnic wage differentials, and increased expenditures for workers' health, housing, recreation, and education. The Big Five also expanded economic opportunities for nonplanter whites. On the plantations, they raised salaries and perquisites for haole managers and haole and Portuguese overseers, increasing an already vast socioeconomic chasm between whites and non-whites. By 1910 managers earned as much as a thousand dollars a month, while field hands toiled for seventy-five cents a day. Elsewhere, the expansion of Big Five investments outside sugar increased haole opportunities for professional and managerial employment. Paternalism toward the Asian working class had a striking counterpart in planter relations with whites of all classes, born of the need to defend a contested white supremacy.[77]

For its part, the HPC ended efforts to lure white settlers and investors.[78] Much like the founders of the HCC and Country Club Park, the territorial government official Lucius Pinkham and the islands' richest and most powerful industrialist and developer Walter Dillingham undertook to build a white-only enclave at Waikīkī Beach. In contrast to Cuba, haole specifically did not intend for the Waikīkī resort area to serve as a conduit for the U.S. capital investment that the Big Five did not want.

In 1906 Pinkham, then head of the health board, had unveiled a plan for transforming Waikīkī into an exclusive Anglo-Saxon community. His report argued that the wetlands that supported the duck and fish ponds and rice and taro fields of Hawaiians, Chinese, and Japanese farmers were "deleterious to the public health." Although mosquitoes (accidentally imported by whites) were plentiful, mosquito-borne diseases were unknown. The "unsanitary, unhygienic, and repellant conditions" described by Pinkham were not medical but rather the "objectionable features and neighbors" that deterred investment by "persons and residents of private fortune, who seek an agreeable climate and surroundings, and who expend large already acquired incomes rather than those who expect the community to furnish them a livelihood." The aquaculture and agriculture that provided Chinese, Japanese, and Hawaiians a living offended the aesthetic sensibilities of privileged whites. These farmers prevented Waikīkī from "fulfil[ling] her destiny" to acquire "a most desirable population" and create "a thoroughbred city instead of a common town." Pinkham cast the choice starkly: make hundreds of acres "attractive and desirable" to wealthy whites or leave them to "a class of population that limited means force onto undesirable and unsanitary land." In 1918, Pinkham (by then governor),

Dillingham, and their allies convinced the legislature to finance a canal to drain Waikīkī and keep it dry.[79]

By the time World War I ended, tourism promoters in Cuba and Hawai'i were prepared to capitalize on a postwar international travel boom driven by U.S. citizens, whose economy prospered as a result of wartime mobilization. The enactment of Prohibition in 1919 provided U.S. tourists an additional incentive to travel abroad. While Prohibition technically extended to the U.S. territory of Hawai'i, it had no legal standing in Cuba. In the summer of 1919 only a handful of states had ratified the Eighteenth Amendment when the *New York Times* announced: "A land that has never known a blue law, Cuba, and its capital, Havana, are preparing with haste to gather to their opulent bosoms this Winter, and all the Winters following, the horde of moneyed Americans who object to being hobbled in the pursuit of pleasure." It predicted that "vast quantities of wines and liquors from Europe" would soon fill the cellars of Havana hotels and casinos financed by New Yorkers and *habaneros* eager to invest in the future "Monaco of America—a playground at the doorstep of a puritanical nation, in which there will be no monitions but 'Be sure you have the price.'"[80]

From the time the *New York Times* announced that "moral bars" in Cuba, "never so high they could not be easily hurdled, have been further lowered," travel writers vied with each other to establish drinking, gambling, and prostitution as normative Cuban habits that legitimized tourists' indulgence in them. "When in Rome applies to the tropics," quipped A. Hyatt Verrill, as he pronounced siesta "the secret of the Spanish-American's fondness for night-life." This attitude condoned all manner of vice in a land "untouched by Puritanism or restrictions of personal liberty." No travelogue written during Prohibition failed to point out that Havana had over seven thousand bars, although some cautioned, "Don't try to drink all the [booze] in Cuba the first day." Charles Chapman asserted that gambling and its "running-mate," prostitution, were "habits which reach into every nook and cranny of the nation."[81] If Cuban wives did not concern themselves with their husband's nights out, neither should the wives of U.S. tourists. The *Times of Cuba* suggested, "Don't question hubby too closely when he stumbles back to the hotel at 5 A.M. It wouldn't do you any good to confirm your suspicions." Even better, it told men, come alone, for "packing a wife to Cuba is like bringing a biscuit to a banquet." Many viewed such panegyrics on 'pleasure' as proof that Havana was "the smart-est city in the world."[82]

In bidding "Adios" to Cuba in 1920, travel writer G. M. Morrill con-demned Havana, where, he thought, "pleasure is a rite, idleness a duty, and depravity an accomplishment."[83] At the time, he was virtually alone in associating these traits not only with commercial vice but with a political crisis and economic depression then descending on Cuba. As Morrill's ship steamed out of Havana Harbor, political crises erupted in both Cuba and Hawai'i. In response to them, their promoters stepped up plans to reconsti-tute their political regimes and harness them to their pleasure regimes in new ways. Visions of transforming Cuba and Hawai'i into resorts like those of the Riviera, catering to an aristocratic, cosmopolitan class of wealthy westerners, came to the forefront of imperial dreams as those of making white republics of these tropical islands died.

Even as the United States abandoned ambitions of an overseas empire comprising many united and happy white republics governed by and for free whites, it remained officially committed to spreading its allegedly spe-cial freedoms and more perfect forms of nationhood to less fortunate peo-ples. Even as U.S. citizens visiting or living in Cuba and Hawai'i came to see themselves as modern-day aristocrats enjoying the pleasures of imperi-alism they associated with the ostensibly corrupt, oppressive monarchical nations and empires of Europe, privileged white U.S. citizens maintained their belief that the United States was an exceptional nation, empire, and people unlike their European counterparts. A key difference, they argued, was the U.S. devotion to remaking benighted peoples everywhere on U.S. lines and preparing them for liberty, freedom, and republican self-government. That this required dismissing as disingenuous other empires' civilizing missions or France's claim that it too was a republican empire dedicated to liberty, equality, and fraternity made them doubt the sincerity of their intentions and actions not a bit.[84]

CHAPTER THREE

Royal Resorts for Tropical Tramps

Havana today is the Sleeping Princess waked by the Kiss of her lover
Freedom.

Havana, the Magazine of Cuba, 1929

The "Merry Monarch" loved his beautiful kingdom and was desirous
that all the world should love it too.

Paradise of the Pacific, 1927

Haole travel writers fashioned King David Kalākaua (r. 1874–1891) into
the founder of Hawaiian tourism in time for the grand opening of the
second Royal Hawaiian Hotel. The *Paradise of the Pacific* proclaimed that it
was the "Merry Monarch" who "first thought to acquaint globe trotters"
with Hawai'i, bestowing "his royal blessing" and "a little something" from
the "monarchical treasury" on this journal and the first Royal Hawaiian
Hotel. The king and his minister of the interior, Lorrin A. Thurston, built
an industry that Queen Lili'uokalani and Sanford Dole later gave their
"royal" and "ardent" support. Charting an unbroken course of state support for tourism from the kingdom's last two monarchs to the republic's
only president and the territory's first governor, *Paradise* proclaimed that
tourism had "a king for a father."[1]

  If Hawaiian tourism boasted a king and queen, Cuban tourism claimed
a prince and princess. In *Havana, the Magazine of Cuba*, Karl Decker
described that city's "leaping progress" toward "health, progress, and above
all beauty" as the second "waking of the Sleeping Princess." Decker's kiss
awoke her the first time, that is, in 1897 when William Randolph Hearst
dispatched him to Havana to secure the freedom of Evangelina Cosio y

Cisneros, a young woman from a leading creole family imprisoned by the Spanish for aiding the cause of Cuban independence. When the "fairy princess" arrived safely in New York, Hearst's *Journal* asked, "We have freed one Cuban girl—when shall we free Cuba?" Three decades later, Decker named Carlos Miguel de Céspedes, a descendent of a revolutionary hero and the public works secretary of President Gerardo Machado y Morales, as his successor. Decker credited the new prince with bringing the fairy tale to a happy end by converting a "tourists' Hell" into a "tourists' Paradise."[2]

During the interwar years, the travel writers and tourism professionals of Cuba and Hawai'i joined others around the Caribbean and the Pacific in constructing a host of royal resorts loosely modeled on those of the European Riviera.[3] Promoters sold their destinations as ideal combinations of the aristocratic and the democratic, the feudal and the modern, the foreign and the familiar. Developers erected resorts fit for kings and queens, while writers merged history and fantasy to cast tourists as aristocrats whose status gave them license to indulge in decadent pleasures created just for them. Tourists attracted to the smartest resorts included rich industrialists, famous politicians, glamorous celebrities, and, of course, titled aristocrats.[4]

Promoters offered U.S. white elites a temptation that often proved irresistible: entrée into credible, if not accredited, American aristocracies. Hawai'i boasted the only palace in the United States, once home to actual kings and queens. Regarded by U.S. tourists as the leading New World home of Spanish counts and countesses, as well as "New York's Gayest Suburb," Havana claimed the seat of a truly pan-American royalty. In this way, Cuba and Hawai'i catered to rich whites who sought to belong to an international class of cosmopolitan pleasure seekers and wanted the deference they felt due those of their station. At a time of intense and often violent domestic struggles in the United States by blacks, immigrants, women, and workers for democratic rights and decent wages, the resorts in Cuba and Hawai'i offered wealthy tourists from the United States venues through which to act out their fantasies of royalty and empire. And herein lay the irony: even as official agents of U.S. expansion sought to effect the "political and cultural seduction of local elites" in the name of democracy, a similar seduction worked in the opposite direction.[5] Tourists who sought out the pleasures of imperialism in Cuba and Hawai'i supported— unwittingly or not—the repressive regimes whose officials and allies built the resorts to fulfill their own desires, as well as those of their guests.[6]

Political Turmoil and the Turn to Tourism

Tourism promoters in Hawai'i and Cuba harnessed aristocratic rhetoric to the restoration of white rule after 1920, when their ruling classes came under attack by those they governed and by the U.S. government. In Cuba, the political class created during the first U.S. military occupation came under assault as a result of a disputed election and an economic crisis; in Hawai'i, Native legislators and Japanese and Filipino workers respectively challenged haole control of cheap land and cheap labor. In Cuba, U.S. State Department officials responded with a diplomatic intervention. They sent General Enoch Crowder to Havana and charged him with bringing stability and honesty to government. Meanwhile, Cubans seized the opportunity to demand the pursuit of national economic independence and the abrogation of the Platt Amendment that limited the nation's political sovereignty. Both demands posed potential threats to U.S. interests. In Hawai'i, U.S. officials responded with sympathy to Hawaiian demands for land rights, and to the news of a strike by workers, by threatening political intervention. Haole publicly rallied to demonstrate that they could govern the territory without additional interference and oversight from Washington; privately, they worked to deny the demands of Asian immigrants for fair wages and working conditions and of Native Hawaiians for their ancestral lands. Both threatened haole authority and power. In the face of these upheavals, white elites in both places turned to travel and tourism to contain threats to their governance from below and above, from within and without.

White elites harnessed tourism promotion to planter paternalism in Hawai'i and business nationalism in Cuba.[7] The victorious candidate in Cuba's 1924 presidential election, Gerardo Machado, pledged to usher in an era of sovereignty and capitalist development through U.S.-Cuban partnerships designed to reconcile and advance U.S. and Cuban interests. He identified tourism as a promising sector for U.S.-Cuban partnerships designed to diversify the economy and satisfy nationalist demands to expand Cuban ownership of and participation in the economy. In Hawai'i, Castle & Cooke and Matson Navigation Lines, Walter F. Dillingham, and the Hawaii Tourist Bureau worked to develop the tourism industry and use it to cast haole governance as benevolent and progressive. In both cases, promoters came to develop and apply narratives of aristocratic pleasures to those of oligarchic political regimes to explain the need for slow, cautious programs of democratization from above of masses deemed immature and unruly.

Even before Machado pledged to reconcile the interests of Cuban nationalism with those of U.S. and Cuban capital, many Cuban and U.S. elites had identified tourism as a growth industry. Leading businessmen and government officials saw an investment opportunity in the continuation of Prohibition at the federal level and bans on horse-race betting by many individual states. In the summer of 1919 the head of the Biltmore hotel empire, John McEntee Bowman, traveled to Havana, where he met his new partner and first manager of Oriental Park racetrack, Charles Flynn, bought the future Sevilla-Biltmore Hotel, and renovated it in time for a Champagne-drenched opening that New Year's Eve. To make Cuban horses competitive enough to attract wealthier U.S. bettors and more prominent stables, Bowman loaned the republic Top Hat, a studhorse sired by the famous racehorse Hastings and grandsired by the legendary Man O'War.[8]

Plans to extend high-stakes betting from horse racing to the roulette and baccarat tables associated with the celebrated resorts of the Riviera proceeded apace. After a nine-year struggle, Carlos Miguel de Céspedes and his business partners, the congressmen José Manuel Cortina and Carlos Manuel de la Cruz, convinced Congress to pass a tourism development bill. It gave a company owned by Céspedes, Cortina, and de la Cruz the exclusive right to operate a casino in Marianao, financed a bridge to connect the hotels of downtown Havana to the environs of the proposed casino and seaside pavilion, and established the Cuban Tourist Commission. The bill offered a textbook case of corruption. Of several casino syndicates, only the one whose owners included congressmen benefited from a bill funding public works that increased the value of their private investments. The president's and senate president's families received lucrative gambling concessions in thanks for their support of the bill. The Gran Casino Nacional and bathing facilities at La Playa de Marianao opened just as two crises struck.[9]

The "Dance of the Millions," a brief period of prosperity occasioned by high sugar prices during World War I, ended abruptly in 1920, when the price of sugar plummeted from twenty-two cents to three cents a pound between May and December. Depression descended on Cuba. Sugar-mill owners could not pay their debts. The government declared a moratorium on loan payments. Foreign, especially U.S., investors acquired insolvent banks, mills, and other enterprises at bargain prices. But as depression deepened, tourism continued to grow, prompting observers to argue that this "crop" offered the best hope for diversifying a moribund monocrop economy.[10]

Economic collapse coincided with a contested presidential election in which both sides claimed victory. The State Department charged Crowder with restoring stability and honesty to a politically, as well as economically, bankrupt government. He got the government on sounder fiscal footing and secured a brief period of honest administration from President Alfredo Zayas in return for Washington's approval of a loan to liquidate debt. After that, Zayas's administration took graft to a level beyond that of all his predecessors. Cubans called for his impeachment. Crowder wanted to threaten military intervention, but the State Department refused to let him. It deemed honest government less important than a stable one that would protect U.S. interests. But Cubans wanted honest as well as stable government, and even more, they wanted government officials more responsive to Cuban than to U.S. interests. Determined to achieve unqualified sovereignty, Cubans made demands for abrogating the Platt Amendment and developing the economy "by and for Cubans" central to the elections of 1924.[11]

In his presidential campaign, Machado addressed a political constituency long neglected in Cuba: its citizens. His "Platform for Regeneration" promised to abrogate the Platt Amendment and lead Cuba into capitalist modernity and liberal democracy. He denounced corruption and pledged to incur no more foreign debt. He averred that public works for "Roads, Schools, and Water" would benefit all. Public works, protective tariffs, and government support of agriculture and industry would generate employment, diversify the economy, and increase Cuban stakes in it.[12]

As Cubans represented only one of Machado's two main constituencies, he took pains to address U.S. business and government concerns. On a postelection visit to Washington, Machado identified the increase of commercial relations between Cuba and the United States as "one of the principal objects of his administration." The State Department replied that with honest administration in Cuba's historically graft-ridden Public Works and Justice Departments, "capital would roll in to any amount needed." Crowder, who became U.S. ambassador to Cuba in 1923, concurred with the State Department that eliminating corruption in public works and providing U.S. firms with more favorable treatment in courts would lead to an influx of U.S. capital. So it was that Washington's definition of honesty came into alignment with its definition of stability while ceding something to Cuban nationalism: the United States henceforth assessed Cuban government by how well it served U.S. capital and improved the material well-being of Cuba and Cubans.[13]

In New York, Machado told businessmen how he would advance the interests of U.S. capital while satisfying nationalist demands by making Cuba and Cubans more prosperous and sovereign. His voice carried weight. He had made a fortune with U.S. businessmen, most notably as vice president of the Electric Bond and Share Company headed by Henry Catlin. At a dinner of the Merchants' Association of New York organized by Catlin and Bowman, Machado said, "One of your class . . . will shortly occupy the presidency of your sister Republic." As president, "I will always be ready to help and to promote . . . our common interests." He offered "full guarantees to all business" concerns: "there is no reason to fear [disorder] because I have sufficient material force to stamp it out." He would make good on this promise.[14]

Many agreed with Machado that tourism represented the most promising opportunity for developing "Cuba for the Cubans with the cooperation and aid of American business." Machado's appointment of Céspedes, an owner of the Gran Casino and La Playa, as his secretary of public works bespoke his commitment to tourism. His administration gained privileged access to the New York financial community when Catlin secured Machado's son-in-law, José E. Obregón, a position at Chase's Havana branch. Machado's plan to build a central highway across the island promised to open the interior of the island to tourism. It would enable Cubans to make, transport, and sell food and goods for Cuban consumption, lessening dependence on their expensive imported counterparts and foreign-owned railroads. Projects to modernize and beautify Havana and build schools, aqueducts, and streets promised jobs for Cuban workers, businessmen, and contractors, and investment opportunities for Cuban and U.S. capital. Through tourism and public works, U.S. and Cuban investors and the government would modernize Cuba to the benefit of all.[15]

While Cuba's promoters placed their faith for expanded tourism in gambling, a pastime and industry recently denounced as inimical to the young republic's virtue, tourism promoters in Hawai'i did likewise with the hula many haole had despised on the grounds that it was barbaric. Renamed and reorganized in 1919, the Hawaii Tourist Bureau (HTB) presented hula as essential to a new strategy of selling Hawai'i as "a name that immediately suggests romance." Interwar-era boosters soon became as determined to showcase hula as previous promoters had been to suppress it. Yet white settler concerns about its place in the moral and political economy in a civilized U.S. territory lingered. In the *Paradise of the Pacific*, a writer voiced dismay over the lack of support for hula promotion: "Are we doing anything to train hula dancers and keep alive the traditions of the most romantic of all Hawaiian customs?" The reply, "We are not; We are striving tooth and nail to kill anything remotely suggestive of the hulas of ancient Hawaii." Thurston continued his antihula campaign in the *Advertiser*, but letters to the editor suggested that the cultural climate had changed. In 1922 the eminent Hawaiian Flora Allen Hayes compared the hula to other popular dances: "Why pick on Hawaiians and the Hawaiian hula in particular? Is any of the Hawaiian hulas more indecent, vicious, degrading, immoral . . . than the cheek to cheek, bosom to bosom, thigh to thigh dances which we witness in the ballroom, roof garden, or steamer dances?" Whereas the haole advocate of supposedly ancient hulas represented Hawaiian culture as not just old but dying and, along with the Hawaiian people, on the path to extinction, the Native Hayes presented hula, and by extension Hawaiians and their culture, as active participants in a contested present and future. As she wrote, debates about hula and tourism were becoming tied to broader struggles over governance and rights.[16]

Hawaiians reasserted claims to their indigenous lands, especially the 1.75 million acres of Crown lands the annexationist government had seized in 1894 and ceded to the United States after annexation. Although these acts were presented by haole as consensual, most Hawaiians regarded both land seizure and title transfer as illegal. In 1920, as many planter leases on Crown lands were set to expire, Hawaiian legislators introduced to the U.S. Congress the first of several bills designed to return Hawaiians to their indigenous lands. Haole rushed to defend planter leaseholds. First, they convinced enough U.S. congressmen that the Hawaiian people had neither right nor title to former Crown lands but agreed that some Natives deserved the opportunity for "rehabilitation" as leaseholders on part of these lands. Then haole moved to limit the number of Hawaiians eligible for said rehabilitation. For their part, the congressmen proposed defining Hawaiians either as the subjects and descendents of King Kamehameha III or by a blood-quantum criterion of one-thirty-second. Haole protested that such an inclusive definition threatened the "white race [and its access to] valuable public lands." Haole prevailed. The 1920 Hawaiian Homes Commission Act defined Hawaiians by a blood-quantum criterion of 50 percent. So it came to be that an act proposed to restore land to Hawaiians became a law that protected the leases of planters. Haole restricted entitlements available in theory to those they deemed the deserving natives of a dying race but denied them to overly mixed Hawaiians whom haole cast either as diluted white Americans or degenerated Asians. According to this legal logic, Hawaiians would disappear in the not-so-distant future. Contests over land rights exhibited a parallel logic to debates over hula: whereas haole cast themselves as guardians of the last vestiges of a dying culture and people, Hawaiians presented themselves as vanguards of the future in laying claims to recognition and rights as the indigenous people of Hawai'i.[17]

As Hawaiians contested haole control of cheap land, Asian immigrant workers threatened their access to cheap labor. In 1920, eighty-three hundred Japanese and Filipino workers in O'ahu, almost 80 percent of its plantation workforce, sought to transcend divides of race and nationality when together they struck for 165 days for better wages and conditions and an end to racialized pay scales. Haole refused to recognize the strikers' interracial and cross-national solidarity. They insisted that the Filipinos were but stooges of the Japanese. The haole press thus cast the strike as a plot by Japan to take over the sugar industry, and then the territory of Hawai'i. The *Advertiser* editorialized, "Is Hawaii to be ruled from Tokio?" The *Star-Bulletin* concurred: "Is Hawaii to remain American or become Japanese?"[18]

Planters pooled resources in order to wait the strikers out. Afterward, haole responded with a mixture of repression and paternalism. The Hawaiian Sugar Planters' Association raised wages and expanded worker perquisites and welfare. The territorial government enacted antilabor and antiorganization laws. Planters and the U.S. military allied to address the "Japanese problem" and spy on alleged activists, radicals, and labor leaders. Haole lobbied to increase the number of U.S. military personnel in Hawai'i. Before the strike, forty-four hundred U.S. military personnel were stationed or homeported there. A few years later, their number nearly quadrupled to seventeen thousand, almost doubling the population of "Other Caucasians," that is, haole, or whites excluding Portuguese or Spanish, on O'ahu, where most haole resided.[19]

Despite these successes, haole miscalculated how others might react to their linking of the 1920 strike and Japanese imperial ambitions. This representational strategy, coupled with haole demands for a larger military presence, prompted metropolitan officials to question the scale and scope of white dominion in Hawai'i. The strike demonstrated to the local head of

U.S. military intelligence the wisdom of placing the territory under a commission form of government, that is, military rule. Although this did not happen at the time, the military did capitalize on the strike to extend its actual powers of surveillance and oversight and potential powers to take control. Likely as distressing to haole, the acting governor asserted that he would ask for a U.S. military takeover if the Japanese again threatened white rule. The federal government's and territorial governor's readiness to consider military rule alarmed leading haole, whose wealth depended on their control of local politics. These reactions compounded haole anxieties about the future, when the children of Asian immigrants born on U.S. soil as U.S. citizens would become the electoral majority of Hawai'i. In responding to the internal specter of Asian-American electoral power and the external specter of direct rule, haole turned to immigration to change the racial demography of the workforce and to tourism to demonstrate their authority and power at home and abroad.[20]

In 1922 the governor told the U.S. president that the territory's "racial elements are out of balance" and "seriously in need of adjustment." Haole sought to balance the races by reducing the number of Japanese and increasing the number of Chinese and Filipinos. In 1920, the Japanese comprised 43 percent of the 256,000 people of Hawai'i. No other racially or nationally defined group exceeded 10 percent. "Other Caucasians" constituted less than 8 percent. The HSPA, Dillingham, and the territorial government asked Congress to amend the Chinese Exclusion Act of 1882. Reintroducing the Chinese, they argued, would drive many Japanese back to Japan. Congress refused. Planters recruited more Filipinos, but they failed in their quest to dramatically alter the racial balance of the plantation workforce.[21]

Recruiting immigrants to divide the workforce was part of a strategy to shore up haole governance in the islands; attracting tourists represented part of a strategy for securing a corps of wealthy whites to whom to showcase haole power on the mainland. The Waikīkī Beach reclamation project opened fourteen hundred acres for development, a broad swath of it for an exclusive recreational and residential enclave. The three-mile Ala Wai Canal built to drain Waikīkī and keep it dry reached completion in 1924. Building it destroyed Hawaiian fish ponds, temples, and dwellings, archaeological remains of which date to 1100 c.e., and erased from memory the centuries when Waikīkī was shared by ordinary and chiefly Hawaiians, long before ali'i became royals.[22]

   Land prices and property values promptly skyrocketed, which led to the sale and razing of nearby farms and homes. Although the estates and trusts of Princess Bernice Pauahi Bishop and Queen Emma retained ownership of most of Waikīkī, their haole trustees controlled decisions about the use of these properties. Rising values enhanced their ability to enforce "informal covenants" that restricted leases and development rights to privileged whites and upper-crust Hawaiians.[23] Physical transformation aided the construction of narratives that presented white settlers and tourists and select Hawaiians as rightful heirs to a royal playground.

Making Fairy Tales Come True

After 1920, the production of narratives of Waikīkī as a place reserved for royalty, once Hawaiian, now Anglo-Saxon, proceeded in tandem with the construction of the Royal Hawaiian Hotel. In design, decor, and staffing, the Royal's owners, managers, and promoters worked to present the white supremacist ruling oligarchy in Hawai'i as an enlightened and benevolent modern feudal order devoted to preparing the nonwhite majority for eventual democracy. In Cuba, by contrast, Bowman and Céspedes needed to install a viable aristocratic society in Havana to attract the capital needed to transform it into a competitive resort and show that tourism would generate returns for all involved in its expansion. They succeeded by staging a successful winter tourist season in 1925–1926 that convinced investors to finance Machado's project of business nationalism. Despite protestations to the contrary, private and public investments in tourism primarily benefited a privileged white minority.

   Upon assuming the presidency in May 1925, Machado presented a public works law to Congress. That July it passed a bill identifying the Central Highway, a national capitol, and the beautification of Havana as its three priorities. To finance them, Congress enacted special sales taxes that accrued in an account outside the regular budget. Although tax revenues could not possibly pay for these projects, they could easily service loans on them, especially in the absence of graft. Although Machado had pledged not to increase Cuba's indebtedness, rumors swirled around the country-club circuit that his administration sought $100 million from U.S. banks. Loans depended on creative financing and a favorable interpretation of the Platt Amendment's Article 2. It forbade the Cuban government from expending more revenues than taxes generated, but it did not specifically prohibit it from contracting for work in excess of revenues. Debate over whether or not certificates of indebtedness constituted debt intensified when the price of sugar declined again, making Machado and his allies eager to alleviate unemployment.[24]

As bankers and diplomats debated financing that would satisfy Article 2, Céspedes and Bowman labored to attract investors. Céspedes began cultivating his reputation as the Tropical Haussmann when he brought city planners from France to design a master plan to make Havana worthy of its reputation as the Paris of the Caribbean. A Bowman syndicate leased the Gran Casino and Oriental Park racetrack. Bowman transformed the private Jockey Club into a sumptuous space, while Céspedes oversaw construction of La Quinta Avenida (Fifth Avenue), a palm-lined boulevard connecting Havana to Oriental Park, the Casino, Havana Country Club, and the Havana Yacht Club. Both were finished before the first race meet that officially opened the season.[25]

Bowman urged members of the northeastern equestrian and country-club set to visit Havana and there openly enjoy the gambling and drinking that were outlawed, albeit widely indulged in, at Saratoga, Belmont, and other U.S. tracks. More than a renowned hotelier, Bowman had built the Biltmore Westchester Country Club; he belonged to the U.S. Turf and Field, Greenwich Country, Indian Harbor Yacht, and Great Neck Golf clubs and had served as president of the National Horse Show and United Hunts Racing associations. Basil Woon, a writer on smart resorts like Deauville and Monte Carlo, characterized Bowman's rise as a sportsman as "more spectacular than his skyrocketing career as a hotel financier." Bowman intended to broker his cultural capital into financial capital.[26]

Efforts to entice New York financiers to visit Cuba came to fruition on opening day of the 1925–1926 racing season. Machado, a breeder whose horses carried the colors of the National Stables of Cuba, presided over the races from a presidential box at the Jockey Club that overlooked the one reserved for the U.S. ambassador and other embassy officials. The next day, three hundred members of the Bankers Investment Association had time to read the *Havana Post*'s effusive praise of the Jockey Club before joining Machado and other prominent Cuban and U.S. citizens at a luncheon there. Afterward, the bankers golfed and sailed and then gambled and danced at the casino. Media coverage of the meeting of the holy trinity of Machado's Cuba—the Cuban cabinet, Washington diplomats, and New

York financiers—broadcast confidence to invest in a resort that promised handsome returns in profit and pleasure.[27]

For years afterward, social and financial commentators heralded the 1925–1926 racing season as the success that opened a new era in a New World high society that compared favorably to that of the Old World. Open to new and old wealth alike, this society was at once "democratic in management" and "quite exclusive." Indeed, "every clubman in Cuba, or members of his family, was present" that day. "His Excellency" Machado, "Cuban Czar" Céspedes, and "Prince of Hotel Fame" Bowman hosted Manhattan "barons of finance," Cuban and European aristocrats, and "Havana's 'Four Hundred.'" The *Cuba Review* appropriated the name "Four Hundred" from the New York society named in 1892 by Mrs. Ward McAllister and dominated by her and Mrs. William Astor. One Cuban, Carlos María de Heredia, made the original list of the Four Hundred. William K. and Vincent Astor and their wives often visited Havana, and Heredia often visited New York, lending credence to the use of the name in Cuba.[28]

Those who had long snubbed Oriental Park suddenly rushed to join the Jockey Club. Industrialist Charles R. Fleishman sent horses from his New York stable. Mrs. Harry Payne Whitney, wife of the industrialist and horse breeder, and her son Cornelius Vanderbilt Whitney, a director of Pan American Airlines (which Machado secretly granted exclusive landing rights), came as spectators. Their peers joined them. Cuban membership in the Jockey Club rose apace. Its splendor and Machado's patronage provided "the dignity, the polish, and the pageantry" required to attract "the best families of Havana."[29]

More than a name and a few transnational connections, the Four Hundred in Havana shared other core characteristics with its predecessor in New York. Both welcomed new wealth and other arrivistes. Neither evinced much interest in intellectual pursuits and civic leadership; tellingly, rich Cubans and North Americans regarded the Jockey Club and the Casino as their "civic institutions." The status of the original and reconstituted Four Hundred relied on publicity, conspicuous consumption, and display, such as the acquisition of European art, titles, and crowns through marriage or purchase. They were not a ruling aristocracy but a social aristocracy or smart set. Havana offered a self-conscious alternative to the royal resorts of the Old World where the New World's old and new rich alike sometimes felt uncomfortable, outclassed, or simply not at home. In Havana U.S.

financial barons and baronesses and Cubans titled and otherwise created an enclave where the wealthy and titled met as equals at the headquarters of an American aristocracy at once selectively inclusive and delightfully exclusive. The use of the term "Havana's Four Hundred" represented a coup for Bowman and Céspedes. The winter season's success convinced sufficient principals to invest in their tourism schemes and provided businessmen and government officials the time to negotiate financing that satisfied Article 2.[30]

In January the following season (1926–1927), Bowman and Machado invited the Jazz Age mayor of New York City, James Walker, to preside over the groundbreaking ceremony of the Havana Biltmore Yacht and Country Club. Once Walker arrived from Key West, the chief of police, Carlos Mendietta, escorted him to the races. The orchestra played "The Sidewalks of New York" as Walker entered the presidential box draped for the occasion with Cuban and U.S. flags. The next day, Walker received the keys to the city. Reporters and photographers from the *New York Times* and the *Havana Post* trailed Walker around the Sevilla-Biltmore, La Playa, Oriental Park, and Casino. Their coverage of the Nightclub Mayor advertised Havana as a fashionable destination where money and taste provided entry into a high society, whose members Woon labeled "foes of hypocrisy and cant and the silly snobbery of America's self-elected society, even though they are members of that society." Media coverage set the stage for the ground-breaking of the future headquarters of the Four Hundred. "Jack" Bowman, "Jimmy" Walker, and "Geraldito" Machado led a motorcade from the Presidential Palace to the Jaimanitas beach, where they turned the first shovels of dirt for the Biltmore clubhouse. They strolled grounds destined for a golf course, casino, marina, and palatial homes. Céspedes announced he would extend Fifth Avenue to the new resort. The media dubbed the directors of the future country and yacht club and residential park "the pleasure trust."[31]

The media that announced the directors of the Cuban Realty Company, the Cuban National Syndicate (which bought the Gran Casino and Oriental Park), and the Havana Biltmore Yacht and Country Club (HBYCC) celebrated Machado's business nationalism as a project that advanced U.S. interests, Cuban participation in the economy, and public works for the people. These firms' directors brought Cubans in business and government together with the U.S. bankers who financed private resorts and public works. Interlocking transnational directorates were not new in Cuba. U.S.

The gay night life of Havana pulses through the CASINO NACIONAL. Its magnificent halls and dining rooms are thronged nightly with dinner parties who remain to dance and woo the Fickle Goddess at the gaming tables. In furnishings and equipment the CASINO NACIONAL sustains a note of grandeur that must be seen to be fully appreciated.

The CASINO NACIONAL represents the zenith of the glorious days of variegated amusement one enjoys in Havana, the wide scope including an early round of golf, surf bathing at LA PLAYA, where one sees the notables of Europe and America; luncheon at the SEVILLA-BILTMORE or the Jockey Club, and an afternoon of racing thrills at ORIENTAL PARK.

CA-SI-NO

39 HOURS FROM NEW YORK

NACIONAL

5. Casino Nacional, 39 Hours from New York. Reconstituting the "Four Hundred" in "New York's Gayest Suburb." *Havana, the Magazine of Cuba*, January 10, 1929. Courtesy General Research Division, the New York Public Library, Astor, Lenox and Tilden Foundations.

6. Gran Casino Nacional, Havana, Cuba. One of the civic institutions of the smart set. Author's collection.

corporations had long named Cuban government officials to their boards. Such arrangements gave Cubans stakes in promoting U.S. interests and provided them with opportunities to acquire wealth. What was new about the HBYCC, the Realty Company, and National Syndicate was the direct access to U.S. financiers they provided Cuban officeholders seeking capital for private and public investments. But what ultimately proved even more important was the political investment that U.S. financiers made in the continuation of a government headed by Machado.[32]

The directors and officers of the pleasure trust collaborated in the pursuit of their mutual financial, political, and social interests. The presence of Walker, known as the people's mayor, at the groundbreaking ceremony of the HBYCC celebrated the business side of business nationalism in a project that increased Cuban investments in and ownership of the national economy. His visit set the stage for the announcement of financing of public works and the contract for the Central Highway, which would ostensibly free all Cubans from dependence on the foreign-owned railroads they despised and expensive imported goods and foodstuffs, thus representing the nationalist side of business nationalism.

The directors of the pleasure trust proved instrumental in securing a $10 million loan for the highway that technically was not a loan.[33] Few expressed surprised that the government selected Chase's bid. At the ceremony announcing the $10 million loan, the secretaries of public works and justice, recently enshrined as the twin symbols of honest and stable government, signed the contract. Chase deposited $2.5 million into the government account as a "guarantee of good faith." A somewhat wary State Department approved an arrangement that lender and debtor hoped would set a precedent for the future. On Catlin's suggestion the little-known Boston-based Warren Brothers received the contract to build the highway. Required to give a quarter of the work to Cubans, it subcontracted to a firm in which Machado held a stake. The media evinced such delight over the loan and contract that they failed to mention that the Machado regime had assassinated nearly 150 critics and labor leaders since taking office.[34]

By the time of the groundbreaking for the Central Highway, Machado's term was half over. Several factors had delayed implementation of his public works program: accruing revenue from the special taxes took time, as did securing the confidence of U.S. investors and a financing the State Department approved. Economic malaise hindered all of these. A rise in sugar prices coincided with the loan's announcement. Recovery boded well for the financial future of public works. But they would not reach completion under Machado in the absence of a second term that he had promised not to seek, but that some had already suggested.[35]

Machado sought Crowder's support for a reelection bid. Crowder thought Machado had the support and the confidence of his two leading constituencies: the "Cuban people" and the U.S. "contractors and creditors of the nation." When Crowder submitted his letter of resignation as U.S. ambassador of Cuba in March 1927 (effective the following September), he noted that he had accomplished all goals set for him: "Today we have a solvent national government, free from graft, an improved national conscience, unquestioned friendship with the United States and a stability of Government never before witnessed in the history of Cuba." While Crowder held an obvious stake in this claim, many Cuban and U.S. observers at the time regarded Machado as the young republic's most popular, honest, and successful president to date.[36]

In contrast to Cuba, where Bowman and Céspedes had to make Havana into a smart-set destination in order to attract investment capital, in

Hawai'i, Castle & Cooke and Matson held or had access to more than enough capital to make Waikīkī competitive with the world's most fashionable resorts. Building the Royal Hawaiian coincided with the writing of narratives that posited Waikīkī as a place once reserved for a Hawaiian royalty that had transferred its titles to an imagined transnational aristocracy. As was the case in Cuba, in Hawai'i haole invested vast sums of capital in enterprises in which political returns on investments were about as important as financial returns. As in Cuba, in Hawai'i the royal resort catered to privileged white settlers, expatriates, and visitors.

The Royal Hawaiian Hotel constituted one of three projects in Castle & Cooke's and Matson's plan for making Waikīkī an upper-class resort and residential community. In 1925, their directors approved a tripartite grand scheme to build an ocean liner to transport 650 first-class passengers (the *Malolo*), erect a four-hundred-room, world-class hotel to accommodate the liner's patrons (the Royal Hawaiian), and construct a golf and tennis club (Waialae Country Club) for the enjoyment of them and their hosts.[37]

The keel of the *Malolo* was laid in May 1925. Its $7.5 million price tag ensured that it was the largest, fastest, and most expensive U.S. ship of the day. No other ship afloat had a swimming pool or one hundred private baths and fifty private showers. With twenty-five thousand horsepower, the liner made the passage between San Francisco and Honolulu in four and a half days, two days faster than other ships. At her christening Herbert Hoover asserted, "Embodying as she does every refinement which modern science can furnish to safety, comfort, and convenience, she perhaps stands for the moment preeminent among American ships." At a time when the luxury liner was synonymous with transatlantic travel, Hoover offered high praise indeed.[38]

The Royal Hawaiian Hotel matched on land the opulence and grandeur the *Malolo* provided at sea. The haole genealogists who forged a royal lineage for the properties on which it would stand counterpoised the luxurious modernity of the future hotel with the primitive simplicity of the residences of ali'i. They noted that the grounds of the Royal occupied sites leased from the Bishop estate, lands that Princess Bernice Pauahi Bishop inherited from the Kamehameha dynasty. They traced the use of Helumoa, an "ancient cocoanut [*sic*] grove" in the "immediate vicinity" of the Royal Hawaiian from the "big grass house of Kalanikapule, King of Oahu" to the coral house of King Kamehameha and Queen Ka'ahumanu, where Hawaiians hosted a lū'au for the Duke of Edinburgh in 1869. Kalākaua, the last Hawaiian king, maintained a Waikīkī residence, where he entertained Robert Louis Stevenson at the most famous lūʻau in haole memory. The well-know firm of Warren & Wetmore (which renovated the Sevilla-Biltmore) echoed the coral motif in a hotel painted coral pink and designed to provide "every known means for the realization of comfort and luxury."[39]

The Spanish-Moorish architecture and Orientalist decor of the "Pink Palace" resembled that of other interwar-era hotels. The Royal was not the only hotel to boast a Persian room—so did the Waldorf Astoria. Hotels throughout the world had Regency rooms, which in the case of the Royal was a theater-ballroom decorated with images of barges floating down the Nile. Egyptian motifs were a popular style found, among other places, at the Jockey Club in Havana. The furniture of the Royal and attire of the bellboys—white shoes, white gloves, white pants with side stripes, and jackets—mimicked British colonial interior design and servant dress. But the Orientalism of the Royal put on display not only a general white colonial fantasy but the specific form of U.S. imperialism in Hawaiʻi. In its staffing, the hotel management replicated the hierarchy of the plantation order. Displaying it as a stable, benevolent, and democratizing regime, the management highlighted the territory's multiracial U.S. citizens but hid from public view its Asian immigrants. Whites managed. Hawaiian U.S. citizens served as hula girls and beach boys. Hawaiian, Chinese, and Japanese Americans staffed positions in public spaces. Japanese and Filipino immigrants worked out of sight in the kitchen and on the grounds.[40]

The gala affair marking the opening of the Royal simulated a coronation that paid tribute to the former Hawaiian monarchy and staged the succession of a haole aristocracy to a court at Waikīkī. The grand opening in the winter of 1927 was the haole social affair of the decade. The twelve hundred invited guests represented the crème de la crème of society: the officers and directors of the firms that built the Royal, prominent planters and businessmen, the governor, high-ranking U.S. military officers, society-page editors, and select wealthy tourists. Few aliʻi received invitations. The day before the opening, the *Honolulu Star-Bulletin* published an eighty-page souvenir edition that, among other things, explained the opening rituals.[41]

The gala affair staged the merging of two worlds: Hawaiian royalty and Anglo-Saxon wealth. It choreographed the end of a reign of Native monarchs and the beginning of a new one for an imagined aristocracy of wealthy white settlers and tourists. Representing the Hawaiian monarchy and directing the transfer of aristocratic privilege and property was Princess Abigail Kawānanakoa, whom elite haole thought of as Honolulu's most celebrated hostess. She was a daughter of James Campbell, a Scots-Irish settler who became one of the wealthiest landowners, planters, and financiers in Hawai'i, and Abigail Kuaihelani Maipinepine Bright, a member of a prominent Anglo-Hawaiian family of Maui and a descendant of the islands' ruling chiefs. The princess, who, it was often said, "could have been Hawaii's queen if the monarchy had survived," was the widow of Prince David Kalākaua Kawānanakoa, a nephew of King Kalākaua's consort, Queen Kapi'olani. A number of identities and genealogies merged in her body. She represented the product of unions between Hawaiian nobility and Anglo-Saxon capital. Her ancestors ranged from premonarchical chiefs to the first and last kings. She was a descendant of Hawaiians and haole who collaborated to bring civilized nationhood to Hawai'i.[42]

After a haute-cuisine dinner at which the soup and fish courses bore the names of the first Hawaiian king, Green Turtle Soup Kamehameha, and the last direct male heir of that line, Supreme of Mullet Albert, Princess Kawānanakoa led the guests to the beach for the ceremony she "arranged and directed." According to the *Star-Bulletin*, "the curtain of time was drawn back" in a re-creation of the landing on Waikīkī of Kamehameha the Great, the "Napoleon of the Pacific," upon completion of his "conquering tour" that brought all the Hawaiian islands under centralized rule. A souvenir booklet proclaimed that here "Kamehameha set up his court as ruler of all Hawaii and established a government which for more than a century commanded the respect of all nations." Five princesses greeted Kamehameha and his retinue of warriors, oarsmen, *kahili* (feather standards of royalty) bearers, and *tapu* bearers who alighted at "the site of Royal Hawaiian." Taking the throne, the king and guests enjoyed an hour of hula and mele.[43]

The "strains of a foxtrot" issuing from the hotel's ballroom marked the end of the historical pageant. "The curtain of time dropped back in place" as Kamehameha and his retinue descended the throne and disappeared into the dark. Princess Kawānanakoa was the first guest to sign the register at the Royal Hawaiian; she did not stay overnight. Haole returned from beach to ballroom, from re-created past to recreational present, from Native Hawaiian kingdom to Anglo-Saxon U.S. territory. Dancing lasted until morning, heralding the dawn of a "Recreational Era" at "a coral-pink castle set amidst a royal grove of old Hawaii." While the "days of kingdoms and tribal principalities [were] far-gone, [the] romance and glamour" of those days "still remain." The publisher of the Honolulu *Advertiser* elevated the tourist industry to the same status the opening ceremony conferred upon its guests: "If Sugar is 'King' and Pineapple 'Queen' of Hawaii," then the "Tourist Trade is Surely the 'Prince Royal.'"[44]

The Royal Hawaiian's opening ceremony naturalized haole dominion as the outcome of a civilizing mission rooted in a long history of consensual marriage and collaborative governance that had apparently begun with the arrival of the first European: "From the time of Captain Cook to the present day white men have played a leading part in the development of the tiny kingdom. Kamehameha I . . . under counsel of white men and with the aid of gunpowder, united all the islands. . . . A year before the missionaries arrived in 1820 from Boston with their permanent civilization, the pagan religion had voluntarily been discarded . . . , so that the Hawaiians were waiting with open arms for Christianity which they readily embraced as a permanent religion and never forsook." A Christian princess who enjoyed an enormous unearned income from stock in sugar and whose Native and haole ancestors had cooperated culturally, economically, and politically to civilize Hawai'i, Kawānanakoa possessed the authority to appoint an aristocracy of modern whites as successors to a former ruling monarchy of an allegedly dying race of Hawaiians and transfer the prerogatives of royal privilege and power to them.[45]

The whole affair offered a lesson in lineage, succession, and state-building that made it seem that haole had not illegally overthrown the sovereign monarch of an independent kingdom, but properly ascended to the royal court. Narratives of Waikīkī as a royal playground, once for Hawaiian ali'i but now for rich whites, masked the slow appropriation of land, power, and wealth by haole and the resistance of Hawaiians dedicated to maintaining the sovereignty of the kingdom. Celebrations of the Royal's location on land originally controlled by the Kamehameha dynasty erased from public memory the severe limitations haole set on Hawaiians' ability to reclaim Crown lands and the recent displacement from Waikīkī of ordinary farmers across the color line and Native royalty alike. Tourist narratives buried the devastations produced by the Mahele of 1848, a land division that dispossessed ordinary Hawaiians from all but 1 percent of the land. They erased the brutality of U.S. imperialism and did further violence by appropriating Hawaiians' genealogical ties *with* the land to legitimize haole acquisitions *of* land in the form of property through marriage, purchase, and conquest. They effaced the opposition of most Hawaiians to the overthrow of Queen Liliʻuokalani and the Hawaiian Kingdom in 1893 and the islands' forcible U.S. annexation in 1898. They elided the fact that Kawānanakoa's mother, her then-future husband, and his brother, Prince Kūhiō Kalanianaʻole, had led the movement to restore queen and kingdom. Kawānanakoa's parents named one of her siblings Royalist, a resistant act of naming like that of Emma Nakuina's great-grandmother.[46]

Kawānanakoa commanded authority and respect from haole for her leadership of Honolulu's high society as its most legendary hostess, a position she used to obligate them to accept her political work on behalf of Hawaiians. Kawānanakoa represented aliʻi to Hawaiians and royalty to Hawaiians and haole. She demanded the respect historically due her station, signing correspondence and answering the telephone with the single word Princess. After her brother-in-law and ten-time delegate to the U.S. Congress, Prince Kūhiō Kalanianaʻole, died in 1922, Kawānanakoa became leader of the Hawaiian community. She promoted women's rights and legislation benefiting women and children. She helped get out the Hawaiian vote. She served as Republican national committeewoman for Hawaiʻi from 1924 through 1936. From 1935 to 1940 she was a member of the Hawaiian Homes Commission. She put it on sound fiscal footing and struggled to make it take seriously its mandate to return Hawaiians to the land.[47]

The theatrical histories chronicled during the construction and grand opening of the Royal Hawaiian Hotel and the reconstitution of New York's Four Hundred in Havana helped tourists and travel writers view Cuba and Hawaiʻi through the lens of the carnivalesque worlds that they inhabited in Marianao and Waikīkī. The reality of these views was reinforced by a process of repetition and replication signaled by the whistle of steamships bringing new arrivals and through tourists' and residents' participation in daily leisured rituals of sunbathing, hula, and surfing at Waikīkī and sunbathing, golfing, and gambling at Marianao.

Latter-Day Conquistadors

Interwar-era tourism promoters harnessed a well-worn global theme to present Cuba and Hawaiʻi as the ideal combination of the traditional and the modern. They celebrated tourism's role in preserving golden ages past and accelerating their drive toward liberal democratic and capitalistic futures. The HTB portrayed greater Honolulu as a place where "native enchantment" and "the progress of civilization" meet, "Primitive Polynesia still casts her ageless spell, but with the added appeal of luxurious, modern comfort," and "Old Polynesia lives against and, strangely, pulses from the heart of a modern, American city." Similar narratives celebrated Havana's "Spanish antiquity and American up-to-dateness," which combined the "glory of one of the greatest colonial empires the world has ever known" and the "latest developments of twentieth century science, industry, commerce, and progress." Leaving colonial Havana for suburban Marianao felt like "stepping abruptly from the middle ages to modernity."[48]

The same narratives that equated the modern and progressive with the United States, and the barbaric and feudal with the Hawaiian and Spanish, posited a trading of stereotypic places. Tourists entered not only new landscapes but new narratives. The opening of the Royal produced a steady influx of tourists configured as the latest in a "mighty procession" of peoples: Polynesian seafarers, British explorers, U.S. missionaries, whalers, and merchants. In like fashion, travel writers imagined tourists to Cuba as "the latest in a long line of invaders from the Spanish Main." Although "yachts and ocean liners" had replaced "galleons," Havana remained "the city of Treasure and Romance." Positing tourists as latter-day conquistadors, explorers, and adventurers positioned them to join their hosts in indulging in all manner of pleasures while intimating that a powerful U.S. empire stood behind to protect their safety and guarantee their freedom to act out overseas fantasies unavailable or censured at home.[49]

Such narratives have transcended particular times and places, but they also served historically specific purposes. U.S. and Cuban supporters of Machado deployed narratives of the personal liberties enjoyed by tourists to posit the increasingly dictatorial chief executive as the champion of a free Cuba, sanction resurgent corruption, efface a growing opposition, and obtain additional financing for public works. Narratives of tourists and their hosts as modern conquistadors affirmed the white power and privilege that united elite Latin- and Anglo-Americans. Erasing the history in between, namely slavery and the slave trade, celebrations of pan-American whiteness worked to erase blacks and blackness from Cuba. Havana's hotels, casinos, and clubs were not merely white only for clients; most employed few or no blacks, nor did they offer entertainment influenced by Afro-Cuban culture. Most cabarets deemed rumba unacceptable during the 1920s. Tourists and their hosts enjoyed the modern amenities of "New

7. Ponce De Leon discovering the fountain of eternal youth in the La
Florida Bar. Tourists as latter-day conquistadors. Author's collection.

York's Gayest suburb," but one stripped of many of Manhattan's "mongrel" features.[50]

The royal welcome Castle & Cooke and Matson provided tourists likewise
affirmed white colonial privilege and power. But in contrast to Cuba, narratives and rituals of the beach in Hawai'i, specifically tourists' encounters
with native hula girls and beach boys, opened spaces for transgressions
across race and class lines that made it seem very much a melting pot.
By linking touristic leisure to educational tours on the Americanization of
Hawaiians and Asians like those with whom they interacted on the beach
or at the hotel, haole recast white supremacy as interracial harmony and
white rule as a multiracial democracy in feeling if not form. Along with
vacations fit for kings and queens, promoters sold their guests a sort of
racial paradise: "Hawaii is a land with true American ideals of democracy
and equality, a world famous melting pot, imbued with the spirit of live
well and let others live well; a land where there is little poverty, hardship,
or disease; a land that is tropical in aspect but temperate in atmosphere and

conduct." Here the plantation hierarchy replicated in the staffing of the Royal Hawaiian permeated celebrations of an internationally renowned multiracial democracy. Hawai'i was tropical yet temperate by virtue of those who governed it, that is, privileged Anglo-Saxon men. The phrase "live well and let others live well" emanated from a planter paternalism that arrogated the right to define and attend to the welfare of the nonwhite majority as haole deemed fit. Yet through the narratives and rituals that introduced tourists to Hawaiian hula girls and beach boys, promoters prepared their guests to meet some members of the many races who "mingle" and "dwell in unity under the American flag."[51]

Matson's and the Royal's welcome situated tourists at the top of the territory's "plantation pyramid." Often in images and sometimes in practice, Hawaiians in outrigger canoes representing Kamehameha and his retinue greeted arriving cruise ships, allegedly much as they had welcomed Captain Cook as a god. While the Royal Hawaiian Band played, lei girls enveloped passengers with fragrant floral garlands. When guests arrived at the Royal, the haole general manager greeted each of them and settled them in for tea (or something stronger) served by Japanese-American "geisha girls" wrapped in kimonos. Meanwhile, Chinese-American baggage handlers in "Cathayan costume" whisked trunks often containing guests' own silver and crystal to rooms where the servants of tourists or the hotel staff unpacked them.[52]

While the royal welcome affirmed the hierarchies that sustained white colonial power and privilege, it also disturbed them, in part through discourses of the sexually liberated "new woman" whom promoters invited to enjoy the sort of "South Seas romances" long deemed a male prerogative.[53] During the 1920s, haole promoters debated whether to promote ancient forms of hula or popular ones visitors knew from Broadway musicals, vaudeville houses, and Hollywood films.[54] While this debate continued, promoters typically portrayed the hula girl as a white woman, one who went native with Hawaiian beach boys.[55]

Waikīkī was the first beach where bathing attire went modern, and women adopted bathing suits that revealed necks, arms, legs, and even waistlines and cleavage. They cultivated suntans, outwardly changing races from Caucasian to Polynesian and enhancing their sensuality with the assistance of a beach boy. "Solicitous 'beach boys'" lavished "every attention" on visitors, recorded the travel writer Clifford Gessler: "Here an eastern lady of fashion lies prone beneath the sun while a smiling Hawaiian youth

8. "Honolulu How Do You Do!" Tourists as latter-day explorers. This sheet-music cover spoofs myriad paintings depicting Hawaiians greeting Captain James Cook as a god. Published by Paul F. Summers, 1932. Courtesy Hawai'i State Library, Honolulu.

anoints her back and legs with coconut oil to encourage protective and ornamental tan." Nearby, "another bronze boy kneels over another fair visitor, kneading and manipulating the muscles in a soothing and relaxing massage." Surfing lessons provided white women with a similarly sexualized encounter with Hawaiian men: "The pupil lies forward on the board, the instructor behind and partly over her, his strong arms providing most of the motive power for the long pull outward bound and the swift fierce struggle to catch the wave. When it is caught he lifts her to her feet, and she has all the feeling of conquering the surf when in reality her brown companion has done most of the work."[56]

Such erotically charged encounters sometimes did lead to romance, but not because life was "so carefree at Waikiki." Sunbathing and surfing took place in broad daylight in front of the Moana and Royal Hawaiian hotels. Beach boys were subject to the discipline of haole managers. As beach boy Harry Robello explained, "The beach boys had to be straight-line. Well mannered. Women were safe with the beach boys." Management forbade beach boys from all hotel areas but the lobby, a prohibition easily circumvented with a tip, but only if a female tourist invited a beach boy to her room. Beach boys could not ask women out. Robello recalled, "She tell her parents, her parents tell the hotel, you out." Tales of torrid affairs—true, false, embellished—between beach boys and female tourists became the stuff of urban legend. Travel writers, tourists, and Hollywood stars, some of whom took beach boys on vacations to their mainland homes or remembered them in their wills, spread this fantasy globally.[57]

Cultural producers also provided male tourists opportunities to enhance their manliness and participate in the colonial project of preserving native culture. In 1909, the anthropologist Nathaniel Emerson lamented, "today it is hard to find a surfboard outside of our museums and cultural collections." He attributed the decline of surfing to the "touch of civilization," quite a euphemism for the coercion and violence employed by missionaries and their ilk over the course of a century to repress surfing and hula on the grounds that they encouraged nudity and gambling and distracted from Protestant worship and the inculcation of its work ethic.[58]

A number of historians credit the novelist Jack London and globetrotter Alexander Hume Ford with the revival of the Polynesian "sport of kings" and its transformation into a leading tourist attraction. In 1908, Ford founded the Outrigger Canoe Club on Waikīkī with several goals in mind. First and foremost, he intended to "preserve surfing on boards and in outrigger canoes." He also endeavored to open the beach and revive the sport among the Hawaiian "boy of limited means," whom fees and discriminatory practices kept off Waikīkī, and to popularize a sport that in Ford's words, "demonstrated that the white man could learn all the secrets of the Hawaiian-born." Because few Hawaiians could afford the annual fee charged by the Outrigger or were willing to allow haole to appropriate this part of Hawaiian culture, in 1911 they formed their own club, Hui Nalu (House of the Waves). Its members came to serve as beach boys, a relatively lucrative vocation that was also quite prestigious, especially for the opportunities it provided to transgress a number of colonial hierarchies.[59]

Glossing over such disparities, London mythologized Ford's vision in "The Royal Sport," a tourist reading staple. Describing a "brown Mercury" whose "heels are winged" and his "riding the sea that roars and bellows and cannot shake him from its back," he concluded: "He has 'bitted the bull-mouthed breaker' and ridden it in, and the pride in the feat shows in the carriage of his magnificent body as he glances for a moment carelessly at you who sit in the shade of the shore. He is a Kanaka—and more, he is a man, a member of the kingly species that has mastered matter and the brutes and lorded it over creation." Yet you the tourist could become such a man, as Jack London did, in part, by learning "the sport of ancient royalty" from the "competent and most entertaining . . . beach boys" in "a week or so." He anchored man and sport in a civilization that traced its genealogy both to ancient Greek gods and Polynesian kings. In such narratives, the white male tourist pursued a masculine quest to recover dormant barbarian virtues by learning primitive secrets and enhancing his sexual appeal for his wife.[60]

Through the narratives and rituals of tourists' interactions with the beach boys, promoters made travelers symbolic participants, on the one hand, in the interracial marriages haole used to legitimate their claims to and governance of Hawai'i, and on the other hand, in the creation both of a "new people," a "golden race" of "neo-Hawaiians," and a new society that had ostensibly solved the problem of the races.[61] However, such narratives of erotic and exotic interracial encounters invariably ended with sexual fulfillment between the white married tourists. Unlike earlier promoters for whom volcanic eruptions symbolized biblical creation and a divinely ordained U.S. manifest destiny in Hawai'i, for interwar-era promoters, volcanic eruptions stood for the revitalized sex life promised by a "South Seas Honeymoon." Vacationing couples would find that passions "that have lain dormant . . . flare into being [and] the fires of romance [play] in the heavens where the coals once smoldered on earth." Like earlier promoters, those of the interwar years found in Anglo-Saxon Protestant values of restraint here symbolized by marital fidelity an antidote to, and measure of superiority over, the sexual temptations of sensuous Polynesians. In like fashion, the freedom white women had in their relationships with the beach boys seemed to provide evidence that Hawai'i was a racial democracy even as it allowed haole to display their power to ensure that beach boys respected white women and their respective places in the plantation pyramid.[62]

The haole ruling class thus exploited evidence of the interracial harmony and democracy that tourists presumably experienced with the beach boys to navigate the horror with which many U.S. tourists must have greeted widespread miscegenation in Hawai'i *and* to reorganize and reentrench a white supremacy recently challenged from below by Native Hawaiians and Asian immigrants and settlers.[63] Promoters further linked tourists' apparently democratic and egalitarian experiences with the beach boys to tours of local schools and plantations to showcase how haole Americanization programs had made Hawai'i a racial democracy and would someday make it a political democracy. Even before guests embarked on such tours, they had learned that the Japanese geisha-girl servers and Chinese baggage handlers at the Royal were upwardly mobile U.S. citizens, whose jobs demanded standard English and paid more for far less grueling work than plantation labor. "Combining study and play," a trip to a school offered tourists the opportunity "to witness the workings of an Americanization program that is making loyal U.S. citizens of a melting pot enrollment," while a tour of a plantation proffered a lesson of the "rags to riches" story of success as the reward of perseverance and hard work.[64]

School tours celebrated diversity by combining performances of traditional Chinese, Japanese, and Korean dances with a demonstration of the progress of Americanization, for example, by Asian children reading essays they composed on "their Pilgrim fathers." For the tourist Grace Harlow, three observations showed how the education system in Hawai'i confirmed that "all nationalities may reach great attainments." First, she found in a debate (which she did not attend) between British students from Oxford and Japanese students from the University of Hawaii proof that educational and civilizational uplift produced intellectual parity, one she equated with the achievement of racial equality. Second, a public celebration of Washington's birthday by members of the "darker races . . . commemorating the

9. Nearby Hawaii. Tourists on the beach at Waikīkī at once among, as, and above the beach boys. Hawaii Tourist Bureau, second printing, 1934. Author's collection.

birth of the adopted Father of their adopted country" underscored the
opportunities that the white ruling class offered for entry into the U.S. body
politic, provided that the U.S. citizens born to Asian immigrants accepted
the responsibility of showing themselves worthy of adoption by the U.S.
nation. Third, her description of a pageant hosted by the Salvation Army
where "a little Korean girl sang 'My country 'tis of thee'" stressed the gratitude of Asian American citizens who followed the example of haole in
reciprocating the "good works" that haole extended to the less fortunate.[65]

Tours of cane plantations followed a script developed by the Hawaiian
Sugar Planters' Association in the 1920s. The tours built upon a practice
the HSPA institutionalized after the strike of 1909, when planters began
offering cash prizes to the workers who kept the most handsome homes
and gardens: "An attractive camp" gives guests "a favorable impression of
the treatment of laborers by the plantations. When taking visitors around,
we always show them the camps that are well kept." *The Story of Sugar in
Hawaii* narrated a tale of success and opportunity on the frontier. The men
who built the sugar industry were of the "same hardy pioneer stock that
built up the great western U.S." They included those with capital and those
who "came here poor, but worked their way up through sheer pluck and
industry." Opportunity for advancement was available to all "races of men"
who came to work the cane fields and mills: "Hawaii's sugar industry has
given all of them steady work. There have been no hard times—prosperity
and development have been constant. . . . Many men from these races have
risen to prominence, wealth and position. . . . Thousands of good citizens
have developed and a Territory has grown up of which we are all proud. A
land for which the future holds great possibilities." Laborers could rise to
wealth and prominence with the help of a planter class that afforded them
more and better chances to achieve success through hard work than were
available to European immigrants on the mainland.[66]

The sugar laborer and his family "dwell amid conditions far above those
of his city brother," specifically the European immigrant working in a U.S.
industrial city. Planters provided working families with a "free house, free
fuel, free medical attention, low cost for food and necessities, and chances
for gardening." As a result, "the plantation laborer has a good opportunity
to save money, and hundreds of them do put away substantial savings
accounts." These were not the only opportunities for accumulating savings
and capital: "Only about 5% work under the minimum guaranteed wage"
of "$1.00 per day." Planters "encourage continuous work" through

10. A tourist enjoys experiencing the harmonious melting pot. Hawaii Tourist Bureau, *The Story of Hawaii*, reprint edition, 1929. Author's collection.

bonuses and overtime pay. For these reasons, the first immigrant group, the Chinese, became "good farmers and good businessmen" who "control many flourishing business enterprises." The most recent immigrants, Filipinos, saved and remitted large sums: "The savings banks have over two million dollars on deposit by Filipino laborers alone, and over one million is sent back each year by Filipino sugar plantation laborers to their parents or relatives in the Philippines." Filipino workers earned enough to return home "after three years," but many who did so came back, "attracted by . . . the fair wage on the plantations, the good housing and general better surroundings." Embedding tours of schools and plantations within the context of the apparent interracial harmony that tourists experienced on the beach contributed to convincing productions of Hawai'i as a melting pot that had solved the problem of the races.[67]

At best, the alleged success of paternalist Americanization projects exaggerated laborers' housing conditions, perquisites, pay, and bonuses and, at worst, lied about the prospects of the poor to become rich, although these facts are less important for this discussion than are the tensions and contradictions they reveal. After the 1920 strike, the haole ruling class invested an enormous amount of cultural, financial, and political capital in the image of Hawai'i as a land of American democracy and opportunity, although both democratization and the upward mobility of Asians and Asian Americans were inimical to its interests. In 1929 the HSPA president offered the baldest statement made about the purpose of the sugar industry: "As has been emphasized over and over again, the primary function of our plantations is not to produce sugar, but to pay dividends." Sugar production underwrote the power, privilege, and wealth of the planter class and a sizeable community of haole and tiny group of Hawaiian stockholders. The production of dividends was at odds with providing more than the lowest wages and minimal benefits required to maintain order, and the lowest taxes needed to fund services the planters thought important, like the police and other patronage jobs that ensured the Hawaiian vote, and those they did not, like education and welfare. It was at odds with securing plantation workers increasingly drawn from the ranks of Asian Americans rather than Asian immigrants. Education particularly came to worry the planter class, which correctly perceived that it offered opportunities for immigrants' children to learn skills that would prepare them for better jobs and ideas about democracy that would inspire demands for liberty and equality.[68]

The planters worked to resolve such contradictions. Perquisites and bonuses offered them more control over workers than did higher wages. Overtime helped keep workers too busy and tired to organize. Although no travel writer failed to boast that Jim Crow laws were absent from Hawai'i, haole institutionalized separate and far from equal schools, ostensibly not on the basis of race but of English-language skills, which correlated closely with racial categories. This was a typical imperial maneuver, as Ann Laura Stoler argues of Dutch schools in the East Indies, "Access to cultural resources was contingent on already having them." The first English-standard school system opened in Honolulu in 1924 with 546 haole students, 135 Hawaiians, 78 Portuguese, 27 Chinese students, and 16 Japanese students. Between 1925 and 1932, Asian children never comprised more than 7 percent of its student body (typical of English-standard schools, for only 8 percent of the population spoke standard English) at a time when Chinese and Japanese students made up 60 percent of school enrollment. The Japanese newspaper *Hawaii Hochi* called standard schools a bastion of the "Nordic caste system," one "utterly at variance with the ideals for which America stands." And by 1929 the planters asked the territorial government to stop overeducating Asian students and instead offer vocational training in hopes of persuading them to join the plantation workforce.[69]

The haole ruling class had a vested interest in promoting the image of the Americanness of Hawai'i and the Americanization of its Chinese, Japanese, Korean, and Filipino immigrants, settlers, and citizens. It sought to balance representations of the territory's immigrants and U.S. citizens of Asian ancestry by deploying the mutually sustaining model minority and yellow peril discourses—the former to stress the Americanization of non-whites and the latter to secure a strong military presence to protect haole from internal and external threats. After the 1920 strike, the planter class focused on demonstrating the success of Americanization and the Americanism of people of color in matters large and small. One such trivial matter reveals the depth of haole preoccupation with image production. In 1927 the Hawai'i governor reproached the HTB for allowing an issue of *Tourfax*, a monthly throwaway publication, to present a "summary of the population of Hawaii that gives the impression that this is a section of the United States made up of aliens." He demanded that future issues "more definitely emphasize the population of this Territory in terms of our American citizenship." The U.S. citizenship held by Hawaiians and U.S.-born Asians demonstrated the progress of the Americanization even as haole worked to limit nonwhites' access to the rights and privileges of U.S. citizenship.[70]

Haole commitments to showcasing equality and democracy in Hawai'i constituted part of a strategy for preventing their achievement. Their relentless efforts to broadcast the Americanization, equality, and democracy of Hawai'i intended nothing less than to preserve the plantation hierarchy. The outcome of the production of cane was sugar; the outcome of the production of dividends was a most privileged way of life indeed.

Whereas the 1920 strike and the U.S. government's response to it led haole to demonstrate to a metropolitan audience their ability to Americanize and democratize the nonwhite majority, at the time no comparable reason compelled Cuba's transnational white elite to do likewise with the *raza de color.* Their elision of the racial inequalities in Cuba that U.S. imperial agents worked to more deeply entrench served the interests of a Cuban elite which frequently presented itself as the defender of racial equality associated with the ideals of Cuba Libre. While tourists often met blacks in public spaces, virtually all private places catering to tourists were segregated. Still, even as they praised the extension of Jim Crow from the United States to Cuba, travel writers invoked the figure of the mulata to imply sexual excess and grant whites sexual license. Waldo Frank, for example, described Cuba and the Cuban woman as a mulata: "The hips and the high heels are jazz; the arms and breasts swath her in Andalusian softness; under the blare of her rouge Africa mumbles." Whites invoked the mulata to sanction their indulgence in commercial sex and other erotic or exotic pleasures tourists regarded as desirable yet debased, while the same time, making whiteness the measure of luxury and refinement.[71]

But much as the haole in Hawai'i celebrated freedom while practicing repression, Cuba's white cultural producers also championed the extension of liberty and modernity by and for Cubans as they worked to secure a second illegal term for Machado. Their celebrations of the freedom available to U.S. citizens in Cuba took on new significance and meaning when Machado moved to extend his term through a constitutional process of the most dubious legality. Members of the pleasure trust engaged the U.S. travel writer Basil Woon as a publicity agent for the Cuban government and the famous Cuban caricaturist, graphic artist, and editor Conrado Walter Massaguer to oversee a new high-society, winter-season, English-language magazine, *Havana, the Magazine of Cuba.* Woon, Massaguer, and other pro-Machado promoters deployed narratives of the personal liberty flaunted by Havana's Four Hundred to posit the increasingly dictatorial president as the champion of a progressive Cuba, sanction graft, erase a growing opposition, and obtain a $50 million "loan" for public works.[72]

After Machado told Crowder he sought a second term in order to complete his public works program, the president approached Congress. In 1927 it passed resolutions that amended the constitution to benefit the executive and legislative branches alike. It established a single six-year presidential term and extended Machado's presidency and representatives' and senators' terms. In a constitutional convention the following May, politicians dropped the provision prolonging Machado's term and specified that the limitation of a president to one term would become effective after the election of November 1928. A new law recognized only three political parties. All three declared Machado their nominee, so he ran for a second term as the sole candidate. For the renowned anthropologist Fernando Ortiz, these acts signaled a "new parenthesis of peril." Even Crowder deemed them a "kind of civil coup d'etat." Cuban support for Machado began to drop precipitously. But as a rising chorus of critics condemned the conversion of a president into a dictator, promoters celebrated Havana as a land of liberty.[73]

Woon for one insisted that "personal liberty to the Nth degree" was a Havana hallmark. It allowed, among other things, that "you may drink as much as you want to. . . . You may lose as much money as you desire in the Casino. . . . You need not carry your marriage certificate with you." Bruce Bliven, a travel writer who admired Machado, declared that Havana "is hot, it is 'wet,' it is, in its easy tropical way, Wide Open." He described the day of "the typical sojourner." He "spends his alcoholiday according to a well tried formula: arise at noon, horse-racing until cocktail time, dinner . . . , and the evening at the National Casino. . . . After he has counted his losses . . . perhaps a nightclub, or, if he wants a place that is more wicked, he can find one as tough as he is." Woon offered a similar program. Drinks at the races preceded a round of golf and drinks at the clubhouse, followed by blackjack and drinks at the casino and a sail before drinks and dinner: "You wonder what to do now. Shall it be Havana and the fleshpots?—Or just another whirl at the Casino?—Or one more bottle of wine with the Lady in Green?"[74]

It was not just the availability of alcohol, gambling, and sex that U.S. tourists and travel writers found so appealing. Led by New York, major U.S.

11. Cuba Libre reinterpreted. *Havana, the Magazine of Cuba,* February 19, 1929. Courtesy General Research Division, the New York Public Library, Astor, Lenox and Tilden Foundations.

cities stopped enforcing laws criminalizing drinking and gambling not long after their enactment, although their practice did become far less public. It was the legality and openness of vice in Cuba and the Machado administration's support of that openness that fueled tourists' and travel writers' conflation of the liberties enjoyed by tourists with the extension of Cuba Libre under Machado. The Cuban Tourist Commission hailed his second term as the continuation of an enlightened and progressive government devoted to "Cuba's welfare and progress," one "duly appreciated" by the Cuban people through his reelection.[75]

As rumors swirled among the country-club set that contractors for the Central Highway were netting profits of 30 percent and that bribes had tripled the projected cost of the Capitol, travel writers presented graft as similar to the gambling enjoyed by U.S. tourists and claimed both as a legacy of Spanish colonialism. Enrique Canova defined Havana's allure as the "glamour of a lurid past, with its pages of piratical plundering, pomp and high adventure with which it is so romantically linked." For Sydney Clark, Havana was where "the conscience takes a holiday." Both remained admirers of Machado after his overthrow in 1933. Both associated plunder and piracy as normative practices of U.S. visitors and Cuban officials. Moreover, Clark said, "Other regimes grafted quite as outrageously and left nothing to show for it. Machado got things done."[76]

Travel writers naturalized graft as intrinsic to the modernization process by pointing to Jimmy Walker, now a frequent guest of Machado and Bowman. The corrupt but popular, dashing yet decadent Nightclub Mayor embodied 1920s New York where "con games were culture." Admirers and detractors agreed that Walker brought such cachet to corruption and glamour to graft that he remained "first choice for mayor" a dozen years after Franklin D. Roosevelt forced him to resign on corruption charges. His visits to Cuba came to symbolize the movement of financial and cultural capital from New York to Havana in a transnational con game of profit, pleasure, and politics.[77]

The comparisons between Céspedes and Walker that proliferated after Machado extended his presidency performed the same work. *Havana, the Magazine of Cuba*, commented that "Charlie Mike," or Carlos Miguel de Céspedes, was "a man who in New York would build a subway over a weekend, and while we were smoking a cigarette erect a statue, and while we were gaping into a subway would build a park." The *New York Times* praised Céspedes for transforming Havana into a beautiful, orderly, and well-policed city. It suggested that Walker hire Céspedes to replicate his success in New York. Explicit comparisons of Walker and Céspedes and implicit ones between the Machado regime and the Tammany machine and New York's and Havana's interwar-era public works programs became commonplace. In the 1920s, the United States acquired power, argues Ann Douglas, "by colonizing the future, defining, monopolizing, and selling at steep rates the modernization process itself," a process that Machado, Céspedes, and their allies attempted to buy at very steep rates indeed. They sought to import New York modernity to Cuba in self-aggrandizing quests for power, prestige, and privilege.[78]

Machado supporters backed his civil coup d'etat to protect and advance their investments. Having developed a tourist industry built on the foundation of racetrack and casino, they gambled that Cuba could meet further obligations to New York banks. They sought to replicate Bowman's and

Céspedes' success in obtaining a $10 million loan by staging another spec-
tacular winter season to secure an additional $50 million. The Sixth Pan
American Conference, scheduled to convene in Havana in January 1928,
offered the Machado administration an opportunity it milked for all it was
worth.

When Machado traveled to the United States in April 1927 to invite
President Calvin Coolidge to inaugurate the conference, he struck deals in
Washington offices and at New York luncheons hosted by the Chase, J. P.
Morgan, and National City banks and by Mayor Walker. Coolidge
approved Machado's bid for a second term secured with or without elections, although he expressed a preference for the former. After Machado
left, the State Department informed J. P. Morgan that it had "no objection"
to a $9 million loan that would allow the Cuban government to retire debt
and enable it to service future loans. Obregón told Chase that the government would accept bids for a $50 million loan after the conference.[79]

While some historians argue that the Machado administration demanded
the abrogation of the Platt Amendment primarily to satisfy its Cuban constit-
uents, it also agitated against it to increase its bargaining power with Washington. Despite Crowder's pleas not to protest the Platt Amendment on his
U.S. visit, Machado and Orestes Ferrera, Cuba's ambassador to the United
States, did just that. U.S. newspapers and Latin American embassies broadcast their pronouncements throughout the hemisphere: the Pan-American
Conference would serve as a forum for opposing the Platt Amendment.[80]

Many Latin American nations were incensed by U.S. policy in Latin
America, especially its recent interventions in Nicaragua, Haiti, and the
Dominican Republic, and planned to boycott the conference. But a
Machado representative convinced them that Cuba needed their assistance
to achieve its sovereignty. Machado secured the participation of all Latin
American nations, the first time that had happened in the history of the
conference. As their delegates and many Cubans prepared to agitate for the
abrogation of the Platt Amendment, Machado worked to ensure that no
protests against it or the United States would occur. He suppressed anti-
U.S. skits in vaudeville houses. Fearing student protests, he closed the University of Havana. He moved Carnival to coincide with the conference.
Its parades and parties helped divert attention from the business of the
conference.[81]

Diplomatically the conference ended in failure. But the support of the
Machado administration and the spectacles of the winter season helped

mollify criticisms of U.S. policy in Latin America, focus attention on Cuba's progress under Machado, and demonstrate the republic's worthiness for additional financing. Cooperative media members headlined the pageantry of transnational high society and relegated criticisms of U.S. interventions to the inside pages of Cuban and U.S. newspapers.

Coolidge opened the conference by invoking the discovery of the New World in 1492: "In the spirit of Christopher Columbus all the Americas have an eternal bond of unity." More delegates saw chains of repression than bonds of unity. But Machado backed Coolidge, averring that the Monroe Doctrine safeguarded hemispheric security and "the territorial integrity of America." When Latin American delegates condemned U.S. interventions, Ferrera defended them: "In my country the word 'intervention' has been a word of honor, a word of glory, a word of triumph, a word of liberty; it has been a word of independence." He asserted that under U.S. tutelage, Cuba had become the most modern nation in Latin America, evidenced by the selection of Havana as host of the Pan American Conference and as a hub of Pan American Airlines.[82]

Coolidge declared the conference in recess so that he and Machado could welcome the inaugural passenger flight of Pan American Airlines from Miami. The flight celebrated Havana's importance as an axis of the Americas, Pan Am's designated embarkation point for all Latin American countries on the eastern seaboard. When the conference resumed, Cuban delegates continued to defend U.S. policy, and most others to denounce it. The media continued to praise the progress of Cuba under Machado.[83]

As the conference drew to a close, Charles A. Lindbergh arrived in Havana on the last leg of a fourteen-nation Pan-American tour sponsored by Pan Am. U.S. Ambassador Noble Judah hosted a reception for the celebrity pilot attended by four thousand of "the best elements of Havana society, Cuban, American, and English." Lindbergh then attended the opening of the Havana Biltmore Yacht and Country Club, which outdid the ambassador's reception for the Prince of the Air. Céspedes completed the extension of Fifth Avenue to it in time for the affair. Commentaries on his work provided opportunities for favorable coverage of the government. Reviewing "the greatest month for tourist travel that Cuba has ever known," the *Cuba Review* urged completion of loan negotiations as it praised the regime's achievements: "There is no break in the program to make Cuba a land of progress and prosperity . . . striving to get into the first rank of cultured, wide-awake independent nations. The driving force, the genius of enterprise . . . is our indefatigable Secretary of Public Works, Carlos M. de Céspedes, backed to the limit by Gen. Gerardo Machado."[84]

As a monthly, *Cuba Review* was not among the ten newspapers that Obregón paid (and for which he billed Chase) for publishing "favorable articles with regard to the loan." The pro-Machado media did not suggest that expenditures for public works that had improved Havana largely for the benefit of privileged Cuban and U.S. citizens left the government short of funds for the Central Highway. Machado prudently waited until U.S. reporters departed before ordering police to drop the bodies of four opponents into Havana harbor to be eaten by sharks, scarcely a practice of a cultured nation. This marked an escalation in the use of violence in struggles between the *machadato* and its growing opposition. The harbor master soon banned shark fishing to prevent fishermen from finding the bodily remains of people assassinated by the army and police.[85]

Nothing could conceal deepening depression. The price of sugar fell; unemployment rose; tax revenues declined. Servicing debt, which Machado deemed a "sacred obligation," required slashing other government expenditures. After servicing debt, the government transferred funds from the public works account to prevent overdrawing the general budget. Bids submitted by Chase, National City Bank, and First Bank of Boston took into account the growing crisis and demonstrated a willingness to invest only in Machado. All proposed loans were payable before his second term ended.[86]

In May 1928 Machado accepted by presidential decree $50 million in financing from a syndicate headed by Chase. It doubled Cuba's annual loan repayments. Congress followed the wishes of the tropical Mussolini and voted to approve a second loan. It gave him "power without limitation to finance works" and establish new taxes until the loan was "totally paid." Following the precedent set by the $10 million advance, and no doubt grateful for Machado's support during the Pan-American Conference, the State Department endorsed the financing. Few were surprised the government accepted Chase's bid. In addition to its close relationship with the Machado regime, Chase apparently made the only proposal that did not tie financing to specific projects.[87]

Most plans for roads, schools, and highways were put on hold. Work on Central Highway and Capitol proceeded, with graft absorbing unknown amounts. Schools received little funding, despite protests by Cubans and U.S. citizens after a study by a University of Havana professor showed that in one decade illiteracy had increased 21 percent among black school-aged children and 15 percent among white children. Even Crowder could not convince the government to invest $5 million in schools. As the U.S. observer Leland Hamilton Jenks noted: "Millions are being spent for the sudden beautifying of Havana, while the extension of education to a half-literate population proceeds very slowly."[88]

The Capitol Building reached completion in time for Machado's second inauguration in May 1929. A slightly larger replica of its counterpart in Washington, D.C., the Cuban Capitol professed a modernity that put Cuba on a par with the United States. The final cost of the building reached $16 million, over five times its original estimate of $3 million. Certainly the project experienced normal overruns and cost increases. But critics argued that the amount of money absorbed by bribes and graft exceeded costs—by several times. Machado's second inauguration coincided with growing criticisms of and protests against his repression and corruption. By the year's end, his regime had spent the $60 million loan from Chase.[89]

As the onset of the Great Depression in the United States plunged the Cuban economy into even deeper crisis, Cuban opposition to the *macha-dato* swelled. Many pointed to the tourism industry and the multinational white elite that had built it for themselves as well as visitors in condemning government corruption and repression, political and economic dependence, and white supremacy. Meanwhile, at a time when revolution seemed imminent in Cuba, haole hegemony appeared secure in Hawai'i. But in 1931, the wife of a junior naval officer stationed in Honolulu alleged that five so-called local boys of color had raped her. The allegation and two ensuing trials rocked the Big Five order. Many in the United States demanded military rule. In Hawai'i, people across the color line began to forge an identity of themselves as locals opposed to haole colonial governance and planter paternalism. On both islands, settlers and citizens organized to protest hollow promises of democratization from above and work for it from below.

Sugar paid the dividends and provided the capital tourism promoters used to build the royal resorts that enabled Havana's and Honolulu's visiting and resident white elites to live like a cosmopolitan leisured class symbolized by European aristocrats. But much like these elites' celebrated lifestyles, their governance of Cuba and Hawai'i proved to be as corrupt and oppressive as that in the European empires U.S. expansionists had long condemned as monarchical and contrasted with their own ostensibly hon-

orable and democratic empire for liberty. As crises exposed the contradictions between republican promises and repressive practices, they provided
opportunities for anti-imperial, antiracist movements from below. As
Cuban citizens mobilized to fulfill the promise of Cuba Libre by building a
sovereign, inclusive, and democratic nation, many of the U.S citizens, settlers, aliens, and Natives in Hawai'i began to articulate an identity of themselves as locals united against colonial rule and demanded recognition, if
not as U.S. citizens, then as patriotic American settlers devoted to constitution and country.

CHAPTER FOUR

Revolutions, Reformations, Restorations

It is well for us to dream of a Havana beautiful. It is well for optimistic futures to be made on how the republic is going to be transformed into a paradise. But first we must live and to live we must eat. . . . While the Prado is being embellished with feverish haste, in many streets hungry children are to be found. Beggars asking for a crust of bread have increased.

El Cubano Libre, 1928

News was flashed to the mainland that Hawaii was unsafe for women. That was serious, for it might injure the tourist trade upon which Hawaii greatly depended for a source of revenue. I was asked by the acting Governor to make official denial, which I refused to do. I told him that, in fact, I subscribed to that belief.

Rear Admiral Yates Stirling, 1939

As recession gave way to depression and repression met armed opposition, more and more Cubans made tourism a symbol of a corrupt dictator and his allies who enriched themselves at the expense of the Cuban nation and its citizens. A year after *El Cubano Libre* criticized the government for beautifying Havana for the rich while ignoring the worsening plight of the poor, the *Cuba Review* sought to counter a rising chorus of criticism. Machado's public works program had prevented, not caused, poverty, and strengthened, not imperiled, Cuba: "From eighty to one hundred thousand poor people, through the efforts of Public Works, have been kept alive and not submitted to the humiliation of a government dole. They have earned their bread and butter by honest toil, freed the country from the danger of revolution, and . . . left monuments to the wisdom and good taste of the Republic." More observers than not thought mounting opposition to the machadato made revolution likely.[1]

In Hawai'i, the haole governing class also found itself embroiled in a political crisis many observers attributed to tourism, specifically the promotion of relationships between Hawaiian beach boys and white women tourists. In September 1931, Thalia Massie, the white wife of a white junior naval officer, alleged that five men of color had raped her. Hollywood actress Dorothy Mackaill blamed a volatile racial-sexual environment fostered by tourism: "The beach boys . . . have had many romances with rich American women. . . . These affairs have been invited by the white women visitors . . . [who] lie on the beach . . . in abbreviated bathing suits and permit the 'beach boys' to rub them with coconut oil so they will receive a good tan. . . . It is a real tribute to the Hawaiian people that none of the men accused of attacking Mrs. Massie was a Kanaka. The five men were mixed breed. . . . [But] what can we expect of these people when they see Kanakas openly receiving the attentions of American white women?" The allegation confirmed a long-held belief of Rear Admiral Yates Stirling, Jr., commandant of the Fourteenth Naval District at Pearl Harbor: "Present government control should be by men primarily of the Caucasian race . . . by men without preconceived ideas of the value and success of the melting pot experiment." He meant military officers and civilians from Washington. Coverage of the two trials relating to the Massie case rivaled the other big story of the year, the Lindbergh baby kidnapping. Small wonder, for they featured "sex, racism, perjury, lynch law, inept cops, two trials, a world-class attorney, demagogic reporting, foaming editorials, political blackmail, loony congressmen, ass-kicking sailors, a homicidally hoity mother-in-law, vacillating bureaucrats, Presidential intervention, a miscarriage of justice, and finally the Pinkerton Detective Agency."[2]

The Great Depression brought tourism to a standstill before Massie's allegation of rape in 1931 and the revolution that ousted Machado in 1933. But by the 1934–1935 winter season, the number of U.S. tourists in Hawai'i and Cuba returned to pre-Depression levels. Travel writers helped tourists forget the recent crises. Hudson Strode, for example, wrote as if little had changed in Cuba since the 1920s: "American women in plenty cluttered the golf links, dotted the club buildings' terraces at cocktail hours, and danced tangos deliriously with sleek young men who looked like gigolos but who carried wads of hundred-dollar bills for pocket change."[3]

But things had changed in Cuba and Hawai'i, irrevocably so. The overthrow of Machado and the two trials stemming from Massie's allegation transformed the political, racial, and social orders of both. The U.S. government acted to reconstruct political order in Cuba and project its power more authoritatively in Hawai'i. Meanwhile, people across lines of color, and often class as well, challenged elite white power and privilege in both places. Cubans embraced an anti-imperial, antiracist nationalism rooted in *mestizaje* in their quest for "antidotes to Wall Street," to cite novelist Alejo Carpentier's famous phrase. Nonwhite "locals" in Hawai'i pursued antidotes to the Big Five as they worked to build an interracial labor and social movement. The struggles of ordinary people and efforts to co-opt or contain them that began in the 1930s persisted well into the 1950s.[4]

"Antidotes to Wall Street" and the Big Five

On the second Saturday of September 1931, a group of U.S. junior naval officers and their wives gathered at a Waikīkī club for a night out. Among them were Lieutenant Thomas Massie and his wife, Thalia. The naval community disliked Thalia, for she refused to play the roles dictated by her and her husband's place in the naval hierarchy. That night, for example, she not only argued with one of his superior officers but slapped him. She left alone before midnight. Two hours later, Thomas located her at home by phone. She told him to return at once. He found her bloodied and bruised. She said that five men had beaten and raped her. That night, police arrested five working-class men, the Hawaiians Benny Ahakuelo and Joseph Kahahawai, the Japanese Americans Horace Ida and David Takai, and the Chinese Hawaiian Henry Chang, for their role in an unrelated car accident. No evidence linked them to Thalia. Nor did doctors find evidence of rape. Thalia said she could not identify her attackers. But when the police showed her these men, she did just that. The police charged all five with rape.[5]

The haole press and U.S. military presumed their guilt. The *Advertiser* and *Star-Bulletin* labeled Massie's alleged attackers "degenerates" and "thugs" and denounced the "crime" against a "white woman of refinement and culture." Stirling told the press, "Our first inclination is to seize the brutes and string them up on trees," but he insisted on giving "the authorities a chance to carry out the law." Stirling brought Thalia into the Navy fold, describing her as "one of the younger set, demure, attractive, quiet-spoken, and sweet," the "daughter of prominent people in the Eastern

States, raised in a cultured American home." Thalia's mother, Grace Fortescue, a Washington socialite and niece of Alexander Graham Bell, took the first ship to Hawai'i.[6]

In December 1931, the jury found the evidence so flimsy that it failed to reach a verdict, resulting in a mistrial. Incorrectly insisting the jury voted along racial lines to protect the guilty and convinced a retrial would not return the verdict it wanted, Stirling in effect sanctioned lynching, stating that he "half suspected" that one or more defendants would soon be "swinging from trees by the neck." Within a week, several sailors abducted Horace Ida and beat him unconscious. In early January 1932, Grace Fortescue, Thomas Massie, and two enlisted men kidnapped Joseph Kahahawai. Intent on forcing a confession, one of them fatally shot him. Fortescue, Massie, and an enlisted man went to dump the body. A policeman stopped them for speeding and found the corpse. The police arrested all four and charged them with murder.[7]

Newspapers across the mainland insisted that the four accused had acted properly. They demanded that the U.S. government intervene to protect the sanctity of white women. The *New York Sunday News* led the U.S. media in proclaiming "Honor Killing in Honolulu Threatens Race War." On the front page of every Hearst paper in the nation, its founder proclaimed, "The situation in Honolulu is deplorable. It is becoming or has become an unsafe place for white women." Hearst insisted that "the whole island . . . be promptly put under martial law and the perpetrators of outrages upon women promptly tried by court martial and executed. Until such drastic measures are taken, Hawaii is not a safe place for decent white women and not a very good place for self-respecting civilized men." Most members of the mainland media agreed.[8]

Fortescue hired Clarence Darrow of Scopes trial fame to defend her and her alleged collaborators. Mainland reporters rushed to Honolulu to cover his performance, and radio stations broadcast his four-and-a-half-hour summation across the nation. But this time, the evidence and testimony left no reasonable doubt. The jury found the four defendants guilty of manslaughter. They recommended leniency, but the judge sentenced all of the convicted to the maximum penalty, ten years at hard labor.[9]

An outraged mainland media again spoke with near unanimity in demanding full pardons for the convicted. The media asked the secretary of the interior to impose military rule on Hawai'i, as did the secretary of the navy and other high-ranking military officers. Letters and phone calls poured into the office of Governor Lawrence Judd. Several senators called for military rule. One hundred three congressmen signed a petition urging Judd to grant full pardons "for the welfare of Hawaii," which he interpreted as a "thinly veiled threat." Judd refused to overturn the guilty verdict. Instead, he commuted the sentence to one hour, served in his office.[10] Walter Dillingham told a private audience of high-ranking military officers, including Stirling, why he supported Judd's decision, despite his belief that the men accused of rape were guilty. He elaborated in a not-so-secret, secret memorandum. Whites unfamiliar with Hawaiʻi could not understand the importance of demonstrating to "the people" that they have "no right to take the law into their own hands." Lynch law "may be condoned" where "whites are in the majority." But in Hawaiʻi, the specter of revolt by the nonwhite majority made it "vital to stress the necessity of abiding by the laws of the country."[11]

The outcome of the two trials split the haole community and Republican Party. It united people across lines of color and class against the haole establishment. The majority who decried the miscarriage of justice that allowed Kahahawai's convicted murderers to go free expressed their outrage in the press, at the polls, and on the street. Princess Abigail Kawānanakoa led the way: "Are we to infer from the Governor's act that there are two sets of laws in Hawaii—one for the favored few and one for the people generally?" The *Hawaii Hochi* asserted that "the Republican party has been discredited and many of the most powerful people in public life stand branded as traitors in the eyes of the common people." The 1932 territorial elections confirmed this view.[12]

For the first time in history, the Republicans did not sweep the territorial legislature. Ninety percent of registered voters elected an unprecedented number of Democrats and Chinese Americans and Japanese Americans, Republican and Democrat, to it. The number of Democrats elected quadrupled. Voters chose a Democrat as the nonvoting delegate from Hawaiʻi to the U.S. Congress. The election results for the Honolulu Board of Supervisors were the most striking, for local politics gave local voters an actual voice in territorial politics and mattered most to them. Prior to the elections, the Republicans held a six-to-one majority; afterward, the Democrats, a three-to-one majority. Two years earlier, some interpreted the election of a Japanese American as the beginning of a trend in which Asian Americans would join haole in further subjugating Natives. That happened in later decades, but in 1932, the Hawaiian vote proved critical to the election of

Asian Americans. And during the Massie trial, "local" became a popular term used to describe the five accused men and distinguish them and their supporters from their white accuser and her haole defenders. For the rest of the interwar period, Hawaiians, Chinese, Filipinos, Japanese, Koreans, and Portuguese struggled to articulate an identity of themselves as locals united by an inchoate interracialism and the experiences of colonialism and racism that Natives and immigrants shared, albeit in crucially different ways.[13] Theon Wright, a son of the *Hawaii Hochi's* English-language section editor and reporter who covered Kahahawai's murder case for the *Honolulu Advertiser*, later argued that the trial left "the missionary-sugar planter faction exposed in all its totalitarian nakedness." He identified it as the harbinger of the "second revolution" in Hawai'i, this one against the Big Five and haole governance.[14]

As Hawai'i locals worked to forge an interracial labor movement in Hawai'i, Cubans launched a revolution to oust Machado. As locals labored to construct interracial identities and politics and assert their rights as U.S. citizens and American settlers, Cubans sought to fulfill the unrealized dreams of Cuba Libre by building a nation *con todos y para todos* (with all and for all), validating *Afrocubanistas* across the color line who presented Cuba and *cubanidad* as a *mestizo* nation. The forces of revolution and antiracism aligned against those of reaction and racism again in Cuba and for the first time in Hawai'i.

The crash of Wall Street made Cuba's already dire situation worse. The sugar industry led a cycle replicated in every economic sector. Salaries and wages fell, businesses closed, workers were laid off. In January 1930, the government slashed salaries for all public employees except, tellingly, the armed forces. It soon joined the private sector in falling behind on payrolls. Opposition to the machadato swelled as economic distress exacerbated political outrage. It came to include workers and students, blacks and women, middle-class professionals and large landowners, communists and fascists, and segments of the armed forces and police, although they did not necessarily agree on anything but the need to oust Machado. Many elite opposition leaders across the color line presented themselves as a vanguard that would rebuild the nation, prepare ordinary Cubans for democracy, and contain the excesses of revolution. Mobilizing, the *clases populares* made a mockery of of the elite view that ordinary Cubans could continue to be repressed, excluded, or ignored. As government repression increased, the opposition retaliated. Violence rose. Assassinations, bombings, and drive-by shootings became so common that Cubans borrowed a term from a Hollywood genre, *gangsterismo*, to describe them.[15]

As U.S. officials launched their own plans to remove Machado, U.S. businessmen defended a regime that continued to make its loan payments. They had predicated their financial investments in Cuba on their political investments in Machado. The untimely death of John McEntee Bowman and closure of his Sevilla-Biltmore Hotel in 1931, due not just to the Depression but, as lawyer Mario Lazo put it, to its "heavy capitalization" and "absolutely indiscriminate" spending, left the Machado regime without its most visible and vocal U.S. ally. So Machado negotiated with the public relations pioneer Carl Byoir. He offered a lucrative contract to Carl Byoir & Associates if it would first spend its own capital to attract tourists to Havana and secure positive U.S. media coverage of Cuba. Byoir helped organize the "Committee of One Hundred" to solicit support from rich U.S. citizens in pursuit of these goals. Chemical industry magnate Irénée du Pont was a not atypical subscriber. A vacation in Cuba led him to join the Havana Country Club, build a mansion on Varadero Beach, sell property from his holdings there to "well-to-do people," and invest in sugar stocks and Chase bonds. Du Pont urged his senators to lower tariffs on Cuban sugar to allevi-ate distress and instability. Using the good name of men like du Pont, the Committee of One Hundred lobbied for more financing to enable the Cuban government to complete public works and service loans. It sup-ported a "Good-Will" tour of Cuba made by five hundred U.S. bankers and businessmen. A Chase-led syndicate loaned the government $20 mil-lion. These efforts may have helped extend Machado's regime.[16]

But then in late July 1933, Havana bus drivers struck. This spark ignited a wildfire. Soon, a general strike paralyzed the island, led to clashes between demonstrators and police, and transformed a series of rebellions into a revolution. U.S. Ambassador Sumner Welles ordered Machado to step down. He refused. Many Cubans demanded, and the United States threat-ened, intervention. Machado defied it to do so. Then the armed forces turned against Machado. He fled on August 12.[17]

In September, a group of sergeants, corporals, and enlisted men led by Fulgencio Batista y Zaldívar moved against the remaining Machado officers in what became known as the "sergeants' revolt." Combined with contin-ued revolt by ordinary civilians, the specter of ordinary white, black, and mulatto soldiers rising up against a corrupt and privileged white officers'

12. Village of the Havana poor. Walker Evans, 1933. Courtesy of J. Paul
Getty Museum, Los Angeles, California. Smart-set members like Karl
Decker saw a completely different Havana: "In no other Capital can one
swing from the heart of the city out into the suburbs and country beyond
without seeing through sordid, squalid sections—poverty-stricken and
depressing. . . . But Havana's outlet from the city is of itself a thing of
beauty. . . . For twelve miles the visitor to the Havana Biltmore Beach front
has never been within sight of a single unpleasing feature of landscape."
Karl Decker, *Havana, the Magazine of Cuba*, January 1, 1929.

corps filled white elites with dread. So did the military junta's selection of
the populist Dr. Ramón Grau San Martín as provisional president. Fearing
the worst and seeking proximity to the marines aboard U.S. warships
patrolling the harbor, Welles directed U.S. citizens to gather at the waterfront Hotel Nacional, a luxury complex backed by Machado that had
opened in 1931. The assembled prayed for a U.S. intervention that did not
materialize. As Machado's former officers and their families descended
upon the Nacional, tourists abandoned it and the island. In November,

soldiers loyal to Batista attacked in a battle that made clear that he controlled the armed forces. He rewarded junior officers and men across the color line with promotions.[18]

U.S. and Cuban white elites revived fears of a black peril as they moved to contain the historically entwined forces of antiracism and revolution. An associate cabled du Pont to say that race riots were possible in Cardenas. Many U.S. residents thought they were imminent in Havana. Some Havana radio stations alleged that black women "of the worst class" had attacked white "ladies" who sought refuge at the Nacional. White elites may have refused to accept the mulatto Batista as a social equal, but they did come to accept that only he could contain the forces of revolution. He in turn accepted that his future depended on collaborating with them.[19]

The United States refused to recognize the populist Grau regime, deeming it revolutionary. Grau unilaterally abrogated the Platt Amendment. His regime established a minimum wage, an eight-hour workday, and a Ministry of Labor, and ordered all businesses to give 50 percent of their jobs to the Cuban-born. It suspended payments on $80 million in loans and nationalized two sugar mills with ties to Machado and his allies. As Batista worked to secure the backing of the United States and find a president it would recognize, U.S. officials signaled their support by racially remaking him. In November 1933, a U.S. military attaché told Washington, "I am very much inclined now to believe that Batista is either of Chilean-Indian extraction or of Chilean-Mexican extraction, and not as first believed, half-negro and one-quarter Chinese." Elite Cubans did not follow suit. On New Year's Eve, Batista, his top aides, and their wives went to Sans Soucí nightclub. Upper-crust Cubans arose and stalked out, the first of many snubs to which they subjected Batista. Still, they agreed with U.S. actors. "Superior though they may have felt, they could no longer rule Cuba without Batista," Frank Argote-Freyre astutely observes.[20]

In January 1934, the United States recognized Carlos Mendieta as provisional president. It also recognized the need to make concessions not only to the new government but to Cubans. To spur economic recovery, the U.S. and Cuban governments negotiated a reciprocity treaty more favorable to Cuba. With the Jones-Costigan Act, the United States increased Cuba's share of the U.S. sugar market, fomenting economic recovery. Perhaps most importantly, the United States abrogated the hated Platt Amendment, making the Republic of Cuba a formally sovereign nation for the first time in its brief history.

The end of the Plattist state provided Cubans with the opportunity to promulgate a new constitution that would serve as the foundation of a new republic. Batista remained receptive to contradictory demands from ordinary Cubans for building a sovereign and inclusive nation and from white elites for maintaining race and class hierarchies. He played the roles, historian Robert Whitney argues, of "a dictator, an American ally, a populist, and a nationalist, and he kept Cubans and Americans alike guessing as to what he might do next." All recognized that the Revolution of 1933 had irrevocably changed Cuba. Many agreed on the need for an interventionist state to reconstitute the Cuban economy and build an honest and sovereign democratic nation-state governed especially by and for the citizens of the republic.[21]

The corruption, dependency, and dictatorship so intimately linked to U.S. capital in general, and the tourism industry in particular, animated nationalist searches for antidotes to Wall Street. Analyzing the entwined and conflicting racist, nationalist, and artistic discourses swirling about Havana in the 1930s, Robin Moore observes that even as "anti-black sentiment remained relatively strong among most commentators," it came under assault by "anti-imperialists who supported all forms of Cuban expression." Even white supremacists whom black and white Afrocubanistas presented as symbols of U.S. subordination understood and accepted mestizaje as a vehicle for pursuing the widely shared goal of Cubanizing Cuba and *cubanidad*.[22]

Although Cubans regarded the *ingenio* (sugar mill) as the national symbol of Wall Street, images of a segregated tourism industry built by and for privileged whites may have resonated more directly with *habaneros*. Snapshots of debates over tourism in general, and *comparsas* (Afro-Cuban music and dance processions) in particular, that raged in the late 1930s provide glimpses into Cuba's charged cultural politics. As Cuban Tourism Commission officials and Havana's mayor debated whether reintroducing *comparsas* to carnival would engender national pride or incite racial unrest, du Pont's lawyer asked the Tourism Commission to establish private beaches to keep the "undesirable classes" away. Meanwhile, Batista entered a partnership with mafioso Meyer Lansky to restore tourists' confidence in a corrupted gambling industry and to acquire the financial capital he needed to improve his cultural and political standing. As *Life* later observed, "Back in the 1930s, when Batista made his first bid for power in Cuba, he learned what a great asset gambling can be to a politician who needs money fast."[23]

Black and white Afrocubanistas targeted the tourism industry, and not just because its patrons, workers, and owners were white and its clubs, casinos, and many other venues, segregated. The Havana Country Club, Jockey Club, and Casino were the premier institutions of white elites of many nations who nonetheless regarded Cuba, an HCC president averred, as "our country." That many of its Cuban members had fought wars for freedom and racial equality only to help the United States limit Cuba's independence and transplant Jim Crow to the land of José Martí still registered as an unforgivable betrayal of Cuba Libre. No wonder Afrocubanismo and mestizaje proved powerful in animating efforts to build a sovereign and inclusive nation. Comparsas became one of many sites (including beaches, parks, and rumba) bound up with tourism where Cubans translated "battles over representation" into "battles for rights and citizenship," as historian Alejandra Bronfman argues.[24]

After receiving assurances from the esteemed anthropologist Fernando Ortiz that reintroducing comparsas to carnival would not incite "racial conflicts and political disturbances," Havana's mayor acted on the Tourism Commission's recommendation to reintroduce them in 1937. The state had banned comparsas from carnival after its brutal repression of the revolt led by the Partido Independiente de Color in 1912. The opportunity comparsas presented to experience a local spectacle and learn about Cuban culture would draw U.S. tourists; the opportunity they presented to experience a collective national identity rooted in mestizaje would lure Cubans. Supporting comparsas offered a way for a reorganized Tourism Commission to distance itself from the machadato, while publicly demonstrating its commitments to building a sovereign and inclusive nation. Reintroducing comparsas to carnival seemed to bring what Ortiz called internal tourism and international tourism into harmonious alignment.[25]

Comparsas emerged as a site of cultural and political contestation over different visions of citizenship and nationhood. Their performance reinforced reactionary whites' view that Afro-Cuban culture and citizens were barbaric, exotic, and primitive, a view to which at least one Tourism Commission brochure lent its full weight, describing comparsas as "typical Afro-Cuban pageants . . . based on the traditional slave celebration of their one day of freedom, granted every year. On that occasion they gave vent to pent-up passions in the form of native Africa, accompanied by exotic music and the throbbing beat of tom-toms." The mayor's demand that Afro-Cuban music be "purified," "elevated," and "perfected" reflected elites' beliefs that they needed to work from above to reform the nation and national culture and prepare the clases populares for self-government. For many critics, stereotypical representations of African traditions in comparsas reproduced in the performative sphere the inequality blacks suffered in the political sphere. For many supporters, the performances validated blackness in national culture, thereby exposing the racism institutionalized in the first republic by Cuban and U.S. imperial agents and preparing the way for its dismantlement in the second.[26] Bronfman shows that as black activists prepared for the upcoming constitutional convention, they applied "issues of marginalization and cultural representation raised by the comparsas to issues of legal and political representation." They made demands that the state legislate against all forms of discrimination central to debates leading up to the constitutional convention.[27]

As Cubans drew on shared histories of racial equality and revolutionary struggle in pursuing antidotes to Wall Street, locals across the color line in Hawai'i began to build an interracial labor movement as an antidote to the Big Five. Unlike Cubans, the diverse people of Hawai'i did not have a shared history of revolutionary struggle or much of a shared identity as Americans or U.S. citizens, the latter not even available to Asian immigrants. Yet even as Cubans worked to build a post-Plattist state freed from U.S. influence, Hawai'i locals found an ally in the U.S. metropolitan state, specifically the New Deal agents charged with advancing labor's rights. In Cuba, tourism became a contested site of cultural politics between multinational white elites and anti-imperial, and according to the group, antiracist, Cuban nationalists. By contrast in Hawai'i, haole turned to tourism to restore an authority and power challenged by an emergent labor movement and calls for U.S. military rule and other forms of U.S. intervention.

After the two trials that resulted from Massie's rape allegation, the U.S. government sought to expand its authority and oversight of Hawai'i. In 1932, Congress introduced two bills to impose military rule. They inspired much debate but died when the U.S. military, which expanded its collaborations with the Big Five as tensions with Japan rose, led the way in withdrawing support for them. Two years later, the Jones-Costigan Act took effect. Designed to foment economic recovery in Cuba, it increased Cuba's share of the U.S. market and decreased that of Hawai'i, the Philippines, and Puerto Rico. It also reclassified Hawai'i as a foreign producer, reversing the domestic status the United States had accorded it since annexation.

Enactment of the Jones-Costigan Act, combined with the most serious calls for U.S. military rule since annexation, persuaded the Big Five that statehood had its merits.[28] In 1935, the Big Five directed the delegate to the U.S. Congress to agitate for statehood. Yet haole remained ambivalent about it, due to fears of empowering a growing nonwhite electorate, fears magnified by concerns of the sort of state government the Democratic administration of President Franklin D. Roosevelt might sponsor. Indeed, to their shock and amazement, his New Deal agents not only documented labor abuses in Hawai'i but actually acted on their findings. Haole were used to the U.S. government serving their interests, not those of workers, especially those of color.[29]

The National Labor Relations Board (NLRB) supported workers' organizing efforts. Metropolitan state intervention opened a space that aided interracial organizing efforts and solidarity, which secret naval intelligence reported on the rise a year after Kahahawai's murder. Sociologist Moon-Kie Jung argues that the Big Five had long "ruthlessly exerted dictatorial powers to eradicate any semblance of organization among island workers." They saw no reason to obey the Wagner Act any more than they did the Desha Bathing Suit Law, a rarely enforced Honolulu statute that prohibited wearing an uncovered bathing suit in public. After arriving in Hawai'i in 1937, the NLRB forced haole to allow waterfront, sugar-mill, and pineapple-cannery workers to organize and gain union recognition. Its agents compelled management to negotiate with strikers for the first time in history. As haole sought to exploit the linguistic, racial, and national divisions that had served their antilabor interests before, workers struggled to transform a vision of themselves as locals into a labor movement built on interracial solidarity. But in the late 1930s, the labor movement remained plagued by anti-Filipino and anti-Japanese racism, as well as continued resistance by employers. During World War II, the military governor outlawed strikes and unions. Yet Jung shows, the "big organizing campaign between 1944 and 1946, was in essence, the union's prewar story . . . writ large and rapid."[30]

Haole turned to tourism to restore their authority in the islands and on the mainland. The Outrigger Canoe Club organized the Waikīkī Beach Patrol to bring the beach boys under centralized control. When Shirley Temple vacationed in Hawai'i in 1935, the Beach Patrol made her its first honorary captain. Widely published photographs of the child star with Olympic swimming champion Duke Kahanamoku testified to the sanctity of all white women and children in the care of the beach boys. The year before, photographs of Franklin Roosevelt, the first sitting president to visit Hawai'i, had offered visual reassurances that Hawai'i was as stable as it was beautiful. His secret plans to spy on Japanese immigrants and U.S. citizens and intern them in the event of war with Japan offered assurances of political and racial order to haole in the know. Between the Massie case and World War II, promoters erased Asians from tourism literature and landscapes. They no longer mentioned, much less celebrated, Japanese Americans, Chinese Americans, and Filipino Americans. The Massie and Kahahawai cases had made a mockery of claims that multiracial Hawai'i had solved the problem of the races, so haole promoted it as a South Sea paradise peopled solely by caring whites and carefree natives or just by whites acting out fantasies of native culture.[31]

The Hawaiian Sugar Planters' Association, the Hawaii Tourist Bureau, and Matson Navigation Lines hired the San Francisco advertising firm Bowman, Deute, Cummings to restore the islands' tarnished image. Sydney Bowman established the Pan-Pacific Press to coordinate the simultaneous appearance in mainland papers and journals of HTB ads and the stories, features, and editorials it produced. Bowman invited editors and reporters on expense-paid vacations. *Atlantic, Harper's, Scribner's, Colliers, Vogue, Woman's Home Companion*, the *New Yorker*, and *Red Book* were among those who sent writers and published favorable articles on Hawai'i as a tourist paradise and statehood candidate, a view Bowman's agents also sought to impress on visiting congressmen. Bowman launched the weekly radio show *Hawaii Calls*. Broadcasting Hawai'i music and tropical delights, it became the most popular and influential medium through which fantasies of Hawai'i traveled to the U.S. mainland.

In a 1939 memoir, Rear Admiral Stirling made a scathing critique of haole mismanagement of the Massie case and the threat both haole and the Japanese posed to national security at a time when war with Japan seemed imminent. In 1940, *Fortune* condemned the Big Five's handling of the Massie case, the "ignorance" in which the HTB kept the "average man" about the importance of Hawai'i to national security, the Pan-Pacific Press's management of reporters, and the sincerity of the sudden haole desire for statehood. Citing the Big Five's "paternalistic semi-feudalism," *Fortune* argued that its pursuit of statehood was a public-relations move designed to block post-Massie interventions by the United States and protest the Jones-Costigan Act. Following Stirling, most damning of all was *Fortune*'s conten-

Matson Line to Hawaii

NEW ZEALAND · AUSTRALIA VIA SAMOA · FIJI

There are so many reasons to be happy in Hawaii

Complete details of fascinating Matson Cruises through the South
Pacific from all Travel Agents or Matson Line-Oceanic Line, New York,
Chicago, San Francisco, Los Angeles, San Diego, Seattle, Portland.

*Hawaiian hotel reservations, at the beautiful Royal Hawaiian and Moana on
Waikiki Beach, can now be made at the same time you book your steamer passage.*

S. S. LURLINE · S. S. MARIPOSA · S. S. MONTEREY · S. S. MALOLO

*Natural color photograph
taken at Waikiki Beach*
© MATSON NAVIGATION CO. 1937

13. The sexually liberated white woman tourist enjoying the company of a
surfer was used to promote different visions of Hawai'i before and after the
Massie case: before, as an introduction to a harmonious multiracial melting
pot that had solved the problem of the races; after, as an advertisement for
a South Seas paradise peopled either by happy whites and carefree natives
together or whites alone under the seductive spell of a tropical island Eden.
Advertisement, Matson Navigation Lines, 1937. Reproduced courtesy of
Matson Navigation Company archives.

tion that the "loyalty" of haole to the United States was as questionable as that of the Japanese. It condemned haole for refusing "to think of themselves as part of any grand scheme of U.S. defense." *Fortune* insisted that haole had much "*civic* pride" but little "*nationalist* pride." They regarded Hawai'i as neither paradise nor bastion of defense "but just a darned good place to live, to make and invest money, and to hand on all its wealth and loveliness to satisfied sons and daughters." The article caused a scandal, confirming for some and convincing other civilian and military officials, media members, and just plain citizens of the lack of haole loyalty to the United States.[32]

Journalist Joseph Barber built upon *Fortune*'s article in a popular 1941 book on the Big Five's quest to maintain its "island monopoly" while countering its image as a "devouring ogre." Barber agreed with *Fortune* that the Massie trials had prompted the Big Five to promote tourism and statehood in a "strategic move" to stave off metropolitan interference in local affairs. He charged that haole hired Bowman to combat the appeal of the New Deal and unions among locals. Even as Bowman labored to convince visitors and congressmen that "Hawaii was truly the tourists' paradise, that it was thoroughly American, loyal, progressive, worthy of statehood," he sought to discredit the New Deal's "championship of the rights of labor" among teachers, workers, and immigrant newspapers. He worked to convince immigrant newspapers to publish articles favorable to the Big Five. He hired operatives to spy on workers' and teachers' meetings, which led to the firing and blacklisting of some deemed "obnoxious to industry." Barber averred that as New Deal agents, the working class, and the middle class of Asian ancestry labored to democratize Hawai'i, Congress remained complicit in maintaining the Big Five's monopoly of wealth and power: "As long as Hawaii is permitted by Federal legislation to raise and market annually upward of a million tons of sugar and ten to fifteen million cases of canned pineapple, . . . there will be small likelihood of the Big Five and the HSPA being pried loose from their control." Big Five executives "have frequently made capital in Washington of their contention that island stability demands the maintenance of the status quo."[33]

Promoting tourism and statehood may have returned tourists to Hawai'i, but it backfired politically. Confronted with ongoing challenges to their authority from above and below, haole breathed a sigh of relief when the United States imposed martial law after the Japanese bombed Pearl Harbor. As Lorrin P. Thurston, son of the leading annexationist and the military governor's public relations advisor put it at the end of World War II, "They did it and we liked it."[34]

In the Shadow of the Constitution and Martial Law

The United States imposed martial law in Hawai'i a year after Cuba promulgated a new constitution. War technically ended tourism in both places. Although the million-plus defense personnel who passed through or were stationed in Hawai'i spent money like tourists and the military used tourism to acculturate them to Hawai'i, their class and often their race marked them as alien to the rich whites whom haole and locals knew as tourists.[35] Postwar plans for tourism in Cuba and Hawai'i developed in the respective shadows of the constitution and martial law. While the constitution provided a framework that Cubans hoped would enable them to build a sovereign and inclusive political economy, martial law deepened the determination of locals to overturn haole governance and build an inclusive U.S. state and economy. The war helped Hawai'i end dependence on sugar but revitalized Cubans' commitment to it.

The Constitution of 1940 was remarkable for both its liberalism and its inclusion of the desires of ordinary people across lines of color and class. It provided for free elections, universal adult suffrage, and the freedom of association, speech, religion, and the press. It guaranteed the right to strike, social insurance, workers' compensation, pensions, paid vacations, minimum wages, maximum hours, and equal pay for equal work. It outlawed racial and other forms of discrimination, including in the workplace, and guaranteed minorities representation in elected bodies. It made the state responsible for full employment and diversified development. But much of the constitution required the enactment of enabling laws. Laws illegalizing racial discrimination never passed. Still, it filled Cubans with the hope that building a sovereign, inclusive, and honest nation was in reach. They elected Batista as president in 1940.[36]

World War II provided the revenues Batista used to increase wages, finance the welfare state during the war, and accumulate capital for development after it. World War II pulled Cuba out of nearly two decades of continuous depression and produced national prosperity. War in Europe and Asia caused world sugar production to fall 60 percent. After the U.S. military announced that it would buy all of the sugar produced by Hawai'i, the U.S. government negotiated to purchase Cuba's entire crop. The industry shifted "from enforced underproduction to all-out production for war." At the war's end, the United States continued to buy most of Cuba's sugar for its troops. Just as the restoration of global production threatened to depress prices and Cuba's share of the U.S. market, the Korean War caused demand and prices to surge upward.[37]

The renewed prosperity of a sugar industry increasingly owned by Cubans revitalized their commitment to an industry that had reached the limits of growth and had never provided steady employment. Between 1934 and 1951, Cubans purchased forty-seven mills for $48 million. These investments were more than financial. Sugar was a leading symbol of Cuban identity, which along with the post-Plattist state, Cubans could finally claim as their own. National pride reinforced economic commitments, for when sugar performed well, it paid fabulous dividends. As Marifeli Pérez-Stable argues, "Breaking the sugar conundrum required social initiative, political action, and national vision." It also required political access.[38]

Tourism professionals worked to build a case for this industry's role in the postwar political economy. The industry's association with corruption, dictatorship, and vice hampered efforts to obtain support of the organizers of a constitutionally mandated central development bank and development experts who sought to end dependence on sugar and reduce high unemployment and underemployment. These efforts were led by prominent leaders of the 1933 revolution, including historian Ramiro Guerra, progressive economists Julián Alienes Uroso and Felipe Pazos, lawyer José Alvarez Díaz, and banker Joaquín Martínez Saénz.[39]

These men were divided over the place of tourism in Cuba's development and compared it to sugar to defend their positions. Guerra for one thought that tourism should become Cuba's "segunda zafra" or second harvest. By contrast, Alienes contended that these industries shared the same problems: seasonal employment, fierce competition, a troubling source of balance-of-payments fluctuations, and dependence on the United States as a primary source of capital and imports. In his 1944 book, El Turismo, engineer Victor Santamarina recast tourism as a national industry, nationalistic project, and a year-round industry that would help the state deliver services to rural areas and raise living standards and generate full-time employment for all Cubans.[40]

Santamarina argued that tourism promotion needed to focus more on "natural wealth" than urban resorts and nightlife, for Cuba possessed extensive mineral springs and mountain regions. Noting that spas and mountain resorts in the eastern United States earned the same amount from tourism that Florida did, Santamarina asserted that Cuba could compete with all of them. Building spas especially required investments in health, medical, and sanitation systems that could be designed to benefit tourists and Cubans. Arkansas's Hot Springs brought such services and jobs to a poor rural area. And France employed 600,000 workers in spas across the nation. In citing France, Santamarina drew on Havana's reputation as the Paris of the Caribbean to set up his point. Cuba's natural wealth awaited development into a *national* tourist industry and "grand public work" that would provide full-time jobs, health-care, and sanitation for all.[41]

Before debates on Santamarina's proposals could take place, tourism and corruption converged again. Taking office in 1944, President Ramón Grau San Martín and his Auténtico Party members assumed responsibility of a full treasury. They pledged to finance public works to promote diversification and create jobs. They instead used state funds to diversify their portfolios. For example, supporting expanded tourism, Grau began construction on a new road from Rancho Boyero Airport to downtown Havana. A scant mile reached completion during his four-year presidency. At his term's end, he faced formal charges that he had embezzled $174 million in state funds.[42] Furthermore, Grau outraged the members of Havana's exclusive country- and yacht-club set by promoting the interests of tourism-industry workers. This set's members had long financed tourism; some of them were organizing the central bank. In 1943, Grau supported the formation of the Gastronomic Workers' Union and raises for its first members, cooks and waiters. Cuba's version of the "Big Five" (HCC, Havana Yacht Club, Havana Biltmore, Miramar Yacht Club, and Casino Español) struck back. During the 1946 holiday season, the clubs cancelled Christmas and New Year's Eve parties rather than concede to workers' demands for better wages and conditions. They dealt similarly with the Musicians' Union.[43]

As the new constitution filled Cubans with hope, martial law in Hawai'i deepened locals' resentments of a haole ruling class whose most powerful members had supported military rule. From the bombing of Pearl Harbor on December 7, 1941, through October 24, 1944, the people of Hawai'i lived under martial law. The U.S. Army suspended the writ of habeas corpus, took over the courts, censored the press, froze wages, regulated the movements and occupations of workers, outlawed strikes and unions, and

took control of most government functions. The army's commanding officer became the military governor and assumed most executive, legislative,
and judicial powers. The Big Five, Dillingham, and other conservative haole
supported military rule, incensing most locals and liberal haole. Their smol-
dering resentments exploded into purposeful action after the lifting of martial law.[44]

The Japanese were the main target of martial law. The military shut
down Japanese-language schools and newspapers. It closed Japanese-owned
banks and froze their deposits and assets. It banned Japanese from many
jobs. Interning the territory's nearly 160,000 Japanese and Americans of
Japanese Ancestry (AJAs) was simply not possible, for they constituted a
majority of the population and workforce. So the United States interned
nearly 3,400 of their community leaders and thereby "held hostage not only
the internees but the entire race."[45] The United States allowed 3,000 of
Hawaiʻi AJAs to serve in the Japanese American 100th Infantry Battalion
and 442nd Regimental Combat Team. When President Roosevelt activated
the 442nd in February 1943, he insisted, "Americanism is not and never
was a matter of race and ancestry."[46] But the previous February, he had
ordered the internment of nearly 120,000 Japanese U.S. citizens and immigrants on the mainland precisely on the basis of race and ancestry.

In four years, the U.S. military transformed Oʻahu from a rural, agricultural society into an urban, service-based one. In contrast to Cuba, where
the renewed prosperity of an increasingly Cuban-owned sugar industry
revitalized faith in monocrop export agriculture, in Hawaiʻi, defense
replaced agriculture as the islands' economic base during, and again soon
after, the war. Hawaiʻi served as the western outpost for the nation's defense
and the staging ground for the million-plus troops who fought in the
Pacific Theater. The military also took control of sugar, pineapple, and
tourism. It purchased virtually all Hawaiian sugar and pineapple. It regulated all aspects of tourism, from hotels to prostitution to photos with hula
girls. The military made the Big Five provide it with land, electricity, water,
equipment, and workers. Planters reaped far more than workers from labor
"loans." The military paid laborers diverted to the docks forty-two cents
an hour and planters sixty-two cents an hour per worker. As workers' wages
remained frozen, planters profited from 514,130 person-days of loaned
labor.[47]

Workers resumed their challenge to the Big Five the moment martial
law ended, aided by the Hawaii Labor Relations Act allowing agricultural

workers to unionize. Their work at building an interracial politics and identity was aided by the implosion of the equation of U.S. nationalism and anti-Japanese racism. Between 1944 and 1946, the International Longshoremen's and Warehousemen's Union (ILWU) transformed Hawai'i from the least to the most unionized U.S. territory or state. In 1946, 1947, and 1949, ILWU workers staged successful industry-wide strikes in sugar, pineapple, and shipping respectively. The 1946 strike so rocked the plantation order that "people began to talk about the One Big Union and the Big Five . . . as if they were equally matched contestants for power." Such statements exaggerated the power of the union, but it did capture the solidarity workers forged in highly selective identity narratives. They wove the history of all the diverse laborers of Hawai'i into a story of unified action of progressive locals against haole white supremacists, eliding workers' recent racism, particularly against the Filipinos and Japanese.[48]

Refusing to be left out of a story of success and progress, haole tourism industry representatives sought to write themselves into the emerging quest of Hawai'i for interracial solidarity and democracy. The Honolulu Chamber of Commerce presented tourism and statehood as the twinned future of Hawai'i in a blueprint report for the future it published in 1946. That January, its members had voted unanimously on a resolution favoring immediate statehood, a move designed to cleanse the chamber of the stain acquired by its support of martial law. In *Hawaii's Postwar Plans*, the chamber did not mention military rule. Instead, it proclaimed that wartime experiences had produced a modern, urban, upwardly mobile, and racially tolerant society characterized by "new ways of living, new wants and desires." Together, the islands' patriotic, democratic, and upwardly mobile U.S. consumer-citizens would build "the Hawaii of Tomorrow . . . a place of new and more unified Americanism; a Territory securely proved worthy of Statehood, and an area where the highest standards of living and the healthiest way of life may be enjoyed." The cover of the chamber's report showed how Hawai'i would achieve these goals. In the foreground, a couple of white tourists stopped their convertible to congratulate local fishermen on their catch. Pleasure boats and cruise ships plied the sparkling waters of the harbor, behind which rose the bustling city of Honolulu. In the distance, a wisp of steam rose from the stack of a lone sugar mill; the cane fields were indistinct. The image made clear that a booming tourism industry would replace a fading plantation regime. Tourism would provide the full employment and mass consumption that would lift all the U.S. citizens of Hawai'i

to economic equality, extend to them all the rights and privileges of consumer-citizenship, and help this part of the consumers' republic demonstrate its worthiness to join the Union as a state.[49]

The labor movement naturally sought better wages and conditions for
workers, but it was part of a broader movement in which locals across class
lines committed themselves to the more ambitious goal of transforming a
haole-controlled plantation society into an egalitarian multiracial political
economy. Among those who sought to overturn the white supremacist
plantation order was a growing managerial and professional class of U.S.
citizens of Chinese and Japanese descent. During the interwar period, the
Chinese had moved into the banking, real estate, construction, and insurance sectors, especially within ethnic and island communities. After the
war, they invested in enterprises in competition with haole across the territory. For example, in 1947 Chinn Ho established Capital Investments and
became the first local to purchase land from the Big Five. Ho challenged
the haole monopoly of land ownership by selling fee-simple lots to homeowners, farmers, and business owners long denied the opportunity to own
land.[50]

Returning AJA veterans became upwardly mobile as well, and many
moved into the public sector. Above all, their service in the war confirmed
the claims of all Japanese to U.S. citizenship. Their service with the 442nd
and 100th made them one of the most decorated units in U.S. Army history. Many AJAs had completed undergraduate degrees before the war.
They took advantage of the GI Bill and Veterans Administration loans to
obtain mainland graduate educations, particularly in law. They returned to
pursue careers in business, the professions, and politics, especially as members of a Democratic Party they helped energize and came to lead.[51]

Invocations of military service permeated representations of their entry
into politics. Katsumi Kometani asserted, "We have helped win the war on
the battlefront but we have not yet won the war on the home front. We
shall have won these things only when we attain those things for which our
country is dedicated, namely equality of opportunity and the dignity of
man." Daniel Inouye remembered, "We were not about to go back to the
plantation. . . . Day after day, rally after rally, we hammered home the
point that there must be no more second-class citizens in the Hawaii of
tomorrow." Matsuo Takabuki concurred, "Many of us were no longer willing to accept the same system. We wanted to change the way things were
in Hawaii. . . . We were not revolutionaries . . . [but] willing to play by the

rules of the game." They were not radicals, as conservative haole alleged. It could not have been otherwise. Although heroic masculine service to the state during war legitimized their standing as first-class U.S. citizens, Cold War constructions of patriotism limited the ability of all citizens, especially those of color, to pursue radical change. Politically influential AJA veterans were reformers, not radicals.[52]

The Democrats sought to redistribute wealth and income through land and tax reform. They advocated property and income taxes to shift the burden "from those least able to pay to those most able to pay" and to make fee-simple ownership the rule, not the exception. They backed higher minimum wages and public expenditures on education, health, housing, workers' compensation, and welfare. They supported opportunities for locals to own and manage diverse businesses at a time when haole banks and firms catered to and employed mainly whites.[53]

As a social and political movement of locals that included progressive haole forged a competitive Democratic Party, the haole-led Republican Party continued to fracture. Its two factions pitted the Big Five, Thurston, Dillingham, and other martial law supporters against moderates, led by the territory's congressional delegate, Joseph R. Farrington, and others who had protested martial law and the handling of the Massie and Kahahawai cases. Many of the latter supported the Democrats' platform. Finally, many moderate Republicans joined Democrats in calling for immediate statehood.[54]

Determined to prevent the further erosion of their power and authority, old-guard haole led the opposition to statehood in Hawai'i (especially immediate statehood), despite frequent declarations of advocacy. Opening the governorship to a vote and enabling Hawai'i to send voting senators and congressmen to Washington promised to diminish the power of haole in the islands and on the mainland. The Big Five and their allies worked to prevent the redistribution of their wealth and their power. Among other things, they accelerated the mechanization of the sugar industry, expanded their investments overseas, and worked to discredit ILWU leaders by labeling them communists and aiding federal prosecutions of them.[55]

Conservative haole played into the hands of statehood opponents on the mainland. While Presidents Truman and Eisenhower, the Departments of Defense, Interior, and State, much of the business and popular press, and Gallup polls publicly supported Hawaiian statehood, powerful opponents rallied against it. Led by, but not limited to southerners, many in Congress refused to countenance statehood for a multiracial territory. Cold warriors charged that organized labor in Hawai'i was radical, communist, or both, and therefore that admission of the territory was unthinkable. Others opposed statehood on the grounds that the Big Five was a feudal oligarchy, which might be acceptable for a plantation colony but not a U.S. state. Antimonopoly and anticommunism charges often stood in for racism. Red-baiting by Lorrin P. Thurston, the first postwar chair of the (Republican) Hawaii Statehood Commission (HSC) and the Hawaii Visitors Bureau (HVB), ensured derailment of a 1947 statehood bill in Congress, although Thurston was well aware of the limited influence communists had in Hawai'i. He revealed his fears in a talk he had with the antistatehood Dillingham in the late 1950s. Dillingham ordered Thurston to resign from the HSC "or else," saying, "he didn't want a goddamn Jap—to quote him exactly—to be governor or members of the Supreme Court, or the other official government offices . . . most of which has come true; and I hated it as much as he, but I'm still glad we got statehood."[56]

An array of haole-dominated institutions united to promote tourism and a conservative vision of eventual statehood. The Honolulu Chamber of Commerce, the Hawaii Visitors Bureau, the Bank of Hawaii, Hawaii Economic Foundation, the *Paradise of the Pacific*, Thrum's *Hawaiian Almanac and Annual,* and Thurston's *Honolulu Advertiser* concurred that tourism represented the future. Ignoring the calls by labor, Chinese and AJA middle classes, and Democrats for developing a highly diversified economy, in 1950 the acting territorial governor championed tourism alone in a letter to the Department of Interior: "There is now complete agreement that the further development of the tourist trade is Hawaii's greatest economic opportunity." In response to demands for political and economic democracy from locals and liberal haole, from Democrats and moderate Republicans, old-guard haole did what they had done before. They turned to tourism to shore up the status quo.[57]

In sharp contrast to Hawai'i, in Cuba, modernizers led by the first president and research head of the Banco Nacional de Cuba (BNC), which opened in 1950, ranked tourism a long-term goal, not a short-term priority. Pazos and Alienes committed to diversifying agriculture and improving living standards for the poor rural majority, which did not ideally position Cuba for competing in a booming Caribbean market. Between 1949 and 1952 the number of tourists visiting Cuba rose from 180,000 to 220,000, but Cuba's share of the Caribbean market fell from 43 to 36 percent. From 1951 to

1955, the number of tourists visiting Cuba increased 18 percent, white those visiting Puerto Rico increased 83 percent; Nassau, 92 percent; and, the Dominican Republic, 118 percent. As Cuban tourism grew a *total* of 18 percent, Hawai'i experienced an *annual* average growth rate of 18 percent.[58]

Shockingly, from a balance-of-payments perspective Cuba did not even have a tourist industry in the first decade after World War II. Although the Cuban Tourism Commission reported that tourists and cruise-ship passengers spent $44 million in Cuba in 1951, the BNC labeled this figure "arbitrary and high." The bank estimated that foreigners spent only $19 million in Cuba that year, while Cubans spent $50 million vacationing and shopping in the United States, resulting in a balance of payments loss of $31 million. Such estimates prompted a London observer to comment, "The moral to be drawn by British exporters is that Miami is a good place in which to make sales to Cubans who find British goods too expensive in Havana." The sums Cubans spent in the United States did not account for the dollars and monetary instruments they smuggled there. Rather than U.S. tourism serving as a source of Cuba's foreign earnings, Cuban overseas tourism funneled a sizable portion of national wealth and income to the United States.[59]

In 1951, six years after the Anglo-American Caribbean Commission presented Cuba as the model for Caribbean tourist development, the International Bank for Reconstruction and Development, which soon changed its name to the World Bank, reached the opposite conclusion. It wasn't the lack of hotels, amenities, infrastructure, or plans for them that troubled the bank's investigators. It was the "government attitude that Cuba is a ready-made tourist attraction. The professional view is that . . . it is not." World Bank investigators complained that Cuban tourist officials failed to grasp modern marketing, consumer desire, planning, and global and regional competition. They insisted that labor was at the root of Cuba's tourism woes. Without mentioning that the cost of living in Havana rivaled that of New York City, the World Bank asserted that the Cuban state so protected the wages of union labor in hotels that in this undeveloped nation, "wage-rates are roughly equivalent to those in first-class American hotels." It concluded on an ironic note of optimism: "So much needs to be done that Cuba is almost in the position of having to start from scratch. . . . Her scope need not be too greatly restricted by the necessity to make the best use of what already exists, because . . . little exists to be used."[60]

The World Bank report must have dismayed Cuban tourism professionals. But once Batista returned to power in 1952, they had reason to celebrate, for he committed to developing tourism. Batista's regime and the
haole in Hawai'i adopted similar positions on tourism. Expanded tourism
would raise the standards of living and mass consumerism and, they hoped,
produce constituencies of contented consumer-citizens. Consumption
would compensate for a lack of, or slow progress toward, civic and civil
rights and inclusive participatory democracy.

Bloodless Restoration, Bloodless Revolution

On March 10, 1952, Fulgencio Batista avoided his certain defeat in the
upcoming presidential election through a coup. On the opening night of
carnival, he and his conspirators took control of the government, he later
crowed, in an hour and seventeen minutes. Batista suspended constitutional guarantees, dissolved Congress, closed the university and many press
offices, occupied union and Communist Party headquarters, and called off
elections until 1954.

Cubans applauded and condemned Batista's coup. Most welcomed the
end of a decade of rule by the corrupt and violent Auténtico Party but
denounced the suspension of constitutional government. A U.S. Embassy
official who traveled across the island reported a "general consensus"
among Cubans "of resentment, if not shame . . . that Cuba does not have
a constitutional government." They believed that their progressive constitution had put them on a par with the United States and distinguished their
enlightened republic from despotic dictatorships elsewhere in the Americas.[61]

Batista's coup coincided with Cuba's then largest sugar harvest of over
seven million tons and a sharp drop in its global price. These two events
compelled his government to stockpile nearly two million tons of sugar to
prevent a collapse of the national economy and world sugar market.
Depression descended. Historically high levels of unemployment and
underemployment rose further. Nicolas Rivero, whose family owned the
conservative newspaper *Diario de la Marina*, offered a chilling comparison:
"In the worst year of the worst depression in United States history there
were about 25 percent unemployed, which is the normal unemployment
percentage for Cuba." Declining real wages and standards of living left

Cubans in about the position they had been in the 1920s. In the first year of Batista's rule, per capita income fell 18 percent.[62]

In addition to producing hardship, economic decline threatened another claim to civilized modernity that many Cubans, especially *habaneros*, enjoyed: a U.S. consumer lifestyle without parallel elsewhere in the world, even Europe. The U.S. Commerce Department noted that the Cuban worker "has wider horizons" than "most Latin American" and "many European workers. . . . His goal is to reach a standard of living comparable with that of the American worker." Batista exploited this desire in courting support for his dictatorship from former allies, especially the middle class and labor, until the promised elections of 1954. Declaring himself a "democratic dictator" and "dictator with the people," he promised "peace, employment, and prosperity" through development programs focused on tourism and light industry.[63]

Rebuilding tourism depended upon Batista's ability both to attract investors and secure U.S. support for his regime. Two weeks after the coup, the Cuban Tourism Commission reported it had proposals from U.S. capitalists to invest $50 million in the industry. Overblown at best, the claim expressed confidence in Batista's ability to reverse declining U.S. investments in tourism. The timing was fortuitous. The U.S. Kefauver Senate Crime Committee had recently prompted many states to crack down or ban gambling. Slot machines rendered useless in Florida had already resurfaced in Cuba. Other Caribbean islands intended to capitalize on this market. But none could claim Havana's reputation as the "vice capital of the world," a distinction not limited to gambling. As *Time* proclaimed when it featured a beaming Batista on its cover after his coup, Havana was also "one of the world's fabled fleshpots." Batista hoped to capitalize on this sex-and-sin reputation, but to do so he needed the backing of the very promoters and developers who blamed labor for the lack of investment in tourism.[64]

Cuban and U.S. tourism observers insisted that labor and state protections of it lay at the root of the lack of investor interest. A U.S. Embassy official criticized the state for failing to recognize that "the principal obstacles to any appreciable growth in Cuban tourist business are two: excessive hotel rates and prices for meals, due largely to the administration of labor laws." He summarized industry observers' complaints: "Hotel and restaurant employees . . . are so expensive, so independent, and so inefficient, that the high prices charged to cover labor costs, when combined with the

poor service given, cannot fail to drive more and more tourists away."
Havana's mayor concurred: "Salaries demanded by the gastronomicos, as
everyone knows in Cuba, are so extraordinary that they do not permit
hotels to operate adequately."[65]

Experiencing the same declining incomes as most Cubans, the *gastronómicos* did not agree. In January 1952, six thousand of them staged a one-day
strike to reinforce previous demands for a 30 percent wage increase. When
the state waived a 2.75 percent tax on gross sales, management agreed to a
lesser raise. Batista could ill afford to alienate organized labor, a historic
ally. But there were other issues. Batista had more confidence in his ability
to revitalize the tourism industry than the U.S. government had in his ability to weather challenges to his political power.[66]

Although worried about his staying power, the United States recognized
the Batista government seventeen days after the coup on the basis of his
Cold War credentials, that is, his pledge to protect U.S. capital, contribute
to the security of the hemisphere, and contain communism. Some Cubans
thought the U.S. government had aided Batista's return. Three days before
the coup, the two nations signed agreements to provide Cuba with equipment, training, and weapons for hemispheric security under the Mutual
Defense Assistance Act. Although the coup apparently came as a "complete
surprise" to the United States, it did not protest Batista's use of U.S. weapons for internal repression rather than collective security. Instead, U.S.
officials urged discretion. In January 1953, the ambassador reported that
since the military was "more preoccupied" with maintaining its "own political position than with contributing to continental defense, [it is] essential
that our military assistance be . . . discreet [and] public ceremonies . . .
sharply limited." In July, twelve days before Fidel Castro led an armed
revolt against the regime, the ambassador reiterated, "Public demonstrations of solidarity between the armed forces of the two countries which are
capable of giving the impression that the armed forces of the United States
sympathize with the existing intervention of the Cuban military in the politics of the country should be enjoined."[67]

Cubans protested the U.S. recognition of the Batista government. How
could the self-proclaimed Cold War leader of the free world support an
unabashed dictator? Elisio Riera-Gomez, a naturalized U.S. citizen who
fought for his adopted country in World War II, wrote the U.S. secretary of
state "with the hope that an informed public opinion in the land of Washington, Jefferson, and Lincoln may be aroused to protest the existence, at

its very door, of a shameful dictatorship, so in conflict with the principles for which these men stood and for which our wars today are being fought." Cubans, he told his congressman, "cannot respect our pose as prime defenders of democracy when we appear disinterested in their loss of liberty and freedom." Carlos Hevia, a candidate for the aborted 1952 presidential elections, denounced the United States for its "defense of Dictator Batista at a moment when the most prominent Americans are speaking of the need to defend liberty and Democracy in the world." Cubans did not just protest to the United States. Some did likewise in Cuba, Castro among them.[68]

The young lawyer challenged the legitimacy of Batista's regime before the Court of Constitutional Guarantees. Declaring Batista's "revolution" the "source of the law," the court ruled, it could not find his presidency "unconstitutional." The ruling convinced Castro that the "only way to set-tle the issue" was through armed revolt. The revolt's first act was the failed attack on the Moncada Barracks on July 26, 1953. In his trial defense (later reconstructed as "History Will Absolve Me"), Castro compared the symbol of justice to its practice under Batista: "If they see her kneeling before some and brandishing the sword against others, they will imagine her a prostitute holding a dagger in her hand." He empathized with the judges "prevented by force" from imparting justice and correctly predicted the outcome of the trial: "This time force again will oblige you to condemn me. The first time you could not punish the guilty; now you will have to punish the innocent—the maiden of justice twice raped." Castro did not explicitly link his condemnation of dictatorship to the sex-and-sin tourism industry, but he had before and would again.[69]

In 1948, Castro had joined other students to protest at the Bogotá Con-ference convened to transform the Pan American Union into the Organiza-tion of American States. Stopping in Panama en route to Colombia, he witnessed a "depressing and unforgettable sight." An "endless succession of brothels, nightclubs, and other lurid amusements" lined the streets near the U.S. naval base. Castro knew of their counterparts in Havana and near Guantánamo Bay, but two aspects of the scene made a lasting impression. First was the large number of Cuban prostitutes—"the famous Panama Canal Zone was the final destination of women from humble families, turned into prostitutes by the Cuban bourgeoisie and its system of corrup-tion, unemployment, hunger, and despair!" Second, "this was the only rea-son that Cuba was so well-liked and well-known beyond its frontiers." Aghast that Cuba's reputation centered on commercial sex, Castro soon exploited this image to his advantage. He and his allies presented their emergent movement as the force that would liberate and redeem a Cuban nation and people prostituted by corrupt Cuban politicians backed by the United States.[70]

When Castro entered prison in 1953, Cuba's tourism industry was in disarray, its casinos beset by scandal, its workers discontented, and financiers reluctant to invest. The next year Batista failed to legitimate his regime politically: the promised elections were a farce. After them, Batista focused on providing employment and consumption to compensate Cubans for the lack of democracy. After his "election," Batista transformed the $350 million Economic and Social Development Program on which he campaigned into a new satellite bank of the BNC, the Banco de Desarrollo Económico y Social (Economic and Social Development Bank, hereafter, Bandes), to develop tourism and light industry. Promises of "peace, employment, and prosperity" underlay Batista's self-representation as a "democratic dictator," but few forgot that the "khaki, blue, and white" (army, police, and navy) allowed him to stay in power.[71]

Batista employed his consummate organizing skills to restore the confidence of hotel investors, forge a compromise between capital and labor, and build support for his regime by the armed forces, middle- and working-class habaneros, and U.S. business and government. After his coup, he consigned his uniforms to the closet and henceforth dressed in coat and tie. With his white linen suits, Batista seemed to distance himself from his bloody repression. The dark suits he favored for negotiations with U.S. investors signaled his resolve to attract foreign capital.[72]

Batista achieved labor cooperation and discipline in the tourism industry with the opportunities he provided unions and their pension funds. For example, the Maritime Workers' Union initially opposed the reopening of the automobile ferry between Havana and Key West. So Batista began to require tourists to buy a $2.50 tourist card, 30 cents of which went to the Maritime Workers pension fund, 20 cents to the Air Retirement Fund, and $2.00 to the Cuban Tourism Institute. The union dropped its opposition, and the ferry returned to service in 1954. By 1957 Key West, with Havana as its one international connection, was the third most important embarkation port for U.S. overseas tourists (New York was first; Miami, second).[73]

A contract with Conrad Hilton secured the discipline of the gastronómicos. In 1952, Batista granted their union an exemption to a law restricting the investment of pension funds to government bonds. It negotiated with

Hilton to build and manage the Havana Hilton hotel and casino, which the union pension fund would own. All parties hoped to replicate the spectacular success of Puerto Rico's El Caribe Hilton, which returned $6 million on a $7.3 million investment in its first four years of operation. Batista granted Hilton tax exemptions for ten years, waivers on import duties, permission for a casino, and guaranteed loans (he made all these national law in 1955). Hilton put up $2 million. The union secured an $8 million loan from Bandes. Its pension fund provided the remaining $4 million. Its need to make loan payments guaranteed that workers would not strike or demand large benefit or wage increases. The signing of the contract in March 1953 by Batista; Francisco Aguirre, the head of the union; and Mario Lazo, whose law firm represented hundreds of U.S. firms in Cuba, signaled that the state, labor, and business would cooperate to promote tourism. The message played well. U.S. investments rose dramatically after the signing of the Hilton contract and then the cleanup of gambling.[74]

Early in 1952 the U.S. Embassy began receiving complaints that the Tropicana and Sans Soucí casino nightclubs were cheating tourists. The scandal broke publicly when Dana C. Smith, a lawyer and controversial campaign sponsor of Senator Richard M. Nixon, lost $4,200 at San Soucí. Nixon asked the embassy to investigate. The *Saturday Evening Post* sent a reporter to do the same.[75] Batista ordered the police to protect tourists and authorized his military intelligence force, the Servicio de Inteligencia Militar (SIM), to deport crooked operators. He hired Mafioso Meyer Lansky to restore honesty to casinos. High-stakes gamblers regarded Lansky's Montmartre as the only legitimate casino in Havana.[76]

Some found it ironic that Batista hired Lansky to end corrupt practices, but not an unnamed contemporary who quipped for *Life*, "Who did you expect to be running the games down here? [Secretary of State] John Foster Dulles?" The ironic result of this partnership was not that it ended corruption by making good Batista's promise to "guarantee the ethical treatment of visitors," but that it shifted the locus of corruption from casino tables to government offices.[77] Beginning in 1954, the Cuban government legislated that casinos pay a $25,000 fee for a concession, a $2,000 monthly fee, and 20 percent of profits. Rather than increasing state revenues, these funds primarily increased the personal wealth of high-ranking military officers and government officials. Criminal capitalist Santo Trafficante (Louis Santos), who opened casinos at the Caprí, Commodoro, Deauville, and Sevilla-Biltmore hotels, reported that $250,000, not $25,000, was the "expected amount to be paid under the table for a lucrative concession." Batista's ministers and officers received shares of these inflated payments and fees and from profits collected from casinos "almost nightly by bagmen . . . for Batista and his cronies." The take from commercial vice extended throughout the ranks of the police, who collected a "tax" from Havana's lottery-ticket booth operators, brothels, and prostitutes. Gambling and lottery receipts had long enriched government officials. But as Jorge Domínguez argues, "The result of [Batista's] creativity in the corruption business was to spread the wealth beyond officeholders" to allies in business, the media, unions, and beyond. Batista and many who invested in his political and tourism regimes extorted state funds loaned by Bandes.[78]

Havana Hilton documents suggest widespread corruption. Management constantly complained that contracts of "purchasing agents" granted their jobs by Batista contained "provisions and conditions never shown to us" and which "only come to light as the contracts are let and payments must be made." A Hilton executive later accused the "government people [of] taking all the pension fund of the gastronomical workers union." A Cuban economist speculated that "so much money was wasted or stolen" that the pension fund "could not yield even a 1 per cent return." Even if the casino at the Hilton, like that at the Riviera, earned $3 from gambling for every other $2 spent in the hotel, loan payments would restrict the growth of the workers' pension fund. Corruption also obtained in the building of Lansky's Hotel Riviera. Bandes never determined the destination of several six-figure checks written against the bank's loan. Loan administrators questioned managers and contractors about the lack of documented expenses, failure to comply with acceptable accounting practices, and differences between payment authorizations and check amounts.[79]

Between 1953 and 1958, Bandes and other BNC banks made loans totaling $86 million for investments in tourism. Receiving 25 percent of all private loans the BNC made, tourism represented the single largest industry in which it invested. Between 1951 and 1957, BNC loans helped finance $173 million in public works projects, the stated purpose of which was tourism. Greater Havana was the main beneficiary, receiving $133 million. Between 1954 and 1958, thirteen new hotels opened in Havana; seven hotels and three motels at an estimated cost of $90 million were projected or under way by 1958. In 1958 and 1959, construction employment rose from sixty-five thousand to eighty-three thousand. Although many jobs were in industry or housing, hotel construction and public works benefited tens of thousands of workers and thousands of architects, contractors, engineers, lawyers, and purveyors.[80]

Batista spurred a tourism boom that underwrote a consumption boom for many Cubans who lived in the city and province of Havana. Between 1950 and 1958, Cuban consumption of imported, mainly U.S., goods rose from $515 million to $777 million. By the mid-1950s, Cubans owned almost as many televisions per capita as U.S. consumers. In 1958, Lazo boasted that Cuba's middle class, which he estimated at between 20 and 30 percent of the population, was among the largest in Latin America. He was proud that Cubans owned one radio for every five inhabitants, one television for every twenty, and one automobile for every twenty-seven.[81]

Growth privileged the province of Havana, where 26 percent of Cuba's 6.5 million people lived, and came at the expense of other areas. Between 1953 and 1958, wages paid to 1.7 million Cubans in Havana province rose 22 percent from $379 million to $463 million, while wages of Cuba's other 4.8 million people fell 23 percent from $337 million to $260 million. In 1959, the urban middle classes had annual incomes of around $2,000. Per capita annual income was $300, and rural per capita annual income, $90.[82]

As Batista's coup returned a U.S.-armed and U.S.-trained military to the center of Cuban politics, the U.S. military came to drive the Hawaiian economy. The military replaced sugar as the territory's economic base and drove the development of Oʻahu, home to three-quarters of the population. By 1954, seventy-three thousand civilian and military defense workers represented one-third of the labor force and earned one-third of its $226 million annual payroll. Military expenditures of $271 million represented almost 40 percent of the islands' income from the United States. During the then-biggest tourism boom, Pearl Harbor employed six thousand civilians, compared to twenty-five hundred total hotel workers. U.S. military spending, combined with tourism receipts and migration to the mainland, allowed Hawaiʻi to maintain a historically low 3 to 5 percent unemployment rate.[83]

In 1954, the same year bogus elections cemented the importance of the military to Batista's dictatorship, AJA veterans figured prominently among the Democrats who swept territorial elections. Their victory ended the haole-controlled Republican's half-century dominance of the territorial legislature. The Democrats secured a two-thirds majority in the House and a nine-to-six majority in the Senate.[84] The so-called Bloodless Revolution dismayed conservative haole. Republican Governor Samuel Wilder King told the new legislature that enacting the Democrats' proposed land, tax, and other reforms would "penalize private enterprise to the detriment of our whole economy." The *Honolulu Star-Bulletin* editorialized, "To interpret the results of the election as a mandate to swing the Territory's rudder to the left is to misread the public will. The people . . . do not need and do not want radical proposals of visionaries." Republicans attacked Democrats who championed their reforms as the means to create equality and democracy in narratives that posited the expansion of private investment as the way to complete the democratization of Hawai'i.[85]

Representing Hawai'i as on the verge of equality and democracy was part of a strategy conservative haole adopted to prevent them. The Bloodless Revolution convinced many former opponents to pursue a statehood that would maintain the status quo. The Democrats presented statehood as the "principal vehicle" for achieving "real democracy." Conservative Republicans and the Hawaii Statehood Commission sought to negotiate the transition to a more open economy and polity that preserved as much haole privilege, power, and wealth as possible.[86]

In the first research report the Bank of Hawaii (BoH) published after the 1954 Democratic victory, bank vice president and business research director James Shoemaker argued that Democrats should abandon goals to redistribute wealth and income through progressive taxation and government spending and cooperate with established haole to expand private investments in tourism and defense-related industries: "We can no longer afford the luxury of industrial, political, or racial disunity. We have reached a point in the economic development of Hawaii, at which working together for higher levels of production, employment, and income is the only possible answer to the problems we face." He added, "Racial cleavages," meaning challenges to the status quo, "block growth by disrupting the economy and the orderly operation of government." Shoemaker thought the Democratic platform inimical to development and full employment.[87]

Yet as he reported, the territory's tax revenues increased sixfold between 1939 and 1954, to $222 million, largely due to taxes paid by the U.S. military, which rose tenfold to $122 million. He knew that the flat 2 percent income tax in Hawai'i made it one of the most regressive in the nation and that property taxes for large landowners were far below market value. As in the antebellum U.S. South, large landowners often provided assessments of their properties to the government, instead of the other way around. Hawai'i earned 17 percent of its revenue from property taxes, 20 percent less than most states. Despite a vastly enlarged tax base and ample evidence of taxation inequities, the BoH embraced the dominant mainland view that expanded private production and consumption alone would lead to "economic democracy."[88]

The Hawaii Visitors Bureau similarly suggested that building "racial aloha" and selling it to tourists constituted symbiotic projects: "The traditional appeal of Hawaii to visitors parallels our desire to create in Hawaii a rich culture based upon the contributions that each of the many racial groups here can make to that culture." The BoH advocated limiting government spending for public services unless proponents could demonstrate "that the benefits from such service will be greater than from the private purposes for which funds would be used." So did the Governor's Advisory Committee on Tourism. In a 1956 report, the committee asserted the inferiority of government expenditures for social services and the superiority of those invested in tourism. The latter constituted "an investment on which government receives direct returns in the form of *increasing government revenues* and indirect returns in form of more income and employment, thus *decreasing government expenditures* for unemployment and relief." Although publicly the committee claimed that "the hotel industry is among the fastest growing industries," between 1956 and 1958, the number of hotel jobs rose only 18 percent as the number of visitors rose 55 percent. Privately the committee acknowledged, "it is over-estimating to believe that tourism employs a great number of people." The BoH, HVB, and Republican governor's office denied structural racial inequalities in efforts to preserve a contested haole power and privilege.[89]

They advocated expanding tourism to advance economic democracy for producers large and small. The BoH and Bishop Bank helped finance Stanley Kennedy's Hawaiian Airlines, new Waikīkī hotels like Kaiser's Hawaiian Village, Matson's SurfRider and Princess Kaiulani, and Roy Kelley's Islander, Edgewater, and Reef, and small businesses like Aloha-shirt makers and taxi companies. Most of their clients were white. The protagonist of Milton Murayama's *Plantation Boy* put it well: "The Bank of Hawaii and the Bishop Bank are haole banks with haole staff for haole clients." Neither practiced the economic democracy it preached, although the HVB voiced alarm over the amount of business lost due to inadequate rooms and services.[90]

The BoH and the HVB devoted more resources to commodifying the success of locals than to underwriting it. For example, a postwar executive director of the HVB and the Hawaii Hotel Association, Mark Egan, helped sponsor the production of *Go for Broke!* a film celebrating the AJAs' war-time service. He also helped sponsor the Hotel Association's night program in hotel management. It lasted only one semester, due to the feeling among students and teachers that "local people would have little chance to advance to managerial positions," an observation borne out by the continued pre-dominance of whites in hotel management.[91]

Statistical analyses were also critical to producing the appearance of multiracial equality. Andrew Lind reported sharp gains in the percentage of men with incomes of five thousand dollars per year or more (solidly middle class or better) between 1949 and 1959. Caucasian men falling into that category rose from 19 to 35 percent of all Caucasian men; for Chinese men, the increase was from 14 to 50 percent, and for Japanese men, from 7 to 39 percent. Many Chinese and Japanese were or became people of plenty in the 1950s. Assertions that the male heads of Chinese and Japanese house-holds earned more than whites were only true, a consultant stressed, "if military personnel are included in this figure." This "if" was key to statisti-cal productions of economic equality in Hawai'i.[92]

The inclusion of U.S. military personnel, mostly white, in income statis-tics also impacted analyses of wage and salary differentials, as did the inclu-sion of the Portuguese into a single Caucasian census group in 1949. U.S. military personnel and the Portuguese received lower wages and salaries than most haole, so the inclusion of both in income statistics made all whites appear less well off than they were. At the same time, nonwhite civilian U.S. military employees generally earned more than peers in the territory's trades, professions, and services; thus, the wages and salaries the military paid them raised their aggregate income levels vis-à-vis whites. This reflected an external stimulus toward economic democracy, not the outcome of the largess of the Big Five, the second largest employer in Hawai'i. And most Hawaiians, Filipinos, and Samoans were excluded from rising prosperity and upward mobility.[93]

Ironically, as tourism professionals made cultural and racial aloha the dominant narrative about Hawai'i, mainland capital and the federal gov-ernment were more likely to offer people of color the better jobs, higher incomes, and loans the BoH and the HVB deemed critical to economic democracy. In Hawai'i, U.S. business and government did not follow many of the discriminatory policies they did on the mainland, for they shared with Hawai'i locals the goal of ending haole economic dominance, if not for the same reasons. With the support of mainland capital, the U.S. government, and the local community, Chinese and AJA firms compelled haole firms to change their discriminatory habits and introduced the competition haole championed but seldom promoted.[94]

The support of the local community and workers, the federal government, and mainland capital converged in the development of Trans-Pacific Airlines (TPA). It broke the monopoly on interisland transportation held by Stanley Kennedy's Hawaiian Airlines. A Chinese-led partnership headed by publisher Ruddy Tongg founded TPA in 1946 to inaugurate service between Hawai'i and China. The communist revolution there and the U.S. response to it ended that dream. So TPA sought approval for interisland service from the U.S. Civil Aeronautics Board (CAB). The poor service and discriminatory practices of Hawaiian Airlines provided TPA with a rationale and an opportunity. During World War II, Hawaiian Airlines often refused people of Asian ancestry service, citing wartime exigencies, but this practice apparently preceded and postdated the war. Nor did Hawaiian employ many Asians. As a result, many locals vowed never to fly Hawaiian. The CAB argued, "Never before has the Board been confronted with a case in which the need for competitive airline service was so clear. . . . The monopoly of Hawaiian Airlines . . . is more than a monopoly. . . . It is an absolute stranglehold." It has a record of "sky-high earnings and fares, poor utilization of equipment, high ratio of earnings to costs, failure to provide adequate aircraft or ticket facilities, and a physical impossibility of accommodating passengers . . . on peak travel days." Shortly after the CAB granted TPA a temporary certificate in 1949, the airline began calling itself TPA Aloha.[95]

The airline worked to earn a reputation that gave rise to the idea that TPA stood for "the people's airline." To win local support, the airline introduced a half-fare family plan, selling half-price tickets to all family members traveling with one who paid full fare. To capture the tourist market, it decorated its planes with Hawaiian themes, installed windows that enabled visitors to take undistorted photographs, and routed flights to showcase scenery and volcanic eruptions. It paid its unionized pilots and workers fairly well. Working conditions at TPA Aloha should not be romanticized. The rubber paychecks its employees sometimes received undoubtedly produced hardship. The airline benefited from a tradition of racialized wages that allowed them to pay its Asian workers less than Hawaiian Airlines paid its haole and Hawaiian ones. Yet workers, shareholders, and passengers shared the feeling that supporting TPA Aloha contributed to economic democracy. That is why Daniel Inouye worked at "the airline of the people" as a sales representative: "There was a sense of ownership and inclusion, a sense of aloha." Locals demonstrated their commitment in 1958. Despite a still shaky financial position that produced a reorganization and new president, Hung Wo Ching, the airline offered a million dollar preferred stock issue to Hawai'i residents. It was oversubscribed in sixteen days.[96]

The support of local consumers and workers, as well as that of the U.S. government and mainland capital, enabled the airline to survive. The firm often relied on air-mail subsidies, which in 1951 provided 9 percent of its revenue. In 1956, the airline earned its permanent certificate, qualifying it for long-term loans. After failing to secure adequate financing, it asked the CAB for a return to subsidy status to avoid raising rates that "would have to be borne by Hawaii's hard-pressed citizens." U.S. military business also helped. In 1954, TPA Aloha secured a contract to maintain, repair, and overhaul military aircraft, a source of income that rose from $35,000 in 1955 to $200,000 in 1959. While not large, these sums were important to a firm that alternated between annual profits and losses of around $100,000. In 1958, Aloha secured financing from two New York firms to purchase three new aircraft. Its success in fomenting the sort of economic competition hailed by the haole business community helped transform the territory's racial economic landscape and increase locals' stakes in the economy.[97]

Japanese and Chinese businessmen similarly worked to transform the insurance and banking industries, obliging haole to alter their historic discriminatory practices.[98] Their economic achievements were critically important after the Bloodless Revolution, for they provided a counterweight to one political defeat after another. Governor King vetoed most laws passed by Democratic legislature on the grounds that they would "soak the rich." In 1955 alone, he vetoed seventy-one bills, including those on tax and land reform and labor legislation.[99]

After Batista's bloodless coup and the Democrats' Bloodless Revolution, defenders of the status quo presented full employment and mass consumption as consumer-citizens' key reward from expanded tourism. They hoped that privileges of consumer-citizenship would compensate for the dearth of political rights of citizenship. Building upon proven strategies of promoting tourism through commercial vice and aloha seemed to offer an opportunity for Batista to legitimate his dictatorship and for conservative haole to work for a statehood that would preserve as much of the status quo as possible. But the majority in Cuba and Hawai'i rejected consumer-citizenship as a trade-off for political citizenship. They wanted both.

CHAPTER FIVE

Travels to Another Revolution and to Statehood

> Cuba's latest revolution was plotted in gun-running missions off the
> coast of Florida, in elegant Havana yacht clubs, in the man-trying
> mountains of eastern Cuba, and in the hushed offices of leading Havana
> lawyers.
>
> *Time*, January 12, 1959

> Struggle ill becomes an island paradise. In a few more years, the worlds
> of Walter Dillingham, Jack Hall, Hiram Fong, and Sakae Takahashi may
> relax together into the old Hawaiian custom of enjoying living.
>
> *Time*, February 18, 1952

Led by *Life* and *Time*, the publishing empire of architect of the American
Century Henry R. Luce portrayed the Cuban revolution and Hawaiian
statehood as national family romances.[1] Just after the triumph of the revolution, *Time* asserted that the combined forces of guerilla fighters, managers, and lawyers had toppled a brutal "strongman" and his "fellow crooks"
whose deeds included "the padlock on the door of Havana University, the
bodies dumped on street corners by casual police terrorists, the arrogant
functionaries gathering fortunes from gambling, prostitution, and a leaky
public till." It favorably compared Fidel Castro, his top command, and
their "prosperous, conservative, and respectable revolution" to the U.S.
founders and their moderate and orderly revolution. By comparison in
Hawai'i, a local movement to enact equality across the color line could
seem far more radical. Yet *Time* insisted, once the conservative haole Walter
Dillingham, radical haole labor leader Jack Hall, Chinese American millionaire Hiram Fong, and AJA Democratic politician Sakae Takahashi completed their struggles for competing visions of society and statehood in "the

most spectacular story of all the incredible stories of Americanization," they would forget their differences and return to living together in harmony.[2]

U.S. support for revolution and statehood emerged in the context of critiques of Cold War containment culture and the deleterious effects of that culture on the nation's global power. Many critics feared that the decline of American manhood and the masculine state were undercutting U.S. influence in the developing and decolonizing world.[3] Others felt smothered by their weight. By the mid-1950s, Van Gosse observes, the "all-encompassing narrative of the Free World and the American Century" had become "very boring. . . . Not only did 'we' never lose, the 'we' was transparently the world of fathers" and of a patriarchal imperial presidency "epitomized by the figure of Ike." Such feelings helped animate a U.S. romance with Cuba's rebels, especially Fidel Castro, who seemed the sort of "superman" and "radical democrat" commentators ranging from Norman Mailer to Arthur M. Schlesinger, Jr., called upon to rejuvenate a political life emasculated by mass society, materialism, and momism. Schlesinger captured this sentiment while watching the six thousand Harvard students who gathered in April 1959 to hear Castro speak: "They saw in him, I think, the hipster who in the era of the Organization Man had joyfully defied the system, summoned a dozen friends and overturned a government of wicked old men." Although by then Castro was under sustained assault in the United States, many continued to see the Cuban revolution as a noble cause rooted in its revolutionary and frontier pasts. Paradoxically many who championed the mission of the Moviemiento 26 de julio (M-26–7) to rescue a Cuba prostituted by corrupt *batistianos* fantasized about visiting the Havana they knew as a "brothelly good time city."[4]

Advocates of Hawaiian statehood cast it as a different sort of national family romance. They invoked patriarchal authority to reassure white U.S. citizens fearful of admitting a multiracial state into a Union that continued to equate national belonging with whiteness. Beneath "the romance of swaying palm trees and hula skirts," argued Ralph Kuykendall and A. Grove Day in a history popular with tourists, lay the deeper "romance of reality." In a "few lifetimes," they declared, "economic initiative and democratic ideals" had made Hawai'i into "a thriving commonwealth of almost half a million Americans of many ancestral stocks, all working together to erect an American state." They predicted that Asian Americans in Hawai'i would soon follow recently whitened European ethnics in securing full incorporation into the nation.[5]

Because many mainlanders viewed high rates of interracial marriage in Hawai'i as reason enough for denying it statehood, tourism-statehood promoters drew on melting-pot narratives to write its mixed-race bodies into narratives of national belonging.[6] If in Cuba the prostitute emerged as twin symbol of tourism and dictatorship, in Hawai'i the interracial woman became a twin symbol of tourism and statehood. A leading symbol of her was Miss Hawaii, in 1953 the "lovely Dorothy Leilani Elliss, of English-Chinese-Japanese-German-Hawaiian-Irish-Scottish ancestry."[7] Appearing as beauty queen, hula girl, student, shopper, and future wife and mother, the interracial woman deployed to attract tourists also represented the future union of Uncle Sam and the Aloha State. Her local counterpart, the Chinese, Japanese, Korean, and Filipino organization man and husband-father-homeowner, moored this multiracial society to the white, middle-class mainstream. If Cuba's hip rebels made the organization men who backed Batista seem boring (but brutal), the banality of the organization men of Hawai'i rendered them safe. Tourism-statehood boosters presented the territory's multiracial people as cousins of stereotypical white, middle-class suburbanites on the mainland and offered these kinship ties as proof that its people were worthy of all the privileges, rights, and responsibilities of national belonging.

The rebel and the organization man coexisted in the 1950s, and in different ways, the hip revolutionaries of Cuba and the square Chinese businessmen and Japanese politicians of Hawai'i challenged the U.S. policy of promising to promote freedom and equality overseas while supporting right-wing dictators and white supremacy. Revolution and statehood activists deployed discourses of tourism to urge the self-appointed global champion of democracy to deliver on its promise to bring the political, as well as cultural, fruits of liberty enshrined in the nation's revolutionary past to the people of the free world. Echoing annexationists of half a century earlier, revolution and statehood advocates presented the people of Cuba and Hawai'i as American enough, civilized enough, republican enough, and white enough to warrant their support by a U.S. nation and people bound to them by affection and kinship, duty and destiny.

"The Full Freedom to Live Abundantly"

Narratives and counternarratives of the Cold War American Century became enmeshed in efforts to enlist U.S. tourists as "diplomats without portfolio" and charge them with exporting "freedom and abundance" and "peace and prosperity."[8] Tourists' overseas expenditures would contribute to the modernization of new nations emerging from colonialism and imperial rule. Tourists would provide overseas peoples a glimpse of their future as modern nuclear families blessed with an abundance of goods. This narrative drove to the heart of critiques of Cold War conformity, domesticity, and materialism, wherein lay a problem: most tourists came from the very ranks of the organization men, smothering moms, and maladjusted teens who, critics charged, had emasculated the citizenry, enfeebled the nation, and imperiled its global leadership.

Many who presented U.S. tourists as "ambassadors of good will" came to fear that travelers instead jeopardized U.S. foreign policy goals much like the "striped-pants" diplomats excoriated by William Lederer and Eugene Burdick in their popular and politically influential 1958 novel, *The Ugly American*. The runaway best-seller condemned a U.S. diplomatic corps and other emissaries of the nation for preferring to lead globe-trotting, country-clubbing, party-going lives in capital cities over working with the people to develop new and aspiring nations and their economies. It is ironic that the obnoxious tourist became synonymous with the ugly American, for in fact the novel's heroes were ugly: down-in-the-dirt, gritty-yet-wholesome, modern-day frontier men and women who worked, lived, and fought alongside ordinary people to spread capitalism and contain communism. Revolution and statehood advocates sought to make tourists more like these ugly Americans, committed to working against the grain of luxury-loving bureaucrats, or at least, to supporting their peoples' aspirations for self-determination.[9]

Still, many boosters in Cuba, Hawai'i, and the United States remained confident that traveling U.S. citizens could help win the Cold War. Addressing a convention of U.S. advertising executives at his Hawaiian Village Hotel in 1957, industrialist Henry J. Kaiser urged them to assume responsibility for "extending the benefits of civilization to the entire human race." He pontificated on a manifest destiny updated by modernization theory: "Americans have the opportunity, given of God, to lead in the revolutionary improvement in the lot of mankind," specifically "into the full freedom to live abundantly." Kaiser asserted that the executives were advancing this goal in their dual roles as consumer-citizens supporting a tourist industry critical to the modernization of Hawai'i and corporate capitalists learning about it "as a remarkable test area" for perfecting the "new advertising and marketing plans" that would help them spread "American know-how in engineering, industry, science, management, [and] marketing" across the decolonizing and developing world. As a bonus, the working managers enjoyed the recently legislated right to deduct their trips as business expenses.[10]

After World War II, conservative consensus academics rewrote the legacy of the Revolutionary War in terms of mass consumerism. As David Potter exhorted at the time, "We have supposed that our revelation was 'democracy revolutionizing the world,' but in reality it was 'abundance revolutionizing the world.'" Historian David W. Noble shows that scholars transformed a revolutionary struggle for a national republic rooted in political liberty into a global one that associated democracy only with the liberty of consumer-individual in the world market. Academics held no monopoly on this narrative's production. Kaiser and American Express, Hilton Hotels International, and Pan American Airlines executives also helped write and popularize it. They argued that incorporating the developing, decolonizing world into a U.S.-led capitalist world economy represented the surest, safest route to modernization, collective security, and the "age of high mass consumption" that modernization theorist W. W. Rostow deemed the end of history. They made tourism and tourists central to these projects.[11]

Modernization, collective security, and mass consumption converged in the promotion of U.S. overseas tourism during the presidency of Dwight D. Eisenhower. Its "trade not aid" policy toward the developing and decolonizing world charged the private sector with primary responsibility for economic modernization and the public sector with that for collective security. Premised on free trade and free travel, trade not aid and its "vacations not donations" component provided incentives, including tax breaks and liberalized tariffs and tourist allowances, for U.S. corporate capitalists and consumer-citizens to invest and spend. Their combined outlays would contribute to capitalist development and establish bulwarks against communism and radical nationalisms. American Express president Ralph T. Reed captured the policies' spirit: "Tourist Dollars are an Economic Tonic for the Free World, the security of which is inextricably linked to our own."[12]

Modernization and collective security converged in Cold War practice and ideology. Modernization theory presented the United States as a universal model of development and its history as a mirror of the path that underdeveloped economies would follow toward capitalist, consumerist

futures; modernization practice sought to accelerate the development process by the application of U.S. knowledge, capital, and military assistance.
Collective-security thinking described the obligation of free world nations
to block the advance of communism by spreading capitalism and mass
consumption globally; the obligation was put into practice through a series
of U.S.-led regional military alliances (like NATO and SEATO) that bound
member states to consider an attack on one an attack on all and meet it
with a collective response. Collective security sought to provide an environment conducive to modernization, and modernization, to security.[13]

Trade not aid and vacations not donations arose in the context of business and government leaders' rejection of New Deal projects to redistribute
wealth and income through progressive taxation and government spending
and embrace of the notion that private investment and enterprise would
fuel sustained economic growth and the upward mobility of most people.
Acceptable domestic government expenditures were not supposed to alter
the economic status quo or resemble communistic intervention into private
lives. These leaders argued that whereas military expenditures contributed
to growth and flowed through existing market channels, welfare spending
redistributed wealth and income and required Soviet-like government
bureaucracies.[14]

The same logic informed U.S. policy overseas. Government expenditures for military assistance would provide the stability needed for capitalism to take root and flourish. By contrast, government assistance for
development was the equivalent of welfare. It resembled "serfdom" to Pan
American Airlines President Juan T. Trippe and was therefore incompatible
with "growth in the American tradition of freedom and free enterprise."
As Reed put it, "The free functioning of economic demand and supply
through tourism" was "far superior to any kind of aid. . . . Benefiting
nations develop far greater self-sufficiency and initiative from such revenue," which "moves more quickly and spontaneously into productive
channels of capital investment." Ironically, military aid promised to under-
write capitalist development overseas, but economic aid seemed sure to
hamper it.[15]

Trippe proposed that aviation would lay the same basis for the modernization of twentieth-century undeveloped nations that railroads had done
for the nineteenth-century United States. Aviation networks and hotels
would open overseas trade and investment opportunities to business travelers. The dollars recreational travelers spent through these same channels,

Secretary of Commerce Sinclair Weeks argued, would "provide new funds for local investment in industry." Kaiser averred that tourist expenditures would enable people overseas to "raise their standards of living." Noting that U.S. tourists spent $1.25 billion overseas in 1955, industry leaders incorrectly boasted that this was more than double U.S. government expenditures on foreign aid. Ignoring that this was the minimum annual sum the Economic Council on Latin America deemed essential for stimulating development on that continent (and where U.S. tourists spent only $22 million), Reed asserted that U.S. citizens were "helping build these countries toward prosperity and true independence." Vacations not donations wedded a belief in the beneficence of growth driven by consumption to a "corporate idiom of public service."[16]

U.S. corporate capitalists and consumer-citizens would also contribute to collective security. Eisenhower made travel promotion a provision of the Mutual Security Act of 1954, symbolically incorporating tourists and the tourist industry into the apparatus of the national security state. A Pan Am vice president declared that 40 percent of the company's aircraft were "available for military assistance within twenty-four hours." Conrad Hilton claimed to have positioned his hotels to contain communism. He built in Cairo because it "holds the key to Africa and the Middle East"; in Tokyo, because Japan "is the key to Asia"; in West Berlin, "because Germany holds the key to the containment of Europe." If embassies represented U.S. government soil, Hilton's "little Americas" were private U.S. spaces abroad where ambassadors without portfolio could gather to "talk peace," specifically the dividend of peace and prosperity certain to result from modernization projects driven by free enterprise, free trade, and free travel.[17]

Faith in free enterprise and the consumer-goods sector credited with fueling sustained growth and rising prosperity acquired almost totemic status in the 1950s. Moreover, Lizabeth Cohen argues, consumption "also seemed to promise a citizenry of economic equals, without necessitating a direct attack on inequality." If the aggregate spending of consumers contributed to economic growth and full employment and raised the standards of living of U.S. citizens, that of U.S. overseas tourists did much the same for people abroad. They also contributed to domestic growth and employment by fomenting demand for U.S. goods. Trippe argued that although "the average man" perceived that "his dollars" were "flying away, the dollars he leaves" overseas "always fly home," for they "cannot ultimately be spent anywhere but here." To contribute to prosperity and employment at home and modernization and security abroad, U.S. citizens need only do what they did best: buy and spend. *Foreign Commerce Weekly*'s quip "World Trade Is More Darn Fun!" presented private salesmanship and public statesmanship as enterprises as mutually sustaining as they were enjoyable.[18]

Business, government, and media representatives nonetheless worried incessantly about efforts to enlist U.S. tourists as missionaries preaching the twin gospels of free enterprise and mass consumption. Given the gendering of consumption as an especially female pursuit, they feared that male tourists might be viewed less as private salesmen than petty shoppers, contributing to perceptions of them and their nation as effeminate. They further feared these narratives lent credence to criticisms of the United States and its people as imperialist, materialist, and morally bankrupt. The State Department expressed alarm that so many people overseas perceived U.S. tourists "as overly rich, insensitive, crude, loud, inconsiderate, uncultured, ignorant of other cultures, and arrogant."[19] Equally alarming was their inability to respond to criticisms that the United States could not lead the free world when it denied basic rights to its own citizens of color.[20] Travel boosters urged tourists respond to questions about racism with the answer that race relations were fast improving and the movement toward racial equality was rapidly advancing. They worked to make tourists better moral representatives of the nation.[21]

U.S. efforts to present consumer-citizens in spreading "freedom and abundance" overseas came up against the limits imposed by leaders all too willing to dispense with stated commitments to democracy when deemed necessary to safeguard capitalism, as exemplified by their overt support of right-wing dictators and covert overthrow of left-leaning governments.[22] Hilton and Eisenhower's promotional efforts sought to identify the nation and its citizens as moral bearers of the republican, revolutionary, and reputed religious ideals of the founding fathers, who established a new nation that would serve as an ideal type for all mankind.[23] Hilton urged his fellow hoteliers to act "smart enough and tough enough—and spiritual enough to match the American Revolution and outmatch the communist revolution" in their efforts to transplant abroad the "American Revolution of freedom, initiated by Washington, Madison, Adams, Jefferson." He helped Eisenhower give voice to a political morality and religious piety that conjoined the nation-building projects of the Founding Fathers to a global Cold War struggle sanctioned by a Christian God against a godless enemy. In 1953, Hilton sponsored the first Prayer Breakfast in Washington, D.C.

Gathered beneath a painting of Uncle Sam kneeling "to do battle for peace" commissioned by Hilton for his "America on its Knees" ad campaign, the president, vice president, cabinet, Supreme Court justices, and Congress prayed for divine intervention in the Cold War. The *Washington Star* reported, "Here, in a 20th century Declaration of Dependence—on GOD—is America on its knees. And America on its knees is invincible." Eisenhower began to enjoin tourists to "portray America as . . . a peace-loving nation living in the fear of God but in the fear of God only, and trying to be partners with our friends."[24]

Although they were intended to present the U.S. nation and its citizens as worthy heirs and defenders of political and religious values bequeathed them by the founders and their virile and virtuous republicanism, it seems as likely that such saccharine paeans to God and Founding Fathers offered critics yet another example of the drift and impotency of an administration that had imperiled the nation and compromised its ability to project its power. For its national and global salvation, the United States needed men of action, not pontification. To ensure the victory of democratic capitalism over communism demanded reanimating a masculine republican virtue first forged by the founders in a revolution for political liberties and continued by those who followed in their mythic footsteps, among them westward pioneers, Rough Riders, heroes of Hollywood Westerns, and most recently, *The Ugly American*'s not-so-fictive heroes. Before John F. Kennedy emerged as the United States' very own political superman, many valorized the rebels of Cuba and the "Golden Men" of Hawai'i as kin of *The Ugly American*'s heroes, the sort of self-sacrificing Americans the United States needed to win the global Cold War.

Upholding the political legacy of the Revolutionary War required leaders and allies of the sort that Castro and the M-26–7 and the Chinese and Japanese elite of Hawai'i were said to embody. These white rebels and U.S. citizens of Asian descent appeared the sort of virile and virtuous people who deserved support for different quests modeled on the moderate, orderly revolution that produced the United States. Supporting revolution and statehood would show foreign peoples that the United States favored democracy over dictatorship and accepted people of color as equals.

Many Cubans and U.S. citizens and settlers of Hawai'i demanded that the United States make good on its promise to advance its revolution's legacy of political liberty. They identified with the American dream of mass consumption and home-ownership, but most did not accept "the full free-dom to live abundantly" as a substitute for civil rights and representative self-government. For example, two U.S. reporters hit the mark when they noted that many Cubans joined or supported the revolution "out of a pro-found sense of embarrassment" that "while they could boast of their air conditioners and television sets that seemed to put them almost on a par with the Americans, they had as a government a shabby military dictator-ship that seemed more worthy of an old banana republic than a country aspiring to join the modern world."[25] Upholding the legacies of the Revolu-tionary War required that the United States support fellow Americans in Cuba and Hawai'i.[26] National narratives of belonging and bonds of mar-riage and brotherhood once again converged in projects that harnessed pleasurable travel to political transformation.

The Family Romances of Revolution and Statehood

Luce and his magazines excelled, Amy Kaplan observes, at making "Ameri-can interests synonymous" with the world's while effacing the "otherness of foreign lands, peoples, and cultures." The best-known U.S. popularizers of revolution and statehood remain, respectively, the veteran *New York Times* reporter Herbert Matthews and the popular and political writer James Michener. Yet *Time* and *Life* especially served as switching points in the broader networks in which Michener, Matthews, the M-26-7, and the Hawaii Visitors Bureau and Hawaii Statehood Commission operated. Their agents worked to transform into revolution and statehood advocates not just the rich tourists but a broad white middle class, much of whose knowl-edge about Cuba and Hawai'i came from travel narratives. For example, while Michener urged "every American who can possibly do so" to visit Hawai'i, he was aware that most would only be able to read about its "glory," one found not in its volcanoes, beaches, or "dazzling flowers [but in] the people [of a] polygot population [who have] devised a manner of life which is a lesson and a reproof to the world." Cheap flights from Miami and the Key West ferry enabled a broader group of U.S. citizens to travel to 1950s Cuba, if only for an evening. But as violence rose, tourism declined. *Time* and *Life* joined others who helped make actual and armchair tourists into symbolic allies of movements that would restore the nation's reputa-tion as the global champion of liberty.[27]

In continuing contrast to Cuba, the HVB proved quite successful in maintaining power over the production of discourses of Hawai'i. A cadre of town-and-gown experts was always on hand to guide reporters, travel writers, and others around the islands and through the archives. The HVB worked closely with reporters, travel writers, and editors. It boasted that in 1958 its press office "directly arranged" 102 pages of tourism-statehood articles published in mainland magazines, including "all of the stories" in Luce's *Time, Life, Fortune,* and *Sports Illustrated.*[28]

Agents of the HVB and HSC collaborated to develop and deploy mutually sustaining discourses of tourism and statehood, well symbolized by Lorrin P. Thurston, a director of both at different points in the 1950s. Following in the footsteps of his annexationist father, Thurston helped coordinate the Hawai'i visits of U.S. media and government officials and ensured that virtually all arriving and mainland-bound tourists received literature asking them to write their congressional representatives "urging favorable action on Hawaiian statehood." Identifying cabdrivers as the "leading purveyors of anti-statehood propaganda," the HSC worked to convince them that because statehood would increase tourism and benefit them financially, they should expound upon its merits to visitors. Although Kaiser refused to become an officer of the partisan HSC, he opened his lobbying organizations to it and spoke to Congress, media, and tourists on Hawai'i as a melting pot, statehood candidate, and bridge between the United States and Asia.[29]

A fairly broad accord emerged on Hawai'i as an integral part of the United States, a harmonious and egalitarian melting pot, and a cultural and political link between "East and West." Businessmen, diplomats, editors, military strategists, musicians, presidents, reporters, senators, and travel writers celebrated the Americanness of the diverse people of Hawai'i, particularly those of Asian descent, and their ability to advance the interests and image of the United States in Asia. They denigrated "pure" Hawaiians, whom haole alleged were the only group which refused to identify mainly as Americans, and celebrated ostensibly more Americanized "part"-Hawaiians. The territory's tourism-statehood promoters put these visions on institutional footing in every possible venue.[30]

Denying the modernity and maturity of "pure" Hawaiians while praising that of "part"-Hawaiians worked to erase a long history of U.S. colonialism, dispossession, and exploitation of Hawaiians, and their opposition to annexation, colonial rule, and, for an as yet unknown number, statehood as well. Public discourse, scattered acts of resistance, and some statistics suggest that Hawaiians were divided over statehood, although this awaits further study. It was, for example, as noted, the opposition of Hawaiian cabdrivers to statehood that led the HSC to devote time and resources to combating this threat. Many Hawaiians thought that statehood would open a new era in their dispossession, new because as U.S. citizens of Asian descent achieved political and economic power, they would join haole in undermining Native claims to indigeneity and Hawaiian nationhood. Alice Kamokila Campbell, a sister of Princess Abigail Kawānanakoa, presented this view to Congress in 1946: "I do not feel . . . we should forfeit the traditional rights and privileges of the natives of our islands for a mere thimbleful of votes in Congress, that we, the lovers of Hawai'i from long association with it should sacrifice our birthright for the greed of alien desires to remain on our shores, that we should satisfy the thirst for power and control of some inflated industrialists and politicians who hide under the guise of the friends of Hawaii."[31]

Tourism-statehood promoters attributed Hawaiian resistance to state-hood to cultural and political immaturity. Michener reported that only a "few die-hard romantics" wanted national independence, before derogato-rily commenting that "since every one of them wants to be prime minister, the plan lags." He cited the plans to "solve it all" tendered by a group of Hawaiians he met at a bar and presumably were drunk: "Complete freedom from the United States so we can get Marshall Aid and Point Four and live like kings." Michener deemed irrational the Hawaiian desire for self-determination, which he championed for other Pacific Islanders under European rule but which he could not fathom for Hawaiians, given his belief in the nonimperial nature of U.S. expansion. This view was common, despite the fact that the United Nations listed Hawai'i among the world's "non-self-governing" territories, a status that obligated the United States to work for its decolonization, a process that the U.N. thought should privi-lege independence. *Life* presented Hawaiians as lacking the modernity and maturity that made the benefits of statehood, consumerism, and desire for them patently obvious. In a photomontage of a group of multiracial busi-nessmen and politicians, *Life* presented visitors and residents watching malo-clad, torch-bearing Hawaiian men fishing at night, "like a fond parent watching the games of children" dependent upon non-Hawaiian adults for protection. The fishermen were one example *Life* used to position Hawai-ians outside a modernity in which "Sears, Roebuck and Coca-Cola have replaced Ka-ne, the god of earth, and Pele, goddess of volcanoes." It cast

Native opposition to statehood as a refusal to accept the gifts of U.S. civilization and citizenship.[32]

The image of Coca-Cola supplanting Pele provided an example of how American influence and annexation had placed Hawai'i on a teleological path toward statehood. According to travel writer Ben Adams, statehood had been "the dream of responsible people" for half a century. Although neither the United States nor most haole entertained very serious thoughts of statehood before World War II, afterward, the idea that Hawai'i had begun a march to statehood fifty or a hundred years before took hold. The *New York Times* dated the origins of the quest for statehood to 1903, while *Time* offered this date and 1854, calling statehood "Kamehameha's dream." Hence statehood was not part of a long history of colonialism. Instead, promoters cast the U.S. refusal to grant decolonization in the form of statehood as its lone imperialist act.[33]

Paeans on the beauty and intelligence of so-called Caucasian Hawaiians and Asiatic Hawaiians also glossed over a long colonial history while bringing Asian settlers into the fold of the future Aloha State. New narratives used marriages to Hawaiians to trace genealogical ties that bound Asians, not just haole, to Hawai'i and Hawaiians. In 1942 and 1945, *Life* photoessays presenting the territory as a "perfect laboratory of race-crossing" used interracial women to dispute charges that miscegenation produced physical and intellectual "inferiors." To the contrary, this "new race" or "new mixed race," one deemed "tolerant, healthy American," that was "energizing and stabilizing" Hawai'i exhibited beauty and intelligence. The Caucasian Hawaiian, Asiatic Hawaiian, and Asiatic Caucasian women depicted boasted an M.A. candidate at Columbia, a U.S. Army translator, the daughter of a territorial senator, and a bevy of hula dancers and beauty-pageant winners. These images lent credence to claims "that someday every inhabitant of Hawaii will be part Hawaiian." Further, because Hawaiians ostensibly had escaped "the servile destiny of other Pacific peoples" colonized by Europeans and instead welcomed wave after wave of foreigners into their "carefree and tolerant" society, they "had much to do with making a polyracial paradise." In presenting part-Hawaiians as the territory's fastest growing group, observers perpetuated the myth of a native race doomed to extinction and conferred upon all settlers genealogical claims to Hawai'i and Hawaiian culture.[34]

In such readings, the Hawaiians who married and otherwise embraced settlers had transmitted a world-renowned aloha spirit to them, their off-

14. This photograph invariably inspired paeans to the beauty of mixed race
women of a Hawai'i presented as at once intriguingly cosmopolitan and
thoroughly American. It was one of the most popular images used to
promote tourism, statehood, or both from the end of World War II until
the admission of Hawai'i into the Union as the Aloha State. Hawaii Visitors
Bureau Photograph reproduced in Helen Bauer, *Hawaii, the Aloha State*,
1960.

spring, and society at large, ensuring the resounding success of the melting
pot experiment of assimilation, Americanization, and whitening. These
narratives had roots in turn-of-the-twentieth-century discourses on annexation, which asserted that it resulted from the mutual desire of the Hawaiians and haole who had married and together governed the kingdom since
the mid-nineteenth century. These representations of annexation, the legal
frameworks of U.S. citizenship, and the 50 percent blood quantum definition of a Hawaiian underlay haole arguments that marriages between haole

and Hawaiians diluted their offspring's Hawaiianness and progressively whitened Hawaiians into Americans. These frameworks provided a foundation upon which tourism-statehood promoters built narratives of the transformation of the U.S. citizens of Asian descent in Hawai'i into normatively white, middle-class suburbanites.[35]

Comparisons of the experiences of the territory's Asian Americans to those of the mainland's recently whitened European ethnics became a staple of tourism-statehood discourse. The Americanization of the diverse people of Asian descent in Hawai'i represented a "repetition of the great immigrant epic," Adams proclaimed, "almost identical" to that of the mainland's "Irish, Germans, Jews, Czechs, Poles, Italians, and a score of other nationalities." Though educational, generational, and occupational succession, Kuykendall and Day argued, the descendents of "oriental and peasant coolies" had become "as capable, as educated, as ambitious, as democratic, as patriotic, and as thoroughly American as are the descendents of, for example, Germans now living in the American middle west." Michener found Hawai'i Chinese and Japanese "precisely as American in custom and form as the descendents of Irish or German or English families." *Time* cited the businessman Hung Wai Ching, who asserted that "the end product" of a territorial public-school education was "just as American as a boy from Virginia or Maine or Wisconsin."[36]

The modernization of a rural plantation economy into an urban postindustrial one was fast propelling Hawai'i into the age of high mass consumption and transforming foreign racial others into whitened Americans, as modernization theorists had predicted. James Shoemaker equated the use of consumer goods with Americanness and whiteness, arguing that "change from Oriental to American modes of living" was well under way and "expressed in a sharp postwar increase in the per capita use of electric appliances, telephones, motor cars, and modern homes."[37] The glue binding the people of Hawai'i to the U.S. body politic was none other than mass consumption, domestic bliss, and patriarchal authority.

Producing and performing "racial aloha" preoccupied the HVB in the late 1940s and 1950s, well symbolized by Aloha Week. Begun in 1947 to offset a traditional travel slump in October, the annual festival quickly became so popular that it taxed hotel capacity. A celebration of the cultures of all the islands' multiracial people, Aloha Week opened with a recreation of the landing on Waikīkī of actors dressed as Kamehameha, his consort, and their retinues. It showcased luau, hula, and other aspects of commodi-

15. "The Hawaii of Tomorrow will be a place of new and more unified Americanism; a Territory securely proved worthy of Statehood, and an area where the highest standards of living and the healthiest way of life may be enjoyed." U.S. tourists enjoy themselves, as their expenditures help transform all the people of Hawai'i into U.S. consumer-citizens and the U.S. territory into the Aloha State. Honolulu Chamber of Commerce, *Hawaii's Postwar Plans*, 1946. Courtesy Hawaiian Collection, Hamilton Library, University of Hawai'i at Mānoa, Honolulu.

tized Hawaiian culture. It generally linked Hawaiians and their culture to the past, in contrast to its presentation of other groups. They appeared as agents of the present and future and as successful representatives of the process of "assimilation of the many Caucasian and Oriental cultures which make up the Hawaii of today." Aloha Week showcased the traditional costumes, cuisines, dances, and music of people of Chinese, Japanese, Korean, and Filipino descent. Yet public performances of these foreign-national pastimes, *Paradise of the Pacific* editor Eileen O'Brien explained, did not portray the domestic life that made the territory's U.S. citizens of Asian descent so thoroughly American. She noted, "a pretty girl of Korean ancestry takes off her costume after appearing in a program for visitors and dons jeans and T-shirt for a homework session." Here was the romance of reality at work in a youth engaged in performing a role different from her life as a typical teenager. For O'Brien, in changing clothes, she literally took off a staged Asian identity and put back on a whitened American one.[38]

Throughout the 1940s and 1950s, texts produced by the HVB and *Life* worked to culturally whiten women and youth of Asian descent in Hawai'i and present public education and consumer culture as twin engines of assimilation and Americanization. In 1959, *Life* photos of a Chinese drum majorette leading the band at an Aloha Bowl football game and a University of Hawai'i fraternity pledge selling ice cream to three sorority sisters of Asian descent during homecoming week presented evidence that the diverse Asians of Hawai'i "definitely consider themselves Americans first, Hawaiians second" (and Asians apparently not at all). In 1954, a *Life* visual essay depicted a Chinese-produced "hit television show" showing scrolls and costumes to its audience of adults and children, and television commercials in which Japanese women advertised consumer durables, while a Filipino couple promoted a local beer. While they addressed their target audience in a language of their national origin, the U.S. technology of television served to incorporate U.S. citizens of Chinese, Japanese, and Filipino descent into a body politic of whitened consumer-citizens. Allowing them to communicate across generations, the medium enabled adults to instill in youth the cultural and linguistic skills that would allegedly help them serve as a bridge between the United States and Asia.[39]

A stable familial, managerial, and political patriarchal order made the islands' multiracial people part of the mainland's stereotypical married, white, middle-class suburban landscape. Beginning in 1954, business, political, and recreational tourists received an HSC publication also sent to and widely cited by mainland editors, reporters, and congressmen. *Hawaii U.S.A.* presented the U.S. citizens of Hawai'i as solidly middle class, with per capita incomes of "$1821, higher than in 24 states." It urged actual and armchair visitors to take a tour of the "show-place of American democracy." The booklet paraded the reader past tidy ranch houses, Little League baseball fields, and Carnegie-endowed public libraries. It presented the territory's diverse U.S. citizens through an ordinary professional, father, and husband who was meant to appear as white as his mainland counterpart: "The average Honoluluan leads the life of a typical mainland suburbanite. . . . He drives a car or rides up-to-date buses to work. He belongs to a Republican or Democrat precinct club. . . . Of an evening he takes his family to the movies. . . . Besides sports . . . one of his main hobbies is his garden. . . . On Sundays, between church and the family swim at the beach, the Honoluluan can usually be seen spraying his lawn. . . . While the weekly watering is relatively unnecessary, he labors under the illusion that the ten minute hosing is the cause for growth. He is a typical American." *Life* presented aspects of such a tour visually, showing a group of Chinese, Filipino, Japanese, Korean, and Hawaiian "professional men" attired in sport coats discussing statehood at a lawn party while "their wives are off gossiping." Such images of Cold War separate spheres combined with countless others presented women and youth as of mixed race but portrayed fathers, husbands, and professionals as coming from a single, presumably pure national, racial, or ethnic group.[40]

Tourism-statehood promoters generally relegated biological miscegenation to the domestic spheres of family, home, or school. While the incorporation of a mixed-race and multiracial Hawai'i into the Union would enable the United States to disavow racism at home and abroad, miscegenation was unique to Hawai'i and would remain contained to a state over two thousand miles off the West Coast. The beauty of mixed-race women and youths figured prominently as a reason U.S. citizens should visit Hawai'i, but interracial marriage and procreation was not a model for the mainland to adopt. A rare southern congressman who supported statehood, Henry Larcade (Democrat–Louisiana), made clear that "it is their way of life, that is their business. . . . In the South we do not approve of this way of life, and this should be our business." *Look* asserted that while "intermarriage is an essential ingredient of Hawaii's harmony," it was neither possible nor desirable to emulate "on the mainland."[41]

While Asian American fathers, husbands, homeowners, and breadwinners made Hawai'i so mainstream and middle class, the elite cosmopolitan "Golden Man" represented those who would become eligible for membership in the foreign-policy establishment upon achievement of statehood. As *Business Week* argued, the "thousands of citizens of Chinese, Japanese, Korean, and Filipino ancestry, who understand the customs, and in some cases, speak the language of the country of their fathers and grandfathers" would provide the United States with "cultural ties" to Asia just like the mainland citizens who had "always [provided] cultural ties to Europe." But the men who would perform the actual work of advancing U.S. policy and investment in Asia would come, as was traditional in the foreign policy establishment, from the ranks of the privileged or those who overcame hardship and prejudice in their rise from rags to riches.[42]

Michener famously personified these figures as Golden Men in ways that echoed Clifford Gessler in the 1930s. In tracing the emergence of a "golden race" of "neo-Hawaiians," Gessler characterized miscegenation as being as likely a product of cultural interaction as of biological reproduction. Two decades later, Michener concurred: "in an age of Golden Men it is not required that their bloodstreams mingle, but only that their ideas clash on equal footing and remain free to cross-fertilize and bear fruit." Michener cast the Golden Men as powerful Cold War weapons by virtue of their alleged cultural and linguistic hybridity and elite status: "influenced by both the west and the east, a man at home in either the business councils of New York or the philosophical retreats of Kyoto," the Golden Man was "wholly modern and American yet in tune with the ancient and the Oriental."[43]

An idea like that of the Golden Man figured in Kaiser's dream of using his Hawaiian Village Hotel to take a "brotherhood of man" already "live[d] and practice[d]" in Hawai'i to the "peoples of the farflung new Pacific era." Whereas designers of the interwar-era Royal Hawaiian Hotel had built an architectural fantasy of white colonial rule in a tropical pink palace, Kaiser's blended Asian, Caucasian, and Polynesian styles to convey interracial harmony and cooperation. W. Clement Stone thought he succeeded: "At the Hawaiian Village you feel the brotherhood of man a reality and not a theory. Europeans, Americans, Polynesians, and Orientals meet on a plane of equality," although the majority of Polynesians found there were entertainers and other workers. Kaiser negotiated with Hilton to manage the Hawaiian Village in the hope that it would become a little America where

businessmen and statesmen from the United States, Hawai'i, and Asia
would gather to negotiate U.S. policy and investment in Asia.[44]

Kaiser's efforts to link the United States and Asia via Hawai'i through
Hilton's hotel chain did not come to fruition, but Thurston's parallel work
did. Thurston undertook to make the Hawaiian tourism industry a model
for "all the countries, colonies, and territories of the Pacific." He asked
Secretary of State John Foster Dulles to inaugurate "an important phase of
economic rehabilitation in the Pacific area which will do much to further
democracy and combat the advances of Communism" by serving as the
keynote speaker at the Pacific Travel Conference. Dulles declined. But the
conference led to the founding of the Pacific Area Travel Association
(PATA) in 1952. A former U.S. colony, the Philippines, became the first
nation to model its tourist industry on Hawai'i. PATA's work helped make
the region the world's fastest growing tourist area. This bolstered claims
that Hawai'i was already advancing U.S. objectives in Asia and the Pacific
and that Hawai'i Asians would prove pivotal to advancing U.S. interests in
the region, working with institutions founded by a haole elite whose ranks
they were joining.[45]

The Asian men destined to bridge East and West as businessmen, diplomats, cabinet members, and congressmen, according to the HVB, *Life*,
Time, and others, were different from the middle classes deployed to sell
the mainland on the kinship of Hawai'i with the national family. Those
identified as future members of the imperial brotherhood especially came
from the class of Chinese businessmen who had earned postgraduate
degrees from elite mainland universities, become self-made millionaires,
been directors of leading business and cultural institutions, and moved to
traditionally elite haole residential enclaves. These men had transformed
the plantation system and simultaneously joined the once all-haole establishment. Although given less prominence, this elite included AJA veterans
whose heroic service to the state during World War II proved their patriotism, as did their later success in politics and government.

Collectively these upstanding Chinese and Japanese U.S. citizens
embodied the sort of self-sacrificing and innovative men needed to supplant the effete, striped-pants diplomats who threatened to undermine a
U.S.-led world order imperiled by communism and radical nationalisms.
The skills honed at capitalist land reform in Hawai'i by the self-made millionaire and real-estate developer Chinn Ho, for example, would serve the
United States well in Asia. As noted in the previous chapter, his Capital

Investment Co. broke haole planters' monopoly on land and built homes and small farms "at prices people could afford." The *Paradise of the Pacific* approvingly quoted Ho's free-enterprise, modernization spirit: "From the first, company policy was directed toward 'extending the benefits of capitalism to more and more people.'" Photographs and articles portrayed Ho with his trademark cigar clamped between his teeth working on the ground at his development sites to advance this goal. His rise as chief executive officer of nine companies; place on the board of Hawaiian Airlines, Seaboard Finance, and Honolulu Rapid Transit Company; and service as president of the Honolulu Stock Exchange, Bishop Museum Association, and Red Cross testified to his prowess, individualism, and commitment to liberal democratic capitalism. Chinn Ho personified both the Golden Man and authentic ugly American. And Ho was not alone.[46]

Assessing the credentials of a poststatehood candidate for U.S. Senate, the Chinese American self-made millionaire Hiram Fong, *Life* noted his Harvard law degree, the law firm he founded, his service as the territory's House Speaker and a framer of the state constitution. The *Life* photo showed an expensively dressed, handsome Fong casually perched on the lanai (balcony) of his home, which boasted a breathtaking view of Honolulu's Nuʻuanu Valley. The magazine displayed the strenuous upper-class masculinity of "Hawaii's Top Chinese," Ruddy Tongg, the founder of Aloha Airlines who "heads several successful corporations," in a photograph of him hunting in the rugged interior of Oʻahu. A photograph of a muscular Sakae Takahashi, "ex-Army major" and the "first Oriental in Hawaii's cabinet," featured him with his elegantly attired Scandinavian wife and their children. In overcoming hardship, men like Ho, Fong, Tongg, and Takahashi had acquired the qualifications needed to join a foreign-policy establishment dominated by investment bankers, lawyers, and patrician academics who glided between the public and private sectors. They had earned the credentials needed to join "a fictive brotherhood of privilege and power" in which service and sacrifice sanctified ambition and power. The Golden Men would reenergize a State Department still suffering from the loss of Asia hands purged by McCarthyites and their ilk and held responsible for the "loss" of China.[47]

Statehood would enable the United States to improve relations with Asia and to demonstrate to the world that it accepted people of color as equals. As Christina Klein argues in a related context, statehood would repudiate "the history of American racism without the difficulties of putting that position into practice." A related logic informed support for the Cuban revolution. Backing it would improve the image of the United States in Latin America by demonstrating a U.S. commitment to promoting democracy without the need of renouncing support for right-wing dictators, including Batista. For many outside the top echelons of the foreign-policy establishment, the risk seemed low. As admirers and detractors of the rebels agreed, Cubans' desire for the "American way of life" and appreciation of the "ties of singular intimacy" that had bound the two nations would, as in the past, put sharp limits on the leftward drift of any revolutionary regime.[48]

Although Castro and other rebel leaders boasted the sort of elite educations, class credentials, and other qualities that might make them worthy of U.S. support, Samuel Farber observes that they neither belonged to Cuba's traditional political class nor were "known and tested" like Batista. Castro and the M-26–7 worked hard to secure the "legitimacy and respectability" needed to earn "the confidence of the Cuban middles classes and allay any concerns in Washington D.C." The M-26–7, Julia Sweig argues, adroitly used the press to cultivate international sympathy. Its members demonstrated their media savvy after their disastrous return to Cuba on the *Granma* in December 1956. Only a handful escaped the landing and assault by Batista's army. The first task they faced was convincing the world that they were alive. Many Cubans believed, some U.S. officials hoped, and Batista insisted they were not. A censored Cuban press was of no use. The rebels called upon the *New York Times*. It sent Herbert Matthews.[49]

After days of publicity, on the front page of the Sunday *Times* on February 24, 1957, Matthews proclaimed: "Fidel Castro, the rebel leader of Cuba's youth, is alive and fighting hard and successfully in the rugged, almost impenetrable fastnesses of the Sierra Maestra. President Fulgencio Batista has the cream of his Army around the area, but the Army men are fighting a thus-far losing battle to destroy the most dangerous enemy General Batista has yet faced in a long and adventurous career as a Cuban leader and dictator."[50] Widely reprinted, the three-part series made Castro a worldwide celebrity and seldom-seen tourist attraction, almost overnight.

Although the *New York Times* and Matthews were authoritative political voices, many Cold Warriors regarded both as soft on communism. By contrast, Luce, *Time*, and *Life* boasted impeccable anticommunist credentials. *Time* and *Life* followed the rebels' lead in interpreting the revolution through the travel narratives that constituted a key source of U.S. citizens' knowledge of Cuba. Although the *New York Times* covered the revolution's effects on tourism, it tended to treat them as separate entities, in separate sections. In May 1957, it did note that conditions in Cuba had come to "border on the bizarre. There is a one-man dictatorial rule . . . [and] an organized guerrilla resistance movement. Yet it is a haven for American tourists who fly there in a jiffy for a happy vacation." But it did not, as *Life* did, assert that tourists contributed to Batista's "private pension plan" each time they placed a bet in casinos "rigged for graft." *Time* and *Life* did not absolve tourists from complicity in Batista's regime. Instead their coverage of Batista's "savage repression" encouraged U.S. citizens to think about how they, as well as their nation, perpetuated his dictatorship.[51]

Time and *Life* also reached a Cuban audience eager for uncensored news. Censorship was in place eighteen of the twenty-five months between Castro's return and Batista's flight on New Year's Eve of 1959. While Batista's censors scissored stories from each daily copy of the *New York Times*, *Time* and *Life* apparently reached mail subscribers intact. Assessing the influence of *Time* and *Life* remains fraught with speculation, but two examples suggest something of their authority. As Matthews interviewed Castro, three U.S. youths (aged seventeen to twenty-one) living with their parents at Guantánamo Bay left the naval base to join the M-26–7. Filmed by Robert Taber for a CBS Special Report broadcast on television and radio, the three embodied popular U.S. support for the Cuban revolution. Two of the young men left with Taber, but the third stayed and went on to fight with the rebels. Batista refused to allow the show to air in Cuba. But *Life*'s reprint of the story and photographs taken by Taber's team documented Batista's ineptitude to Cubans. How could a news crew, laden with bulky equipment, escape the scrutiny of soldiers at not one but numerous check-points? The rebels also worried about how these magazines influenced their ability to transform popular opposition to the dictator into concrete support by rural and urban workers and the poor. In January 1958, the National Directorate coordinator argued, " 'If the 26th wants to win over labor, we have to do it defending their interests. Remember . . . that the magazines *Time* and *Life* have called our revolution a middle-class revolution.' "[52]

Between February 1957 and January 1959, *Time* and *Life* often portrayed Castro and his top command as the leaders of a moderate revolution. They presented the streamlined organization of rebels as a force comprising hardened guerillas and innovative managers capable of producing impressive returns on a shoestring budget. They interpreted the revolution through popular critiques of the organization man, Cold War, and vice tourism that Castro and the M-26-7 also used to present themselves to U.S. and Cuban audiences.

While corruption, tourism, and their links to dictators backed by U.S. capital and the state were scarcely new to Cuba, Fidel Castro was the first public figure to merge these images and present the M-26-7 as their antithesis and Cuba's salvation. Castro and the M-26–7 constructed themselves, their code of conduct, and their revolution as the antithesis of Batista, his dictatorship, and its corruption, which merged in tourism development. As Batista expanded the industry, Castro kept critical pace. In his trial-defense speech for the Moncada Barracks attacks in 1953, Castro asserted that "tourism could be an enormous source of wealth." In 1956, he criticized the batistianos who rebuilt the industry on gambling and sex and condemned a regime whose allies enriched themselves at the expense of the nation and people: "with the hundreds of millions removed by foreign trusts from our country, plus the hundreds of millions that the embezzlers have stolen, plus the graft that thousands of parasites have enjoyed without rendering service or producing anything . . . , plus the losses of all types due to gambling, vice, and the black market, . . . Cuba would be one of the most prosperous . . . countries of America." Castro pledged to reform the republic's moral and political economy.[53]

The spartan code of conduct elaborated by and for the M-26 likewise offered a contrast to the dictatorship. Batista, his chiefs of the army, police, and SIM regularly wined, dined, and gambled at greater Havana's hotels, casinos, and country clubs. As the liberal economist Rufo López-Fresquet observed, "a relatively small number of landowners, rentiers, businessmen and corrupt politicians and tourists constituted the clientele of Havana's luxurious nightspots." They were among Batista's loyal supporters. It was no accident that the 1956 assassination of the head of SIM, Colonel Antonio Blanco Rico, occurred at the Montmartre casino-nightclub. The embassy urged the U.S. military to refrain from public displays of support of Batista. But after the Directorio Revolucionario launched a disastrous attempt to assassinate Batista in March 1957, the rear admiral who was commanding officer of Guantánamo enjoyed a dinner party with him at the Tropicana to cement good will between base and regime. It may have distracted attention from the one U.S. tourist killed and one wounded when the attack spilled into the streets.[54]

By contrast, M-26–7 members were forbidden to patronize nightclubs and bars. Gambling, whoring, and "lavish living" were strictly against the rules. Castro boasted that none who joined him in exile was a "millionaire" and that each man sustained himself on "far less" than it cost Batista's army to feed a horse. The famous beards sported by rebels wearing crumpled fatigues contrasted with clean-shaven batistianos turned out in dress uniforms and business suits. According to the rebel journalist Carlos Franqui, the *barbudos* invoked the religiohistorical figure of El Apostál José Martí and his figurative reincarnation in the figure of Castro and his "Twelve Apostles," the name given to those who survived the return to Cuba on the *Granma* (and who may have numbered twelve, sixteen, or twenty). The beards also evoked the "epic quality of the American Wild West" as portrayed by Hollywood, where rugged men drew on revolutionary and frontier traditions to validate struggles against injustice.[55]

The Western focuses on the legitimate use of violence by modern, masculine heroes to overthrow backward, illegitimate regimes. As "a myth of American origins," Richard Slotkin argues, the Western validates violence as essential to the formation of the U.S. republic and entitles the "better" classes to a "privileged form of violence." During the Cold War, the Mexican Revolution became for foreign-policy elites and Hollywood directors the symbol of a model revolution that responded to popular needs while protecting U.S. interests. Hollywood Mexican Westerns proved wildly popular with Cuban as well as U.S. audiences. But whereas U.S. audiences might experience "regeneration through violence" of the past, Cubans might discern ways to pursue the historic goals of Cuba Libre in the future. Cuban and U.S. citizens viewed the same cinematic and political performances through different temporal lenses.[56]

Castro averred that the rebels struggled against tyranny, not the armed forces. Rebel planes dropped ground troops photographs of Batista's army officers in brothels and Havana nightclubs, enjoying themselves while their enlisted men risked their lives in the Sierra Maestra. A *Sierra Maestra* manifesto told rebel sympathizers, "Batista's sons do not come to the mountains, [the chief of the General Staff, General Francisco] Tabernilla's sons do not come to the mountains, the sons of ministers and senators . . . [and] millionaires do not come to the mountains." Castro praised the "ability and courage" and lamented the losses of the men sent by Batista to fight the M-26–7, while high-ranking officers remained in Havana, growing rich "through the exploitation of gambling, vice, extortion, and shady business."

Removal of "these plundering army chieftains" was a top priority. As Castro told *Look*, "Our revolution is as much a moral as a political one," again contrasting it to Batista's tourism and political regimes.[57]

Time and *Life* drew on such images to portray a virtuous revolutionary movement fighting for justice against a corrupt dictatorship growing rich from gambling, prostitution, and graft. If Castro was a "well-born, well-to-do-daredevil," his "top leadership" boasted similar credentials: "four are lawyers, three are physicians, two are financiers, and one a mill owner," each of whom "earns more than $20,000 a year," as much as the richest 1 percent of U.S. citizens. *Time*'s Sam Halper portrayed their patrician status after attending a M-26–7 meeting where leaders "conspire[d] behind brocaded curtains in air-conditioned homes. . . . Silent servants opened the doors, poured the drinks, and arranged the foam-cushioned arm chairs in a neat plotters' circle. The only proletarians were the help." The revolution helped finance itself through bonds, ranging from "$1 bonds" purchased by workingmen to "$100 bonds," by professionals. When it could not pay peasants for goods and services rendered, it gave them receipts for payments due. The M-26–7's honest accounting practices contrasted with the Batista regime's, which set "new records for corruption," no mean feat in Cuban history.[58]

By contrast according to *Time*, austerity and frugality manifested on the field in the rebels' quest "for a single, basic political goal: the return of constitutional government." Contributions of money and arms did not enable rebels to match the professionalism and weaponry of a U.S.-trained and U.S.-equipped Cuban Army. Instead, rebel leaders and their "unpaid volunteer troops" dressed in "Truman shirts or Eisenhower jackets" marched "often dry and thirsty" and ate "irregular meals." Only "about 10%" had modern weapons. Their "real strength lies in the fact that they are willing to die—and for nothing a month." In June 1957, a month after Batista launched "a campaign of extermination" against the rebels, *Time* snickered, "Since then the rebel band has not yet been sighted, let alone exterminated." By October, Batista had deployed twenty-five hundred well-outfitted troops, as well as B-26 bombers and F-47 fighters, to vanquish the rebels. Still, *Time* reported, "Castro, his army grown from a rag-tag band of less than 100 to 600 wily sharp-shooters, claimed victory in recent skirmishes."[59]

If critics cast Eisenhower as a soft organization man presiding over a bloated imperial presidency, the outnumbered and outgunned Cuban

rebels recalled the heroic exploits of the Yankee colonists against the imperial forces of King George: "The government troops, trained on flat, open
land, had to fight in mountainous terrain in which the rebels were thoroughly at home."[60] At once gritty guerilla fighters *and* respectable business
and professional men, the rebel leaders showed that managerial elites could
pursue virile political life through streamlined organizations dependent on
self-actualization and self-sacrifice. Contrasting the white, elite respectability of a rebel movement fighting against Batista's regime, *Time* and *Life*
criticized the U.S. policy of supporting dictators like him as symptom and
fact of the debasement of an American Century whose architect had voiced
opposition to all forms of totalitarianism.

In *Time, Life*, and other venues, Castro compared Cuba's most recent
revolution to the Revolutionary War. Defending the M-26–7's program to
destroy the sugar crop and disrupt tourism and other economic sectors as
a strategy for overthrowing the Batista dictatorship, he told Andrew St.
George in a famous 1958 interview, was like the "American colonists
throw[ing] tea into Boston Harbor as a legitimate defense measure." Castro
asserted that the U.S. support of the dictator constituted betrayal of the
U.S. promise to uphold and defend liberty and sovereignty—both sacred
principles of the American Revolution: "by arming Batista you are really
making war against the Cuban people." In the civil war between Batista's
regime and the "Free Territory of Cuba," the United States once again
abandoned its promise to champion democracy and instead publicly
backed a dictator, making a mockery of representations of the Cold War as
a global struggle between Soviet-style slavery and American-style freedom.[61]

Time and *Life* documented Batista's "brutal counter-terrorism campaign" that was driving "thousands of Cubans from neutrality to opposition." After the failed attempt to assassinate Batista, *Time* condemned the
"irresponsible police thugs" who retaliated by murdering the lawyer Pelayo
Cuervo Navarro, "a respected, nonviolent leader of the anti-Batista Ortho-
dox Party." Batista reminded the country-club set that their safety, as well
as portfolios and pleasure, depended on him. Every few months, his men
deposited the corpse of a torture victim near the artificial lake of the
Havana Country Club. Navarro was one of these. In rebuilding tourism,
Batista gambled state funds. But this house of cards could not last forever,
Life commented in 1958: "Batista's days appear to be numbered. But with
his new gambling boom rigged for graft, his financial future is secure if he

can just hang on long enough. 'Just give him one more year of these casi-nos,' said one Havana observer, 'and he can retire to Texas. His Texas.' "[62]

For all the cultural dialogue of tourists as diplomats without portfolio, their outward trappings visually marked them as seekers of pleasure. Acting as a tourist to detract attention from oneself was like hiding the purloined letter in plain sight. U.S. reporters posed as and relied on tourists to elude Batista's censorship. When the former president of the Banco Nacional de Cuba, Felipe Pazos, asked *New York Times* correspondent Ruby Hart Phil-lips to recruit a journalist to prove that Castro was alive, she requested Matthews. To escape the scrutiny of Batista's soldiers at checkpoints along the Central Highway, Matthews and his wife dressed like "a middle-aged couple of American tourists." Andrew St. George boasted that he escaped the scrutiny of customs officials and Batista's police by stuffing the equip-ment he needed to interview Castro "into a pair of golf bags which fairly screamed 'tourist.' "[63]

When Matthews's story broke, the first uncensored editions of it may well have arrived with tourists who carried them to Havana from New York and Miami. The process worked in the other direction as well. When Batis-ta's censors blocked Jules Dubois from filing his stories with the *Chicago Tribune*, he persuaded tourists to transport his copy to the States. The flow of outbound tourists carrying news copy to the United States and inbound tourists bringing news stories to Cuba had the potential to engage all U.S. citizens visiting Cuba in a network of rebel sympathizers.[64]

Some other U.S. youths sought to join the rebels. Jules Dubois and Herbert Matthews received letters from young men asking them how to follow those from Guantánamo Bay. College students flocked to the New York offices of the M-26–7, seeking to enlist in the revolution for the sum-mer with the caveat that they "had to be back in the States in September before school starts." A few actually did join. Far more reveled in a touristic personal liberty quite different from the rebels' political liberation move-ment. School vacations offered students a seemingly perfect opportunity to imagine the adventure of revolution while exploring the nightlife of Havana. Spring-break revolutionaries seemed to find nothing contradictory in fantasizing about liberating Cuba while they downed Cuba Libres in bars haunted by Ernest Hemingway or frequented brothels that expressly catered to college students, where "boys from the University of Miami would come," as the novelist John Sayles later put it, "to fuck little blondie Cuban girls who spoke good English and wore ponytails and blue jeans just like the little blondie town girls they were afraid to fuck back home." Spring-break revolutionaries fueled the same sort of anti-Americanism among Cubans that other tourists did, a feeling some of their compatriots recognized. Schlesinger expressed disgust at the ways Havana had been "debased into a great casino and brothel for American businessmen over for a big weekend from Miami. My fellow countrymen reeled through the streets, picking up fourteen year old Cuban girls and tossing coins to make men scramble in the gutter. One wondered how any Cuban—on the basis of this evidence—could regard the United States with anything but hatred."[65]

If the imaginary exploits of tourists in service of the revolution contributed to its popularity as romance, some businessmen found themselves compelled to extend a hand for more pragmatic reasons. Conrad Hilton began construction on the Havana Hilton in collaboration with batistianos but later opened a door to potential cooperation with the *fidelistas*. One month before the hotel's grand opening in mid-March 1958 and on the eve of Havana's second annual Gran Premio, M-26–7 representatives kidnapped the international celebrity and Argentine race-car driver Juan Manuel Fangio. Hoping to recover the star, Batista delayed the race for hours, to no avail. During it, a car crashed into the grandstand, killing four and injuring fifty spectators. Released that night, Fangio thanked the rebels for saving his life and praised their cause. The number of tourists arriving in Havana immediately began to plummet, as violence in Havana continued to rise. The Batista regime responded by organizing a "NEW CUBA, Pro Tourism Committee" to "counteract the effects of newspaper accounts of political unrest." To make matters worse, just before the Hilton opened, the rebels called upon supporters to employ all available tools to overthrow Batista and staged a "Tea Party" for the hotelier. Members of the M-26–7 shifted from Key West, where activists had been warning tourists that Cuba was unsafe to visit, to California, near Hilton's home. The M-26–7 took to the streets and newspapers, urging U.S. citizens to boycott Cuban travel to disrupt the economy and help oust Batista. Fearing sabotage, Hilton management consulted with the embassy and State Department. Given a green light, it stepped up security and scaled back festivities. Four days before the opening, so many bombs exploded between Havana and Vedado, where it, the Caprí, Riviera, and other hotels were located, that it became known as the "Night of One Hundred Bombs."[66]

In a carefully written speech, Hilton cast the joint venture between Hilton International and the Cuban Hotel and Restaurant Workers' Union as "a whole new world of economic opportunity and industrial cooperation." Departing from the "usual relationship" of corporate governance, he boasted, "here we have reversed the picture; Capital is working for Labor; Employers are working for Employees." He concluded, "With . . . our Havana Hilton, we are, I think, pushing The Revolution a little farther down the road towards greater happiness and plenty for everyone." Hilton raised a question he could not answer: pushing which revolution down what road?[67]

The speech made the news, so the M-26-7 was able to note what may have been an opening gesture by Hilton. The hotelier boasted credentials the rebels admired. He spoke fluent Spanish and read Cuban papers in English and Spanish, both of which set him apart from a number of recent U.S. ambassadors. He worked hard to keep the Mafia out of the hotel's casino. His lease agreements ensured that a majority of casino and hotel profits stayed in Cuba (and greatly reduced Hilton's investment and minimized his risk). Hilton had worked with the revolutionary government of Gamal Abdel Nasser in Egypt, which the M-26-7 had studied and at times emulated. It seemed possible that he would do the same in Cuba. In addition to the ambiguity of the hotelier's speech, Castro scored two other public relations victories. First, after working for years on this centerpiece of his tourism program, but fearing for his safety and office, Batista did not attend the opening. Second, after it, U.S. tourist arrivals to Cuban continued to drop, due to the inability of Batista to maintain the fiction that the revolution was "600 miles away" in light of the violence that had engulfed Havana. A few weeks after the grand opening, the 630-room hotel had only forty-four guests. Hilton soon joined other hoteliers in laying employees off. The historian Thomas Paterson wryly notes, "With a symbolism surely not lost on the observant, the hotel industry and Batista were collapsing together."[68]

By mid-1958, Cuba's highly celebrated but often illusory prosperity ground to a halt. Many observers concurred with *Time*: "Prosperity is a key weapon in President Fulgencio Batista's struggle to remain in office." Rebels simultaneously waged guerrilla and economic warfare through general strikes planned by Frank País, who was assassinated in July 1957. In response, a general strike briefly paralyzed Oriente. Efforts to extend it to Havana were mixed, but *Time* called it a failure: "Hotheaded partisans of Rebel Fidel Castro tried to close down the Cuban economy last week and quickly discovered that well-paid workers do not become ardent revolutionaries. . . . Most Havana workers, making near record wages, ignored the call. Going up were four new skyscraper hotels." Speaking of the truly disastrous general strike in Havana in April 1958, *Time* predicted that a new "attempt will be harder to mount, particularly bucking the prosperity of Cuba's current $2 billion-a-year national income."[69]

Like *Time* and *Life*, many observers insisted that even without Batista's repression, Cubans' commitment to the "American dream" would have made them unwilling to openly support the revolution. But such faith also prevented them from understanding the depths of Cuban support, even if it was tacit due to fears of reprisal. Two economists for the M-26–7, Felipe Pazos and Regino Boti, presented the tourism industry as a microcosm of the economy. They charged the Batista regime and U.S. economists with the "prostitution of statistics" that, on the one hand, made Cuba appear "a western paradise of abundance and prosperity" and, on the other hand, claimed that Cuba lacked the resources to address deep unemployment and underemployment: "The science of Statistics thus prostituted serves the Malthusian in his plan to lead the citizens to a point of moral prostration and to a feeling of impotence and it serves to maintain the privileges of those who prosper at the expense of our people."[70]

Habaneros came to agree with the M-26–7 that tourism embodied much of what was wrong in Cuba. They had expected that expanded tourism would bring prosperity, but rising tourist receipts could not offset economic stagnation and rising prices in one of the world's most expensive cities. They experienced frustration as they tried to live First World lifestyles in a Third World economy. Cubans found U.S. tourists a tangible reminder of the inability of the Perezes to keep up with the Joneses. And consuming increasingly resembled gambling. Gracia Rivera Herrera described her father's plan for buying a television: "He'd pay 10 pesos down and the first month's installment, then he'd keep the set for a few more months without paying until finally they'd take it away. As soon as papá managed to get another 10 pesos together, he'd make a down payment and the whole thing would start again." After her parents divorced and three family members secured full-time jobs, "we had more money than we ever had, but our expenses were still larger than our income." So one month they would "pay the installment on the TV but not on the bedroom set," the next month "pay on the bedroom set but not on the TV." Corporate accounts confirmed personal anecdotes of floating televisions and cars. Between 1953 and 1958 Ford's credit subsidiary reported brisk retail sales, but its repossession rate averaged 17 percent annually. Ford's second largest overseas market produced no dividends after Batista took power. Tourism helped create consumer desire, but it did not provide Cubans with sufficient means to live the American dream.[71]

Middle-class Cubans regarded the present and future with trepidation. Before Batista closed its doors, graduates of the University of Havana received diplomas that more often than not guaranteed them unemployment. The owner of the Hotel Riviera, Mafioso Meyer Lansky, opened a croupier school in Havana. It was intended to attract high-school graduates, his biographer reported, but instead the typical students held undergraduate and graduate degrees, among them some of the "ten thousand young professionals—doctors, engineers, lawyers, veterinarians, dentists, teachers, pharmacists, journalists, painters, sculptors" whom Castro addressed in "History Will Absolve Me." They helped make Castro's tourism-dictator critique a standard of public discourse. Standing outside the Riviera, a Cuban told *Life*: "That cost *us* $6 million. It cost the owners $8 million. If it makes money, *all* the profits will be siphoned off to the U.S. If it loses money, we Cubans have a $6 million white elephant. . . . What kind of deal is that for Cuba?" The tourist industry became the subject of critical cultural dialogue that served as substitute for the political commentary quashed by censorship and repression.[72]

Batista and his allies had again rebuilt a tourism industry anchored in commercial vice. They again betrayed a quest to fulfill the ideals of Cuba Libre and dashed dreams of building a sovereign and inclusive political economy, dreams revived by the overthrow of Machado, the abrogation of the Platt Amendment, and the Constitution of 1940. In ways, the two dictators followed similar programs. But in sharp contrast to the Machado dictatorship, in Batista's Cuba U.S. businessmen and government officials, the Cuban upper and middle classes, and Cuban armed forces did not constitute a cohesive ruling class devoted to maintaining mutually gratifying relationships of politics and pleasure. They remained socially and politically isolated from the Batista regime and one another until its excesses and abuses united them in the common cause of removing the dictator from power.

New States, New Tourisms

On New Year's Eve 1958, Cubans and U.S. residents of Havana reported the mood tense and gloomy, a fact either lost on or ignored by most of the tiny number of two thousand tourists there for gala events. While Batista shared a final meal with guests at Camp Columbia hours before flight into exile, the Tropicana opened its floor show with an act depicting Cubans scurrying to the airport, mockingly chronicling the end of the dictatorship on one of the most important nights of the travel season. All awoke the next day to a general strike. Cubans took to the streets, smashing parking meters and slot machines, twin symbols of a dictator whose officials illegally pocketed revenues from both sources. Hilton employees convinced crowds to go elsewhere, as did former Hollywood actor George Raft, a greeter at the Capri. But as destruction gave way to celebration, nervousness turned to curiosity. Tourists joined the revelry. The situation approached the surreal. Tourists in evening-dress mingled with barefoot Cubans streaming in from the countryside; Errol Flynn roamed the crowds with bottle in hand in defiance of Castro's ban on alcohol; tourists gushed about the gracious manners of the barbudos; gangster Lansky joined Ambassador Earl E. T. Smith to coordinate efforts to get tourists home; bellhops wearing M-26–7 armbands guarded tourists sleeping in hotel lobbies.[73]

On January 8, 1959, Fidel Castro and the rebels triumphantly swept into Havana. He and his entourage moved into the Hilton, which for months could be the best place to find them. From the Continental Suite, Castro, Pazos, and others formulated plans to diversify the economy, a program to which tourism remained central. On January 13, 1959, Castro invited U.S. tourists and investors "back to Cuba . . . which can now be counted among the countries where freedom and democracy is a reality." To foment the recovery of tourism, the Castro government appropriated $6 million for renovations and new construction for 1959. His government advanced loans and credits worth nearly $1 million to Hilton to cover rent and expenses until tourism picked up, the only loan and credit extension the revolutionary government ever made to a U.S. firm.[74]

Castro initially shut down casinos and brothels, claiming he was "not only disposed to deport the gangsters" but also "to shoot them." But the nearly ten thousand employees who had worked in casinos protested the loss of their jobs. One month after they were closed, casinos reopened without gangsters and slot machines, subject to higher taxes and other terms far more favorable to Cuba than they ever were under the Batista regime.[75]

Following tradition, tourism constituted one of three economic sectors (along with diversified agriculture and light industry) to which the new government committed. A 1959 tourism and investment booklet entitled

Cuba: Land of Opportunity, Playground of the Americas promised U.S. tourists a "pleasant, long-to-be-remembered vacation" and presented tourism as "the strongest single factor in further cementing good relations between our two nations" and the way to "provide a better life and a higher standard of living for all Cubans." More than "an ideal place for recreation and enjoyment," the booklet proclaimed, Cuba was "the land of opportunity for foreign investors." It "holds virtually unlimited possibilities for profit-making ventures." The advantages Cuba now offered investors included tax and tariff concessions, lower tax rates for foreign firms and citizens, capital from private and public sources, a strong domestic market, an intelligent labor force, and "perhaps most importantly, generally favorable attitudes toward private initiative." If any asset outranked the last, it was the end of corruption. This made it "possible to budget without the big 'if' of official blackmail. The way for legitimate competition in which initiative and efficiency will receive their due reward is open."[76]

The government also moved to reform the consumption regime. The implementation of agrarian reform, the revision of the tax code, the curtailment of tax evasion (Rufo López-Fresquet, the minister of the treasury from 1959 to 1960, found that only five thousand of the thirty thousand Cubans belonging to luxurious clubs were registered taxpayers), wage increases, taxes on imported luxury and semiluxury goods, and the reduction of rents, utilities, medicines, and foodstuffs promised a consumption order to which all would have access. These laws lowered the incomes and purchasing-power of many middle- and upper-class Cubans; at the same time, the reduction of rents alone increased the purchasing power of most other Cubans by more than 120 million pesos (one peso was worth one dollar) in 1959.[77]

Reform of the consumption regime prompted the first serious conflict over the course of revolution within Cuba, symbolized by a famous debate between Fidel Castro and José Ignacio Rivero, editor of the *Diario de la Marina*. Rivero asserted that import controls threatened middle-class consumption and, by extension, civilization, in Cuba: "The level of civilization . . . is not measured only by the enjoyment of prime necessities . . . but also by the use and enjoyment of certain technical advances that . . . can be called luxurious, but that indicate a high level of individual and collective well-being of a nation." Castro countered that Rivero should measure civilization not by the yardstick of automobiles, radios, refrigerators, and televisions but by that of unemployment, illiteracy, infant mortality, tuberculosis rates, and the number of children infested with parasites. Then, "what would the illustrious *Diario de la Marino* say to me? It would have to say that we are a barbaric country, an uncivilized country." Cuba would remain uncivilized as long as a few enjoyed "more luxury than Americans and had more Cadillacs per capita than Americans [while] vast numbers [of Cubans] cannot daily earn enough to live.'" As conservative critics of the New Deal in the postwar United States had, Rivero and like-minded Cubans rejected the pursuit of economic equality through the redistribution of wealth and income and embraced private enterprise as the means of upward movement toward mass consumption by more people. Yet this strategy depended upon increased productivity and sustained growth, neither of which typically characterized Cuban postwar economic performance, especially outside the city and province of Havana.[78]

U.S. business confidence initially ran high, especially in tourism. For 1959, U.S. direct investment in Cuba totaled $63 million, representing an annual increase greater than any other year since World War II. Hilton, Pan Am, and the American Society of Travel Agents joined a reorganized Cuban Tourist Commission as financial partners in a massive publicity campaign. Grace Lines reestablished Havana as a port of call, and fifty-five cruise ships included it in their winter itineraries for 1959. Hilton told the State Department that his firm enjoyed "excellent relations" with Castro and that he and his allies understood "the importance of the tourist business for economic recovery and the future of Cuba."[79]

The joint efforts of the Castro government and U.S. business sought to demonstrate compatibility between a pro-U.S. business climate and an anti-imperial revolutionary government. They served as a counterbalance to the government's agrarian, rent, tax, utility, and other reforms. This was an important counterweight given the contentious state of U.S.-Cuban diplomatic relations. Cubans were taken aback by the unwillingness of the U.S. government to lend its enthusiastic support to a government that had just ousted one of Cuba's most hated dictators. Nor could they fathom a U.S. intolerance for the reforms implemented by Cuban economists, many of whom had studied in the United States, considered themselves devoted friends and admirers of the United States, and modeled their programs on the New Deal.[80]

Few tourists visited Cuba in early 1959, but the Castro government and U.S. tourism firms placed hopes for recovery in the American Society of Travel Agents annual convention, scheduled for October in Havana. Work-

ers gave Havana's tourist districts a complete face-lift while the tourist commission planned elaborate entertainment. Castro played the perfect host,
delivering stirring speeches and mingling with the crowd. He endeared
himself to the travel agents, who made him the society's first honorary
member.[81]

But midway through the convention, the former commander of the air
force flew a B-25 bomber from the United States to Cuba and blanketed
Havana with leaflets claiming that Castro was a communist. The air force
took pursuit and fired at the plane, missing. On live television, Castro
denounced the United States for its alleged involvement in the "air attack."
The next day, *Revolución* headlines announced "Bomb Attack." There had
been no bombs. ASTA president Max Allen despaired, "It is absolutely . . .
no use to offer . . . tourists splendid hotels, casinos, sumptuous nightclubs
. . . unless [the tourist] feels that he is coming to a place where he is welcome." Travel agents departed deeply disappointed. Castro escalated his
anti-U.S. invectives. It was in the aftermath of this event that Eisenhower
administration officials "began to prepare for a definitive break." Even
before the Cuban government nationalized airlines, hotels, casinos, country
clubs, and other industries in 1960 and the United States declared its travel
and trade embargo in 1961, U.S. tourism in Cuba had died. In stark contrast, statehood and the jet age came to Hawai'i the same year, ushering in
its then biggest tourist boom in history. [82]

A decade of planning and a dose of spontaneity characterized the public
celebration of Hawaiian statehood in Honolulu. The news that Congress
passed a bill for statehood reached the islands mid-morning on March 12,
1959. As arranged in advance, the tolling of church bells, the blasting of
air-raid sirens, and the blowing of steamship whistles broadcast the imminent arrival of statehood. Workplaces, schools, houses, and shops emptied
as people took to the streets for a celebration that lasted into the night.
Kaiser lit a string of twenty thousand firecrackers; spectators watching hula
dancers created a traffic jam in Waikīkī. As undoubtedly seemed fitting to
those who cast statehood as marriage, a columnist for Thurston's *Honolulu
Advertiser*, Bob Krauss, described the spectacle as a "gigantic, exuberant
wedding party." Yet the celebration did not formalize statehood. In March
1959, Eisenhower signed the admission bill, and in June, 94 percent of
voters checked "yes" on a ballot asking, "Shall Hawaii immediately be
admitted into the Union as a State?"[83]

Krauss did report that "there were mothers that cried at the wedding." One of them was "Aunt Jennie Wilson . . . who began her career as the favorite hula dancer in the royal court of Kalakaua in 1886." The announcement of statehood reminded Wilson of the "sad day" in 1898 that she and her mother watched the Hawaiian flag descend on 'Iolani Palace grounds when the United States officially annexed Hawai'i. She was hardly alone. The Hawaiians who voted for statehood did not necessarily share the view that it was the process by which Natives would reclaim a meaningful measure of sovereignty or land. The construction of statehood as a consensual marriage rested upon both an illegal act and manufactured amnesia that mirrored the turn-of-the-century claim by haole that Hawai'i and Hawaiians had voluntarily annexed themselves to the United States, despite the fact that an overwhelming majority of Native Hawaiians protested annexation. In 1945, the United Nations Charter had stipulated that colonial administrators work to develop self-government in non-self-governing territories. In 1953, it resolved that "independence is the primary form of self-rule unless another status is selected under conditions of 'absolute equality.'" Until 1959, the United Nations and the United States recognized Hawai'i as a non-self-governing territory. But months before statehood, the United States removed Hawai'i from this list. Illegally under international law, the United States exempted itself from offering independence as a choice on the referendum on statehood.[84]

For the vast majority of Chinese, Japanese, and Koreans, statehood represented a large step toward first-class citizenship and their incorporation into "a thriving and contented middle-class—the realization of the high ideal of Americanism," to recall the words of striking Japanese worker-settlers in 1909. Yet the quest by haole Republican tourism-statehood promoters to produce a statehood that preserved white power and privilege and the desire by most locals for the full rights of U.S. citizenship and political participation in the affairs of the nation had an effect unforeseen by its most optimistic proponents. Between World War I and statehood, virtually all in Hawai'i helped make racial and cultural aloha ideologically, but not structurally, normative. A diverse group of actors who struggled against white supremacy and for racial equality were thereby among those who reinforced the "tradition of tolerance," Jonathan Y. Okamura argues, that has allowed "Hawaii's people to avoid acknowledging" much less "confronting the institutionalized inequality among ethnic groups." Key leaders of the Democratic Party that soon came to dominate party politics in Hawai'i initially pursued the goals of economic and political equality from within the U.S. ideologies and structures of which Hawai'i became a part. As Matsuo Takabuki said in the mid-1950s, "We were not revolutionaries" but "willing to play by the rules of the game." Daniel Inouye too credited his election to the U.S. Senate in 1962 as a result of continuing a tradition of "not making big waves." The Japanese-led Democratic Party blunted its reformist impulses as some of its leading members came to commit themselves to promoting and profiting from tourism. Much like haole before them, it led other elite locals, to embrace aloha in appeals to shared values of interracial harmony and love that have worked to maintain the new status quo and contain political resistance. [85]

Whereas incorporation into the Union was the intended result of Hawaiian statehood, it was an unintended result of the Cuban revolution. In understanding this phenomenon, the childhood recollections of the literary critic Gustavo Pérez-Firmat are instructive. Like so many privileged whites who left Cuba in the early years of the revolution, he and his family were confident that if Cubans did not "get fed up with the Revolution and overthrow Castro," then "the Marines would show up" and "wrest the government from him." After all, the United States had never long tolerated a Cuban government that it and its allies did not support. Privileged Cubans had long relied on a variety of U.S. interventions to thwart the radicalization of previous revolutions and gone into temporary exile in the United States to await the restoration. No wonder the first waves of Cubans who left fully expected to spend, as the title of Pérez-Firmat's memoir observes, *Next Year in Cuba.*

　　Yet there was a sense that things were different. For example, when the Pérez-Firmat family left Havana in 1960, they placed their house in the care of an uncle. Before joining them in exile, the uncle spent a day ripping out the toilets, sinks, and electrical fixtures and wiring in his home and the former home of his nephew's family, hardly the act of one imagining imminent return. Pérez-Firmat recorded a moment of bittersweet triumph in his family's personal blow against the revolution: "To the victors belong the spoiled fixtures." Consumption commitments were a key reason why the family could not remain in Cuba. His family embraced the notion that "Grand Cuban style meant big: big houses, big cars, a big yacht, big jewelry, big furs, big cigars. . . . Thus it was with my father, who loved the outward signs of wealth more than wealth itself." His example influenced his sons:

"Already in Cuba, my brothers and I were being trained to become Americans; without knowing it, our parents were grooming us for exile."[86]

Although revolution and statehood were radically different forms of decolonization in most ways, the more than 200,000 mainly privileged white Cubans who migrated to the United States in the first years after 1959 became as deeply incorporated into the Union as the people of Hawai'i did. In an unexpected way, they fulfilled plans that nineteenth-century U.S. imperial architects and privileged white creoles had formulated to make Cuba and Hawai'i parts of the white republic and states of the Union in the nineteenth century. Indeed, as much as the U.S. nation needed multiracial Hawai'i during the Cold War and backed statehood to show the world that the United States embraced people of color as equals and first-class citizens, most mainlanders predicated their support of statehood on reconstructions of the diverse population of Hawai'i, particularly its Asian American majority, as white. When U.S. actors lent their support to the Cuban revolution, they did so by casting it as a drama in the ongoing family romance rooted in a white republican manhood and moderate revolutionary tradition first forged by the Founding Fathers of the United States and continued by nineteenth-century U.S. and Cuban white elites committed to annexing Cuba. As the United States came to reject the leftward course of the Cuban revolution, it wrote Castro, his revolutionary compatriots, and the Cubans who supported them out of narratives of national belonging. It did not do the same with the privileged white Cubans who chose U.S. exile; they were instead cast as patriots of both Cuba and the United States, in a rare U.S. affirmation of dual nationality. As in the mid-nineteenth century, so too in the mid-twentieth did assessments of the worthiness of the people of Cuba and Hawai'i for incorporation into the Union hinge upon demonstrations that they were American enough, civilized enough, republican enough, and white enough to deserve the full rights and privileges of national belonging. As at the turn of the twentieth century, at its midpoint, architects of U.S. empire deemed national self-determination and sovereignty for Cuba and Hawai'i unacceptable outcomes of a long history in which the pleasures of imperialism served as rewards for those entrusted with the politics of empire.

CONCLUSION

The Ugly American has haunted this project, in part owing to confusions over who the ugly American was (and is). In popular parlance the term refers to the arrogant, insensitive, and rude U.S. tourist abroad. This figure is the twin of the party-going, country-hopping, globe-trotting diplomats, executives, officers, and others disparaged by Eugene Lederer and William Burdick and a dead ringer for the book's European colonial officials. Yet these jet-setters are polar opposites of the ugly Americans who are Lederer's and Burdick's heroes and heroine, the hard-working, plain-living, self-sacrificing emissaries of democratic, capitalist modernity to the decolonizing and developing world. The authors' denial that these "true" Americans bear a resemblance to agents of other empires is part of a broader U.S. denial that its empire bears any resemblance to those empires. That is another reason the novel has haunted this project. Lederer and Burdick wrote *The Ugly American* to counter Graham Greene's critique of U.S. imperialism in *The Quiet American*. Greene may have later offered his own rejoinder to them: "I enjoyed the *louche* atmosphere of Batista's city and I never stayed long enough to be aware of the sad political background of arbitrary imprisonment and torture."[1] Was this critic of imperial politics and aficionado of imperial pleasures aping *The Quiet American*'s protagonist to mock the U.S. envoys who knew just how much their pleasure depended on *their* man in Havana (to paraphrase another Greene title)?

Reflecting on the U.S. imperial histories of Cuba and Hawai'i suggests how the comparative study of societies within the U.S. empire can contribute to the comparative and global study of the United States and other empires. The long-standing U.S. denial, not that it was an empire, but that it was an empire like other empires informed the insistence by interwar tourism promoters that the polities and resorts of Cuba and Hawai'i were at once democratic and aristocratic. The "aristocratic" served as a shorthand signifier for belonging to an exclusive club comprising the citizens of the world's imperial powers and their allies, an international class of privileged whites racially endowed with the right to rule, and a cosmopolitan order of pleasure for the leisured few. The "democratic" sought to distinguish and distance the U.S. nation and empire from its European counterparts. The blessing of providence and absence of a feudal and monarchical past situated the United States outside the laws of history, making it the best example of a polity based on universal rights and a republic destined to extend these rights to benighted peoples everywhere. Still, U.S. imperial agents came to insist that they could indulge in what they deemed decadent aristocratic pleasures and repressive monarchical politics without compromising their and their nation's republican principles or its special mission to spread them globally. Cultural producers cast the United States as a virtuous imperial republic by contrasting it with corrupt European nations and empires.

Abetting such displacements and denials, agents of U.S. empire justified their support of exclusionary, repressive regimes by presenting them as necessary evils required for achieving a liberty that they came to equate more with the freedom of capital than with the freedom of citizens. The elite insistence that ordinary people across the color line had the potential to acquire universal rights like liberty and equality rationalized the indefinite deferral of these rights. Discourses of imagined aristocracy in interwar-era Cuba and Hawai'i again offer a case in point. During a period of intense class, racial, and labor strife in the United States, and intensifying anticolonial and antiracist agitations around the globe, these discourses promised rich white U.S. citizens membership in truly American aristocracies that offered them the privilege, hierarchy, and deference they believed their due. These same elites simultaneously presented themselves as torchbearers of a republicanism forged in the New World, far from the decaying influences of the Old World. Their rhetorical devotions to and ritual displays of republican virtue aided efforts not just to elide responsibility for the tyrannical regimes the United States backed but to recast them as enlightened states dedicated to preparing all for truly democratic and representative self-government in some foggy future. The United States contrasted itself with the very empires it imitated to deny that it was anything like them.

Despite such denials, the United States was much like other empires, beginning with a steadfast belief in its exceptional nature that predated the nation's founding. In fact, claims to exceptionalism are a hallmark of virtually every empire.[2] When Jefferson declared the United States an empire for liberty, he could hardly lay claim to originality. Well before the American Revolution produced many happily united states, the British regarded theirs as an empire of liberty. So did the Dutch. They saw their liberal, Protestant empires as polar opposites of the empire of despotic, Catholic Spain and thought, as the U.S. founders later did, its "priest-ridden" people incapable of liberty.[3] Yet in different ways, all these were empires of liberty for the free white men who were their intended benefi-ciaries. Still, Jefferson's insistence that the United States was an empire and a republic, as were Rome and France, stood in marked contrast to the U.S observers and scholars of many generations who thought them diametri-cally opposed. Their assertions of incommensurability have baffled their counterparts outside the United States. They have readily accepted that republics are as suited for empire as, for example, monarchies, and that the leading historic fear of republican empire was how to combine the twin pursuits of liberty and conquest while maintaining a proper balance between the people and the palace, as the Romans put it of their republican empire.[4]

Over time and space, the United States came to prefer informal empire, commercial imperialism, and indirect governance over formal colonialism, territorial annexation, and direct rule. Again, many of its architects and emissaries claimed exceptionalism. Once again, other contemporaries and historians, especially outside the United States, found this not at all excep-tional.[5] Over the course of modern world history, most empires became less colonial and more imperial, although, of course, even the most indi-rectly ruled peoples and places have been "subordinate to, and fitted into, an overarching colonial state."[6] The United States began a slow, uneven shift from colonialism and toward imperialism around the mid-nineteenth century when it made states of territories in the Pacific West and protector-ates of a number of islands in the Caribbean and Pacific.[7] That said, terms like "territories" and "protectorates" or "informal" and "formal" empire or "direct" and "indirect" rule say little about the concrete forms and prac-tices of imperial governance.[8]

It would seem likely, or at least logical, that empires hold and exercise greater power in formal, directly governed colonies than they do in infor-mal, indirectly ruled imperial dependencies. Yet the histories of the last U.S. territory modeled squarely on its settler colonial frameworks and the first protectorate of its informal empire suggest, if not entirely otherwise, some-thing less clear-cut. For much of its history, the independent nation of Cuba enjoyed less political and economic autonomy and sovereignty in its imperial relationship with the United States than the annexed territory of Hawai'i did. Hawai'i was subject to less U.S. oversight and fewer interventions than Cuba, and only one military occupation, which resulted as much from fears of Japan as fears about the Japanese of Hawai'i. Hawai'i possessed more autonomy than Cuba vis-à-vis the U.S. political capital of Washington, D.C., and financial capital of New York. With scant U.S. direct capital investment until after World War II, the haole of Hawai'i never became accountable, much less beholden, to U.S. financial interests. By contrast in Cuba, U.S. business and government measured the performance of the Cuban government by how well it protected U.S. corporate interests, a gauge that often translated into the degree of freedom accorded Cuban government officials.[9]

U.S. governance of Hawai'i stood in marked contrast to Cuba, where during the first of two military interventions and occupations (as well as numerous political interventions), the United States labored to create and install in power a political class of mostly English-speaking, white elites, many educated in and naturalized citizens of the United States. At the same time, in turn-of-the-twentieth-century Hawai'i, U.S. imperial architects created for an existing, if then fragmented, haole ruling class a governorship with more power than any other U.S. territory or state. Although in theory the U.S. president chose territorial governors, the United States generally allowed haole to select their own. U.S. officials allowed haole to govern as they saw fit more often than not until they imposed martial law on Hawai'i during World War II. Haole dominion was aided by the fact that only a minority of adults in the U.S. territory had the right to vote or was eligible for U.S. citizenship until the broad eve of World War II. In the Republic of Cuba, 1902 to 1959, adult Cuban men, and beginning in 1934 women as well, across the color line elected many presidents and suffered several dictators, but they had the luxury of backing only one president the United States did not support, and that a provisional president who as a result lasted only weeks. By contrast, in the U.S. territory of Hawai'i, 1900 to 1959, haole perhaps had one governor of whom they did not approve, over whom they did not exercise power, or both.

The power to represent oneself that is both measure and manifestation of political power likewise emerged from and sustained the different kinds of imperial relationships of the United States in Cuba and Hawai'i.[10] These powers of representation first took recognizable institutional form in two annexationist organs, *La Verdad* and the Hawaii Bureau of Information. *La*

Verdad was founded and produced by elite white Cubans and U.S citizens in New Orleans and New York (to promote annexation in Havana in the mid-nineteenth century was to court imprisonment or death); the Hawaii Bureau of Information was established and run by haole divided over annexation but united in the determination to secure white dominion in Hawai'i. These patterns persisted. The three successor agencies of the HBI—the Hawaii Promotion Committee, the Hawaii Tourist Bureau, and the Hawaii Visitors Bureau—commanded more power and far more resources than the Cuban Tourism Commission, founded only in 1919, and its successors ever did, with the possible exception of in 1959. Cuban travel writing and tourism promotion generally operated as a joint project or partnership of Cuban and U.S. actors of varying degrees of intimacy; by contrast, successive generations of haole acquired and, after various crises, reacquired the upper hand in the local production and dissemination of representations of Hawai'i. Differential powers of representation reflected and reinforced the greater autonomy Hawai'i had in its imperial relationship with the United States in comparison to Cuba.

Although Hawai'i may seem to have begun an inexorable march to U.S. statehood in 1900, when it was made a U.S. territory and became eligible for eventual statehood, there, as in Cuba, the forms of U.S. imperial rule shaped the forms of revolt against them.[11] In working for statehood for Hawai'i, local U.S. citizens and settlers, on the one hand, and agents of U.S. mainland capital and the state, on the other hand, had to challenge the haole dominion of the territory's political economy. By contrast, the dependency of Cuba had to wage an anti-imperial revolution to achieve political independence from the United States, in ways comparable to France's colonies of Algeria and Vietnam. Unlike revolutionaries in Algeria and Vietnam, those in Cuba did not wage war against the metropole. For Cuba, it took a civil war against a U.S.-armed and U.S.-backed Cuban dictator *and* a diplomatic revolution waged variously with and against the United States for Cuba to win independent nationhood and economic sovereignty.[12] William F. Buckley, Jr., certainly overstated the case when he said of Castro, "I got my job through the *New York Times*." Yet the rebels' support by a broad cross-section of the U.S. media aided the widespread success of their diplomatic revolution on the U.S. public-relations front until sometime in 1959.[13]

If Cuba's rebels needed the assistance of the U.S. media to win their revolution, in the struggle for statehood for Hawai'i, local and mainland actors needed each other to break the historic haole hold on the political economy. Their efforts took the form of informal collaborations and networks as well as business and military contracts. At the most basic level, U.S. firms and the military needed workers and managers, and U.S. businesses needed consumers of their goods and services. More importantly here, U.S. capital and the state offered locals the jobs, wages and salaries, and access to capital they used to pursue upward mobility and increase their stake and participation in economic sectors outside the plantation order. For different reasons, they shared with locals the goal of breaking haole hegemony and integrating Hawai'i more deeply into the U.S. political economy via statehood. The benefits of statehood were unevenly distributed. For Chinese, Japanese, and Korean Americans, U.S. Hawai'i was home. Accordingly, they held high stakes in their acculturation and assimilation to America and acceptance as Americans in a nation that continued to equate belonging and whiteness. For the most part, they experienced statehood as the process through which they finally secured all the privileges, rights, and responsibilities of U.S. citizenship and nationhood. By contrast, many Hawaiians, Filipinos, and Samoans experienced statehood as another phase of an ongoing imperial history. Not only did it exacerbate competitions and conflicts between their identifications and loyalties as Natives and Americans, but in old and new ways, statehood hampered ongoing quests to assert their collective identities and rights as the once sovereign indigenous peoples of formerly independent states.

A fairly coherent, if ever-changing, set of beliefs about race, whiteness, and the rule of difference that the United States shared with other Western nations shaped the very different forms of imperial governance it designed for and practiced in Cuba and Hawai'i. Even after efforts to transform Cuba and Hawai'i into settler republics failed and were aborted, the logics and legacies of white republicanism and settler colonialism continued to shape the ways that U.S. officials viewed and governed their empire and its peoples. Key conceptual lenses through which U.S. officials and citizens viewed their empire and its peoples endured and shaped the United States' gradual abandonment of settler colonialism and consolidation of a decided preference for informal imperialism.

Across two oceans and two centuries, the notion that the U.S. imperium was created and governed especially by and for free white persons bound by a shared devotion to American civilization and U.S. republicanism survived all manner of imperial realignments. In the mid-nineteenth century,

Cuba and Hawai'i became twinned in the U.S. imperial imagination as desirable additions to the white republic and future states in the Union. Annexationists of the second half of the nineteenth century and advocates of revolution and statehood in the mid-twentieth cast the rebels of Cuba and the diverse people of Hawai'i as actually or potentially American enough, civilized enough, republican enough, and white enough to warrant their support by a U.S. nation and people bound to them by ties of kinship and affection. The U.S. embrace of the radically different forms of decolonization represented by statehood and revolution constitutes less of a break and more a continuity with the past. The founders went to great lengths to build decolonization into an expansive empire for liberty by and for its growing free white citizenry. They embedded this eventuality in the nation's imperial frameworks to ensure that decolonization resulted not in independence from, but further integration into, the Union. Although the founders envisioned U.S. statehood as the ideal type of decolonization, beliefs in the permanence of the bonds of affection and kinship forged in expanding the imperial republic endured alterations to and then abandonment of the territorial system.

From the nineteenth-century fraternity of white men through the Cold War imperial brotherhood, class remained a crucial marker for determining belonging in the imperial republic, one that could and frequently did trump race.[14] Beginning in the mid-nineteenth century, class and racial bonds of brotherhood between Cuban and U.S. annexationists could and did override a prevailing hierarchy of whiteness that situated Anglo Americans above Latin Americans; at the turn of the twentieth century in Hawai'i, haole exploited the widespread view that Polynesians were Aryans to present marriages between Anglo-Saxon haole and Hawaiian ali'i as a founding fiction of the new colonial state and U.S. territory. Between the world wars, the desire of white U.S. elites to become part of American aristocracies in Cuba and Hawai'i again could and often did supersede prevailing views of upper-crust Cubans and Hawaiians as racial inferiors. By the mid-twentieth century, the class credentials acquired by the privileged Golden Men of Asian descent in Hawai'i made them desirable members of the nation's elite foreign policy establishment. Class and race mingled and merged in the production of civilized Americans worthy of rights and privileges of belonging in the imperial republic.

At the same time, exclusionary visions of cultural and racial purity and universal principles of freedom and equality that met in the original empire for liberty endured in altered forms. The U.S. founders likely would have understood the faith that Cold War actors placed in the power of American, civilized, republican whiteness to nurture and sustain imperial relationships. These elite white men imagined and committed to building a racially and culturally homogenous society comprising happily united free white peoples, states, and territories devoid of Indians, blacks, and others deemed racial threats to the nation. But during the Cold War, the United States needed multiracial Hawai'i to demonstrate to the people of the world, especially those in the decolonizing and developing world, that it was capable of accepting persons of color as equals and first-class citizens. The United States supported statehood for Hawai'i to demonstrate its commitment to racial equality as it conditioned this support on racially reconstructing the islands' Asian ethnics as cousins and brothers of the mainland United States' recently whitened European ethnics. At the same time, the United States was under pressure to demonstrate that it was the global champion of liberty and democracy, a claim belied by its frequent support of right-wing dictators and overthrows of popularly elected left-leaning governments. U.S. admirers and supporters of the Cuban revolution premised their support of it on the idea that the rebels had modeled themselves and their movement on the sort of virile republican manhood and moderate, orderly revolution first forged during the Revolutionary War and later along numerous factual and fictional frontiers. Admirers and detractors alike believed that the devotion of white, middle- and upper-class Cubans to the American way of life would enable them and their U.S. allies to prevent this revolution from taking a permanent leftward turn, as with so many previous revolutions. They turned a blind eye to the unfulfilled revolutionary promises of Cuba Libre.

Indeed, as Cubans have known all too well since the United States imposed its travel and trade embargo on the island-nation in 1961, it is unacceptable to break away from a U.S. imperium ostensibly entered into freely and sustained by bonds of affection and kinship. Belief in the consensual nature and the irrevocability of imperial ties helps explain why the break between two nations long regarded as bound by ties of singular intimacy was met with outrage and disbelief in the United States, and why many U.S. and some Cuban citizens came to regard the leftward turn of the revolution as an inexplicable act of betrayal. It helps explain why so many U.S. citizens and Cubans who fled to the United States were certain that the breakup could only be temporary. It helps explain why some hope, even believe, that when Fidel Castro dies the relationship between the United States and Cuba will return to much the way it was before the triumph of a revolution that many in the United States had admired and supported.

Belief in the consensual, irrevocable nature of imperial relationships also helps explain why the United States could not fathom offering Hawai'i the choice of independence in 1959 and resorted to illegal means under international law to avoid having to present such a choice, even though many observers believed, likely correctly, that most people living in Hawai'i and eligible to vote at the time would have cast their ballot for statehood. It helps explain why the U.S. apology to Native Hawaiians in 1993 for its role in the overthrow of the queen and kingdom was made precisely "in order to provide for a *proper reconciliation* between the United States and the Native Hawaiian people" but expressly not in order to recognize Native claims to their indigenous lands and national sovereignty. Deliberations about the wording centered on how to offer an apology while not accepting the responsibility to attempt to right wrongs done, a position upheld by a number of U.S. Supreme Court decisions.[15] This refusal has roots in a broader U.S. stance that will not acknowledge publicly that it has perpetrated the same kinds of violences and injustices as other empires. So too does the inability of the United States to acknowledge publicly that it helped create the conditions that led to an anti-imperial revolution that many U.S. observers compared to their own nation's revolution for independence. The United States' refusal to admit that it is an empire like other empires has long supported its citizenry's demands for the pleasures deemed the reward—and the right—of imperial destiny and duty, as well as disavowals of the devastations they have wrought.

Introduction

1. On islands as contained and bounded spaces upon which westerners have projected and pursued all manner of capacious dreams and schemes, see John Gillis, *Islands of the Mind: How the Human Imagination Created the Atlantic World* (New York: Palgrave Macmillan, 2004); K. R. Howe, *Nature, Culture, and History: The "Knowing" of Oceania* (Honolulu: University of Hawai'i Press, 2000); for a powerful critique, see Epeli Hau'ofa's now classic "Our Sea of Islands," originally published in Eric Waddell, Vijay Naidu, and Hau'ofa, eds., *A New Oceania: Rediscovering Our Sea of Islands* (Suva: School of Social and Economic Development, University of the South Pacific, 1993).

2. In 1881 and 1894 James G. Blaine and John Tyler Morgan respectively used the terms the "same position" and "analogous places" to describe the position of Cuba and Hawai'i in the mental and material geography of U.S. empire. Similar sentiments were voiced earlier in the 1850s by expansionists like William Marcy and Benjamin F. Pierce and later in the 1890s by imperialists that included Theodore Roosevelt and Alfred T. Mahan. The idea of selecting contemporaries and neighbors for comparison comes from the eminent comparativist Marc Bloch, "A Contribution Towards a Comparative History of European Societies," in *Land and Work in Medieval Society: Selected Papers of Marc Bloch*, trans. J. E. Anderson (1928; reprint, London: Routledge and K. Paul, 1967). By neighbors, Bloch meant adjacent or abutting societies. But since the nation's founding, U.S. citizens have had a much more expansive understanding of neighbors and backyards. As Louis Pérez eloquently explains in discussing these ideas, "Metaphorical representation of proximity [has] enabled the Americans to imagine the United States as a presence everywhere, sharing contiguous space with every country in the world." Louis A. Pérez, Jr., *Cuban in the American Imagination: Metaphor and the Imperial Ethos* (Chapel Hill: University of North Carolina Press, 2008), 268.

3. George Steinmetz, *The Devil's Handwriting: Precoloniality and the German Colonial State in Qingdao, Samoa, and Southwest Africa* (Chicago: University of Chicago, 2007), is a brilliant study of the ways precolonial imaginaries shape colonial governance.

4. Edward Said, *"Kim*, the Pleasures of Imperialism," *Raritan* (1987): 27–64.

5. For most of the nineteenth and twentieth centuries, various nations of Europe were U.S. tourists' most popular overseas destinations. But Cuba and Hawai'i were their most popular tropical overseas destinations between 1898 and 1959. While Mexico could count as a tropical destination, it was not overseas. More importantly, first the railroad and then the automobile tied Mexico and Canada to the United States in ways that rendered them much more part of the domestic than the foreign market, a reason contemporaries preferred the term overseas travel to foreign travel.

6. Robert Campbell, *In Darkest Alaska: Travel and Empire Along the Inside Passage* (Philadelphia: University of Pennsylvania Press, 2007), 12.

7. Reid to McKinley, December 5, 1896, and Reid to Donald Nicholson, December 17, 1896, in "Rise to World Power: Selected Letters of Whitelaw Reid, 1895–1912," David R. Contosta and Jessica R. Hawthorne, eds., *Transactions of the American Philosophical Society* 76, 2 (1986), 22, 23.

8. Laura Wexler, *Tender Violence: Domestic Visions in an Age of U.S. Imperialism* (Chapel Hill: University of North Carolina Press, 2000), is a wonderful study of the domestication of empire and the erasure of imperial violence.

9. For amazing analyses of performance that McKinley would have understood well, see Greg Dening, *Performances* (Chicago: University of Chicago Press, 1996); William McKinley, "Speech at the Citizens' Banquet in the Auditorium, Chicago, October 19, 1898," in *Speeches and Addresses of William McKinley, from March 1, 1897 to May 30, 1900* (New York: Doubleday and McClure, 1900), 134; President William McKinley, "State of the Union Address," December 5, 1898, and December 5, 1899, http://stateoftheunion.onetwothree.net (accessed April 1, 2007); Ada Ferrer, *Insurgent Cuba: Race, Nation, and Revolution, 1868–1898* (Chapel Hill: University of North Carolina Press, 1999); Noenoe Silva, *Aloha Betrayed: Native Hawaiian Resistance to American Colonialism* (Durham, N.C.: Duke University Press, 2004).

10. The term "Hawaiian" refers to the indigenous people of Hawai'i.

11. Thomas Jefferson called the United States an "empire of liberty" and an "empire for liberty." Although sometimes used interchangeably, the former term best describes the empire's essence and the latter term, its purpose. Brook Thomas offers an excellent precise and concise distinction: "If an 'empire of libery' is one in which liberty exists, an 'empire for liberty' is one in the service of liberty." Thomas, "A Constitution Led by the Flag: The *Insular Cases* and the Metaphor of Incorporation," in Christina Duffy Burnett and Burke Marchall, eds., *Foreign in a Domestic Sense: Puerto Rico, American Expansion, and the Constitution* (Durham, N.C.: Duke University Press, 2001), 89.

12. The classic study of these ideas remains Albert Weinberg, *Manifest Destiny: A Study of Nationalist Expansion in American History* (1935; reprint, Chicago: Quadrangle Books, 1963).

13. On the interconnections among these visions and the people who worked to realize them, see James T. Campbell, Matthew Pratt Guterl, and Robert G. Lee, introduction to Campbell, Guterl, and Lee, eds., *Race, Nation, and Empire in American*

History (Chapel Hill: University of North Carolina Press, 2007), 1–16; it is a theme ʋɪ Gary Y. Okihiro, *Island World: A History of Hawai'i and the United States* (Berkeley: University of California Press, 2008).

14. Such thinking is at the heart of Frederick Jackson Turner's "frontier thesis." Henry Nash Smith classically explores as it as a culmination, as well as an innovation, of Anglo-Saxon U.S. thought. Henry Nash Smith, *Virgin Land: The American West as Symbol and Myth* (1950; reprint, Cambridge, Mass.: Harvard University Press, 1978).

15. Eric Love and Gerald Horne focus on the centrality of whiteness to U.S. overseas imperialism at the turn of the twentieth century and how considerations of whiteness hindered U.S. imperial ambitions overseas as much as they drove them, but Love and Horne do not frame their analyses in terms of republicanism or settler colonialism. Eric T. L. Love, *Race over Empire: Racism and U.S. Imperialism, 1865–1900* (Chapel Hill: University of North Carolina Press, 2004); Gerald Horne, *The White Pacific: U.S. Imperialism and Black Slavery in the South Seas* (Honolulu: University of Hawai'i Press, 2007).

16. For a compelling critique of the newness of the "new" imperialism, see Susan Gillman, "The New, Newest Thing: Have American Studies Gone Imperial?" *American Literary History* 17, 1 (Spring 2005): 196–214. Four important works that locate the roots of the new imperialism in the nineteenth century and on the North American continent are Walter LaFeber, *The New Empire: An Interpretation of American Expansion, 1860–1898* (Ithaca, N.Y.: Cornell University Press, 1963); Shelley Streeby, *American Sensations: Class, Empire, and the Production of Popular Culture* (Berkeley: University of California Press, 2002); Amy Kaplan, *The Anarchy of Empire in the Making of U.S. Culture* (Cambridge, Mass.: Harvard University Press, 2002); Walter Nugent, *Habits of Empire: A History of American Expansion* (New York: Alfred A. Knopf, 2008).

17. Peter Onuf, *Jefferson's Empire: The Language of American Nationhood* (Charlottesville: University Press of Virginia, 2000); Dana D. Nelson, *National Manhood: Capitalist Citizenship and the Imagined Fraternity of White Men* (Durham, N.C.: Duke University Press, 1998).

18. On the preference of the United States for moderate and orderly revolutions as measured by its own, see Michael H. Hunt, *Ideology and U.S. Foreign Policy* (New Haven, Conn.: Yale University Press, 1987); Hunt expands upon this argument in his most recent and brilliant book, *The American Ascendancy: How the United States Gained and Wielded Global Dominance* (Chapel Hill: University of North Carolina Press, 2007).

19. Matthew Frye Jacobson, *Barbarian Virtues: The United States Encounters Foreign Peoples at Home and Abroad, 1876–1917* (New York: Hill and Wang, 2000).

20. Vicente F. Rafael, *White Love and Other Events in Filipino History* (Durham, N.C.: Duke University Press, 2000), provides a wonderful analysis of how the colonization of the self was a prerequisite of self-government.

21. Dane Kennedy, *Magic Mountains: Hill Stations and the British Raj* (Berkeley:

University of California Press, 1996), 1; Eric T. Jennings, *Curing the Colonizers: Hydrotherapy, Climatology, and French Colonial Spas* (Durham, N.C.: Duke University Press, 2006).

22. On the ways U.S. consumers fashioned themselves as European aristocrats, see Kristan L. Hoganson, *Consumers' Imperium: The Global Production of American Domesticity, 1865–1920* (Chapel Hill: University of North Carolina Press, 2007); on ignorance as a privilege of power, Michol Seigel, *Uneven Encounters: Making Race and Nation in Brazil and the United States* (Durham, N.C.: Duke University Press, 2009).

23. David F. Schmitz, *Thank God They're on Our Side: The United States and Right-Wing Dictatorships, 1921–1965* (Chapel Hill: University of North Carolina Press, 1999).

24. On similar themes in rather different contexts, see Paul A. Kramer, *The Blood of Government: Race, Empire, the United States and the Philippines* (Chapel Hill: University of North Carolina Press, 2006), esp. ch. 5.

25. William W. Stowe, *Going Abroad: European Travel in Nineteenth-Century American Culture* (Princeton, N.J.: Princeton University Press, 1994); Marguerite S. Shaffer, *See America First: Tourism and National Identity, 1880–1940* (Washington, D.C.: Smithsonian Institution Press, 2001), 5.

26. Larzer Ziff, *Return Passages: Great American Travel Writing, 1780–1910* (New Haven, Conn.: Yale University Press, 2000), 7, 8; Cindy S. Aron, *Working at Play: A History of Vacations in the United States* (New York: Oxford University Press, 1999), esp. 5, 9.

27. Campbell, *In Darkest Alaska*; Valerie Fifer, *American Progress: The Growth of the Transport, Tourist, and Information Industries in the Nineteenth Century as Seen Through the Life and Times of George A. Crofutt* (Chester, Conn.: Globe Pequot Press, 1988); Christopher Endy, *Cold War Holidays: American Tourism in France* (Chapel Hill: University of North Carolina Press, 2004); Christina Klein, *Cold War Orientalism: Asia in the Middlebrow Imagination, 1945–1961* (Berkeley: University of California Press, 2003). I wish I had had the time to make better use of the most recent monograph of Dennis Merrill, *Negotiating Paradise: U.S. Tourism and Empire in Twentieth-Century Latin America* (Chapel Hill: University of North Carolina Press, 2009).

28. Melani McAlister, *Epic Encounters: Culture, Media, and U.S. Interests in the Middle East, 1945–2000* (Berkeley: University of California Press, 2001), 8.

29. Daniel Boorstin, "From Traveler to Tourist: The Lost Art of Travel," in *The Image: A Guide to Pseudo-Events in America* (New York: Atheneum, 1980); David Engerman, "A Research Agenda for the History of Tourism as a Foreign Relation: Towards an International Social History," *American Studies International* 32, 2 (1994): 3–31; Endy, *Cold War Holidays*; Klein, *Cold War Orientalism*.

30. In 1954, *U.S. News and World Report* informed its advertising client Conrad Hilton that nearly half its readers had traveled abroad in the past five years, and more than a quarter, in the past year. They were hardly average Americans. Three-quarters of its readers were "managerial men," who earned average annual incomes of $14,500

(in 1957, 7.5 percent of U.S. families earned $10,000 or more; 1 percent earned $20,000 or more). Four years later, the New York Port Authority reported that the median annual income of U.S. tourists flying to the Caribbean, where Cuba was the most visited destination, was over $15,000; 41 percent earned at least $20,000. At the same time, nearly a quarter of U.S. travelers to Hawai'i earned at least $20,000, and over half at least $10,000. See "A Memorandum Report to Hilton Hotels Corporation from 'U.S. News & World Report,'" November 1954, 5, 6, Conrad N. Hilton Papers, Conrad N. Hilton School of Hotel and Restaurant Management, University of Houston; *New York's Overseas Travelers: Report of a One Year Survey Conducted in Collaboration with Overseas Airlines April 1956 Through March 1957* (Port of New York Authority: Aviation Department, Forecast and Analysis Division, May 1958), 18, 98; Hawaii Visitors Bureau, semifinal draft of the 1959 Annual Report, "Tourism in Hawaii 1959," 13, Henry J. Kaiser Papers, carton 180, Bancroft Library, University of California at Berkeley; William D. Paterson, "The Big Picture," *ASTA Travel News* June 1956, 45, and Paterson, "The Big Picture, Part II," *ASTA Travel News* July 1956, 130; June 1958, 146; May 1959, 130.

31. To borrow the title of Walter Nugent's important recent book, cited in n. 15.

32. Haole considered the Portuguese and Spanish white but not haole. Haole were proud to call themselves by this name to connote their position as self-conscious and self-consciously superior white creoles of Hawai'i.

33. Matthew Frye Jacobson, *Roots Too: White Ethnic Revival in Post–Civil Rights America* (Cambridge, Mass.: Harvard University Press, 2006), 7; David Roediger, *Working Toward Whiteness: How America's Immigrants Become White: The Strange Journey from Ellis Island to the Suburbs* (New York: Basic Books, 2005).

Chapter 1. First Fruits of a Tropical Eden

1. Adams to Hugh Nelson, April 28, 1823, *Writings of John Quincy Adams*, ed. Worthington Chauncey Ford, 7 vols., 1820–1823 (1917; reprint, New York: Greenwood Press, 1968), 7: 373; Winthrop cited in William Cronon, *Changes in the Land: Indians, Colonists, and the Ecology of New England* (New York: Hill and Wang, 1983), 90; San Francisco *Alta California*, April 22, 1851, reprinted by the *Honolulu Polynesian*, May 17, 1851, cited in Ralph S. Kuykendall, *The Hawaiian Kingdom: 1778–1854*, 3 vols. (Honolulu: University of Hawai'i Press, 1938–1967), vol. 1, *Foundation and Transformation* (1938), 408; toast cited in Kuykendall, *The Hawaiian Kingdom*, 1: 410; Anders Stephanson, *Manifest Destiny: American Expansion and the Empire of Right* (New York: Hill and Wang, 1995), 18. Pierce's vice president, William King, was sworn into office by a U.S. consul at King's estate in Matanzas, Cuba. Luis Martínez-Fernández, *Torn Between Empires: Economy, Society, and Patterns of Political Thought in the Hispanic Caribbean, 1840–1878* (Athens: University of Georgia Press, 1994), 33.

2. Stevens to John W. Foster, February 1, 1893, U.S. Department of State, *Foreign Relations of the United States, 1894*, appendix 2, *Affairs in Hawaii* (Washington, D.C.: Government Printing Office, 1895), 402.

3. *New York Independent*, February 2, 1893, cited in Julius W. Pratt, *Expansionists of 1898* (Baltimore: Johns Hopkins University Press, 1936), 147–148; newspapers across the nation cited in E. Berkeley Tompkins, *Anti-Imperialism in the United States: The Great Debate, 1890–1920* (Philadelphia: University of Pennsylvania Press, 1970), 35–36.

4. John W. Foster, "The Annexation of Hawaii," address to the National Geographic Society at Washington, D.C., March 26, 1897 (Washington D.C.: Gibson Bros, 1897).

5. Adams to Nelson, April 28, 1823, *Writings of John Quincy Adams*, 7: 372.

6. Greg Dening, *Performances* (1992; reprint, Chicago: University of Chicago Press, 1996); Patricia Seed, *Ceremonies of Possession: Europe's Conquest of the New World, 1492–1640* (Cambridge, Mass.: Cambridge University Press, 1995).

7. Peter Onuf, *Jefferson's Empire: The Language of American Nationhood* (Charlottesville: University Press of Virginia, 2000), 12; on the endurance of marriage as a trope of territoriality and statehood, see Kerry Wynn, "'Miss Indian Territory' and 'Mr. Oklahoma Territory': Marriage, Settlement, and Citizenship in the Cherokee Nation and the United States," in Tony Ballantyne and Antoinette Burton, eds., *Moving Subjects: Gender, Mobility, and Intimacy in an Age of Global Empire* (Urbana: University of Illinois Press, 2008), 172–189.

8. Wai-chee Dimock, *Empire for Liberty: Melville and the Poetics of Individualism* (Princeton, N.J.: Princeton University Press, 1989), 3–41, passim, cited portion, 4; Richard W. Van Alstyne, *The Rising American Empire* (1960; reprint, New York: W.W. Norton, 1974), Jefferson cited on 81; Kirsten Silva Gruesz, "The Gulf of Mexico System and the 'Latinness' of New World Studies," *American Literary History* 18, 3 (Fall 2006): 468–495; Gesa Mackenthun, "Chartless Voyages and Protean Geographies: Nineteenth-Century American Fictions of the Black Atlantic," in Bernhard Klein and Mackenthun, eds., *Sea Changes: Historicizing the Ocean* (New York: Routledge, 2003), 131–148; Thomas Schoonover, *Uncle Sam's War of 1898 and the Origins of Globalization* (Lexington: University Press of Kentucky, 2003); Walter D. Mignolo, "Coloniality at Large: The Western Hemisphere in the Colonial Horizon of Modernity," *CR: The New Centennial Review* 1, 2 (Fall 2001): 19–54; M. Consuelo León W., "Foundations of the American Image of the Pacific," in Rob Wilson and Arif Dirlik, eds., *Asia/Pacific as Space of Cultural Production* (Durham, N.C.: Duke University Press, 1995), 17–29.

9. John O'Sullivan, "The Great Nation of Futurity," *United States Magazine and Democratic Review*, November 1839, 426–430; *Democratic Review*, 1848, cited in Dimock, *Empire for Liberty*, 9.

10. Walter LaFeber, "The American View of Decolonization, 1776–1920: An Ironic Legacy," in David Ryan and Victor Pungong, eds., *The United States and Decolonization: Power and Freedom* (New York: St. Martin's Press, 2000), 25; Lanny Thompson, "The Imperial Republic: A Comparison of the Insular Territories Under U.S. Dominion After 1898," *Pacific Historical Review* 71, 4 (November 2002): 535–574; Matthew Frye Jacobson, *Whiteness of a Different Color: European Immigrants and the*

Alchemy of Race (Cambridge, Mass.: Harvard University Press, 1998), 22–25; Gervasio Luis García, "I Am the Other: Puerto Rico in the Eyes of North Americans, 1898," *Journal of American History* 87, 2 (June 2000): 39–64, esp. 44; Thomas Bender, *A Nation Among Nations: America's Place in World History* (New York: Hill and Wang, 2006), 186.

11. Thomas R. Hietala, *Manifest Design: American Exceptionalism and Empire*, rev. ed. (Ithaca, N.Y.: Cornell University Press, 2003); John C. Weaver, *The Great Land Rush and the Making of the Modern World, 1650–1900* (Montreal and Kingston: McGill–Queen's University Press, 2003); A. Gallenga, *The Pearl of the Antilles* (London: Chapman and Hall, 1873), 5, 117.

12. John A. Logan, Jr., *No Transfer: An American Security Principle* (New Haven, Conn.: Yale University Press, 1961); Louis A. Pérez, Jr., *The War of 1898: The United States and Cuba in History and Historiography* (Chapel Hill: University of North Carolina Press, 1998), ch. 1; Adams to Nelson, April 28, 1823, in *Writings*, 7: 374; Ramiro Guerra y Sánchez, *The Territorial Expansion of the United States, at the Expense of Spain and the Hispanic-American Countries*, trans. Fernando E. Pérez Peña (Lanham, Md..: University Press of America, 2003), ch. 6.

13. Sylvester Stevens, *American Expansion in Hawaii, 1842–1898* (Harrisburg, Pa.: Archives, 1945), ch. 1; John Quincy Adams's report is reproduced in Hiram Bingham, *A Residence of Twenty-One Years in the Sandwich Islands; or the Civil, Religious, and Political History of Those Islands* (Hartford, Conn.: Hezekiah Huntington and New York: Sherman Converse, 1847), cited portion, 588–589.

14. Preface to Abiel Abbot, *Letters Written in the Interior of Cuba, Between the Mountains of Arcana, to the East, and of Cusco, to the West, in the Months of February, March, April, and May, 1828* (Boston: Bowles and Dearborn, 1829), v.

15. Abbot, *Letters*, xiv, emphasis in original, 160.

16. Abbot, *Letters*, 161, 167; on white Cubans' and Spaniards' views of the monteros, see Robert L. Paquette, *Sugar Is Made with Blood: The Conspiracy of La Escalera and the Conflict Between Empires over Slavery in Cuba* (Middletown, Conn.: Wesleyan University Press, 1988), 42, 43.

17. Paquette argues of this circle of annexationist white creoles, "Their vision of *cubanidad* would have emptied Cuba of its blacks, not only its slaves." *Sugar Is Made with Blood*, 91, 101. Hietala similarly argues for Texas about the same time, "The expansionists did not seek to emancipate the slave, but rather, through annexation, to emancipate the United States from the blacks." *Manifest Design*, 54. Richard Gott, *Cuba: A New History* (New Haven, Conn.: Yale University Press, 2004), 55.

18. Francis Steegmuller, *The Two Lives of James Jackson Jarves* (New Haven, Conn.: Yale University Press, 1951); James Jackson Jarves, *Scenes and Scenery in the Sandwich Islands, and a Trip Through Central America* (Boston: J. Munroe, 1843), 15–16. Jarves was also a U.S. signatory to a treaty of navigation, commerce, and friendship between Hawai'i and the United States at this time.

19. T. Walter Herbert, Jr., *Marquesan Encounters: Melville and the Meaning of*

Civilization (Cambridge, Mass.: Harvard University Press, 1980), 55; Jarves, *Scenes and Scenery in the Sandwich Islands*, 16–18, 183–184.

20. Prasenjit Duara, "Transnationalism and the Challenge to National Histories," in Thomas Bender, ed., *Rethinking American History in a Global Age* (Berkeley: University of California Press, 2002), 25–46; Jarves, *Scenes and Scenery in the Sandwich Islands*, 203–204; Louis A. Pérez, Jr., "Incurring a Debt of Gratitude," *American Historical Review* 104, 2 (April 1999): 356–398; Sally Engle Merry, *Colonizing Hawai'i: The Cultural Power of Law* (Princeton, N.J.: Princeton University Press, 2000).

21. William Henry Hurlbert, *Gan-Eden, or Pictures of Cuba* (Boston: John P. Jewett, 1854), 233; Robert E. May, *The Southern Dream of a Caribbean Empire, 1854–1861* (1973; reprint, Athens: University of Georgia Press, 1989), 261.

22. Richard Henry Dana, *To Cuba and Back: A Vacation Voyage*, ed. Harvey C. Gardiner (1850; reprint, Carbonale: Southern Illinois University Press, 1966), 132; Charles Francis Adams, *Richard Henry Dana, A Biography*, 2 vols. (Boston: Houghton, Mifflin, 1890), 2: 172–177. The lone example of "true Yankee" republicanism Dana found in Cuba took the form of a Lowell mechanic temporarily working there. Dana, *To Cuba and Back*, 59–60. Rodrigo Lazo shows how Dana "looped" Cuba "into a southern region of slavery with the U.S. South so that an opposition emerges between New England on the one hand and Cuba and the U.S. South on the other." Rodrigo Lazo, *Writing to Cuba: Filibustering and Cuban Exiles in the United States* (Chapel Hill: University of North Carolina Press, 2004), 154.

23. Lazo, *Writing to Cuba*, 14; Amy S. Greenberg makes this point as well in *Manifest Manhood and the Antebellum American Empire* (New York: Cambridge University Press, 2005), 43–53.

24. Paquette, *Sugar Is Made with Blood*, 264; Basil Rauch, *American Interest in Cuba, 1848–1855* (New York: Columbia University Press, 1948), 61–65, cited portion, 65; Lazo, *Writing to Cuba*, 11, 74–85.

25. Lazo, *Writing to Cuba*, 75; *The Island of Cuba by Alexander von Humboldt*, trans. from the Spanish with notes and preliminary essay by J. S. Thrasher (1856; reprint, New York: Negro Universities Press, 1969), preliminary essay, 86; Rauch, *American Interest in Cuba*, 54–55.

26. Thomas Holt, "Marking: Race, Race-making, and the Writing of History," *American Historical Review* 100, 1 (February 1995): 1–20; Kirsten Silva Gruesz, *Ambassadors of Culture: The Transamerican Origins of Latino Writing* (Princeton, N.J.: Princeton University Press, 2002), xiii, 59, 140; Matthew Pratt Guterl argues that Jamaica and Haiti represented "the Scylla and Charybdis of the American Mediterranean" in *American Mediterranean: Southern Slaveholders in the Age of Emancipation* (Cambridge, Mass.: Harvard University Press, 2008), 35–43.

27. Lazo, *Writing to Cuba*, 76, 79; *A Series of Articles on the Cuban Question* (New York: La Verdad, 1849), 3: 8–10. The pamphlet states that it is divided into two parts, but its page numbers restart from 1 on four separate occasions. So I use the format "1: 8–10" or "3: 8–10" to make the location of each reference clear.

28. *Articles on the Cuban Question*, 1: 5, 6; 2: 1; 4: 1, 5.

29. Joanne Pope Melish, *Disowning Slavery: Gradual Emancipation and "Race" in New England, 1780–1860* (Ithaca, N.Y.: Cornell University Press, 1998). Representations of New England as a model for emancipation became entwined with U.S. imperialism during the drafting of the Northwest Ordinance of 1787. Its architects passed an article prohibiting slavery in new territories. Debates over interpreting the article gave rise to a tradition of invoking emancipation in New England to promote the admission of lands as slaveholding territories. In debates over Indiana, a participant asserted that allowing slaves there would place them on the road to freedom: "they would be so dispersed, that they would be emancipated with the same ease and safety that they have in New England." Peter S. Onuf, *Statehood and Union: A History of the Northwest Ordinance* (Bloomington: Indiana University Press, 1987), esp. xiv, 110, 111, 121, 141–146, cited portion, 121.

30. *Articles on the Cuban Question*, 1: 5, 6; 2: 1; 4: 1, 5.

31. *Articles on the Cuban Question*, 2: 11; see also 1: 6, 21; 4: 9.

32. Cora Montgomery was the pen name of Jane McManus Storm Cazneau; Laura S. Hudson, *Mistress of Manifest Destiny: A Biography of Jane McManus Storm Cazneau, 1807–1878* (Austin: Texas State Historical Association, 2001), 60–64; *Articles on the Cuban Question*, 1: 14.

33. Shelley Streeby, *American Sensations: Class, Empire, and the Production of Popular Culture* (Berkeley: University of California Press, 2002); 88; Robert Campbell, *In Darkest Alaska: Travel and Empire Along the Inside Passage* (Pennsylvania: University of Pennsylvania Press, 2007), 76.

34. Maturin M. Ballou, *History of Cuba, or Notes of a Traveler in the Tropics* (Boston: Phillips, Sampson, 1854), 190, 199.

35. Hurlbert, *Gan-Eden*, 101–102, 175–180; Ballou, *History of Cuba*, 142, 143, 220, 226, 229.

36. Cronon, *Changes in the Land*; Henry Nash Smith, *Virgin Land: The American West as Symbol and Myth* (1950; reprint, Cambridge, Mass.: Harvard University Press, 1978); Howard Mumford Jones, *American Culture: The Formative Years* (1952; reprint, New York: Viking, 1967).

37. Richard B. Kimball, *Cuba and the Cubans* (New York: Samuel Hueston, 1850), 206; John S. C. Abbott, *South and North: Impressions Received During a Trip to Cuba and the South* (New York: Abbey and Abbot, 1860), 55; Dana, *To Cuba and Back*, 127; Thrasher, preliminary essay, 78.

38. Hurlbert, *Gan-Eden*, 177; Ballou, *History of Cuba*, 217, 219, 220, 230; Kimball, *Cuba and the Cubans*, 190; Abbott, *South and North*, 56–57; Dana, *To Cuba and Back*, 132. The lone discordant note came from a British traveler not familiar with the precise terms of the debate. In 1860, Anthony Trollope asserted that because "no Cuban himself will do anything" to bring independence or annexation about, the United States should annex Cuba without Cuban help. Anthony Trollope, *The West Indies*

and the Spanish Main (1860; reprint, New York: Carroll and Graf, 1999), 133, 134, 148.

39. On the development of this discourse and the process by which a free, white New England came to "stand" for the nation, see Melish, *Disowning Slavery*, 210–237.

40. Louis A. Pérez, Jr., *Cuba: Between Reform and Revolution* (New York: Oxford University Press, 1988), 136–139.

41. Merze Tate, *Hawaii: Reciprocity or Annexation?* (East Lansing: Michigan State University Press, 1969); Amy S. Greenberg, *Manifest Manhood and the Antebellum Empire* (New York: Cambridge University Press, 2005), 231–260, passim; William Seward cited in Noel Kent, *Hawaii: Islands Under the Influence* (Honolulu: University of Hawai'i Press, 1983), 42.

42. The idea that the sugar planters led the annexation movement persists, despite being well-documented otherwise by Van Alstyne, *The Rising American Empire* and William Adam Russ, Jr., *The Hawaiian Revolution (1893–1894)* (1959; reprint, Selinsgrove, Pa.: Susquehanna University Press, 1992); Tom Coffman, *Nation Within: The Story of America's Annexation of the Nation of Hawai'i* (Kāne'ohe, Hawai'i: EpiCenter Press, 1998), figures on percentage of people who supported annexation, 124.

43. Kuykendall, *The Hawaiian Kingdom*, vol. 3, *1874–1893: The Kalakaua Dynasty* (1967), 47; Coffman, *Nation Within*, 64–65.

44. My analysis of Twain is indebted to Rob Wilson, "Exporting Christian Transcendentalism, Importing Hawaiian Sugar: The Trans-Americanization of Hawai'i," *American Literature* 72, 3 (September 2000): 521–552, and Amy Kaplan, "The Imperial Routes of Mark Twain," ch. 2 of *The Anarchy of Empire in the Making of U.S. Culture* (Cambridge, Mass.: Harvard University Press, 2002), 51–91; Mark Twain, *Mark Twain's Letters from Hawaii*, ed. A. Grove Day (New York: Appleton, 1966), 12.

45. Twain, *Letters*, 270, 273, 274.

46. George Chaplin,. *Presstime in Paradise: The Life and Times of the Honolulu Advertiser, 1865–1995* (Honolulu: University of Hawai'i Press, 1998), 49–52; see also Walter Francis Frear, *Mark Twain and Hawaii* (Chicago: Lakeside, 1947), 156–159. The best treatment of the election of Kalākaua, his opposition, and search for legitimacy is Jonathan Kay Kamakawiwo'ole Osorio, *Dismembering Lāhui: A History of the Hawaiian Nation to 1887* (Honolulu: University of Hawai'i Press, 2002), 145–192.

47. Coffman, *Nation Within*, 63; Jacob Adler, *Claus Spreckels: The Sugar King in Hawaii* (Honolulu: Mutual, 1966).

48. Osorio, *Dismembering Lāhui*, 146, *Pacific Commercial Advertiser*, June 10, 1876, cited on 178, my emphasis.

49. Noenoe Silva, *Aloha Betrayed: Native Hawaiian Resistance to American Colonialism* (Durham, N.C.: Duke University Press, 2004), ch. 3; Merry, *Colonizing Hawai'i*, 13.

50. Osorio, *Dismembering Lāhui*, 199–295; Silva, *Aloha Betrayed*, 108–112.

51. Kuykendall, *The Hawaiian Kingdom*, 3: 347–366, cited portion, 348.

52. *Hawaiian Gazette*, November 22, 1876; Katherine Coman, *The History of Con-*

tract Labor in the Hawaiian Islands (New York: MacMillan, 1903), 37; Ethel M. Damon, *Sanford Ballard Dole and His Hawaii* (Palo Alto, Calif.: Pacific Books, 1957).

53. *Pacific Commercial Advertiser*, March 29, 1879. For similar examples, see the *Pacific Commercial Advertiser*, June 23, 1877; the *Hawaiian Gazette*, November 22, 1876, and January 24, 1877.

54. Osorio, *Dismembering Lāhui*, Thrum's *Saturday Press* cited on 201–202; Silva, *Aloha Betrayed*, 110–115, *Daily Bulletin* cited on 115; Lydia Kaulapai, "The Queen Writes Back: Liliʻuokalani's *Hawaii's Story by Hawaii's Queen*," *Studies in American Indian Literatures* 17, 2 (Summer 2005): 32–62.

55. Kuykendall, *The Hawaiian Kingdom*, 3: 347–366, cited portion, 348.

56. Osorio, *Dismembering Lāhui*, 243–245.

57. *Honolulu Daily Bulletin*, November 19, 1887, February 18, 1888, May 15, 1888, and May 6, 1889; L. J. Crampon, "Hawaii's Visitor Industry" (University of Hawaiʻi School of Travel Industry Management, 1976, photocopy), 221.

58. Unlike Thurston, Dillingham remained ambivalent about annexation until after the overthrow of the queen. Dillingham's biographer argues that his absence from Hawaiʻi between March 1892 and May 1893 spared him the need of making a "painful decision." After the overthrow of the queen, however, Dillingham threw his support behind the annexationist cause. Paul T. Yardley, *Millstones and Milestones: The Career of B. F. Dillingham* (Honolulu: University of Hawaiʻi Press, 1981), 174–179. Kuykendall, *The Hawaiian Kingdom*, 3: 68, 69; Lorrin A. Thurston, *Writings of Lorrin A. Thurston*, ed. Andrew Farrell (Honolulu: Honolulu Publishing, 1936), 59, 81–82; *Honolulu Daily Bulletin*, March 21, 1891; *Pacific Commercial Advertiser*, March 19, 1891.

59. Kilauea Volcano House Co. and Oahu Railway and Land Co., *The Hawaii Bureau of Information, The Objects and Proposed Basis of Organization* (Honolulu: Hawaiian Gazette, 1892), 4; Henry M. Whitney, *The Tourists' Guide Through the Hawaiian Islands* (Honolulu: Hawaiian Gazette, 1890), 155–166; Lorrin A. Thurston, ed., *Vistas of Hawaii*, "*The Paradise of the Pacific and Inferno of the World*" (St. Joseph, Mich.: A. B. Morse, 1891), esp. 28. See also the OR&L's advertisements on the back cover of *Thrum's Hawaiian Almanac and Annual* during the 1890s; *Pacific Commercial Advertiser*, November 10, 1891.

60. J. Kēhaulani Kauanui, *Hawaiian Blood: Colonialism and the Politics of Indigeneity and Sovereignty* (Durham, N.C.: Duke University Press, 2008), 27.

61. Kuykendall, *The Hawaiian Kingdom*, 3: 476–487; Stevens, *American Expansion in Hawaii*, 188–189; Thomas Kemper Hitch, *Islands in Transition: The Past, Present, and Future of Hawaii's Economy* (Honolulu: First Hawaiian Bank, 1992), 96; *Pacific Commercial Advertiser*, October 20, 1891; *Hawaiian Gazette* October 27, 1891; Thurston, *Writings*, 59, 81–82; Honolulu *Daily Bulletin*, March 21, 1891; *Pacific Commercial Advertiser*, March 19, 1891, and October 20, 1891.

62. *Pacific Commercial Advertiser*, October 20, 1891, and October 30, 1891.

63. Pratt, *Expansionists of 1898*, 51–54; Kuykendall, *The Hawaiian Kingdom*, 3:

534; Lorrin A. Thurston, *Memoirs of the Hawaiian Revolution*, ed. Andrew Farrell (Honolulu: Advertiser, 1936), 228–244, cited portion, 232; Stevens, *American Expansion in Hawaii*, 207–208, cited portion, 208.

64. *Pacific Commercial Advertiser*, August 9 and August 26, 1892. The organizing committee of the HBI comprised William R. Castle (Annexation Club and Annexation Commission of the Provisional Government), Charles M. Cooke (Annexation Commission), H. F. Glade (Annexation Club), John Ena (one of the rare Hawaiian annexationists), and John H. Soper (commander of the Provisional Government Army).

65. Stevens to Foster, no. 74, November 20, 1892, *FRUS 1894*, appendix 2: 192, 193.

66. By the mid-nineteenth century, the word had also come to refer to the Native monarchs and other royals of the Kingdom of Hawai'i.

67. Lili'uokalani, *Hawaii's Story by Hawaii's Queen* (1897; reprint, Honolulu: Mutual, 1990), 388; Silva, *Aloha Betrayed*, 134–135, cited portion, 135.

68. Russ, *The Hawaiian Revolution*, 184; Chicago *Inter-Ocean*, April 30, 1893; Norman Bolotin and Christine Laing, *The Chicago World's Fair of 1893: The World's Columbian Exposition* (Washington, D.C.: Preservation Press, 1992), 138.

69. Chicago *Inter-Ocean*, May 2, 1893; J. C. Furnas, *Anatomy of Paradise: Hawaii and the Islands of the South Seas* (New York: William Sloane Associates, 1937), 418; Aeko Sereno, "Images of the Hula Dancer and 'Hula Girl:' 1778–1960" (Ph.D. dissertation, University of Hawai'i, 1990), 159, 165–167, 181; Lilikalā Kame'eleihiwa, "The Role of American Missionaries in the 1893 Overthrow of the Hawaiian Government: Historical Events, 1820–1893," in Ulla Hasager and Jonathan Friedman, eds., *Hawaii: Return to Nationhood* (Copenhagen: International Work Group for Indigenous Affairs, document no. 75, 1994), 106–119, esp. 117. *Vistas* was republished for the Fair as *Paradise of the Pacific and Inferno of the World*; Russ, *The Hawaiian Revolution*, 173, 220.

70. Robert W. Rydell, *All the World's a Fair: Visions of Empire at American International Expositions, 1876–1916* (Chicago: University of Chicago Press, 1984), 38–71; Gail Bederman, *Manliness and Civilization: A Cultural History of Gender and Race in the United States, 1880–1917* (Chicago: University of Chicago Press, 1995), 31, 32; Sereno, "Images of the Hula Dancer and 'Hula Girl,'" 181; Houston Wood, *Displacing Natives: The Rhetorical Production of Hawai'i* (Lanham, Md.: Rowman & Littlefield, 1999), 63–78; Pratt, *Expansionists of 1898*, 167–170.

71. Blount report cited in Pratt, *Expansionists of 1898*, 134; Morgan report cited by Russ, *The Hawaiian Revolution*, 336; Coffman, *Nation Within*, 151, 152.

72. William Adam Russ, Jr., *The Hawaiian Republic and Its Struggle to Win Annexation* (1961; reprint, Sellingsgrove, Pa.: Susquehanna State University, 1992), 1–49 passim; Coffman, *Nation Within*, ch. 12; Silva, *Aloha Betrayed*, 137.

73. John L. Stevens and W. B. Oleson, *Picturesque Hawaii, a Charming Description of Her Unique History, Strange People, Exquisite Climate, Wondrous Volcanoes, Luxurious Productions, Beautiful Cities, Corrupt Monarchy, Recent Revolution, and Provisional*

Government (Philadelphia: Hubbard, 1894), 14. The authors acknowledged their deep debt to the works of the annexationist and historian William Alexander.

74. Stevens and Oleson, *Picturesque Hawaii*, 12, 14, 18, 34, 36, 37; Mary Louise Pratt, *Imperial Eyes: Travel Writing and Transculturation* (New York: Routledge, 1992), 53, 61; Michael Adas, *Machines as the Measure of Men: Science, Technology, and Ideologies of Western Dominance* (Ithaca, N.Y.: Cornell University Press, 1989), esp. 205–207.

75. Stevens and Oleson, *Picturesque Hawaii*, 38–39; Jarves, *Scenes and Sceneries in the Sandwich Islands*, 76–77.

76. Stevens and Oleson, *Picturesque Hawaii*, 66, 110; Eric T. Jennings offers wonderful analyses of how French imperialists appropriated and reencoded indigenous sites of pilgrimage and worship as civilized, modern, and white in his *Curing the Colonizers: Hydrotherapy, Climatology, and French Colonial Spas* (Durham, N.C.: Duke University Press, 2006).

77. Stephen Greenblatt, *Marvelous Possessions: The Wonder of the New World* (Chicago: University of Chicago Press, 1991), 6; Carl Schurz, "Manifest Destiny," *Harper's New Monthly Magazine*, October 1893, 737–746, 743; Silva, *Aloha Betrayed*, ch. 4; Kaulapai, "The Queen Writes Back."

78. Henry Cabot Lodge, "Our Blundering Foreign Policy," *Forum* 19, March 1895; John T. Morgan, "The Duty of Annexing Hawaii," *Forum* 25, March 1898; John R. Proctor, "Hawaii and the Changing Front of the World" *Forum* 24, September 1897; John R. Musick, "Should Hawaii Be Annexed?" *Arena*, February 1897; Musick, *Hawaii . . . Our New Possessions: An Account of Travels and Adventures, with Sketches of the Scenery, Customs and Manners, Mythology and History of Hawaii to the Present, and an Appendix Containing the Treaty of Annexation to the United States* (New York: Funk and Wagnalls, 1898); Professor George H. Barton, "Hawaii and Annexation," *National Magazine*, January 1898; Mary H. Krout, "The United States and Hawaii," *Chautauquan*, May 1898. Krout and Musick claimed that they opposed annexation until visiting Hawai'i.

79. LaFeber, "The American View of Decolonization," 32; Clark cited in Russ, *The Hawaiian Republic*, 318; Senate Foreign Relations Committee report cited in Eric T. L. Love, *Race over Empire: Racism and U.S. Imperialism, 1865–1900* (Chapel Hill: University of North Carolina Press, 2004), 147.

80. A. Lawrence Lowell, "The Government of Dependencies," *Handbook of the American Academy of Political and Social Science* (Philadelphia: American Academy of Political and Social Science, 1898): 46–59, cited portion, 46–47; Rubin Francis Weston, *Racism in U.S. Imperialism: The Influence of Racial Assumptions on American Foreign Policy, 1893–1946* (Columbia: University of South Carolina Press, 1972), 1–3; José A. Cabranes, *Citizenship and the American Empire* (New Haven, Conn.: Yale University Press, 1979); Rogers M. Smith, *Civic Ideals: Conflicting Visions of Citizenship in U.S. History* (New Haven, Conn.: Yale University Press, 1997), 434, 438; Thompson, "The Imperial Republic."

81. Robert C. Schmitt, *Historical Statistics of Hawaii* (Honolulu: University of

Hawai'i Press, 1968), 25; Thos. G. Thrum, *Hawaiian Almanac and Annual for 1900* (Honolulu: Hawaiian Gazette, 1900), 40; U.S. Bureau of Labor, *Fourth Report of the Commissioner of Labor on Hawaii*, bulletin no. 94 (Washington, D.C.: Government Printing Office, 1911), 675.

82. Pérez, *The War of 1898*, 21–28, Richard Olney, "The Growth of Our Foreign Policy," *Atlantic Monthly*, March 1900, cited on 28.

83. Pulaski F. Hyatt and John T. Hyatt, *Cuba: Its Resources and Opportunities* (New York: J. S. Ogilvie, 1898), 51; Foraker cited in Louis A. Pérez, Jr., *Cuba Between Empires, 1878–1902* (Pittsburgh: University of Pittsburgh Press, 1983), 350; Senator Chauncy Depew, *Congressional Record*, December 12, 1903, cited in Leland Hamilton Jenks, *Our Cuban Colony: A Study in Sugar* (New York: Vanguard Press, 1928), 328–29, n. 2. For other examples on Americanization as a strategy for pursuing annexation and the ways it was modeled on Hawai'i, see Philip S. Foner, *The Spanish-Cuban-American War and the Birth of American Imperialism, 1895–1902*, 2 vols. (New York: Monthly Review Press, 1972), 517–518, 651.

84. Charles Pepper, *To-Morrow in Cuba* (New York: Harper & Brothers, 1899), 149; Robert T. Hill, *Cuba and Porto Rico, with the Other Islands of the West Indies* (New York: Century, 1909), 98, 101, 105, 106.

85. Alexander Saxton, *The Rise and Fall of the White Republic: Class Politics and Mass Culture in Nineteenth Century America* (New York: Verso, 1990).

86. "New York Greets Victorious Navy," *New York Times*, August 21, 1898, 1.

87. John Parkinson, Jr., *The History of the New York Yacht Club, from Its Founding Through 1973*, 2 vols. (New York: New York Yacht Club, 1973), 1: 159, 170–176; Anson Phelps Stokes, *Cruising in the West Indies*, 2nd ed. (New York: Dodd, 1903), 9.

Chapter 2. Garden Republics or Plantation Regimes?

1. Emma Metcalf Nakuina, *Hawaii, Its People, Their Legends* (Honolulu: Hawaii Promotion Committee, 1904); Hawaii Promotion Committee, *Hawaii* (Honolulu: Hawaii Promotion Committee, 1903a), 8; "Promotion Committee Progress," *Paradise of the Pacific*, December 1908, 24; Kerry Wynn, "'Miss Indian Territory' and 'Mr. Oklahoma Territory': Marriage, Settlement, and Citizenship in the Cherokee Nation and the United States," in Tony Ballantyne and Antoinette Burton, eds., *Moving Subjects: Gender, Mobility, and Intimacy in an Age of Global Empire* (Urbana: University of Illinois Press, 2008), 172–189; Elizabeth A. Povinelli, "Notes on Gridlock: Genealogy, Intimacy, Sexuality," *Public Culture* 14, 1 (Winter 2002): 215–238; Sally Engle Merry, *Colonizing Hawai'i: The Cultural Power of Law* (Princeton, N.J.: Princeton University Press, 2000); Noenoe K. Silva, *Aloha Betrayed: Native Hawaiian Resistance to American Colonialism* (Durham, N.C.: Duke University Press, 2004). The best study of domestication and the erasure and naturalization of U.S. imperial violence remains Laura Wexler, *Tender Violence: Domestic Visions in an Age of U.S. Imperialism* (Chapel Hill: University of North Carolina Press, 2000).

2. Such imaginaries span the early national period to the Cold War. Dana D.

Nelson, *National Manhood: Capitalist Citizenship and the Imagined Fraternity of White Men* (Durham, N.C.: Duke University Press, 1998); Mary Renda, *Taking Haiti: Military Occupation and the Culture of U.S. Imperialism, 1915–1946* (Chapel Hill: University of North Carolina Press, 2001); Robert D. Dean, *Imperial Brotherhood: Gender and the Making of Cold War Foreign Policy* (Amherst: University of Massachusetts Press, 2001).

3. Matthew Pratt Guterl, *American Mediterranean: Southern Slaveholders in the Age of Emancipation* (Cambridge, Mass.: Harvard University Press, 2008); María DeGuzmán, *Spain's Long Shadow: The Black Legend, Off-Whiteness, and Anglo-American Empire* (Minneapolis: University of Minnesota Press, 2005); Walter D. Mignolo, "Coloniality at Large: The Western Hemisphere in the Colonial Horizon of Modernity," *CR: The New Centennial Review* 1, 2 (Fall 2001): 19–54.

4. Robert T. Hill, *Cuba and Porto Rico, with the Other Islands of the West Indies* (New York: Century, 1909), 98–106; Leonard Wood, William H. Taft, Charles A. Allen, Perfecto Lacoste [*sic*], and M. E. Beall, *Opportunities in the Colonies and Cuba* (New York: Lewis, Scribner, 1902), 271.

5. Philip Foner was an early proponent of the view that Cuba became the prototype of a flexible U.S. imperial order in which the "form of intervention and control" varied, but the goal of "domination without outright seizure of colonies" assumed primacy. Philip S. Foner, *The Spanish-Cuban-American War and the Birth of American Imperialism 1895–1902*, 2 vols. (New York and London: Monthly Review Press, 1972), 671. For Foner, the varieties of U.S. imperialism range from "a compulsory customs receivership, frequently guaranteed by a treaty arrangement, to a 'financial protectorate' imposed upon a country, to forcing an 'undesirable' political leader out of office by withdrawing or withholding diplomatic recognition, to promoting revolutions favorable to American interests, to the transformation of a nation into a 'client state' run by American appointed officials, to armed intervention to protect American propertied interests." Yet Cuba was not the only "prototype" of the "new imperialism." Walter LaFeber for one tells of a treaty that Secretary of State James G. Blaine attempted to negotiate during 1889 and 1890 that would have made Hawai'i a U.S. protectorate. He argues that "the pact presaged nearly all the famous articles of the Platt Amendment." Walter Lafeber, *The New Empire: An Interpretation of American Expansion, 1860–1898* (1962; reprint, Ithaca, N.Y.: Cornell University Press, 1998), 142.

6. The literature on representations of Hawaiians and Cubans as barbaric, racially inferior, and childlike is enormous; for a particularly influential example focused on political cartoons, see John Johnson, *Latin America in Caricature* (Austin: University of Texas Press, 1980).

7. Louis A. Pérez, Jr., *Cuba Between Empires, 1878–1902* (Pittsburgh: University of Pittsburgh Press, 1983), 269–283.

8. Louis A. Pérez, Jr., *The War of 1898: The United States and Cuba in History and Historiography* (Chapel Hill: University of North Carolina Press, 1998), 81–134, pas-

sim; Amy Kaplan, *The Anarchy of Empire in the Making of U.S. Culture* (Cambridge, Mass.: Harvard University Press, 2005), 121–145, passim.

9. Ada Ferrer, *Insurgent Cuba: Race, Nation, and Revolution, 1868–1898* (Chapel Hill: University of North Carolina Press, 1999), 170–194, passim, cited portion, 198; Merry, *Colonizing Hawai'i*, 13.

10. Pérez, *The War of 1898*, 30, 32; Trumbull White, *Our New Possessions* (Philadelphia: Elliot, 1898), 583–586.

11. Maturin M. Ballou, *Due South, or Cuba Past and Present* (Boston: Houghton, Mifflin, 1885), 99.

12. Pérez, *Cuba Between Empires*, 236; discussions of Cuba's "pure white voices" were a staple of travel writing between 1898 to 1911, as bookended by White, *Our New Possessions*, and Charles Harcourt Forbes Lindsay, *Cuba and Her People of Today* (Boston: L. C. Page, 1911); the *New York Times* cited in Louis A. Pérez, Jr., *Cuba and the United States: Ties of Singular Intimacy* (Athens: University of Georgia Press, 1990), 99; Marifeli Pérez-Stable, *The Cuban Revolution: Origins, Course, and Legacy* (New York: Oxford University Press, 1993), 37; Amy S. Greenburg, *Manifest Manhood and the Antebellum American Empire* (New York: Cambridge University Press, 2005).

13. Robert Porter, *Industrial Cuba: Being a Study of Present Commercial and Industrial Conditions, with Suggestions as to the Opportunities Presented in the Island for American Capital, Enterprise, and Labour* (New York: G. P. Putnam's Sons, 1899); Ferrer, *Insurgent Cuba*, 193; White, *Our New Possessions*, 550, 584; Franklin Matthews, *The New-Born Cuba* (New York: Harper and Brothers, 1899), 43.

14. Edward Atkins cited in Mary Speck, "Prosperity, Progress, and Wealth: Cuban Enterprise During the Early Republic, 1902–1927," *Cuban Studies* 36 (2005): 50–86, cited portion, 63; Porter, *Industrial Cuba*, 33.

15. The phrase "annexation by acclamation," used by the biographer of General Leonard Wood (governor of the U.S. military occupation), is cited in Pérez, *Cuba Between Empires*, 279; McKinley cited in Albert Weinberg, *Manifest Destiny: A Study of Nationalist Expansion in American History* (1935; reprint, Chicago: Quadrangle Books, 1963), 286; Porter, *Industrial Cuba*, 33; José de Olivares, *Our Islands and Their People as Seen with Camera and Pencil*, 2 vols. (New York: N. D. Thompson, 1899), 1: 114; Hill, *Cuba and Porto Rico*, 134; *New York Times*, March 26, 1901; on honor and "trial" government, see also Charles M. Pepper, *To-morrow in Cuba* (New York: Harper and Brothers, 1899).

16. Pérez, *Cuba Between Empires*, 278; Leland Hamilton Jenks, *Our Cuban Colony: A Study in Sugar* (1928; reprint, New York: Arno Press and New York Times, 1970), 153; William van Horne cited in Hudson Strode, *The Pageant of Cuba* (New York: Harrison Smith and Robert Haas, 1934), 331.

17. Matthews, *New Born Cuba*, 203; *New York Times*, May 7, 1900; Lindsay, *Cuba and Her People of Today*, 119; White, *Our New Possessions*, 591.

18. Aline Helg, *Our Rightful Share: The Afro-Cuban Struggle for Equality, 1896–1912* (Chapel Hill: University of North Carolina Press, 1995), 89–98; Alejandro de la

Fuente, *A Nation for All: Race, Inequality, and Politics in Twentieth Century Cuba* (Chapel Hill: University of North Carolina Press, 2001), 57–59.

19. Pérez, *Cuba Between Empires*, chs. 16, 17, 20; *New York Times*, July 7, 1901.

20. Louis A. Pérez, Jr., "Incurring a Debt of Gratitude," *American Historical Review* 104, 2 (April 1999): 356–398.

21. U.S. official cited in Gary Y. Okihiro, *Cane Fires: The Anti-Japanese Movement in Hawaii, 1865–1945* (Philadelphia: Temple University Press, 1991), 13.

22. *Thrum's Hawaiian Almanac and Annual for 1901* (Honolulu: Thos. G. Thrum, 1900), 173; Ronald Takaki, *Pau Hana: Plantation Life and Labor in Hawaii* (Honolulu: University of Hawai'i Press, 1983), 148–150.

23. The U.S. Congress granted citizenship to "all white persons . . . and all persons descended from the Hawaiian race . . . who were citizens of the Republic of Hawaii immediately prior to the transfer of sovereignty." Although most Hawaiians did not have or want citizenship in the republic, it seems likely that most Hawaiians became U.S. citizens and most Hawaiian men became voters in the territory. Lauren L. Basson, "Fit for Annexation but Unfit to Vote? Debating Hawaiian Suffrage Qualifications at the Turn of the Twentieth Century," *Social Science History* 29, 4 (Winter 2005): 575–598; J. Kēhaulani Kauanui, "'A Blood Mixture Which Experience Has Shown Furnishes the Very Highest Grade of Citizen-material': Selective Assimilation on a Polynesian Case of Naturalization to U.S. Citizenship," *American Studies* 45, 3 (Fall 2004): 33–48; the calculation that registered voters comprised 7 percent of the population comes from Robert C. Schmitt, *Historical Statistics of Hawaii* (Honolulu: University of Hawai'i Press, 1977), 599; the figure of 12,550 voters in 1902 comes from the "Third Report of the Commissioner of Labor of Hawaii," *Bulletin of the Bureau of Labor* 13, 66 (September 1906): 411.

24. J. Kēhaulani Kauanui, *Hawaiian Blood: Colonialism and the Politics of Sovereignty and Indigeneity* (Durham, N.C.: Duke University Press, 2008), 18.

25. Tom Coffman, *Nation Within: The Story of America's Annexation of the Nation of Hawai'i* (Kāne'ohe, Hawai'i: EpiCenter Press, 1998), 315, 322; White, *Our New Possessions*; 652; William D. Boyce, *United States Colonies and Dependencies* (Chicago: Rand McNally, 1914), 143.

26. Noel J. Kent, *Hawaii, Islands Under the Influence* (1983; reprint, Honolulu: University of Hawai'i Press, 1993), 68; Gavan Daws, *Shoal of Time: A History of the Hawaiian Islands.* (Honolulu: University of Hawai'i Press, 1968), 294–295; Lawrence Fuchs, *Hawaii Pono: An Ethnic and Political History* (Honolulu: Bess Press, 1961), 156–160; Silva, *Aloha Betrayed*, 139, 189–190.

27. Jonathan Kay Kamakawiwo'ole Osorio, *Dismembering Lahui: A History of the Hawaiian Nation to 1887* (Honolulu: University of Hawai'i Press, 2002), 237; Lydia Kaulapai, "The Queen Writes Back: Lili'uokalani's *Hawaii's Story by Hawaii's Queen*," *Studies in American Indian Literatures* 17, 2 (Summer 2005): 55, 56. The queen's inclusive definition was used to identify the Hawaiians to whom the United States apolo-

gized for the illegal act of the overthrow of the Hawaiian Kingdom on the occasion of
its centennial in 1993.

28. Peter S. Onuf, *Jefferson's Empire: The Legacy of American Nationhood* (Charlottesville: University Press of Virginia, 2000), 51, 52; Denis Diderot expressed a similar idea. See Anthony Pagden, *European Encounters with the New World, From
Renaissance to Romanticism* (New Haven, Conn.: Yale University Press, 1993), 169; on
intermarriage and dispossession in comparative settler colonial contexts, see especially
Katherine Ellinghaus, "Intimate Assimilation: Comparing White-Indigenous Marriage
in the United States and Australia, 1880s-1930s," in Ballantyne and Burton, *Moving
Subjects*, 211–228; Patrick Wolfe, "Land, Labor, and Difference: Elementary Structures
of Race," *American Historical Review* 106, 3 (June 2001): 866–905.

29. Kauanui, "'A Blood Mixture,'" 40.

30. Tony Ballantyne, *Orientalism and Race: Aryanism in the British Empire* (New
York: Palgrave, 2002); Nakuina, *Hawaii, Its People, Their Legends*, preface; Stephanie
Barczewski, *Myth and National Identity in Nineteenth-Century Britain: The Legends of
King Arthur and Robin Hood* (New York: Oxford University Press, 2000). This analysis
is indebted to Christina Bacchilega, *Legendary Hawai'i and the Politics of Place* (Philadelphia: University of Pennsylvania Press, 2007), 102–136, although she attributes
authorship of the preface of *Hawaii, Its People, Their Legends* to Nakuina.

31. Reginald Horsman, *Race and Manifest Destiny: The Origins of American Racial
Anglo-Saxonism* (Cambridge, Mass.: Harvard University Press, 1981), part 1; Sargent
Bush, Jr., "America's Origin Myth: Remembering Plymouth Rock," *American Literary
History* 12, 4 (Winter 2000): 745–756; Hawaii Promotion Committee, *Hawaii* (Hono-
lulu: Hawaii Promotion Committee, 1903b), 10.

32. Nakuina, *Hawaii, Its People, Their Legends*, preface; on the institutionalization
of bourgeois marriage in Hawai'i, see Merry, *Colonizing Hawai'i*, 221–257, passim.

33. Bacchilega, *Legendary Hawai'i*, 103; HPC, *Hawaii*, 1903a, 7; Hawaii Promotion Committee, *Hawaii* (Honolulu: Hawaii Promotion Committee, 1904), n.p.

34. HPC, *Hawaii*, 1903a, 7; HPC, *Hawaii*, 1904, n.p; HPC, *Hawaii*, 1903b, 7, 10.

35. Ann Laura Stoler, "Intimidations of Empire: Predicaments of the Tactile and
Unseen," in Stoler, ed., *Haunted by Empire: Geographies of Intimacy in North American
History* (Durham, N.C.: Duke University Press, 2006), 3.

36. Jonathan Kay Kamakawiwoʻole Osorio, "'What Kine Hawaiian Are You?' A
Moʻolelo about Nationhood, Race, History and the Contemporary Sovereignty Move-
ment in Hawaiʻi," *Contemporary Pacific* 13, 2 (Fall 2001): 359–379, cited portion, 371;
Vicente Diaz and J. Kēhaulani Kauanui, "Native Pacific Cultural Studies on the Edge,"
Contemporary Pacific 13, 2 (Fall 2001): 315–342. See also James Clifford, "Indigenous
Articulations," *Contemporary Pacific* 13, 2 (Fall 2001): 468–490.

37. Nakuina, *Hawaii, Its People, Their Legends*, 7, 8; Ballantyne, *Orientalism and
Race*, 164–167.

38. Nakuina, *Hawaii, Its People, Their Legends*, 11; Barbara Bennett Pearson, ed.,
Notable Women of Hawaii (Honolulu: University of Hawaiʻi Press, 1984), 281.

39. K. R. Howe, *Where the Waves Fall: A New South Seas History from First Settlement to Colonial Rule* (Honolulu: University of Hawai'i Press, 1996), 154–158; Lilikalā Kame'eleihiwa, *Native Land and Foreign Desires: Pehea lā e Pono ai?* (Honolulu: Bishop Museum Press, 1992) 58–60,

40. Nakuina, *Hawaii, Its People, Their Legends,* 20–21; Kame'eleihiwa, *Native Land and Foreign Desires,* 80; Bacchilega, *Legendary Hawai'i,* 108; Greg Dening, "Sharks That Walk on the Land," reprinted in Dening, *Performances* (1992; reprint, Chicago: University of Chicago Press, 1996), 64–78.

41. Nakuina, *Hawaii, its People, their Legends,* preface; Julia Clancy-Smith, "Saint or Rebel? Resistance in French North Africa," in Alice L. Conklin and Ian Christopher Fletcher, eds., *European Imperialism, 1830–1930* (Boston: Houghton Mifflin, 1999), 197. This idea is more fully developed in the book from which it is drawn; see Julia Clancy-Smith, *Rebel and Saint: Muslim Notables, Populist Protest, Colonial Encounters, Algeria and Tunisia, 1800–1904* (Berkeley: University of California Press, 1994), 251–153.

42. Nakuina, *Hawaii, its People, their Legends,* 54, 62.

43. "Information for Tourists and Others," *Thrum's Hawaiian Almanac and Annual for 1904* (Honolulu: Thos. G. Thrum, 1903) 209; "Advertise Cuba," *Havana Post,* July, 21, 1900; Walter G. Smith, "How to Get Tourists," *Paradise of the Pacific,* December 1903, 55.

44. Louis A. Pérez, Jr., *Cuba Under the Platt Amendment 1902–1934* (Pittsburgh: University of Pittsburgh Press, 1986), 34–36; Pérez, *Cuba and the United States,* 126; Alejandro de la Fuente, "Two Dangers, One Solution: Immigration, Labor, and Race in Cuba, 1900–1930," *International Labor and Working Class History* 51 (Spring 1987): 30–49.

45. Susan Sontag, *Illness as Metaphor* (New York: Penguin Books, 1987).

46. Olivares, *Our Islands and Their Peoples,* 1: 27; Porter, *Industrial Cuba,* 108.

47. François Delaporte, *The History of Yellow Fever: An Essay on the Birth of Tropical Medicine* (Cambridge, Mass.: MIT Press, 1991), esp. 138–139.

48. Jenks, *Our Cuban Colony,* 63–66; Foner, *The Spanish-Cuban-American War,* 475–476; Louis A. Pérez, Jr., *Lords of the Mountain: Social Banditry and Peasant Protest in Cuba, 1878–1919* (Pittsburgh: University of Pittsburgh Press, 1989), 79–85, 90–101.

49. Pérez, *Cuba and the United States,* 118; *Commercial and Financial World,* April 7, 1906, 10; Pulaski F. Hyatt and John T. Hyatt, *Cuba: Its Resources and Opportunities* (New York: J. S. Ogilvie, 1898), n.p.; Foner, *The Spanish-Cuban-American War,* 466; *New York Times,* August 3, 1898; *Havana Post,* July 13, 1900; James M. Adams, *Pioneering in Cuba: A Narrative of the Settlement of La Gloria, the First American Colony in Cuba and the Early Experiences of the Pioneers* (Concord, N.H.: Rumford Press, 1901); Louis A. Pérez, Jr., *On Becoming Cuban: Identity, Nationality, and Culture* (Chapel Hill: University of North Carolina Press, 1999), 107–108.

50. "Advertise Cuba" and letter of reply by James H. Dorman, Jr., *Havana Post,* July 21 and July 28, 1900; Hill, *Cuba and Porto Rico,* 134; Scott A. Sandage, *Born*

Losers: A History of Failure in America (Cambridge, Mass.: Harvard University Press, 2005).

51. Foner, *The Spanish-Cuban-American War*, 517, 518, 643; "Put Cuba at Buffalo," *Havana Post*, August 10, 1900; "This Tourist Is Pleased," *Havana Post*, February 22, 1902; "Advertising the Island," *Havana Post*, November 5, 1906; "Many Tourists Are Expected," *Havana Post*, November 19, 1906; minutes of special meeting of the Board of Directors, June 17, 1904, 159, series 7, box 155, packet 2, Cuba Company Papers, University of Maryland, College Park; Lindsay, *Cuba and Her People of Today*, 124–125.

52. Caspar Whitney, *Hawaiian America, Something of Its History, Resources, and Prospects* (New York: Harper and Brothers, 1902), 179–180; Thurston cited in Helen Geracimos Chapin, *Shaping History: The Role of Newspapers in Hawai'i* (Honolulu: University of Hawai'i Press, 1996), 105–110; Gavan Daws, *Shoal of Time: A History of the Hawaiian Islands* (New York: Macmillan, 1968), 302, 303; Clarence L. Hodge and Peggy Ferris, *Building Honolulu: A Century of Community Service* (Honolulu: Chamber of Commerce of Honolulu, 1950), 60, 61; James C. Mohr, *Plague and Fire: Battling Black Death and the 1900 Burning of Chinatown* (New York: Oxford University Press, 2005).

53. J. Kēhaulani Kauanui, "'For Get' Hawaiian Entitlement: Configurations of Land, 'Blood,' andAmericanization in the Hawaiian Homes Commission Act of 1921," *Social Text* 17, 2 (Summer 1999): 123–141; Hodge and Ferris, *Building Honolulu*, 61; Richard A. Overfield, "The Agricultural Experiment Station and Americanization: The Hawaiian Experience, 1900–1910," *Agricultural History* 60, 2 (Spring 1986): 256–266, cited portion 260. As Theon Wright argues, "The desire for tourists was minimal while the oligarchy was entrenching itself economically and politically during the early years of the Territory. Any substantial influx of *malihini haoles* (white newcomers) was unwelcome since they might dilute the power of the *kamaaina haoles*." Theon Wright, *The Disenchanted Isles: The Story of the Second Revolution in Hawaii* (New York: Dial Press, 1972), 37.

54. J. G. Rothwell, J. F. Humburg, Wm. Lishman, "Inviting Tourists," published as a letter to the Honolulu Merchants Association in the *Paradise of the Pacific*, August 1902; Louis Crampon, *Hawaii's Visitor Industry*, unpublished manuscript (University of Hawai'i School of Travel Industry Management, 1976), 223–227; Hodge and Ferris, *Building Honolulu*, 60–61; "A Message [from Governor Sanford Dole] to the Legislature of the Territory of Hawaii, 1903," *The Second Legislative Assembly of the Territory of Hawaii, Regular Session, Journal of the Senate, 1903* (Honolulu: Robert Grieve, 1903), 11–19, cited portion, 13; *The Second Legislative Assembly of the Territory of Hawaii. Extra Session. Journal of the Senate. 1903* (Honolulu: Hawaiian Gazette, 1903), 55, 159.

55. Sereno E. Bishop, *Beauty Spots Hawaii, Business Hawaii* (Honolulu: Hawaii Promotion Committee, 1903); Jared G. Smith, *Agriculture in Hawaii* (Honolulu: Hawaii Promotion Committee, 1903), 13;

56. Whitney, *Hawaiian America*, 146; Victor Clark cited in Andrew W. Lind, *An*

Island Community: Ecological Succession in Hawaii (Chicago: University of Chicago Press, 1938), 271; see also Matthew Guterl and Christine Skwiot, "Atlantic and Pacific Crossings: Race, Empire, and the 'Labor Problem' in the Late Nineteenth Century," *Radical History Review* 91 (Winter 2005): 40–61.

57. Gail Bederman, *Manliness and Civilization: A Cultural History o f Gender and Race in the United States, 1880–1917* (Chicago: University of Chicago Press, 1995), 199; Theodore Roosevelt cited in Gerald Horne, *The White Pacific: U.S. Imperialism and Black Slavery in the South Seas After the Civil War* (Honolulu: University of Hawai'i Press, 2007), 173; Ralph S. Kuykendall and A. Grove Day, *Hawaii, a History* (New York: Prentice Hall, 1948), 211; Katherine Bjork, "Incorporating an Empire: From Deregulating Labor to Regulating Leisure in Cuba, Puerto Rico, Hawaii, and the Philippines, 1898–1909" (Ph.D. diss., University of Chicago, 1998), 139–150, Theodore Roosevelt cited on 139; Matthew Frye Jacobson, *Whiteness of a Different Color: European Immigrants and the Alchemy of Race* (Cambridge, Mass.: Harvard University Press, 1998).

58. De la Fuente, *A Nation for All,* 100–102, Wood cited on 100; Bjork, "Incorporating an Empire," 61.

59. Wood et al., *Opportunities in the Colonies and Cuba,* 271; Carmen Diana Deere, "Here Come the Yankees! The Rise and Decline of United States Colonies in Cuba, 1898–1930," *Hispanic American Research Review* 78, 4 (November 1998): 729–765, esp. 741; Helg, *Our Rightful Share,* 99, 103–105, Rafael M. Portuondo cited on 91; Helg, "Race in Argentina and Cuba, 1880–1930," in Richard Graham, ed., *The Idea of Race in Latin America, 1870–1940* (Austin: University of Texas Press, 1990), 37–70.

60. Charles E. Chapman, *A History of the Cuban Republic: A Study in Hispanic American Politics* (1927; reprint, New York: Octagon Books, 1969), 9, 165; Irene A. Wright, *Cuba* (New York: Macmillan, 1910), 161–162, caption of cartoon reprinted on 411.

61. Deere, "Here Come the Yankees!" 740–743; Pérez, *Cuba and the United States,* 124.

62. Wright, *Cuba,* 322; *Times of Cuba,* March 1914, 15; Boyce, *United States Colonies and Dependencies,* 559.

63. Lindsay, *Cuba and Her People of Today,* 161.

64. Crampon, *Hawaii's Visitor Industry,* 221; Fuchs, *Hawaii Pono,* 251–256; Kent, *Hawaii,* 78–80; David Keanu Sai, "American Migration to the Hawaiian Kingdom and the Push for Statehood into the American Union," *Focus on Hawaiian History,* http://www.HawaiianKingdom.org; Thomas Hitch, *Islands in Transition: The Past, Present, and Future of Hawaii's Economy* (Honolulu: First Hawaiian Bank, 1982), 100; Lind, *An Island Community,* appendix A, 318.

65. Fuchs, *Hawaii Pono,* 252; Okihiro, *Cane Fires,* 37, 38.

66. Cindy S. Aron, *Working at Play: A History of Vacations in the United States* (New York: Oxford University Press, 1999), 7.

67. Pérez, *Cuba Under the Platt Amendment*, 117, 121, 122, 138, 139, 143; Emily S. Rosenberg, *Financial Missionaries to the World: The Politics and Culture of Dollar Diplomacy* (Cambridge, Mass.: Harvard University Press, 1999).

68. Helg, "Race in Argentina and Cuba," esp. 54–57.

69. De la Fuente, *A Nation for All*, 79; Wright, *Cuba*, 97; *The Cuba Magazine*, January 1912, 310.

70. *Cuba Review*, June 1911; "Golf Introduced to Cuba," *Cuba Review*, May 1912, 16–17; "A Magnificent Course Near the City—Club Competitions for the Coming Months," *Cuba Review*, November 1912, 13–14; *Times of Cuba*, January 1913, 21.

71. Country Club Park Investment Company advertisement, *Times of Cuba*, July 1916, 9; "Country Club Park Investment Co., Havana Cuba" (Havana: Country Club Park Investment Co., n.d.), 27; Eric Paul Roorda, "Desarraigando la tierra de clubes: La extinction de la 'colonia americana' en La Habana," *Secuencia* 60 (September–December 2004): 111–134, "our country" on 114.

72. Estrada Palma cited by Bjork, "Incorporating an Empire," 123 and 83; Rosalie Schwartz, *Pleasure Island: Tourism and Temptation in Cuba* (Lincoln: University of Nebraska Press, 1997), 48–49.

73. Anson Chong, "Economic Development of Hawaii and the Growth of Tourism" (M.A. thesis, Columbia University, 1963), 56–66.

74. My discussions of hula owe a great debt to Cathy van Horne, who generously shared with me her knowledge, the fruits of her research, and her terrific paper "The Evolution of the Hula in Hawaii's Early Tourism Advertising from Censure to Commercialization," unpublished paper in my possession.

75. "The St. Louis Fair," *Paradise of the Pacific*, June 1902; "Exit the Hula," *Paradise of the Pacific*, March 1912; Hawaii Promotion Committee Annual Report for 1912, 33; Aeko Sereno, "Images of the Hula and the 'Hula Dancer': 1778–1960" (Ph.D. diss., University of Hawai'i, 1990); Hans Johannes Hoefer, Leonard Lueras, Jerry Hopkins, and Rebecca Crockett-Hopkins, *The Hula* (Hong Kong: Apa Productions, 1982).

76. Workers cited by Ronald Takaki, *Strangers from a Different Shore: A History of Asian-Americans* (New York: Penguin Books, 1989), 151; Henry Yu offers a wonderful definition of settlers: "Settlers are migrants who fantasize about stopping and making an organic tie between themselves and the land they occupy." Henry Yu, "Los Angeles and American Studies in a Pacific World of Migrations," *American Quarterly* 56, 3 (September 2004): 540.

77. Okihiro, *Cane Fires*, 45; Edward D. Beechert, *Working in Hawaii: A Labor History* (Honolulu: University of Hawai'i Press, 1985), 169–176; Fuchs, *Hawaii Pono*, 62.

78. Its last attempt to do so in 1914 drew the wrath of Governor Lucius Pinkham: "We have more demand for land from people now resident than we can meet. It is wicked to so misrepresent opportunities here." Pinkham to A. P. Taylor, March 3, 1914, Papers of Governor Lucius Eugene Pinkham, November 29, 1913–June 22, 1918, Hawai'i State Archives, Honolulu, Hawai'i.

79. Lucius Eugene Pinkham, "Reclamation of the Waikiki District" (Honolulu: Board of Health, T.H., 1907), esp. 3, 6, 7, 9 20.

80. "Cuba, Refuge of the Frivolous and Thirsty," *New York Times*, August 31, 1919.

81. "Cuba, Refuge of the Frivolous and Thirsty;" "Don'ts for Tourists," *Times of Cuba*, January 1920, 95; Chapman, *A History of the Cuban Republic*, 603.

82. A. Hyatt Verrill, *Cuba: Past and Present* (New York: Dodd, Mead, 1924), 55–56; "Come to Cuba!" *Times of Cuba*, February 1920, 81–83; these pieces of marital advice were first printed in "Don'ts for Tourists," *Times of Cuba*, February 1920, 91, and reprinted throughout the 1920s by that journal and by travel writers.

83. G. L. Morrill, *Sea Sodoms: A Sinical Survey of Haiti, Santo Domingo, Porto Rico, Curacao, Venezuela, Guadeloupe, Martinique, Cuba* (Minneapolis: Pioneer Printers, 1921), 177–178.

84. For a brilliant meditation on these themes, see Louis A. Pérez, Jr., *Cuba in the American Imagination: Metaphor and the Imperial Ethos* (Chapel Hill: University of North Carolina Press, 2008). For two wonderful studies of France as a republican empire, see Todd Shepard, *The Invention of Decolonization: The Algerian War and the Remaking of France* (Ithaca, N.Y.: Cornell University Press, 2006), and Alice L. Conklin, *A Mission to Civilize: The Republican Idea of Empire in France and West Africa, 1895–1930* (Stanford, Calif.: Stanford University Press, 1997).

Chapter 3. Royal Resorts for Tropical Tramps

1. "Publicity for Hawaii—Consider 'Paradise'!" *Paradise of the Pacific*, April 1927, 3, 5; "Says Our Tourist Bureau Advertising Is All Wrong," *Paradise of the Pacific*, March 1924, 20; "A King for a Father," *Paradise of the Pacific*, July 1932, 7, 37.

2. Karl Decker, "The Waking of the Sleeping Princess," *Havana, the Magazine of Cuba*, January 1, 1929, 8, 44, 45; Kristin L. Hoganson, *Fighting for American Manhood: How Gender Politics Provoked the Spanish-American and Philippine-American Wars* (New Haven, Conn.: Yale University Press, 1998), 58–61; *New York Journal* cited in Amy Kaplan, *The Anarchy of Empire in the Making of U.S. Culture* (Cambridge, Mass.: Harvard University Press, 2002), 109.

3. For impressions of what I call the royal resort, Larry R. Youngs, "The Sporting Set Winters in Florida: Fertile Ground for the Leisure Revolution, 1870–1930," *Florida Historical Quarterly* 84, 1 (Winter 2005): 28–56; Orvar Löfgren, *On Holiday: A History of Vacationing* (Berkeley: University of California Press, 1999); Mary Blume, *Cote d'Azur: Inventing the French Riviera* (New York: Thames and Hudson, 1994); Basil Woon, *From Deauville to Monte Carlo: A Guide to the Gay World of France* (New York: Horace Liverwright, 1929).

4. On European aristocrats as privileged white U.S. citizens' symbol of a cosmopolitan leisured class, see Kristin L. Hoganson, *Consumers' Imperium: The Global Production of American Domesticity, 1865–1920* (Chapel Hill: University of North Carolina Press, 2007).

5. Odd Arne Westad, *The Global Cold War: Third World Interventions and the Making of Our Times* (New York: Cambridge University Press, 2007), 25.

6. On these themes, see especially Eric Paul Roorda, *The Dictator Next Door: The Good Neighbor Policy and the Trujillo Regime in the Dominican Republic* (Durham, N.C.: Duke University Press, 1998), 149–191, passim.

7. The starting points for the study of planter paternalism in Hawai'i and business nationalism in Cuba are, respectively, Edward D. Beechert, *Working in Hawaii: A Labor History* (Honolulu: University of Hawai'i Press, 1985); Jules R. Benjamin, *The United States and Cuba: Hegemony and Dependent Development, 1880–1934* (1974; reprint, Pittsburgh: University of Pittsburgh Press, 1977).

8. Basil Woon, *When It's Cocktail Time in Cuba* (New York: Horace Liverwright, 1928), 78–86; "Bowman Buys Cuban Hotel," *New York Times*, October 30, 1919; "Top Hat Goes to Cuba," *New York Times*, April 26, 1920.

9. Rosalie Schwartz, *Pleasure Island: Tourism and Temptation in Cuba* (Lincoln: University of Nebraska Press, 1997), 17, 18, 25–27, 30–34; Carlton Beals, *The Crime of Cuba* (Philadelphia: J. P. Lippincott, 1933), 224; *Cuba Review*, May 1920, 11; *Cuba Review*, July 1920, 11.

10. Luis E. Aguilar, *Cuba 1933: Prologue to Revolution* (Ithaca, N.Y.: Cornell University Press, 1972), 43; Robert Freeman Smith, *The United States and Cuba: Business and Diplomacy, 1917–1960* (New York: Bookman Associates, 1960), 29–31; Benjamin, *The United States and Cuba*, 16, 17; on tourism as Cuba's future second crop, see "Eggs in One Basket," *Times of Cuba*, April 1922, 68; Joseph Durrell, "The National City Bank of New York in Cuba," *Cuban Commercial and Financial Magazine*, October 1924, 32–33; for similar arguments in Hawai'i, see Harold H. Yost, "Hawaii's Leading Crop of the Future," *Paradise of the Pacific*, April 1921, 27–29.

11. Louis A. Pérez, Jr., *Cuba: Between Reform and Revolution* (Oxford: Oxford University Press, 1988), 225–228.

12. Machado borrowed the name of his platform from the Asociación Nacional de Industriales de Cuba (National Association of Industrialists), which in 1923 had organized under the banner "For the Regeneration of Cuba" to fight for protection of industry, a government free from corruption, and the abrogation of the Platt Amendment. Marifeli Pérez-Stable, *The Cuban Revolution: Origins, Course, and Legacy* (Oxford: Oxford University Press, 1993), 18; Jules R. Benjamin, *The United States and the Origins of the Cuban Revolution: An Empire of Liberty in an Age of National Liberation* (Princeton, N.J.: Princeton University Press, 1990), 81; Pérez, *Cuba*, 249–251; Jorge Domínguez, "Seeking Permission to Build a Nation," *Cuban Studies / Estudios Cubanos* 16 (1986): 33–48.

13. Crowder to Dwight D. Morrow, August 26, 1924; Francis White to Crowder, April 23, 1925; Crowder to White, April 30, 1925. All citations from Enoch H. Crowder (1859–1932) Papers, 1884–1942, C1046, Western Historical Manuscripts Collection, University of Missouri, hereafter, Crowder Papers.

14. *The Visit of the President-Elect of Cuba, General Gerardo Machado, to the United States in April 1925* (Washington, D.C.: n.p., 1925), 31, 56.

15. *The Visit of the President-Elect of Cuba,* 18; *New York Times,* February 26, 1928.

16. "Cashing in on Advertising," *Paradise of the Pacific,* October 1921, 17; Flora Allen Hayes, "Why Not Ban Some of Our Modern Ball Room and Roof Garden Dances Too?" *Honolulu Advertiser,* September 27, 1922; for more on these debates, see Aeko Sereno, "Images of the Hula Dancer and 'Hula Girl': 1778–1960" (Ph.D. diss., University of Hawai'i, 1990); Hans Johannes Hoefer, Leonard Lueras, Jerry Hopkins, and Rebecca Crockett-Hopkins, *The Hula* (Hong Kong: Apa Productions, 1982).

17. J. Kēhaulani Kauanui, "'For Get' Hawaiian Entitlement: Configurations of Land, 'Blood,' and Americanization in the Hawaiian Homes Commission Act of 1921," *Social Text* 17, 2 (Summer 1999): 123–141, especially, 134, 136, 137; see also Susan Y. Najita, "History, Trauma, and the Discursive Construction of 'Race' in John Dominis Holt's *Waimea Summer,*" *Cultural Critique* 47 (Winter 2001): 167–214.

18. Gary Okihiro, *Cane Fires: The Anti-Japanese Movement in Hawaii, 1865–1945* (Philadelphia: Temple University Press, 1991), 65–81; Ronald Takaki, *Pau Hana: Plantation Life and Labor in Hawaii, 1835–1920* (Honolulu: University of Hawai'i Press, 1983), 164–176; *Honolulu Star-Bulletin,* February 13, 1920, cited in Okihiro, *Cane Fires,* 80; *Honolulu Advertiser,* January 30, 1920, cited in George Chapin, *Presstime in Paradise: The Life and Times of the Honolulu Advertiser, 1865–1995* (Honolulu: University of Hawai'i Press, 1998), 142.

19. Beechert, *Working in Hawaii,* 183, 193, 209, 214, 215; Okihiro, *Cane Fires,* 80, 81, 108–118; Robert C. Schmitt, *Historical Statistics of Hawaii* (Honolulu: University of Hawai'i Press, 1977), 660; Thomas Kemper Hitch, *Islands in Transition: The Past, Present, and Future of Hawaii's Economy* (Honolulu: First Hawaiian Bank, 1991), 125; Andrew Lind, *Hawaii's People,* 3rd edition (Honolulu: University of Hawai'i Press, 1967), 53.

20. Okihiro, *Cane Fires,* 108, 109; Lawrence F. Fuchs, *Hawaii Pono: An Ethnic and Social History* (Honolulu: Bess Press, 1971), 178, 186–188. See also Masayo Umezama Duus, *The Japanese Conspiracy: The Oahu Sugar Strike of 1920,* trans. Beth Cary (Berkeley: University of California Press, 1999).

21. Governor Wallace Rider Farrington cited in Okihiro, *Cane Fires,* 93, 94; John Reinecke, *Feigned Necessity: Hawaii's Attempt to Obtain Chinese Contract Labor, 1921–1923* (San Francisco: Chinese Materials Center, 1979). In 1920, the Portuguese represented 10.6 percent of the population, Hawaiians, 9.3 percent, the Chinese, 9.2 percent, Filipinos, 8.2 percent, and part-Hawaiians 7.0 percent. See Lind, *Hawaii's People,* 28.

22. Houston Wood, *Displacing Natives: The Rhetorical Production of Hawai'i* (Lanham, Md: Rowman and Littlefield, 1999), especially 95, 98–99. Also crucial are Andrea Fesser with Gaye Chang, *Waikīkī: A History of Forgetting and Remembering* (Honolulu: University of Hawai'i Press, 2006); Don Hibbard and David Franzen, *The View from*

Diamond Head: Royal Residence to Urban Resort (Honolulu: Editions Limited, 1986); George S. Kanahele, *Waikiki, 100* B.C. to 1900 A.D.: An Untold Story (Honolulu: University of Hawai'i Press, 1995).

23. Richard Walter Coller, "Waikiki: A Study of Invasion and Succession as Applied to a Tourist Area" (M.A. thesis: University of Hawai'i, 1952), 54–60; Helen Geracimos Chapin, *Shaping History: The Role of Newspapers in Hawai'i* (Honolulu: University of Hawai'i Press, 1996), 149; F. W. Thrum, "The Waikiki Reclamation Project," *Thrum's Hawaiian Almanac and Annual for 1923* (Honolulu: Thos. G. Thrum, 1922), 65–67; Donald D. Johnson, *The City and County of Honolulu: A Governmental Chronicle* (Honolulu: University of Hawai'i Press, 1991), 309, 314, 315.

24. The taxes generated $13.6 million the first year and did not reach their estimated annual collection of $18 million until the fourth year. Aguilar, *Cuba 1933*, 55, 56; U.S. Senate Committee on Banking and Currency, *Hearings on Stock Exchange Practices*, 73rd Congress, 2nd Session, Part 5, Chase Securities Corporation, October 17–25, 1933 (Washington, D.C.: Government Printing Office, 1933), 2548, 2549, 2585, 2821; Crowder to Martin Egan, August 5, 1925, Crowder Papers.

25. Roberto Segre, Mario Coyula, and Joseph L. Scarpaci, *Havana: Two Faces of the Antillean Metropolis* (New York: John Wiley and Sons, 1997), 61–64; *New York Times*, October 31, 1925; Smith, *The United States and Cuba*, 123; *Cuba Review*, February 1926, 15.

26. "Who's Who in Havana: John McE. Bowman," *Times of Cuba*, April 1920, 94–95; Woon to Irénée du Pont, January 11, 1928, box 8, accession 228, Irénée du Pont Papers, Hagley Museum and Library, Wilmington, Delaware, hereafter Irénée du Pont Papers; Woon, *When It's Cocktail Time in Cuba*, 79, 80.

27. "10,000 See Opening of Havana Racing," *New York Times*, December 13, 1925; *Havana Post*, December 13, 1925, and December 14, 1925.

28. George Reno, "The King of Sports: Winter Racing in Havana," *Cuba Review*, January 1927, 17–22; Conrado W. Masaguer, "Sure They're Cubans," *Havana, the Magazine of Cuba*, January 1, 1929, 18, 40, 41. Photographs showing the arrival of the Vanderbilts' yacht routinely made Cuban and U.S. newspapers and journals.

29. Fleishman and Whitney stayed at the Sevilla-Biltmore on their visits to Havana and may have been among those whose ears pricked when rumors circulated that Bowman would soon be offering stock shares in an incorporated Cuban National Syndicate that would buy Oriental Park and the Casino. Bernard Livingston, *Their Turf: The Intimate, In-Depth, Behind-the-Scenes Story of America's Horsey Set and Its Princely Dynasties* (New York: Arbor House, 1973); Edward Hotaling, *They're Off! Horse Racing at Saratoga* (Syracuse, N.Y.: Syracuse University Press, 1995); *Havana Post*, January 1, 1928, and January 1, 1929; *Cuba Review*, January 1928, 13.

30. Reno, "The King of Sports," 17–22; Frederick Jaher, *The Urban Establishment: Upper Strata in Boston, New York, Charleston, Chicago, and Los Angeles* (Urbana: University of Illinois Press, 1982) 478–480; Alfred Padula, "The Fall of the Bourgeoisie:

Cuba, 1959–1961" (Ph.D. dissertation, University of New Mexico, December, 1974), 5–7.

31. *Havana Post* and *New York Times,* January 29, 30, 31, 1929; *Cuba Review,* March 1927, 14, 15; Woon, *When It's Cocktail Time in Cuba,* 31; Schwartz, *Pleasure Island,* 56, 57.

32. The officers of Cuban American Realty Company were Bowman, president; his partner, Charles Flynn, vice president; Juan Arellano, a private contractor and the Cuban transport commissioner, secretary; and Rafael Sánchez, Machado's secretary of communications, treasurer. The president and vice presidents of the Cuban Tourist Commission were respectively the congressman and real-estate and law-firm partner of Céspedes, Carlos Manuel de la Cruz, and Miguel Suárez. José Obregón became the commodore of the Yacht and Country Club. Bowman was the HBYCC's president; Miguel Suárez, its treasurer; Fernando and Nestor Mendoza, of the powerful banking, real-estate, and contracting family, its secretary and vice-secretary. Catlin was named a director, as were José Gomez Mena (sugar industrialist, real-estate developer, and organizer of the contemporary Liberal leadership), Alberto Mendoza and Juan Arellano (partners of a leading contracting firm), Guillermo de Zaldo, Jr. (banker, real estate developer, and Tourist Commission director), and C. H. Stapleton (the vice president of the Country Club Realty Company and the Havana Country Club). Arellano and Mendoza received the contract to build the club. *Havana Post,* February 7, 1927, and January 13, 1928; Woon, *When It's Cocktail Time in Cuba,* 185; Louis A. Pérez, Jr., *Cuba Under the Platt Amendment, 1902–1934* (Pittsburgh: University of Pittsburgh Press, 1986), 228, 229.

33. The Cuban government issued deferred-payment certificates to contractors; then Chase purchased the certificates from contractors and held them until revenues in the public works account could pay for them.

34. Benjamin, *The United States and Cuba,* 41; U.S. Senate Committee, *Stock Exchange Practices,* 2542, 2650, 2652; *Cuba Review,* March 1927, 15, and April 1927, 14; Hugh Thomas, *Cuba: The Pursuit of Freedom* (New York: Harper and Row, 1971), 584, 585.

35. Crowder to Secretary of State Frank B. Kellogg, February 14, 1927, Crowder Papers.

36. Crowder to Kellogg, February 14, 1927, and March 8, 1927, Crowder Papers; Aguilar, *Cuba 1933,* 57.

37. As Anson Chong observes, "Since investment capital, sugar capital, and Matson control were essentially synonymous, control of transportation, as embodied by Matson, was undoubtedly the crucial factor determining large-scale investment into the tourist industry." Anson Chong, "Economic Development of Hawaii and the Growth of Tourism" (M.A. thesis, Columbia University, 1963), 163; Thomas Kemper Hitch and Mary Ishii Kuramoto, *Waialae Country Club: The First Half Century* (Honolulu: Waialae Country Club, 1981), 5–10; Frank J. Taylor, Earl M. Welty, and David

W. Eyre, *From Land and Sea: The Story of Castle & Cooke in Hawaii* (San Francisco: Chronicle Books, 1976), 125–126, 150–152.

38. William L. Worden, *Cargoes: Matson's First Century in the Pacific* (Honolulu: University of Hawai'i Press, 1981), 61; Hitch, *Islands in Transition*, 120; Glen Grant, *Waikiki Yesteryear* (Honolulu: Mutual, 1996), 58; F. W. Thrum, "Launching of the *Malolo*," *Thrum's Hawaiian Annual for 1928* (Honolulu: Thos. G. Thrum, 1927), 90–92, cited portion, 90.

39. Elsie Kuhn Brown, "Hawaii—Where Romance Is Enthroned," *Paradise of the Pacific*, December 1926, 31; "Royal Hawaiian Hotel Souvenir Edition," *Keeler's Hotel Weekly*, August 26, 1927, 7, 47; for a critical treatment, see Andrea Feeser, *Waikīkī: A History of Forgettng and Remembering* (Honolulu: University of Hawai'i Press, 2006) 63–71.

40. Stan Cohen, *The Pink Palace: The Royal Hawaiian Hotel, a Sheraton Hotel in Hawaii* (Missoula, Mont.: Pictorial Histories, 1986); "Royal Hawaiian Hotel, Honolulu, T.H., Souvenir Edition," *Keeler's Hotel Weekly*, August 6, 1927, 7, 30–37.

41. *The Hawaiian Annual for 1928*, 32; Cohen, *The Pink Palace*, 41–50; *Honolulu Star-Bulletin*, January 31, 1927.

42. Richard A. Hawkins, "Princess Abigail Kawānanakoa: The Forgotten Territorial Native Hawaiian Leader," *Hawaiian Journal of History* 37 (2003): 163–177; John S. Whitehead, "The Anti-Statehood Movement and the Legacy of Alice Kamiokila Campbell," *Hawaiian Journal of History* 27 (1993): 43–64. Alice Kamiokila Campbell was a sister of Abigail Kawānanakoa.

43. "Ancient Pageantry, Music, and Dancing to Feature Opening," *Honolulu Star-Bulletin*, January 31, 1927; "Royal Hawaiian Hotel," 47; "Perfection in Every Detail," *Honolulu Star-Bulletin*, February 2, 1927; Jane Desmond, *Staging Tourism: Bodies on Display from Waikiki to Sea World* (Chicago: University of Chicago Press, 1999), 89–91; *Paradise of the Pacific*, February 1927, 25; the Royal had its own *mele inoa* (name chant suitable for royalty), Rob Wilson, *Reimagining the American Pacific: From South Pacific to Bamboo Ridge and Beyond* (Durham, N.C.: Duke University Press, 2000), xiv.

44. Desmond, *Staging Tourism*, 91; "All the Glamour and Glory of Old Hawaii Remain," *Honolulu Star-Bulletin*, January 31, 1927; *Honolulu Advertiser*, February 1, 1927; Chapin, *Shaping History*, 148.

45. Hawaii Tourist Bureau, *The Story of Hawaii* (Honolulu: Hawaii Tourist Bureau, December 1926), 26.

46. This analysis is indebted to two books with the same title: Matt K. Matsuda, *Empire of Love: Histories of France and the Pacific* (New York: Oxford University Press, 2005), and Elizabeth A Povinelli, *The Empire of Love: Toward a Theory of Intimacy, Genealogy, and Carnality* (Durham, N.C.: Duke University Press, 2006). See also Noenoe K. Silva, *Aloha Betrayed: Native Hawaiian Resistance to American Colonialism* (Durham, N.C.: Duke University Press, 2004), 189–90; Tom Coffman, *Nation Within: The Story of America's Annexation of the Nation of Hawai'i* (Kāne'ohe, Hawai'i: Epi-

Center Press, 1998), 315; Barbara Bennett Peterson, ed., *Notable Women of Hawaii* (Honolulu: University of Hawai'i Press, 1984), 209.

47. Hawkins, "Princess Abigail Kawānakoa," 167, 168, 170, 172; Peterson, *Notable Women of Hawaii*, 209–211.

48. Hawaii Tourist Bureau, *Nearby Hawaii* (Honolulu: Hawaii Tourist Bureau, 1923 and 1934), 4; Hawaii Tourist Bureau, *Nani O Hawaii* (Honolulu: Paradise of the Pacific, n.d.), n.p.; Hawaii Tourist Bureau, *Story of Hawaii* (Honolulu: Hawaii Tourist Bureau, 1932), 30; Frank G. Carpenter, *Lands of the Caribbean* (Garden City, N.Y.: Doubleday, Page, 1926), 179; "Travel," *Bulletin of the Pan American Union*, January 1935, 32; *Journal of the Cuban Chamber of Commerce of the United States*, June 1930, 24.

49. *Honolulu Star-Bulletin*, January 31, 1927; Woon, *When It's Cocktail Time in Cuba*, 18; *Havana, the Magazine of Cuba*, February 19, 1929, 6.

50. Robin Moore, *Nationalizing Blackness: Afrocubanismo and Artistic Revolution in Havana, 1920–1940* (Pittsburgh: University of Pittsburgh Press, 1997), 84–86, 141; "The Quest of Winter Ease," *Literary Digest*, December 16, 1922, cites the *New York Herald* as the source of the phrase "New York's Gayest Suburb" on 56; Ann Douglas, *Terrible Honesty: Mongrel Manhattan in the 1920s* (New York: Noonday Press, 1995), 5–6.

51. Hawaii Tourist Bureau, *Story of Hawaii* (1926), 31; Hawaii Tourist Bureau, *Nani O Hawaii*, n.p; Lori Pierce, "Creating a Racial Paradise: Citizenship and Sociology in Hawai'i," in Paul Spickard, ed., *Race and Nation: Ethnic Systems in the Modern World* (New York: Routledge, 2005), 69–86; Henry Yu, *Thinking Orientals: Migration, Contact, and Exoticism in Modern America* (New York: Oxford University Press, 2001), 80–90; Eileen H. Tamura, "Using the Past to Inform the Future: An Historiography of Hawai'i's Asian and Pacific Islander Americans," *Amerasia Journal* 26, 1 (2000): 55–85; Jeff Chang, "Local Knowledge(s): Notes on Race Relations, Panethnicity, and History in Hawai'i," *Amerasia Journal* 22, 2 (1996): 1–29.

52. The phrase "plantation pyramid" comes from the wonderful historical novel of Milton Murayama, *All I Asking For Is My Body* (1959; reprint, Honolulu: University of Hawai'i Press, 1988); *Paradise of the Pacific*, February 1927, 25; Cohen, *The Pink Palace*, passim; Desmond, *Staging Tourism*, 89; "Royal Hawaiian Hotel"; *Honolulu Star-Bulletin*, January 31, 1927.

53. Hawaii Tourist Bureau, *Story of Hawaii* (1926), 31; Hawaii Tourist Bureau, *Nani O Hawaii*, n.p.; for a sort of precursor of the white "new woman" in the colonial tropics who remained popular in the 1920s United States, see Louise Michele Newman, "A Feminist Explores Africa: May French-Sheldon's Subversion of Patriarchical Protection," ch. 4 of *White Women's Rights: The Racial Origins of Feminism in the United States* (New York: Oxford University Press, 1999), 102–115.

54. On the cultural politics of hula, I'm indebted to Cathy van Horne, "The Evolution of the Hula in Hawaii's Early Tourism Advertising, from Censure to Commercialization," unpublished paper; see n. 75 to Chapter 2.

55. Examples include "The Real Hawaiian Hula," *Paradise of the Pacific*, August 1927, 31; "An Advertising Analysis and Recommendation," *Paradise of the Pacific*, December 1922, 91–95; "Hawaiian Music as Publicity," *Paradise of the Pacific*, March 1921, 9; van Horne, "The Evolution of the Hula"; Sereno, "Images of the Hula Dancer," 195–212; Hoefer et al., *The Hula*, 70–74; De Soto Brown, *Hawaii Recalls: Selling Romance to America, Nostalgic Images of the Hawaiian Islands, 1910–1950* (Honolulu: Editions Limited, 1982), 58–61; Desmond, *Staging Tourism*, 80–82.

56. Löfgren, *On Holiday*, 223; Grant, *Waikiki Yesteryear*, 42; Clifford Gessler, *Hawaii: Isles of Enchantment* (New York: D. Appleton-Century, 1937), 148, 150.

57. Gessler, *Isles of Enchantment*, 150; Grady Timmons, *Waikiki Beachboy* (Honolulu: Editions Limited, 1989), 135–140, cited portions, 140.

58. Ben R. Finney and James D. Houston, *Surfing: The Sport of Hawaiian Kings* (1966; reprint, Rutland, Vt.: Charles E. Tuttle, 1971), ch. 4, Nathaniel Emerson cited on 64.

59. Finney and Houston, *Surfing*, 70; Alexander Hume Ford, "Outdoor Allurements," *Thrum's Hawaiian Almanac and Annual for 1911* (Honolulu: Thos. G. Thrum, 1910), 143; Timmons, *Waikiki Beachboy*, 25; Isaiah Helekunihi Walker, "Hui Nalu, Beach Boys, and the Surfing Boarder-lands of Hawai'i," *Contemporary Pacific* 20, 1 (Spring 2008): 89–113.

60. "A Royal Sport," ch. 6 of Jack London, *The Cruise of the Snark* (London: Mills and Boon, 1911), 82–96, cited portions, 83, 84; Hawaii Tourist Bureau, *Story of Hawaii* (Honolulu: Hawaii Tourist Bureau, 1931), 6.

61. Gessler, *Isles of Enchantment*, 303, 307.

62. Hawaii Tourist Bureau, *Nani o Hawaii*, n.p.; Hawaii Tourist Bureau, *Hawaii Eternally Enchanting* (Honolulu: Hawaii Tourist Bureau, 1923), 5.

63. Henry Yu, "Tiger Woods Is Not the End of History: Or, Why Sex Across the Color Line Won't Save Us All," *American Historical Review* 108, 5 (December 2003): 1406–1414.

64. Hawaii Tourist Bureau, *Hawaii Nei* (Honolulu: Hawaii Tourist Bureau, 1932), back cover; Hawaii Tourist Bureau, *Story of Hawaii* (1926), 15, 21, and (1931), 28, 31.

65. S. Grace Harlow, *Hawaii by a Tourist* (Los Angeles: West Coast, 1928), 99, 102, 107.

66. Hawaiian Sugar Planters' Association cited in Ronald Takaki, *Strangers from a Different Shore: A History of Asian-Americans* (New York: Penguin, 1989), 159; Hawaiian Sugar Planters' Association, *The Story of Sugar in Hawaii*, rev. ed. (Honolulu: Advertiser Press, 1929), 14, 15, 26, 27.

67. HSPA, *The Story of Sugar*, 29, 70–75. These discourses influenced and were influenced by academic discourses produced by sociologists Romanzo Adams and Andrew Lind and popularized by their many advocates. Pierce, "Creating a Racial Paradise"; Yu, *Thinking Orientals*, 80–90; Tamura, "Using the Past to Inform the Future"; Chang, "Local Knowledge(s)."

68. President Richard A. Cooke, HSPA Annual Report for 1929, cited in Beechert, *Working in Hawaii*, 241.

69. Ann Laura Stoler, *Carnal Knowledge and Imperial Power: Race and the Intimate in Colonial Rule* (Berkeley: University of California Press, 2002), 17; Fuchs, *Hawaii Pono*, 276, 277; Beechert, *Working in Hawaii*, 243, 244; Okihiro, *Cane Fires*, school figures, 140, cited portion, 159; 112; 110–113, Eileen H. Tamura, "Power, Status, and Hawai'i Creole English: An Example of Linguistic Intolerance in American History," *Pacific Historical Review* 65, 3 (August 1996): 431–454; Tamura, *Americanization, Acculturation, and Ethnic Identity: The Nisei Generation in Hawaii* (Urbana: University of Illinois Press, 1994), 110–113, *Hawaii Hochi* cited on 112.

70. Gary Okihiro, *Margins and Mainstreams: Asians in American History and Culture* (Seattle: University of Washington Press, 1994), 141; Governor Wallace Rider Farrington to Hawaii Tourist Bureau, June 6, 1927, Tourist Bureau, Hawaii, Governor Wallace Rider Farrington Papers, July 5, 1921–July 5, 1929, Hawai'i State Archives, Honolulu; Wallace Rider Farrington, "Hawaii, Remarkable for Achievements of All," *Paradise of the Pacific*, December 1925, 29–35.

71. Waldo Frank, "Habana of the Cubans," *New Republic*, June 23, 1926, 140; Alejandro de la Fuente, *Race, Inequality, and Politics in Twentieth-Century Cuba* (Chapel Hill: University of North Carolina Press, 2001), 156; Louis A. Pérez, Jr., *On Becoming Cuban: Nationality, Identity, Culture* (Chapel Hill: University of North Carolina Press, 1999), 322.

72. Woon to du Pont, January 11, 1928, box 8, Irénée du Pont Papers; *New York Times*, March 31, 1929; Vicki Gold Levi and Steven Heller, *Cuba Style: Graphics from the Golden Age of Design* (New York: Princeton Architectural Press, 2002), 126–149, passim.

73. Russell H. Fitzgibbon, *Cuba and the United States, 1900–1935* (Menasha, Wisc.: George Banta, 1935), 187–188; Crowder to Stockley W. Morgan, chief of Latin American Affairs Division, State Department, April 19, 1927, Crowder Papers.

74. Woon, *When It's Cocktail Time in Cuba*, 4, 6, 7, 91–93; Bruce Bliven, "And Cuba for the Winter," *New Republic*, February 1928, 61–65, cited portion, 61.

75. Timothy J. Gilfoyle, *City of Eros: New York City, Prostitution, and the Commercialization of Sex, 1790–1920* (New York: W. W. Norton, 1992), 307–310; Decker, "The Waking of the Sleeping Princess," 8; *The Miami-Palm Beach-Havana Gimlet, Season of 1928–1929* (Miami: John Ashe Scott, n.d.) 65.

76. L. E. Myers to Crowder, February 21, 1928, Crowder Papers; Enrique C. Canova, "Cuba—the Isle of Romance," *National Geographic*, September 1933, 344–380, 345; Sydney Clark, *Cuban Tapestry* (New York: National Travel Club, 1936), 98.

77. Douglas, *Terrible Honesty*, 11–14, 20, cited portions, 12, 20; Gene Fowler, *Beau James: The Life and Times of Jimmy Walker* (New York: Viking Press, 1949); Herbert Mitgang, *Once Upon a Time in New York: Jimmy Walker, Franklin Roosevelt, and the Last Great Battle of the Jazz Age* (New York: Free Press, 2000).

78. Fred Searing, "What Then Is Mañana," *Havana, the Magazine of Cuba*, January 1, 1929, 16; *New York Times*, January 22, 1928; Douglas, *Terrible Honesty*, 185.

79. Thomas, *Cuba*, 586–587; Benjamin, *The United States and Cuba*, 57; Smith, *The United States and Cuba*, 74, 121, 125.

80. Crowder to Catlin, February 15, 1927, and Crowder to Kellogg, February 17, 1927, Crowder Papers.

81. Fitzgibbon, *Cuba and the United States*, 146; Beals, *The Crime of Cuba*, 256–258; Robert Whitney, *State and Revolution in Cuba: Mass Mobilization and Political Change, 1920–1940* (Chapel Hill: University of North Carolina Press, 2001), 58.

82. *The Miami—Palm Beach—Havana Gimlet, Season of 1929–1930* reprinted Coolidge's opening remarks, 60; George Black, *Good Neighbor: How the United States Wrote the History of Central America and the Caribbean* (New York: Pantheon Books, 1988), 49, 52–54, Machado cited on 52; Ferrera cited in Aguilar, *Cuba, 1933*, 89.

83. *Cuba Review*, February 1928, 15–16, and March 1928, 18.

84. Black, *Good Neighbors*, 49, 53; Schwartz, *Pleasure Island*, 65–67; *New York Times*, January 22, 1928; *Cuba Review*, March 1928, 16–19, and April, 1928, 13; Schwartz, *Pleasure Island*, 91.

85. T. M. Findley, assistant manager, Chase National Bank, Havana, to Carl P. Biggerman, assistant cashier, Main Office, New York City, July 18, 1928, both in U.S. Senate Committee, *Stock Exchange Practices*, 2644; on privileging expenditures for beautification of Havana and Capitol over those for the Central Highway, see U.S. Senate Committee, *Stock Exchange Practices*, 2591; Thomas, *Cuba*, 587; Pérez, *Cuba Under the Platt Amendment*, 378, n. 70.

86. *The Visit of the President-Elect of Cuba*, 19; Beals, *The Crime of Cuba*, 270; Pérez, *Cuba Under the Platt Amendment*, 281; Benjamin, *The United States and Cuba*, 42.

87. Luis B. Deschaplesses to Crowder, June 13, 1928, and June 16, 1928; Myers to Crowder, June 27, 1928; [illegible] from embassy to Crowder, May 8, 1928, Crowder Papers.

88. Crowder to Morrow, May 3, 1928; Crowder to de la Torre, May 14, 1928, and May 15, 1928; F[rank] S[teinhart] to Crowder, October 13, 1928; Céspedes to de la Torre, February 25, 1929, Crowder Papers; Leland Hamilton Jenks, *Our Cuban Colony: A Study in Sugar* (1928; reprint, New York: Arno Press, 1970), 273.

89. Clark, *Cuban Tapestry*, 65; Whitney, *State and Revolution in Cuba*, 56; Gonzalez to Crowder, December 8, 1929, Crowder Papers.

Chapter 4. Revolutions, Reformations, Restorations

1. "Food First," *El Cubano Libre*, August 28, 1928; *Cuba Review*, September 1929, 16.

2. Dorothy Mackaill cited in Grady Timmons, *Waikiki Beachboy* (Honolulu: Editions Limited, 1989), 33; Rear Admiral Yates Stirling, Jr., *Sea Duty: The Memoirs of a Fighting Admiral* (New York: G. P. Putnam's Sons, 1939), 233–234; John Gregory

Dunne, "The American Raj: Pearl Harbor as Metaphor," *New Yorker*, May 7, 2001, 46–54, cited portion, 50.

3. Hudson Strode, *The Pageant of Cuba* (New York: Harrison Smith and Robert Haas, 1934), 247.

4. Alejo Carpentier, *The Lost Steps*, trans. Harriet de Onis (Minneapolis: University of Minnesota Press, 2001).

5. The most extensive historical treatments of the Massie and Kahahawai affairs are David E. Stannard, *Honor Killing: How the Infamous "Massie Affair" Transformed Hawai'i* (New York: Viking, 2005) and Theon Wright, *Rape in Paradise* (New York: Hawthorn Books, 1966).

6. Newspapers cited in Helen Geracimos Chapin, *Shaping History: The Role of Newspapers in Hawai'i* (Honolulu: University of Hawai'i Press, 1996), 154; Stirling, *Sea Duty*, 234, 245–246.

7. Stirling cited in Gavan Daws, *Shoal of Time: A History of the Hawaiian Islands* (Honolulu: University of Hawai'i Press, 1968), 323.

8. *New York Sunday Review* and Hearst papers cited in Stannard, *Honor Killing*, 264, 267.

9. Dunne, "The American Raj," 53.

10. Lawrence M. Judd, as told to Hugh W. Lytle, *Lawrence M. Judd and Hawaii* (Rutland, Vt: Charles E. Tuttle, 1971), 167, 201.

11. Walter F. Dillingham, "A Memorandum" imprinted "For Private Circulation and Not for Publication," Honolulu, 1932, 9.

12. Kawānanakoa cited in Edward Joesting, *Hawaii: An Uncommon History* (New York: W. W. Norton, 1972), 301; Theon Wright, *The Disenchanted Isles: The Story of the Second Revolution in Hawaii* (New York: Dial Press, 1972), 80–83, *Hawaii Hochi* cited on 82; on the differential applications of unified legal codes in colonial contexts, Lauren Benton, *Law and Colonial Cultures: Legal Regimes in World History, 1400–1900* (New York: Cambridge University Press, 2002).

13. Stannard, *Honor Killing*, 411–415; John P. Rosa, "Local Story: The Massie Case Narrative and the Cultural Production of Local Identity in Hawai'i," *Amerasia Journal* 26, 2 (2000): 93–115. "The events of the Massie story certainly make for a compelling 'local origins story" Rosa argues, but "the Massie Case narrative should not be told in reaffirming local identity at the expense of Native Hawaiian: historical narratives in Hawai'i have too often been mobilized against the very people that they were originally meant to empower" (110). Scholarly literature on the local has exploded in recent years; two now-classic starting points are Jeff Chang, "Local Knowledge(s): Notes on Race Relations, Panethnicity, and History in Hawai'i," *Amerasia Journal* 22, 2 (1996): 1–29, and Jonathan Y. Okamura, "Aloha Kanaka Me Ke Aloha 'Aina: Local Culture and Society in Hawai'i," *Amerasia Journal* 7, 2 (1980): 119–137.

14. Stannard, *Honor Killing*, 421; Wright, *The Disenchanted Isles*, 83.

15. Louis A. Pérez, Jr., *Cuba: Between Reform and Revolution* (New York: Oxford University Press, 1988), 253–262; Luis E. Aguilar, *Cuba 1933: Prologue to Revolution*

(New York: W. W. Norton, 1974), 98–107; Robert Whitney, *State and Revolution in Cuba: Mass Mobilization and Political Change, 1920–1940* (Chapel Hill: University of North Carolina Press, 2001), 84–93; Pérez, *On Becoming Cuban: Identity, Nationality, and Culture* (Chapel Hill: University of North Carolina Press, 1999), 297.

16. Rosalie Schwartz, *Pleasure Island: Tourism and Temptation in Cuba* (Lincoln: University of Nebraska Press, 1997), 61; Peñas de Hicacos, S.A., to du Pont, November 28, 1934, box 8, accession 228, Irénée du Pont Papers, Hagley Museum and Library, Wilmington, Delaware, hereafter Irénée du Pont Papers; Museum of Public Relations, "Carl R. Byoir, A Retrospective," www.prmuseum.com/byoir/cb20–30.html, accessed July 6, 2005; du Pont to George W. Platt, treasurer, Cuban-American Bancorporation, April 24, 1930; "History of My Real Estate Venture in Cuba," dictated by du Pont, May 1944, box 18; du Pont to Senator John G. Townsend; du Pont to Senator Daniel O. Hastings, both dated April 10, 1929, box 8, all in Irénée du Pont Papers; "Plan to Aid Cuba on Good-Will Tour," *New York Times*, September, 30, 1930; Robert Freeman Smith, *The United States and Cuba: Business and Diplomacy, 1917–1960* (New York: Bookman Associates, 1960), 120–129. Irénée du Pont came to feel that the Committee of One Hundred had hoodwinked him and his peers.

17. Pérez, *Cuba: Between Reform and Revolution*, 262–264.

18. Hugh Thomas, *Cuba: The Pursuit of Freedom* (New York: Harper & Row, 1971), 658–665; Richard Gott, *Cuba, A New History* (New Haven, Conn.: Yale University Press, 2002), 136–141; Alejandro de la Fuente, *A Nation for All: Race, Inequality, and Politics in Twentieth-Century Cuba* (Chapel Hill: University of North Carolina Press, 2001), 135–137, 198.

19. Hugo "Lippy" S. Lippman to du Pont, undated cable sent between September 5 and September 12, 1933, box 8, Irénée du Pont Papers; de la Fuente, *A Nation for All*, 198–200.

20. Morris H. Morley, *Imperial State and Revolution: The United States and Cuba, 1952–1986* ((New York: Cambridge University Press, 1987), 34, 35; U.S. military attaché cited in de la Fuente, *A Nation for All*, 208; Frank Argote-Freyre, *Fulgencio Batista: From Revolutionary to Strongman* (New Brunswick, N.J.: Rutgers University Press, 2006), 124–126.

21. Pérez, *Cuba: Between Reform and Revolution*, 279–281; Whitney, *State and Revolution in Cuba*, 181–182.

22. Robin Moore, *Nationalizing Blackness: Afrocubanismo and Artistic Revolution in Havana, 1920–1940* (Pittsburgh: University of Pittsburgh Press, 1997), 133; de la Fuente, *A Nation for All*, 188.

23. Alejandra Bronfman, *Measures of Equality: Social Science, Citizenship, and Race in Cuba, 1902–1940* (Chapel Hill: University of North Carolina Press, 2004), 159; du Pont to Luis Machado, May 23, 1938, and Machado to du Pont, June 16, 1938, box 9, Irénée du Pont Papers; Robert Lacey, *Little Man: Meyer Lansky and the Gangster Life* (Boston: Little, Brown, 1991), 133–135; Ernest Haveman, "Mobsters Move in on

Troubled Havana and Split Rich Gambling Profits with Batista," *Life*, March 10, 1958, 39.

24. Eric Paul Roorda, "Desarraigando la tierra de clubes: la extinction de la 'colonia americana' en La Habana," *Secuencia* 60 (September–December 2004), 114; Bronfman, *Measures of Equality*, 171.

25. Bronfman, *Measures of Equality*, 159–160; Schwartz, *Pleasure Island*, 94–99; Moore, *Nationalizing Blackness*, 84.

26. Cuban National Tourism Commission, *Cuba: Ideal Vacation Land* (n.p., 1937), 35–36; Moore, *Nationalizing Blackness*, 83; Bronfman, *Measures of Equality*, 168–171.

27. Vera Kutzinski, *Sugar's Secrets: Race and the Erotics of Cuban Nationality* (Charlottesville: University Press of Virginia, 1993), 9; de la Fuente *A Nation for All*, 183; Bronfman, *Measures of Equality*, 171.

28. Pérez, *Cuba: Between Reform and Revolution*, 279–281; Daws, *Shoal of Time*, 332.

29. Roger Bell, *Last Among Equals: Hawaiian Statehood and American Politics* (Honolulu: University of Hawai'i Press, 1984), 57–66; Edward D. Beechert, *Working in Hawaii: A Labor History* (Honolulu: University of Hawai'i Press, 1985), 256–258, 270–273.

30. Moon-Kie Jung, *Reworking Race: The Making of Hawaii's Interracial Labor Movement* (New York: Columbia University Press, 2006), 106–144, passim, cited portions, 106, 141; see also Stannard, *Honor Killing*, 415.

31. Timmons, *Waikiki Beachboy*, 33–34; Gary Y. Okihiro, *Cane Fires: The Anti-Japanese Movement in Hawaii, 1865–1945* (Philadelphia: Temple University Press, 1991), 123–128; Adria L. Imada, "Hawaiians on Tour: Hula Circuits Through the American Empire," *American Quarterly* 56, 1 (March 2004): 111–149.

32. The Massie case and haole governance in fact seemed to have provided Stirling's *Sea Duty* with its raison d'etre, for they dominate the text. "Hawaii, Sugar-Coated Fortress," *Fortune*, August 1940, 31–37, 78, 81, 82, emphasis in original. The HTB threatened to stop advertising in *Fortune*, although it did not. *Honolulu Star-Bulletin*, August 3, 1940, and August 6, 1940.

33. Joseph Barber, Jr., *Hawaii, Restless Rampart* (Indianapolis: Bobbs-Merrill, 1941), 78, 84, 87, 95, 96, 111, 262.

34. Thurston cited in John S. Whitehood, *Completing the Union: Alaska, Hawai'i and the Battle for Statehood* (Albuquerque: University of New Mexico Press, 2004), 74.

35. On tourism in wartime Hawai'i, see Adria L. Imada, "The Army Learns to Luau: Imperial Hospitality and Military Photography in Hawai'i," *Contemporary Pacific* 20, 2 (Fall 2008): 328–361; David Farber and Beth Bailey, "The Fighting Man as Tourist: The Politics of Tourist Culture in Hawaii During World War II," *Pacific Historical Review* 65, 4 (November 1996): 641–660; Beth Bailey and David Farber, *The First Strange Place: Race and Sex in World War II Hawaii* (Baltimore: Johns Hopkins University Press, 1992).

36. Russell H. Fitzgibbon et al., eds., *The Constitutions of the Americas* (Chicago: University of Chicago Press, 1948); Thomas, *Cuba*, 719–720; Whitney, *State and Revolution in Cuba*, 149–176, passim; Bronfman, *Measures of Equality*, 179; de la Fuente, *A Nation for All*, 222.

37. Jules R. Benjamin, *The United States and the Origins of the Cuban Revolution: An Empire of Liberty in an Age of National Liberation* (Princeton, N.J.: Princeton University Press, 1990), 100, 106, cited portion, 100; Harold Sims, "Cuba," in Leslie Bethell and Ian Roxborough, eds., *Latin America Between the Second World War and the Cold War, 1944–1948* (Cambridge: Cambridge University Press, 1992), 224; Jorge F. Pérez-Lopez, *The Economics of Cuban Sugar* (Pittsburgh: University of Pittsburgh Press, 1991), 7, 179; Thomas, *Cuba*, 760–761, 765.

38. Louis A. Pérez, Jr., *Cuba and the United States: Ties of Singular Intimacy* (Athens: University of Georgia Press, 1990), 207; Alfred Padula, "The Fall of the Bourgeoisie: Cuba, 1959–1961" (Ph.D. dissertation, University of New Mexico, December 1974), 48; Philip C. Newman, *Cuba Before Castro: An Economic Appraisal* (Ridgewood, N.J.: Foreign Studies Institute, 1965), 61; Marifeli Pérez-Stable, *The Cuban Revolution: Origins, Course, and Legacy* (Oxford: Oxford University Press, 1993), 16.

39. Padula, "The Fall of the Bourgeoisie," 252; Pérez-Stable, *The Cuban Revolution*, 17–22.

40. Julian Alienes Urosa, *Economia de Post-Guerra y Desempleo* (Havana: Lex for La Junta Nacional de Economía, 1949); Alienes Urosa, *Los Problemos de la Economía de la Paz y las Soluciones que se apuntan* (Havana: Molinay Compañía, 1945); Victor Santamarina, *El Turismo: Industria nacional* (Havana: Cultural, SA, 1944).

41. Santamarina, *El Turismo*, 17, 43, 45, 50, 58, 79, 89, 155, 225.

42. Ruby Hart Phillips, *Cuba: Island of Paradox* (New York: McDowell, Obelensky, 1959), 264; Thomas, *Cuba*, 737–758.

43. Roorda, "Desarraigando la tierra de clubes," 129, 130.

44. One of the most compelling firsthand accounts and retrospective inquiries into Hawai'i under martial law remains J. Garner Anthony, *Hawaii Under Army Rule* (1955; reprint, Stanford, Calif.: Stanford University Press, 1975). Anthony was attorney general of Hawai'i from 1942 to 1943, a vocal critic of military rule, and a leader of the legal challenge that resulted in the decision by the U.S. Supreme Court that martial law was unconstitutional, a decision the Court made two years after martial law ended. Wright, *The Disenchanted Isles*, 103; Bell, *Last Among Equals*, 84–86.

45. Okihiro, *Cane Fires*, 209, 223–226, 240, 267, cited portions, 223–224.

46. Kathy E. Ferguson and Phyllis Turnbull, *Oh, Say, Can You See? The Semiotics of the Military in Hawai'i* (Minneapolis: University of Minnesota Press, 1999), Roosevelt cited on 159.

47. Thomas Kemper Hitch, *Islands in Transition: The Past, Present, and Future of Hawaii's Economy* (Honolulu: First Hawaiian Bank, 1992,) 135–156, passim; Gwenfread Allen, *Hawaii's War Years, 1940–1945* (Honolulu: Advertiser, 1950), 288–289;

U.S. Department of Labor, *The Economy of Hawaii in 1947* (Washington, D.C.: Government Printing Office, 1948), 12–27; Jung, *Reworking Race*, 134, 137–139.

48. U.S. Department of Labor, *The Economy of Hawaii in 1947*, 188; Daws, *Shoal of Time*, 367; Jung, *Reworking Race*, 154.

49. Postwar Planning Committee of the Chamber of Commerce, *Hawaii's Postwar Plans* (Honolulu: n.p., 1946), 4, 5; Lizabeth Cohen, *A Consumers' Republic: The Politics of Mass Consumption in Postwar America* (New York: Knopf, 2003).

50. Jonathan Y. Okamura, "Why There Are No Asian Americans in Hawai'i: The Continuing Significance of Local Identity," *Social Process in Hawaii* 35 (1994): 161–178; Clarence E. Glick, *Sojourners and Settlers: Chinese Migrants in Hawaii* (Honolulu: University of Hawai'i Press, 1980), esp. 207; Julius Spellman, "Chinn Ho: Hawaii's Horatio Alger," *Finance*, June 1970, 8–13; Mazeppa Costa, "Spotlight on Chinn Ho," *Paradise of the Pacific*, December 1961, 95–96, 112, 114; William R. Tansill, *Hawaii and Statehood* (Washington, D.C.: Library of Congress Legislative Service, July 1948), 9; George Cooper and Gavan Daws, *Land and Power in Hawaii: The Democratic Years* (Honolulu: Benchmark Books, 1985), 150.

51. Wright, *Disenchanted Isles*, 112, 137–138; Lawrence Fuchs, *Hawaii Pono: An Ethnic and Political History* (Honolulu: Bess Press, 1961), 397–401.

52. Katsumi Kometani cited in Okihiro, *Cane Fires*, 274; Daniel Inouye, *Journey to Washington* (Englewood Cliffs, N.J.: Prentice Hall, 1967), 246; Matsuo Takabuki, *An Unlikely Revolutionary: Matsuo Takabuki and the Making of Modern Hawai'i* (Honolulu: University of Hawai'i Press, 1998) 45; Ferguson and Turnbull, *Oh, Say, Can You See?* ch. 5.

53. Bell, *Last Among Equals*, 142–144.

54. Bell, *Last Among Equals*, 84–86; Allen, *Hawaii's War Years*, 174.

55. Hitch, *Islands in Transition*, 163–165; Fuchs, *Hawaii Pono*, 386–396.

56. Bell, *Last Among Equals*, 133–140; Fuchs, *Hawaii Pono*, 407–414; Daws, *Shoal of Time*, 383–390; Wright, *The Disenchanted Isles*, 192–194; George Chapin, *Presstime in Paradise: The Life and Times of the Honolulu Advertiser, 1856–1995* (Honolulu: University of Hawai'i Press, 1998), Lorrin P. Thurston cited on 239.

57. Hawaii Visitors Bureau, *Visitors Become Big Business* (Honolulu: Hawaii Visitors Bureau, 1946), 44–45; Claude A. Jagger, president of the Hawaii Economic Foundation, "Address Before the Sales Executives of Hawaii," June 14, 1948; *Business Week*, August 7, 1948; *Honolulu Star-Bulletin*, February 14, 1948; Bank of Hawaii (prepared by James Shoemaker), *Earning, Spending, Saving in Hawaii* (Honolulu: Bank of Hawaii, May 1951), 22; Bank of Hawaii, *Opportunities for Hawaii to Produce More and Live Better* (Honolulu: Bank of Hawaii, December 1950), 19; Secretary and Acting Governor of the Territory of Hawaii Oren E. Long to James P. Davis, director, Division of Territories and Island Possessions, January 12, 1950, RG 126, Office of the Territories, box 730, Department of the Interior, National Archives II, College Park, Md.

58. Charles P. Leon, "The National Bank of Cuba: A Study in Institutional Change" (Ph.D. dissertation, New York University, 1964), 155, 157; "Economic and

Financial Review: First Quarter of 1953"; Reinhold P. Wolff and Oscar Marcenaro, "Caribbean Tourist Trade Index: A Comprehensive Study of Tourist Trends in the Caribbean for the Past Six Years," unpublished manuscript, Bureau of Business and Economic Research, University of Miami, Coral Gables, Florida, February 1955, 2; Wolff and Robert J. Voyles, "Tourist Trends in the Caribbean, 1951 to 1955," unpublished manuscript, Bureau of Business and Economic Research, University of Miami, Coral Gables, Florida, April 1956, n.p.; Hitch, *Islands in Transition*, 177.

59. Banco Nacional de Cuba information from "Economic and Financial Review * First Quarter of 1953," American Embassy, Habana, April 10, 1953 837.00/4–1053, Confidential Central Files, Cuba, Internal Affairs, U.S. Department of State, General Records, 1950–1954, Record Group 59, National Archives (hereafter, IA, 1950–1954); Susan Schroeder, *Cuba: A Handbook of Historical Statistics* (Boston: G. K. Hall, 1982), 463; T. Brimelow, "Cuba: Economic and Commercial Conditions in Cuba," *Overseas Economic Surveys*, September 1949 (London: HMSO for the Commercial Relations and Exports Department, Board of Trade, 1950), 30.

60. Anglo-American Caribbean Commission, *Caribbean Tourist Trade: A Regional Approach* (Washington, D.C.: Anglo-American Caribbean Commission, 1945), 32; International Bank forReconstruction and Development, *Report on Cuba* (Baltimore: Johns Hopkins University Press, 1951), 182, 767–775.

61. "Revolution at Dawn," *Time*, March 17, 1952, 36; Harold M. Randall, "Observations on Political Thinking Encountered in Eastern and Central Cuba," desp. 1545, April 12, 1953, 737.00/4–253 IA, 1950–1954; Pérez, *On Becoming Cuban*, 446–449.

62. Nicolas Rivero, *Castro's Cuba: An American Dilemma* (Washington, D.C.: Luce, 1962), 71; IBRD, *Report on Cuba*, 6–8; U.S. Department of Commerce, *Investment in Cuba: Basic Information for United States Businessmen* (Washington, D.C.: Government Printing Office, 1956), 7; Samuel Farber, *Reaction and Revolution in Cuba, 1933–1960: A Political Sociology from Machado to Castro* (Middletown, Conn.: Wesleyan University Press, 1976), 153.

63. U.S. Department of Commerce, *Investment in Cuba*, 24; *Time*, March 24, 1952, 38; Thomas, *Cuba*, 790; John Dorshner and Roberto Fabricio, *Winds of December: The Cuban Revolution, 1958* (New York: Coward, McCann and Geoghegan, 1980), ch. 1.

64. *El Mundo*, March 26, 1952, cited by David S. Green, "American Capital Reported Ready to Invest $50,000,000 in Development of Cuban Tourist Facilities," March 31, 1952, 837.181/3–3152, IA, 1950–1954; LeRoi Jones, *Home, Social Essays* (New York: William Morrow, 1966), 21; *Time*, April 21, 1952, 38.

65. R. M. Connell, first secretary of embassy, "National Tourism Development Plan Submitted to President of Cuba," 837.181/9–1450, September 14, 1950, IA, 1950–1954; David S. Green, "Tourist Movement to Cuba—Recent Developments," desp. 1422, March 3, 1952, 837/181/3–352, IA, 1950–1954; Earl T. Crain, acting counselor of embassy to Department of State, "Views of Justo Luis del Pozo, Mayor of Habana," desp. 1518, March 30, 1953, p. 4, 737.00/3–3053, IA, 1950–1954.

66. "Economic and Financial Review"; David S. Green, "Cuban Tourist Commission Superseded by a Cuban Tourist Institute," July 2, 1952, 837.181/7–252, IA, 1950–1954; Fulgencio Batista y Zaldívar, *The Growth and Decline of the Cuban Republic*, trans. Blas M. Rocafort (New York: Devin-Adair, 1964), 193.

67. "Memorandum by the Secretary of State to the President, March 24, 1952," in *Foreign Relations of the United States, 1952–1954*, vol. 4, *The American Republics* (Washington, D.C.: Government Printing Office, 1983), 871–872, hereafter, *FRUS, 1952–1954*; Thomas G. Paterson, *Contesting Castro: The United States and the Triumph of the Cuban Revolution* (Oxford: Oxford University Press, 1994), 58; Louis A. Pérez, Jr., *Army Politics in Cuba, 1898–1959* (Pittsburgh: University of Pittsburgh Press, 1976), 128–132; "Ambassador in Cuba (Beaulac) to the Department of State, Habana, January 9, 1953 and July 14, 1953," *FRUS, 1952–1954*, 882, 895.

68. Elisio Riera-Gomez to the secretary of state, "Report of Economical, Political and Social Conditions in Cuban Under the Present Government of F. Batista," January 20, 1953, 737.00/1–2653; Riera-Gomez to William Lantaff, U.S. representative from Florida, May 8, 1953, 737.00/5–1153; Carlos Hevia to Jack Moors Cabot, assistant secretary of state, July 31, 1953, 737.00/7–3153 all IA, 1950–1954.

69. Jules Dubois, *Fidel Castro: Rebel—Liberator or Dictator?* (Indianapolis: Bobbs-Merrill, 1959), 30; Fidel Castro, "History Will Absolve Me," in Rolando E. Bonachea and Nelson P. Valdés, eds., *Revolutionary Struggle, 1947–1958*, vol. 1 of *The Selected Works of Fidel Castro* (Cambridge, Mass.: MIT Press, 1972), 164–220.

70. Castro cited in Carlos Franqui, *Diary of the Cuban Revolution* (1976; reprint, New York: Viking Press, 1980), 11.

71. Green, "Cuban Tourist Commission"; Enrique Collazo Pérez, *Cuba: banca y crédito, 1950–1958* (Havana: Editorial de Ciencias Sociales, 1989), 49; *Time*, March 24, 1952, 38; Thomas, *Cuba*, 790.

72. Dorshner and Fabricio, *Winds of December*, ch. 1.

73. "Economic and Financial Review; Law-Decree no. 825, *Gaceta Oficial*, May 30, 1953; Morton P. Winsberg, "Overseas Travel by American Civilians Since World War II," *Journal of Geography* 65, 1 (February 1966): 73–79, 78.

74. Minutes of special meeting of Board of Directors of Hilton Hotels, International, March 16, 1952, box 10, Record Group 1, Conrad N. Hilton Archives, Conrad Hilton School of Hotel and Restaurant Management, University of Houston, hereafter, Hilton Archives; Newman, *Cuba Before Castro*, 121; Schwartz, *Pleasure Island*, 154–156. On the El Caribe Hilton, see Dennis Merrill, "Negotiating Cold War Paradise: U.S. Tourism, Economic Planning, and Cultural Modernity in Twentieth-Century Puerto Rico," 25, 2 *Diplomatic History* (Spring 2001): 179–214.

75. Philip Chapman, "Gambling Move," *American Weekly*, November 9, 1952, 9; "U.S. Says Nixon Asked Help for 'Trustee,'" *New York Times*, October 30, 1952; P. J. Reveley, American Embassy, Havana, "Inquiry from Mr. Dana C. Smith Concerning Certain Gambling Practices in Cuba," February 2, 1952, 837.4536/2–253, IA, 1950–

1954; Lester Velie, "Suckers in Paradise," *Saturday Evening Post*, March 1953, 31–33, 181, 183.

76. P. Reveley, "Additional Orders Stopping Gambling," February 11, 1953, 837.4536/2–1153, I/A, 1950–1954; Lacey, *Little Man*, ch. 13.

77. Ernest Havemann, "Old Familiar Faces from Las Vegas Show Up in Plush Casinos with Plenty of Fast 'Action' to Take Tourist Dollars," *Life*, March 10, 1958, 33; Green, "Cuban Tourist Commission Superseded."

78. Frank Ragano and Selwyn Raab, "Havana 1958: Out on Town with the Mob," in Alan Ryan, ed., *The Reader's Companion to Cuba* (New York: Harcourt Brace, 1997), cited portions, 165, 166; Ramón Bonachea and Marta San Martín, *The Cuban Insurrection, 1952–1959* (New Brunswick, N.J.: Transaction Books, 1974). 31–34; Jorge I. Domínguez, *Cuba: Order and Revolution* (Cambridge, Mass.: Harvard University Press, 1978), 94.

79. "The Hilton Hotel Organization," February 1959, p. 7, box 4, Cathleen Baird, "Oral History of Sidney H. Wilner," n.d., 12; John Houser? to Hilton, September 21, 1955, box 1, Hilton Hotels International, Conrad N. Hilton Archives; Rufo López-Fresquet, *My Fourteen Months with Castro* (Cleveland: World, 1966), 18; Schwartz, *Pleasure Island*, 154–158.

80. Collazo Pérez, *Cuba: banca y crédito*, Banco Nacional de Cuba, "Programa de desarrollo económico," Informe no. 4, *Desarrollo del turismo en Cuba*, October 1958, 46; Morris H. Morley, *Imperial State and Revolution: The United States and Cuba, 1952–1986* (Cambridge: Cambridge University Press, 1987), 51; Schroeder, *Cuba: A Handbook of Historical Statistics*, 166. The only two firms financed by Cuba's national bank were Cuban, Cubana Airlines and the Rancho Boyeros airport. José López Vilaboy purchased both from Pan Am in the mid-1950s.

81. Pérez, *Cuba and the United States*, 229; Mario Lazo, *Dagger in the Heart: American Policy Failures in Cuba* (New York: Funk and Wagnalls, 1968), 86, 92.

82. Roberto Segre, Mario Coyula, and Joseph L. Scarpaci, *Havana: Two Faces of the Antillean Metropolis* (New York: John Wiley and Sons, 1997), 77; Pérez-Stable, *The Cuban Revolution*, 30, table 1.3; López-Fresquet, *My Fourteen Months with Castro*, 10, 97.

83. Bank of Hawaii, *Hawaii and the Business of Defense* (Honolulu: Bank of Hawaii, December 1954), 19; Bank of Hawaii, *Growing Islands* (Honolulu: Bank of Hawaii, June 1955), 35.

84. Fuchs, *Hawaii Pono*, 322; Karleen Chinen and Arnold T. Hiura, eds., *From Bento to Mixed Plate: Americans of Japanese Ancestry in Multicultural Hawai'i* (Los Angeles: Japanese American National Museum, 1997), 79.

85. Governor Samuel Wilder King and *Honolulu Star-Bulletin*, February 16, 1955, cited in Dennis M. Ogawa, *Kodomo no tame ni, For the Sake of the Children: The Japanese American Experience in Hawaii* (Honolulu: University of Hawai'i Press, 1978), 379. Whereas Democrats presented America, argues Robert G. Lee in a related context, "as a contradiction between the promise of justice and the historical reality of oppres-

sion," many haole insisted that the "American creed [w]as a set of ideals that had already shaped the course of American history" in Hawai'i. Robert G. Lee, *Orientals: Asian Americans in Popular Culture* (Philadelphia: Temple University Press, 1999), 224.

86. Wright, *The Disenchanted Isles*, 175–179, 187–191; Cooper and Daws, *Land and Power in Hawaii*, 5–6, 35–37; Bell, *Last Among Equals*, 235.

87. The Bank of Hawaii president E. W. Carden ranked this "Report of our Research Department" as "one of their most important." Bank of Hawaii, *Growing Islands*, preface, 4, 8.

88. Bank of Hawaii, *Growing Islands*, 4, 8, 26, 36, 37; Cooper and Daws, *Land and Power in Hawaii*, 35–37; Eric Foner, *Nothing but Freedom: Emancipation and Its Legacies* (Baton Rouge: Louisiana State University Press, 1983), 67.

89. Hawaii Visitors Bureau, Moving Forward in Balance: A Preliminary Report on Essential Programs of Action for the Development of Hawaii's Visitor Industry, 1955–1965 (Honolulu: Hawaii Visitors Bureau, July 1955), 35; Bank of Hawaii, Growing Islands, 36; Territorial Department of Labor and Industrial Relations, "Manpower Needs of the Hotel Industry in Oahu," September, 1957, 3; "Economic Base Study, Oahu, Hawaii, Prepared for the City Planning Commission of the City and County of Honolulu by Charles B. Bennett & Associates," May 1959, 28–29, carton 171, Henry J. Kaiser Papers, 83/42c, Bancroft Library, University of California, Berkeley, hereafter Kaiser Papers; minutes, Tourist Industry Committee, Chamber of Commerce of Honolulu, August 21, 1956, 1; the Governor's Advisory Committee on the Tourist Industry, "Essential Areas of Action for the Development of Hawaii's Visitor Industry," interim report to Governor Samuel Wilder King (Honolulu: Territory of Hawaii, April 1956), 3, emphasis in the original; Governor's Advisory Committee on the Tourism Industry, 1956–1957, Hawai'i State Archives, Honolulu, Hawai'i.

90. Hawaii Visitors Bureau, *Moving Forward in Balance*, 4; Milton Murayama, *Plantation Boy* (Honolulu: University of Hawai'i Press, 1998), 105.

91. Robert W. Bone, "Loli'iana: Seeds of Transformation," *Hawaii Hospitality*, special commemorative edition, *Hawai'i ka'oihana hokele, The History of Hawaii's Hotel Industry, 1840s–1990* (1990): 50–82, 66; Territorial Department, "Manpower Needs of the Hotel Industry on Oahu," cited portion, 14.

92. Andrew W. Lind, *Hawaii's People*, 3rd ed. (Honolulu: University of Hawai'i Press, 1967), 100; at the time Caucasian men were roughly 25 percent of the population; Chinese men, 6 percent; and, Japanese men, 35 percent; John Child & Co., "Economic Growth for Hawaii," report for State Planning Office, Hawaii, December 1960, 6.

93. Lind, *Hawaii's People*, 21, 22, 99, 101; Bell, *Last Among Equals*, 99.

94. As Takabuki observes, "The introduction of mainland enterprises such as Sears and Kaiser to Hawai'i in the 1950s and 1960s did much to change and diversify the economy" (*An Unlikely Revolutionary*, 65). Kaiser brought to Hawai'i his support for unions, high wages, medical and retirement plans, etc., support that prompted

Mike Davis to argue that "Kaiserism" would have been a "more apt name" than "Fordism" for the "postwar social contract between labor and management." Mike Davis, *City of Quartz: Excavating the Future in Los Angeles* (New York: Vintage Books, 1992), 385.

95. Bill Wood, *50 Years of Aloha: The Story of Aloha Airlines* (Honolulu: Aloha Airlines, 1996), 10, 11, 15, 16, 18, 21–24; Ray Thiele, *Kennedy's Hawaiian Air: Hawaii's Pioneer Airline* (Kailua, Hawai'i: Olomana, 1994), 122–129; U.S. Civil Aeronautics Board, docket 2390, et al., In the Matter of Applications for Certificates of Public Convenience and Necessity: Intra-Territorial Service in Hawaii Case (Washington, D.C.: Government Printing Office, 1948), 37, 38.

96. Trans-Pacific Airlines, Ltd., Annual Reports for 1949, 1950, 1952, 1954, no page numbers; Wood, *50 Years of Aloha*, 25, 32, Inouye from his foreword to it, 3; Aloha Airlines, Annual Report for 1958, no page numbers.

97. Wood, *50 Years of Aloha*, 10; Trans Pacific Airlines, Ltd., 1950, Annual Report, 1951, 1954 and 1955, 1956, n.p.; Aloha Airlines, Annual Report, 1958, n.p., 1959, 7, 10.

98. Takeo Kagawa and the Japanese American founders of the Central Pacific Bank provided opportunities for people across the color line to open businesses, pursue home ownership, and buy consumer durables on credit. Their introduction of consumer and commercial financing for nonwhites compelled the Bank of Hawaii and Bishop bank to alter their lending, employment, and customer policies. The insurance executive Kagawa solicited the support of A. P. Giannini, founder of the Transamerica Corp. and the Bank of America. With Giannini's backing, Kagawa introduced long-term and Federal Housing Administration mortgages to Hawai'i,where the then-standard mortgage term was seven years. A group of Japanese American veterans strategized replacing the Japanese American banks permanently closed by the U.S. military after Pearl Harbor but in an institution that provided "equitable service . . . to all communities," not just the Japanese, as Inuoye put it. Backed by mainland, local, and Japanese capital, the Central Pacific Bank opened in 1954. As the protagonist of *Plantation Boy* noted, "Right away the Bishop Bank and the Bank of Hawaii start hiring nonhaole clerks." Right away too Walter Dillingham and the Big Five directors of the BoH brought Rudolph Peterson from the mainland's Transamerica Corp. to be the bank's president. Charged with reversing declining deposits and profits, phenomena directly related to its racist practices, Peterson targeted nonwhites as clients, depositors, and employees. Chinen and Hiura, *From Bento to Mixed Plate*, 67–70, Daniel Inouye cited on 68; Fuchs, *Hawaii Pono*, 398; Marion Kelly, "Foreign Investment in Hawai'i," *Social Processes in Hawai'i* (1994): 14–39, esp. 22, 23; Murayama, *Plantation Boy*, 105; Rudolph A. Peterson, "A Career in International Banking with the Bank of America, 1936–1970, and the United Nations Development Program, 1971–1975," an oral history conducted in 1992 and 1993 by Germaine LaBerge, Regional Oral History Office, Bancroft Library, University of California, Berkeley, 171, 176, 179–185, cited

portion, 179; Noel J. Kent, *Hawaii: Islands Under the Influence* (1983; reprint, Honolulu: University of Hawai'i Press, 1993), 109; Fuchs, *Hawaii Pono*, 400.

99. Gary Y. Okihiro, *Margins and Mainstreams: Asians in American History and Culture* (1994; reprint, Seattle: University of Washington Press, 1996), 175; Bell, *Last Among Equals*, 229, 260.

Chapter 5. Travels to Revolution and Statehood

1. Luce supported statehood for a territory whose Caucasian and Asian U.S. citizens especially were leading it to liberal capitalist democracy, and whose Chinese, Japanese, and Korean men in particular could advance U.S. interests in Asia, where it was losing nation after nation to communism. Luce was a son of missionaries born and raised in China and lifelong defender of Chiang Kai-Shek, and so his support of statehood is not surprising. It may seem surprising that *Time* and *Life* praised Fidel Castro and the Moviemiento 26 de julio (M-26-7), especially since *Time* later "became nearly obsessed with uncovering any damning fact that they could find or invent about Cuba." Samuel Farber, *The Origins of the Cuban Revolution Reconsidered* (Chapel Hill: University of North Carolina Press, 2006), 94; see also Richard E. Welch, Jr., *Response to Revolution: The United States and the Cuban Revolution, 1959–1961* (Chapel Hill: University of North Carolina Press, 1985), 167–168.

2. *Time*, January 12, 1959, 32, 33, and December 9, 1957, 43; on the U.S. willingness to support only revolutions that seemed to resemble it own moderate, orderly revolution, see Michael H. Hunt, *Ideology and U.S. Foreign Policy* (New Haven, Conn.: Yale University Press, 1987), 92–124, passim; "The Brown and White Mosaic," *Time*, February 18, 1952, 22, 27; *Time* and *Life* incorrectly told their readers that Dillingham had reversed his opposition to statehood.

3. Elaine Tyler May, *Homeward Bound: American Families in the Cold War Era* (New York: Basic Books, 1988); Robert D. Dean, *Imperial Brotherhood: Gender and the Making of Cold War Foreign Policy* (Amherst: University of Massachusetts Press, 2001).

4. Van Gosse, *Where the Boys Are: Cuba, Cold War America, and the Making of a New Left* (New York: Verso, 1993), 52, emphasis in original; K. A. Cuourdileone, *Manhood and American Political Culture in the Cold War* (New York: Routledge, 2005), 29–35, 190, 191; Arthur M. Schlesinger, Jr., *A Thousand Days: John F. Kennedy in the White House* (Boston: Houghton Mifflin, 1965), 230; Graham Greene, "Shadow and Sunlight in Cuba," reprinted in Greene, *Reflections*, selected and introduced by Judith Adamson (London: Reinhardt Books, 1990), 247.

5. Ralph S. Kuykendall and A. Grove Day, *Hawaii: A History, From Polynesian Kingdom to American Commonwealth* (1948; reprint, New York: Prentice Hall, 1950), v–vi; David R. Roediger, *Working Toward Whiteness: How America's Immigrants Became White, The Strange Journey from Ellis Island to the Suburbs* (New York: Basic Books, 2005); Matthew Frye Jacobson, *Roots Too: White Ethnic Revival in Post–Civil Rights America* (Cambridge, Mass.: Harvard University Press, 2006); Susan Koshy,

"Morphing Race into Ethnicity: Asian Americans and Critical Transformations of Whiteness," *boundary 2* 28, 1 (Summer 2001): 153–194.

6. Rates of interracial marriage in Hawaiʻi were 40 percent in 1945 and 30 percent in 1959.

7. A. Grove Day, *Hawaii and Its People* (New York: Duell, Sloan and Pearce, 1955), 236.

8. "Peace and prosperity" and "freedom and abundance" were the two most common slogans describing the advantages of U.S. overseas tourism in the 1950s. The best analyses of Cold War tourism discourses are found in Christopher Endy, *Cold War Holidays: American Tourism in France* (Chapel Hill: University of North Carolina Press, 2004); Christina Klein, *Cold War Orientalism: Asia in the Middlebrow Imagination, 1945–1961* (Berkeley: University of California Press, 2003), esp. ch. 3; Dennis Merrill, "Negotiating Cold War Paradise: U.S. Tourism, Economic Planning, and Cultural Modernity in Twentieth-Century Puerto Rico," *Diplomatic History* 25, 2 (Spring 2001): 179–214; Neal Moses Rosendorf, "Be El Caudillo's Guest: The Franco Regime's Quest for Rehabilitation and Dollars after World War II via the Promotion of U.S. Tourism to Spain," *Diplomatic History* 30, 3 (June 2006): 367–407.

9. William J. Lederer and Eugene Burdick, *The Ugly American* (New York: Fawcett, 1958); Jonathan Nashel, "The Road to Vietnam: Modernization Theory in Fact and Fiction," in Christian G. Appy, ed., *Cold War Constructions: The Political Culture of United States Imperialism, 1945–1966* (Amherst: University of Massachusetts Press, 2000), 132–156; Courdileone, *Manhood and American Political Culture*, 220–225; Dean, *Imperial Brotherhood*, 172–198, passim.

10. Henry J. Kaiser, "The Advertising Man's Ever New Horizons," address to the Advertising Association of the West Convention, Hawaiian Village Hotel, June 26, 1957, 4, 12, carton 264, Henry J. Kaiser Papers, accession 83/42c, Bancroft Library, University of California, Berkeley, hereafter Kaiser Papers; on modernization theory's roots in the civilizing mission, see Michael Adas, "Modernization Theory and the American Revival of the Scientific and Technological Standards of Social Achievement and Human Worth," in David C. Engerman, Nils Gilman, Mark H. Haefele, and Michael E. Latham, eds., *Staging Growth: Modernization, Development, and the Global Cold War* (Amherst: University of Massachusetts Press, 2003): 25–46.

11. David M. Potter, *People of Plenty: Economic Abundance and American Character* (Chicago: University of Chicago Press, 1954), 134; David W. Noble, "The Anglo-Protestant Monopolization of 'America,'" in Jeffrey Belnap and Raúl Fernández, eds., *José Martí's "Our America": From National to Hemispheric Cultural Studies* (Durham, N.C.: Duke University Press, 1998), 266; Peter Novick, *That Noble Dream: The 'Objectivity Question' and the American Historical Profession* (Cambridge: Cambridge University Press, 1988), 313, 332–337; W. W. Rostow, *The Stages of Economic Growth: A Non-Communist Manifesto* (1960; reprint, Cambridge: Cambridge University Press, 1965), 166–167. Rostow did not use the phrase "the end of history," but he could not imagine

a stage beyond the "age of high mass consumption," only two problems this age might generate: "secular spiritual stagnation" (boredom) and war.

12. Melvyn Leffler, *A Preponderance of Power: National Security, the Truman Administration, and the Cold War* (Stanford, Calif.: Stanford University Press, 1992); Burton I. Kaufman, *Trade and Aid: Eisenhower's Foreign Economic Policy* (Baltimore: Johns Hopkins University Press, 1982); Robert Griffith, "Dwight D. Eisenhower and the Corporate Commonwealth," *American Historical Review* 87, 1 (February 1982): 87–122; Blanche Weisen Cook, *The Declassified Eisenhower: A Divided Legacy* (Garden City, N.Y.: Doubleday, 1981); American Express Company, *Travel Dollars: Their Growing Impact upon the Economy of the Free World, a Progress Report* (New York: American Express Company, 1954), 29.

13. Michael E. Latham, *Modernization as Ideology: American Social Science and "Nation Building" in the Kennedy Era* (Chapel Hill: University of North Carolina Press, 2000), 215; Christina Klein, "Family Ties and Political Obligation: The Discourse of Adoption and the Cold War Commitment to Asia," in Appy, ed., *Cold War Constructions*, 35–66.

14. Robert M. Collins, *The Business Response to Keynes, 1929–1964* (New York: Columbia University Press, 1981); Elizabeth A. Fones-Wolf, *Selling Free Enterprise: The Business Assault on Labor and Liberalism, 1945–1960* (Urbana: University of Illinois Press, 1994); Laura McEnaney, *Civil Defense Begins at Home: Militarization Meets Everyday Life in the Fifties* (Princeton, N.J.: Princeton University Press, 2000), 11–39.

15. Stephen G. Rabe, *Eisenhower and Latin America: The Foreign Policy of Anticommunism* (Chapel Hill: University of North Carolina Press, 1988), 64–83, passim; Juan T. Trippe, "Aviation and the Cold War," address to the Aero Club of Washington, December 17, 1954, 11, Pan American World Airways Inc., Archives and Special Collections Department, Otto G. Richter Library, University of Miami, Coral Gables, Florida, hereafter Pan Am Papers; Ralph T. Reed, "New Role for U.S. Tourism Abroad," *ASTA Travel News*, February 1956, 42.

16. Trippe, "Aviation and the Cold War," 9–11; Sinclair Weeks, secretary of commerce, "The Importance of International Travel in Advancing World Peace," address to the inaugural meeting of the Permanent Executive Committee of the Inter-American World Travel Congress, Washington, D.C., June 20, 1955, reprinted in *Foreign Commerce Weekly*, July 4, 1955, and the *Department of State Bulletin*, July 18, 1955; Kaiser, address to the American Society of Travel Agents, World Travel Congress, New York, November 7, 1958, 3, Kaiser Papers; Reed, "New Role for Tourism Abroad," 42; "American Travelers Spend More Abroad," *Foreign Commerce Weekly*, May 30, 1955, 21; Jackson Lears, *Fables of Abundance: A Cultural History of Advertising in America* (New York: Basic Books, 1994), 248.

17. *Department of State Bulletin*, March 21, 1955, 494; Willis G. Lipscomb, vice president, traffic and sales, Pan American World Airways, in testimony before the U.S. Congress reprinted in "H.J.R. 350," *ASTA Travel News*, April 1954, 33; Conrad N. Hilton, *Be My Guest* (New York: Prentice Hall Press, 1957), 265; Hilton, "Toward a

Foreign Policy for Hotels," address to the Los Angeles Rotary Club, July 27, 1956, Speeches, box 2, Conrad N. Hilton Archives, Conrad N. Hilton School of Hotel and Restaurant Management, University of Houston, hereafter Hilton Archives.

18. John Kenneth Galbraith, "The Vested Interest in Output," ch. 12 of *The Affluent Society* (New York: Mentor Books, 1958), 132–142; Lizabeth Cohen, "The New Deal State and the Making of Citizen Consumers" (111–126), and George Lipsitz, "Consumer Spending as State Project: Yesterday's Solutions and Today's Problems" (127–148), both in Susan Strasser, Charles McGovern, and Matthias Judt, eds., *Getting and Spending: European and American Consumer Societies in Twentieth Century* (New York: Cambridge University Press, 1998); Juan Trippe, "World Prosperity Through Foreign Travel," address to the American Tariff League, October 27, 1948, Juan T. Trippe Speeches, box 460, Pan Am Papers; *Foreign Commerce Weekly*, May 10, 1947, 5; Victoria de Grazia, *Irresistible Empire: America's Advance Through Twentieth-Century Europe* (Cambridge, Mass.: Harvard University Press, 2005).

19. U.S. Department of State, *The American as International Traveler and Host* (U.S. National Commission for UNESCO, December 1954), 13. *Saturday Review* published numerous articles during the early 1950s criticizing U.S. tourists for failing to act like ambassadors without portfolio; for one example, see Horace Sutton, "Our Dollars and Manners Abroad," *Saturday Review*, May 13, 1950, 20–21. On worries of tourist industry leaders, see the minutes of the plenary meeting of the Business Council for International Understanding, September 26, 1956, Samuel W. Meeks Papers, box 5, J. Walter Thompson Archives, John W. Hartman Center for Sales, Advertising, and Marketing History, Duke University, hereafter J. Walter Thompson Archives. The Business Council for International Understanding was an organization of business leaders and the United States Information Agency (USIA) who collaborated on projects "to improve America's overseas relationships," in large part by working to make business and pleasure travelers better representatives of America abroad. While many industries were represented in the organization, the participating firms that dealt with tourism included American Express, Brainiff Airways, W. R. Grace & Co., Henry J. Kaiser, Northwest Airlines, Pan American Airlines, J. Walter Thompson, and the United Fruit Company.

20. The literature on the relationship between African Americans' struggles for rights and U.S. foreign policy has grown quite large; see especially Mary L. Dudziak, *Cold War Civil Rights: Race and the Image of American Democracy* (Princeton, N.J.: Princeton University Press, 2000); Penny von Eschen, *Race Against Empire: Black Americans and Anti-Colonialism, 1937–1957* (Ithaca, N.Y.: Cornell University Press, 1997).

21. For example, American Express distributed a copy of "Ambassadors of Good Will," (n.p., n.d), American Express Co. Archives, New York, New York) to its clients during the 1950s. On industry collaborations with the USIA to promote better foreign relations, in part, through overseas travel, again see the minutes of the plenary meeting of the Business Council for International Understanding, Samuel W. Meeks Papers,

box 5, J. Walter Thompson Archives. Prescriptive literature that focused on making tourists better agents of U.S. foreign policy proliferated during the 1950s; two examples include Alice Leons Moats, *At Home Abroad* (New York: Viking Press, 1954); Robert Root, *How to Make Friends Abroad* (New York: Association Press, 1954). On commercial tours and special interest group tours focused on "interpreting America's aims to the world" through travel, see Department of State, *The American as International Traveler and Host* and U.S. House Subcommittee on Foreign Economic Policy of the Committee on Foreign Affairs, Hearings on H.J. Resolution 350 [To Promote the Foreign Policy of the United States by Fostering International Travel and the Exchange of Persons and to Establish the United States Travel Commission], 83rd Congress, 2nd Session (Washington D.C.: Government Printing Office, 1954).

22. David Schmitz, *Thank God They're on Our Side: The United States and Right-Wing Dictatorships* (Chapel Hill: University of North Carolina Press, 1999); Zachary Karabell, *Architects of Intervention: The United States, the Third World, and the Cold War, 1946–1962* (Baton Rouge: Louisiana State University Press, 1999).

23. On U.S. nationalism, religion, corporate culture, and anticommunism during the Cold War, see Stephen J. Whitfield, *Culture of the Cold War* (Baltimore: Johns Hopkins University Press, 1991), 83–90; Alan Nadel, *Containment Culture: American Narratives, Postmodernism, and the Atomic Age* (Durham, N.C.: Duke University Press, 1995), 90–102; Melani McAlister, *Epic Encounters: Culture, Media, and U.S. Interests in the Middle East, 1945–2000* (Berkeley: University of California Press, 2001), 43–83.

24. Hilton, "The Fifth International Freedom," address to the annual convention of the American Hotel Association, New York, November 5, 1954, Hilton Archives, 5; Hilton, *Be My Guest*, 273. The first annual Prayer Breakfast, a tradition that continues to this day, made the cover of *Hotel Gazette*, February 14, 1953; *New York Times*, February 6, 1953; *Washington Star*, February 8, 1953, my emphasis. Hilton's sponsorship of the Prayer Breakfasts continued to receive coverage after the first one. See, for example, "Hilton's Private Statesmanship," *Sales Management*, October, 19, 1956; Eisenhower's speeches on tourists as representatives of America were widely reprinted in national magazines, prescriptive literature for tourists, and in a letter that accompanied passports. For one example, see American Express, "Ambassadors of Good Will," frontispiece.

25. John Dorshner and Roberto Fabricio, *Winds of December: The Cuban Revolution, 1958* (New York: Coward, McCann and Geoghegan, 1980), 132.

26. Van Gosse, "'We Are All Highly Adventurous': Fidel Castro and the Romance of the White Guerilla, 1957–1958," in Appy, ed., *Cold War Constructions*, 238–256.

27. Amy Kaplan, *The Anarchy of Empire in the Making of U.S. Culture* (Cambridge, Mass.: Harvard University Press, 2002), 168; Klein, *Cold War Orientalism*, 117–122; Anthony DePalma, *The Man Who Invented Fidel: Castro, Cuba, and Herbert L. Matthews of the New York Times* (New York: PublicAffairs, 2006); James Michener, "Hawaii: The Case for Our Fiftieth State," in *A Michener Miscellany, 1950–1970*,

selected and edited by Ben Hibbs (New York: Random House, 1973), 122. This article was originally published in *Reader's Digest* in 1953.

28. Paul Lyons, *American Pacificism: Oceania in the U.S. Imagination* (New York: Routledge, 2006), 195, 196; Annual Report of the Hawaii Visitors Bureau, 1958, contained in the Governor William Francis Quinn Papers, 1957–1962, Hawai'i State Archives, Honolulu, Hawai'i.

29. Thurston, minutes, HSC, February 23, 1957, 3–5; June 20, 1947, 34; July 25, 1957. One comprehensive collection of HSC minutes is held by the Hawaiian Collection, Special Collections, Hamilton Library, University of Hawai'i Mānoa. Folder on Hawaiian Statehood, 1957–1967, carton 180, Kaiser Papers.

30. For a brilliant, sustained analysis of politics and Hawaiian-ness, see J. Kēhaulani Kauanui, *Hawaiian Blood: Colonialism and the Politics of Indigeneity* (Durham, N.C.: Duke University Press, 2008); see also Klein, *Cold War Orientalism*, 223–264, passim; Lyons, *American Pacificism*, 145–179, passim; Gretchen Heefner, "'A Symbol of the New Frontier:' Hawaiian Statehood, Anti-Colonialism, and Winning the Cold War," *Pacific Historical Review* 74, 4 (November 2005): 545–574; Giles Scott-Smith, "From Symbol of Division to Cold War Asset: Lyndon Johnson and the Achievement of Hawaiian Statehood in 1959," *History* 89, 2 (April 2004): 256–273. Lyons is the only of these authors to discuss Hawaiians and their role in discourses for or against statehood.

31. Candace Fujikane and Jonathan Y. Okamura, eds., *Asian Settler Colonialism: From Local Governance to the Habits of Everyday Life in Hawai'i* (Honolulu: University of Hawai'i Press, 2008); Jocelyn Linnekin, "Consuming Cultures: Tourism and the Commoditization of Cultural Identity in the Island Pacific," in Michael Picard and Robert E. Wood, eds., *Tourism, Ethnicity, and the State in Asian and Pacific Societies* (Honolulu: University of Hawai'i Press, 1997), 215–250; John S. Whitehead, "The Anti-Statehood Movement and the Legacy of Alice Kamokila Campbell," *Hawaiian Journal of History* 27 (1993): 43–63, Alice Kamokila Campbell cited on 50.

32. Michener, "Hawaii: The Case for Our Fiftieth State," 140; "'The 49th State:' Hawaii, Now Grown Up, Makes Bid to Join Union," *Life*, February 9, 1948, 97, 99.

33. Ben Adams, *Hawaii, the Aloha State* (New York: Hill and Wang, 1959), 124; "Statehood Plea Dates Back to '03," *New York Times*, March 13, 1959; "Fading Star," *Time*, March 22, 1954, 29; "Kamehameha's Dream," *Time*, January 4, 1954, 11, 12.

34. "Speaking of Pictures . . . ," *Life*, June 22, 1942, 8–9; "Hawaii: A Melting Pot, a Score of Races Live Together in Amity," *Life*, November 6, 1945, 103–111, cited portions, 104, 110.

35. J. Kēhaulani Kauanui, "'A blood mixture which experience has shown furnishes the very highest grade of citizen-material': Selective Assimilation on a Polynesian Case of Naturalization to U.S. Citizenship," *American Studies* 45, 3 (Fall 2004): 33–48; Koshy, "Morphing Race into Ethnicity."

36. Adams, *The Aloha State*, 134; Kuykendall and Day, *Hawaii*, 286; Day, *Hawaii*

and its People, 237; Michener, "Hawaii: The Case for Our Fiftieth State," 124; "The Brown and White Mosaic," 27.

37. Bank of Hawaii, *Islands at Work* (Honolulu: Bank of Hawaii, June 1954), 7.

38. The best synopsis of Aloha Week is Sydney Clark, *All the Best in Hawaii*, rev. ed. (New York: Dodd, Mead, 1951), 223–228. Beginning in 1947, the October issue of *Paradise of the Pacific* devoted the bulk of its advertising, articles, and pictures to Aloha Week; Eileen O'Brien, "It's Aloha Week in Hawaii," *Paradise of the Pacific*, October 1957, 11–15, cited portion, 11.

39. "Hawaii—Beauty, Wealth, Amiable People," *Life*, March 23, 1959, 67, 68; "Decision Approaches for Hawaii," *Life*, February 22, 1954, 26.

40. Hawaii Statehood Commission, *Hawaii USA: Showcase for Americanism* (Honolulu: Hawaii Statehood Commission, 1959), 13; Hawaii Statehood Commission, *Hawaii U.S.A. . . . Statehood* (Honolulu: Hawaii Statehood Commission, n.d.), 72; (first published in 1954, this booklet went through a number of editions); " 'The Forty-Ninth State,' " *Life*, 108.

41. Heefner, " 'A Symbol of the New Frontier,' " 569–571, Larcade and *Look* cited on 571.

42. *Business Week* cited in Klein, *Cold War Orientalism*, 251.

43. Clifford Gessler, *Hawaii: Isles of Enchantment* (New York: D. Appleton-Century, 1937), 303, 307; James A. Michener, "Birth of Hawaii," *Life*, October 26, 1959, 54–56; Michener, *Hawaii* (New York: Random House, 1959), 807, 937.

44. Henry J. Kaiser, address, Presidents Dinner, Hawaiian Village Long House, April 5, 1959, carton 264, Kaiser Papers; W. Clement Stone, "The Man Whose Work Will Never End," *Success Unlimited*, August 1957, 4–6, 24–26, cited portion, 8; press release on proposed contract with Hilton, January 23, 1956, carton 264, Kaiser Papers.

45. Thurston to Oren E. Long, March 27, 1952; Governor's Advisory Commission on the Tourist Industry, *Role of Government in the Development of Hawaii's Tourist Industry* (Honolulu: n.p., 1957), 6; Thurston to Dulles, September 26, 1951, all in HVB Folder, Governor Oren E. Long Papers, Hawai'i State Archives; *ASTA Travel News*, February 1952, 18; "PATA," *ASTA Travel News*, November 1953, 188–193.

46. Bob Kraus, "Capitalist Chinn Ho, Figures Come Easy in the Multi-Millions," *Paradise of the Pacific*, January 1957, 25, 32; Adams, *The Aloha State*, 134–136; "Power in Business, Labor, Government," *Life*, March 23, 1959, 64.

47. "Decision Approaches for Hawaii," 23; "The 49th State," 108; "Hawaii—A Bridge to Asia," *Business Week*, May 13, 1950, 128; Dean, *Imperial Brotherhood*, 4, 5, 12, 89, 95.

48. Klein, *Cold War Orientalism*, 153.

49. Farber, *The Origins of the Cuban Revolution Reconsidered*, 74, 65; Julia E. Sweig, *Inside the Cuban Revolution: Fidel Castro and the Urban Underground* (Cambridge, Mass.: Harvard University Press, 2002), 184–185.

50. *New York Times*, February 24, 1957.

51. DePalma, *The Man Who Invented Fidel*, 219–220; *New York Times*, May 20,

1957, cited in Gosse, *Where the Boys Are*; Ernest Haveman, "Mobsters Move in on Troubled Havana and Split Rich Gambling Profits with Batista," *Life*, March 10, 1958, 36; *Time*, April 28, 1958, 37.

52. Jules Dubois, *Fidel Castro, Rebel—Liberator or Dictator?* (Indianapolis: Bobbs-Merrill, 1959), 159; Thomas Paterson, *Contesting Castro: The United States and the Triumph of the Cuban Revolution* (New York: Oxford University Press, 1994), 85, 86, 248; Sweig, *Inside the Cuban Revolution*, the National Directorate's Marcelo Fernández cited on 97; *Time*, April 28, 1958, 37.

53. Fidel Castro, "History Will Absolve Me" and "Frente a todos!" *Bohemia* January 8, 1956, translated as "Against Everyone," both in Rolando E. Bonachea and Nelson P. Valdés, eds., *Revolutionary Struggle, 1947–1958*, vol. 1 of *The Selected Works of Fidel Castro*, (Cambridge, Mass.: MIT Press, 1972), 207, 300–301.

54. Rufo López-Fresquet, *My Fourteen Months with Castro* (Cleveland: World, 1966), 11; Ruby Hart Phillips, *Cuba: Island of Paradox* (New York: McDowell, Obolensky, 1959), 283, 284; Paterson, *Contesting Castro*, 83.

55. Fidel Castro, "Speech in New York," November 1, 1955, and "Against Everyone," both in Bonachea and Valdés, *Revolutionary Struggle*, cited portions, 281, 300–301; Carlos Franqui, *Family Portrait with Fidel*, trans. Alfred MacAdam (New York: Random House, 1984), 13–15; Gosse, *Where the Boys Are*, 39–45.

56. Richard Slotkin, *Gunfighter Nation: The Myth of the Frontier in Twentieth-Century America* (New York: HarperCollins, 1992), 352, 353, 408–411; Louis A. Pérez, Jr., *On Becoming Cuban: Identity, Nationality, and Culture* (Chapel Hill: University of North Carolina Press, 1999), 292; Farber, *The Origins of the Cuban Revolution Reconsidered*, 56, 57.

57. Louis A. Pérez Jr., *Army Politics in Cuba* (Pittsburgh: University of Pittsburgh Press, 1976), 206, n. 7, and *Sierra Maestra* [Miami], June 1958, 4, cited on 153–154; Andrew St. George, "Cuban Rebels," *Look* February 4, 1958, 30.

58. *Time*, June 24, 1957, 40; December 9, 1957, 43.

59. *Time*, December 9, 1957, 43; April 14, 1958, 36; June 24, 1957, 40; October 28, 1957, 41.

60. *Time*, June 17, 1957.

61. St. George, "Cuban Rebels," 30. See also Fidel Castro, "Why We Fight," *Coronet*, February 1958, 80–86.

62. *Time*, December 9, 1957, 43; Pablo Medina, *Exiled Memories: A Cuban Childhood* (Austin: University of Texas Press, 1990), 99–100; Mario Lazo, *Dagger in the Heart* (New York: Funk and Wagnalls, 1968), 123; Haveman, "Mobsters Move In,"36.

63. *New York Times*, February 24, 1957; Phillips, *Cuba: Island of Paradox*, 299–301; *Time*, March 4, 1957, 40; Andrew St. George, "A Visit with a Revolutionary," *Coronet*, February 1958, 74–80, cited portion, 78.

64. DePalma, *The Man Who Invented Fidel*, 102;Phillips, *Cuba: Island of Paradox*, 299–301; Paterson, *Contesting Castro*, 140.

65. Dubois, *Fidel Castro*, 159; Neil Macaulay, *A Rebel in Cuba: An American's*

Memoir (Chicago: Quadrangle Books, 1970), 15–16, cited portion, 16; John Sayles, *Los Gusanos, A Novel* (New York: HarpersCollins, 1991), 73. The adventures of spring-break revolutionaries are best memorialized in novels; see especially Glendon Swarthout, *Where the Boys Are* (New York: Random House, 1960); Richard Fariña, *Been Down So Long It Looks Like Up to Me* (1966; reprint, New York: Penguin Books, 1983); Thomas Pynchon, *V.* (1963; reprint, New York: Bantam Books, 1977). Two memoirs of U.S. citizen-soldiers who fought with the M-26-7 are Macaulay, *A Rebel in Cuba*, and Jack Youngblood and Robin Moore, *The Devil to Pay* (London: Anthony Gibbs & Phillips, 1961); Schlesinger, *A Thousand Days*, 165.

66. Rosalie Schwartz, *Pleasure Island: Tourism and Temptation in Cuba* (Lincoln: University of Nebraska Press, 1997), 186–189; "Unhappy Cuba's Cockeyed Week," *Life* March 10, 1958, 28–31; Leonard H. Price, commercial attaché, American Embassy, Havana, "Formation of the NEW CUBA Pro Tourism Committee," May 9, 1958, 837.181/5–958, U.S. Department of State, Confidential Central Files, Cuba, Internal Affairs, General Records, Record Group 59, 1955–1958, hereafter IA, 1955–1958; Paterson, *Contesting Castro*, 57, 100; Earl E. T. Smith, *The Fourth Floor: An Account of the Castro Communist Regime* (New York: Random House, 1962), 90; Robert Caverly to Joseph Cioch, July 2, 1990, Hilton Archives; Sweig, *Inside the Cuban Revolution*, 112.

67. Conrad N. Hilton, "Columbus Started Something," address at opening of Havana Hilton, Havana, Cuba, March 22, 1958, Speeches, box 2, Hilton Archives.

68. Enrique Meneses, *Fidel Castro*, trans. J. Halcro Ferguson (New York: Taplinger 1966), 58–59; Cathleen Baird, "Oral History of Sidney H. Wilner," n.d., 11, Hilton Archives; Lazos y Cuba, "Lease Between Hilton Hotels International and La Caja de Retiro y Asistencia Social de los Trabajadores Gastronomicos," both at Hilton Archives; Catherine Baird Huck, "Egypt's Modern Hotels: From the Historic Shepheard's to the Nile Hilton" (M.A. thesis, University of Houston, 1994); Leonard H. Price, commercial attaché, American Embassy, Havana, "Cuban Tourist Commission Issues Statistics on Travel," December 12, 1958, 837.181/12–1258, IA, 1955–1958; Susan Schroeder, *Cuba: A Handbook of Historical Statistics* (Boston: G.K. Hall, 1982), 462; *Time* April 7, 1958, 32; Paterson, *Contesting Castro*, 57.

69. Sweig, *Inside the Cuban Revolution*, 47–50; *Time*, August 19, 1957, 23, and April 21, 1958, 27.

70. Pazos and Boti wrote the economic program of the M-26-7 in 1957 or 1958. It was published in Spanish and English in April 1959 as part of Fidel Castro, *Pensamiento Político, Económico y Social de Fidel Castro* and *The Political, Economic, and Social Thought of Fidel Castro* (Havana: Editorial Lex, 1959), citations, 88 in the Spanish edition and 138 in the English.

71. Louis A. Pérez, Jr., *Cuba and the United States: Ties of Singular Intimacy* (Athens: University of Georgia Press, 1990), 207–213, 222–225; Pérez, "So Near and Yet So Foreign: Cuba and the United States, 1860–1960," *Culturefront* 2 (Winter 1993): 4–8, 23, 61; Gracia Rivera Herrera in Oscar Lewis, Ruth M. Lewis, and Susan M.

Rigdon, *Four Women Living the Revolution: An Oral History of Contemporary Cuba* (Urbana: University of Illinois Press, 1977), 155, 171; "Summary of Financial and Operating Results," Havana, Cuba (Credesco), Wholesale and Retailing Financing, Ford International Division, January 19, 1960, roll 2 of *The United States and Castro's Cuba, 1950s–1970s: The Paterson Collection*, Thomas G. Paterson's collection of archival material, microfilmed and distributed by Scholarly Resources, Wilmington, Delaware.

72. Robert Lacey, *Little Man: Meyer Lansky and the Gangster Life* (Boston: Little, Brown, 1991), 311; Castro, "History Will Absolve Me," 184; Haveman, "Mobster's Move In," 36, emphasis in original; Pérez, *On Becoming Cuban*, 469–471.

73. Rodolfo "Rudy" Caspari to Arthur Elmiger, January 1, 1959, box 10, RG 1, Hilton Archives; Phillips, *Cuba, Island of Paradox*, 394–402; Dorshner and Fabricio, *Winds of December*, 362, 363, 385; Paterson, *Contesting Castro*, 226–28; Smith, *The Fourth Floor*, 190–193; *Time*, January 12, 1959, 32. Letters praising the politeness of the barbudos and the Hilton's handling of events following the rebel victory (often contrasted to the ineptitude of the U.S. Embassy) poured into Hilton offices in January and February 1959.

74. "Castro Assures Welcome to American Tourists," January 13, 1959; Sidney H. Wilner to Hilton, June 9, 1959; Caverly to Hilton, June 10, 1959; Letter to Fletcher, September 3, 1959; Baird, "Oral History," 13; Caverly to Cioch, July 2, 1990, all from Hilton Archives.

75. Press release, Fidel Castro Ruz, January 10, 1959, Hilton Archives; Lansky, *Little Man*, 252; E. A. Gilmore, Jr., counselor of embassy for economic affairs, American Embassy, Havana, "Cuban Government Modifies Its Opposition to Gambling," February 12, 1959, 837.45/2–1259, U.S. Department of State, Confidential Central Files, Cuba, IA, General Records, Record Group 59, 1959–1960.

76. Cuban Tourist Commission, *Cuba, Land of Opportunity, Playground of the Americas* (Havana: Transcuba News S.A., 1959), cited portions, 6, 50, 51. I thank Van Gosse for sharing his copy of this document with me.

77. López-Fresquet, *My Fourteen Months with Castro*, 85, 97.

78. *Diario de la Marina*, September 26, 1959; *Revolucion*, September 29, 1959; Alfred Padula and Louis Pérez have analyzed this debate respectively in "The Fall of the Bourgeoisie: Cuba, 1959–1961" (Ph.D. dissertation, University of New Mexico, December 1974), 291–294, and *On Becoming Cuban*, 481–482.

79. Padula, "The Fall of the Bourgeoisie," 273; Caverly to Hilton, September 14, 1959 and Conrad N. Hilton conference with State Department, March 9, 1959, Hilton Archives. This view was shared by many Hilton executives.

80. Morris H. Morley, *Imperial State and Revolution: The United States and Revolution in Cuba, 1952–1986* (Cambridge: Cambridge University Press, 1982), 100. On cooperation among the Castro government, U.S. industry, and ASTA, see José Menendez to Mr. Hoffman, January, 31, 1959; Felipe Pazos to Caja de Retiro y Asistencia Social de los Trabajadores Gastronómicos, June 2, 1959; Menendez to Caverly, August

5, 1959, all in Hilton Archives. *New York Herald Tribune*, September 10, 1959, and *ASTA Travel News*, October 1959.

81. Horace Sutton, *Travelers: The American Tourist from Stagecoach to Space Shuttle* (New York: 1980), 259–261; Hugh Thomas, *Cuba: The Pursuit of Freedom* ((New York: Harper and Row, 1971), 1436.

82. Max Allen, *ASTA Travel News*, December 1959; Robert E. Quirk, *Fidel Castro* (New York: W. W. Norton, 1993), 271.

83. Harry Owens, "Hawaii Is the Fiftieth Star in the Flag of the U.S.A.," cited in Lance Tominaga, "Statehood Souvenirs: Recapturing the Memories of '59," *Aloha: The Magazine of Hawaii and the Pacific*, July/August 1989, 53–57; Bob Krauss, *Here's Hawaii* (New York: Coward-McCann, 1960), citation from 249; Roger Bell, *Last Among Equals: Hawaiian Statehood and American Politics* (Honolulu: University of Hawai'i Press, 1984), 276–277; statehood ballot cited in Poka Laenui (Hayden F. Burgess), "Statehood, a Second Glance," http://www.hawaii-nation.org/statehood2.

84. Krauss, *Here's Hawaii*, 249, 250; Nakoa Prejean, "Kanaka Maoli and the United Nations," in Ulla Hasager and Jonathan Friedman, eds., *Hawai'i: Return to Nationhood* (Copenhagen: International Work Group for Indigenous Affairs, 1994), 276–285; Poka Laenui, "Statehood, a Second Glance"; James Podgers, "Greetings from an Independent Hawai'i," article from the *American Bar Association Journal* (June 1997), available at http://www.hawaii-nation.org/abaj.html.

85. Workers' demand cited by Ronald Takaki, *Strangers from a Different Shore: A History of Asian-Americans* (New York: Penguin Books, 1989), 151; Jonathan Y. Okamura, "Why There Are No Asian Americans in Hawai'i: The Continuing Significance of Local Identity," *Social Processes in Hawaii* (1994): 161–178; Matsuo Takabuki, *An Unlikely Revolutionary: Matsuo Takabuki and the Making of Modern Hawai'i* (Honolulu: University of Hawai'i Press, 1998), 45; Jeff Chang, "Local Knowledge(s) : Notes on Race Relations, Panethnicity, and History in Hawai'i," *Amerasia Journal* 22, 2 (1996), 14; Noel J. Kent, "Myth of the Golden Men: Ethnic Elites and Dependent Development in the 50th State," in Michael C. Howard, ed., *Ethnicity and Nation-Building in the Pacific* (Tokyo: United Nations University, 1990), 98–117; Keiko Ohnuma,"'Aloha Spirit' and the Cultural Politics of Sentiment as National Belonging," *Contemporary Pacific* 20, 2 (Fall 2008), 365–394, esp. 369–374; Linnekin, "Consuming Cultures," 228.

86. Gustavo Pérez Firmat, *Next Year in Cuba: A Cubano's Coming-of-Age in America* (New York: Anchor Books, Doubleday, 1995), 19, 27, 32–33, 52.

Conclusion

1. Graham Greene, "Shadow and Sunlight in Cuba," reprinted in Greene, *Reflections*, selected and introduced by Judith Adamson (London: Reinhardt Books, 1990), 247.

2. Ann Laura Stoler, introduction to Stoler, ed., *Haunted by Empire: Geographies*

of Intimacy in North American History (Durham, N.C.: Duke University Press, 2006), 13.

3. Anthony Pagden, *Peoples and Empires: A Short History of European Migration, Exploration, and Conquest, from Greece to the Present* (New York: Modern Library, 2001), 81–98, passim.

4. As Craig N. Murphy recently noted, "Empire grows well in republican soil." Murphy, "Agriculture, Industry, Empire, and America," in Craig Calhoun, Frederick Cooper, and Kevin W. Moore, eds., *Lessons of Empire: Imperial Histories and American Power* (New York: New Press, 2006), 244. Although not focused on republican empire, see also Frederick Cooper's discussion of the "empire-state" as a model for the comparative history of these and other empires in "States, Empires, and Political Imagination, ch. 6 of Cooper, *Colonialism in Question: Theory, Knowledge, History* (Berkeley: University of California Press, 2005), 153–204.

5. I have in mind the contemporaries like V. I. Lenin and J. A. Hobson and historians such as Ronald Robinson and John Gallagher. Lenin and Hobson studied leading U.S. proponents of informal, commercial imperialism as they labored on their famous critiques of Western imperialism and capitalism. Robinson and Gallagher had the United States in mind when they formulated their famous "imperialism of free trade" to analyze the British Empire. See Martin J. Sklar, *The Corporate Reconstruction of Capitalist America: The Market, the Law, and Politics* (Cambridge: Cambridge University Press, 1988), 78–85; Carl Parinni, "Theories of Imperialism," in Lloyd C. Gardner, ed., *Redefining the Past: Essays in Diplomatic History in Honor of William Appleman Williams* (Corvallis: Oregon State University Press, 1986), 65–84; Matthew Connelly, "The New Imperialists," in Calhoun, Cooper, and Moore, eds., *Lessons of Empire*, 23.

6. George Steinmetz, "Imperialism or Colonialism? From Windhoek to Washington, by Way of Basra," in Calhoun, Cooper, and Moore, *Lessons of Empire*, 135–156, cited portion 146.

7. Walter Nugent, *Habits of Empire: A History of American Expansion* (New York: Alfred A. Knopf, 2008). In charting the uneven forms and practices of empire, Nugent observes that the biggest wave of settlement of U.S. continental conquests occurred after the United States formally abandoned settler colonialism.

8. Ann Laura Stoler, "Imperial Formations and the Opacities of Rule," in Calhoun, Cooper, and Moore, *Lessons of Empire*, 48–62.

9. That said, Cubans became masters at manipulating U.S. interests to serve their own purposes and goals.

10. In a now classic work of postcolonial theory, Partha Chaterjee argues, "The power to represent oneself is political power itself." Chaterjee, *The Nation and Its Fragments: Colonial and Postcolonial Histories* (Princeton, N.J.: Princeton University Press, 1993), 76.

11. To paraphrase Mahmood Mamdani, *Citizen and Subject: Contemporary Africa and the Legacy of Late Colonialism* (Princeton, N.J.: Princeton University Press, 1996), 24.

12. Matthew Connelly, *A Diplomatic Revolution: Algeria's Fight for Independence and the Origins of the Post-Cold War Era* (New York: Oxford University Press, 2002).

13. William F. Buckley, Jr., "I Got My Job through the *New York Times*," *American Legion Magazine*, March 1961, 18–19, 46–48.

14. Dana D. Nelson, *National Manhood: Capitalist Citizenship and the Imagined Fraternity of White Men* (Durham, N.C.: Duke University Press, 1998); Robert D. Dean, *Imperial Brotherhood: Gender and the Making of Cold War Foreign Policy* (Amherst: University of Massachusetts Press, 2001).

15. United States Public Law 103–150, 103rd Congress Joint Resolution 19, November 23, 1993, to acknowledge the one hundredth anniversary of the January 17, 1893, overthrow of the Kingdom of Hawaii, and to offer an apology to Native Hawaiians on behalf of the United States for the overthrow of the Kingdom of Hawaii, available at http://www.hawaii-nation.org, accessed February 24, 2007; for debates on how to apologize without incurring responsibilities, see *Congressional Record*—Senate, October 27, 1993, 103rd Congress, 1st Session, 139 Cong. Rec. S 14477, available at www.hawaii-nation.org, accessed February 24, 2007.

140, 203; Bloodless Revolution and, 161–62; contrasts with Cuba, 1, 4–5, 46, 176–77, 209; Democratic Party in, 144–51; demography of, 4, 33, 164; discourse of racial democracy and harmony in, 112–14, 116, *117*, 118, 133, 164; Home Rule Party, 59; interracial democracy as goal in, 12, 62, 134, 185; Kingdom of, 15, 18, 22, 31–33, 64, 107; martial law in, 144–49, 151, 209; planter paternalism in, 77, 82, 89, 93–94, 109–20, 127, 140–52, 186, 211; property taxes in, 162–63; Provisional Government of, 39–41, 71; "racial aloha" in, 150–51, 162, 164–66, 188; racism in, 95, 104, 118–20, 127, 130–34, 141, *143*, 149, 152, 165; Republican Party in, 59, 133, 151; Republic of, 41; schools in, 118–19; suffrage in, 34, 41, 59; tourism as postwar economic salvation of, 152–53, 162–63; unionization in, 144–52; U. S. military as economic base of, 148–52, 161, 164, 209; U.S. statehood and, 1, 6, 12–13, 144, 149–52, 167–69, 176–87, *182*, 188, 202, 205, 210. *See also* annexation; Big Five; Chinese; Filipinos; haole; immigration; Hawaiians; Hawaiian statehood; Japanese; Koreans; labor; Portuguese; republicanism; settler colonialism; sugar industry; U.S. foreign policy; U.S. imperialism; whiteness; whitening; *specific islands, cities, publications, resorts, and people*

Hawaiian Airlines, 163, 165, 187
Hawaiian Board of Immigration, 72–73, 76
Hawaiian Homes Commission Act, 93, 107
Hawaiian League, 35
Hawaiians: apology to, of U.S. government for overthrow of kingdom, 214; devastation by imported diseases, 14–15, 22, 31–32, 60, 62; genealogy and,33–35, 49–50, 60, 65–66, 105–6, 113, 179; nationalism of, 4, 33–34, 40; opposition to U.S. annexation, 3, 31–33, 39–41, 43, 49–50, 203; perceptions of U.S. statehood and, 167, 177–79, 211, 214, 262n30; representations of, by haole, 21, 34–35, 40, 42–43, 51, 58, 60–65, 83–84, 92–94, 96, 103, 105–7, 110, 111, 113, 133, 177, 178–81, 183, 185, 212, 229n6; resistance of, to haole governance and U.S. colonial rule, 22, 31, 32–33, 34, 35, 39, 50, 51, 58–59; as sugar industry

laborers, 4–6, 32, 34. *See also* citizenship; haole; U.S. imperialism; *specific people*
Hawaiian statehood: Cold War and, 151, 170, 184–85, 205, 212–13; "Golden Men" and, 175, 185, 187, 212; interracial women as symbol of, 169, 179, *180*; opposition to, 141–42, 144, 151–52, 169, 177–79, 211, 257n2, 262n30; tourism and, 6, 10, 12, 144, 149, 152, 169–70, 176–78, 180–85, 202, 203; vote on, 202–3, 214
Hawaiian Sugar Planters' Association (HSPA), 71–72, 82, 94–95, 116–18, 142–44
Hawaiian Village Hotel, 163, 170, 185–86
Hawaii Bureau of Information (HBI), 38
Hawaii Hochi, 119, 133–34
Hawaii Hotel Association, 163–64
Hawaii Labor Relations Act, 148–49
Hawaii Promotion Committee (HPC), 49–50, 60–62, 66, 76, 82–84, 210
Hawaii Statehood Commission (HSC), 152, 162, 176–78, 183–84
Hawaii Tourist Bureau (HTB), 89, 92, 107, *115*, *117*, 119, 142, 210
Hawaii Visitors Bureau (HVB), 152, 163–64, 176–77, 181–83, 186, 210
Hayes, Flora Allen, 93
Hearst, William Randolph, 48, 87, 132
Hemingway, Ernest, 194
Heredia, Carlos María de, 98
Herrera, Gracia Rivera, 197
Hevia, Carlos, 157
Higher Wages Association, 83
Hill, Robert, 46, 50, 56
Hilton, Conrad, 158–59, 173–75, 185–86, 195–96, 201, 218n30
Ho, Chinn, 150, 186–87
Hoar, George Frisbie, 44
Home Rule Party, 59
Honolulu, 4, 6, 11, 32, 71, 84, 107
Honolulu Advertiser, 134, 152, 202
Honolulu Chamber of Commerce and Merchants Association, 71–72, 149, 152
Honolulu Star-Bulletin, 35, 94, 105, 131, 162
Hoover, Herbert, 103
Horne, Gerald, 217n15
hotels, 159, 195, 199; Commodoro, 159; Deauville, 97, 159; Edgewater, 163; El Caribe, 159; Islander, 163; Moana, 112; Nacional, 136; Reef, 163; Riviera, 160, 195,

ACKNOWLEDGMENTS

Colleagues and mentors at three universities have shared their wisdom with me and made crucial contributions to this project. At Rutgers, my advisors Michael Adas, Jackson Lears, Matt Matsuda, and Mark Wasserman set the standards of intellectual engagement, boundless generosity, and powerful prose to which I aspire. Paul Clemens, Allen Howard, and Tom Slaughter taught me more than they realize, as did John Gillis, often from afar. Among the many incredible and exceptionally talented graduate students at Rutgers, Erika Bsumek, Roseanne Currarino, Sara Diamond, David Engerman, Van Gosse, Glen Kuecker, Linda Reeder, Ann Rubenstein, Scott Sandage, and Martin Summers especially helped make me the historian I am today. The Center for the Critical Analysis of Contemporary Culture provided a fellowship, an intellectual home, and an engaging year devoted to investigating "The American Century in the Americas"; special thanks to co-directors Pedro A. Cabán and Bruce Robbins and fellows Kim Butler, Jane Junn, and Neil Smith. At Georgia State, the history department provided financial support, and my colleagues, equally important intellectual support. Duane Corpis (now at Cornell) and Joe Perry were my keenest critics. A semester as Visiting Research Scholar in the Program of American Studies at Indiana University made possible completion of the manuscript. So did the support of Matthew Pratt Guterl, Deborah Cohn, Nick Cullather, Ilana Gershon, Katie Lofton, and Amrita Meyers and the kindness of David Thelen.

I was fortunate also to receive research grants and travel awards from the American Studies Association, the Society for the History of American Foreign Relations, the Center for Latin American Studies at the University of Florida, and the John W. Hartman Center for Sales, Advertising, and Marketing History at Duke University. The Hagley Museum and Library provided, in addition to a grant, wonderful symposiums on business and cultural history and a memorable research seminar led by Timothy Lee

Burke at which participants critiqued my work. At the Hagley, I am grateful to Roger Horowitz, Carol Lockman, Marge McNinch, and Phil Scranton.

I owe much to many other archivists and librarians (some of whom are no longer at the institutions named) for their help and advice, especially David Kessler and Wayne Silka at the Bancroft Library of the University of California Berkeley, Chieko Tachihata at the Hawaiian and Pacific Collection at Hamilton Library at the University of Hawai'i at Mānoa, Ellen Gartrell at the J. Walter Thompson Archives at Duke University, Bill Brown at the Special Collections and Archives at the University of Miami, Cathleen Baird at the Conrad N. Hilton Archives at the University of Houston, and Tomás Fernández Robaina at the Biblioteca Nacional José Martí. Thanks also to the wonderful staffs at the Bangor Public Library, the Boston Public Library, the Library of Congress, the National Archives, and the New York Public Library.

Commentators and co-panelists at conferences and seminars improved this project immeasurably, as have participants some of whose names I know and some of whose I don't. Thanks to Victoria Allison, Laura Belmonte, John Carroll, Julia Clancy-Smith, Frank Costigliola, Chris Endy, David Engerman, Durba Ghosh, Philippa Levine, Eric Roorda, and Eric Zolov. One conference paper evolved into an essay in *Moving Subjects: Gender, Mobility, and Intimacy in an Age of Empire,* edited by Tony Ballantyne and Antoinette Burton (Urbana: University of Illinois Press, 2008). I thank the volume editors and the anonymous reviewers for their insightful critiques of an early draft and to the University of Illinois Press for permission to reprint material contained in it here.

At key moments, many others have offered enthusiastic support, constructive criticism, or both, including David Hanlon, J. Kēhaulani Kauanui, James Kraft, Alecia Long, Emily Rosenberg, and Pete Wilcox. For more a decade, Louis A. Pérez, Jr., has shared ideas, research materials, and many memorable meals with me at the AHA. Over the years, Joe Perry generously read many chapters many times. Matt Guterl has helped me in more ways than I can fathom and has become one of my most astute critics and a dear friend. The faith he and Mary Blewett had in me and in this project never wavered, and because of them I soldiered on. Mara Kiere, Chris McKenna, and Scott Sandage offered wise counsel and kept me going in dark times, and they cheered me on.

Bob Lockhart of Penn Press is a wise and judicious editor. I am delighted to have had the privilege of working with him and everyone else at Penn.

My brothers, Paul and John Skwiot, my sister, Diana Smith, and my mother, Joanna Skwiot, always believed that I would finish, although they often wondered when. My mother served as a kind of private foundation at critical times as well as support group of one. My brother-in-law, David Gross, taught me a lot about criticism and theory, usually in the garden at Hancock Pond. Jeff Gross always made me laugh, not least at myself. For two decades, Larry Gross has put me up, put up with me, and provided all manner of support. He has read everything I have written and made me see history and the world in new ways. He has made me a better scholar and a happier person. For these reasons, and many more, I dedicate this book to him.